P9-CIU-019

PARADISE LOST

Paradise Lost

A Life of F. Scott Fitzgerald

DAVID S. BROWN

The Belknap Press of
Harvard University Press
Cambridge, Massachusetts
London, England
2017

Copyright © 2017 by the President and Fellows of Harvard College
All rights reserved
Printed in the United States of America

First printing

Several chapter epigraphs herein are reprinted with the permission
of Scribner, a division of Simon & Schuster, Inc. and are drawn
from the following sources, all edited by Matthew J. Bruccoli:

The Short Stories of F. Scott Fitzgerald. Copyright © 1931 by
The Curtis Publishing Company. Copyright renewed 1959 by
Frances Scott Fitzgerald Lanahan. All rights reserved.

A Life in Letters, by F. Scott Fitzgerald. Copyright © 1994 by
The Trustees under agreement dated July 3, 1975, created by
Frances Scott Fitzgerald Smith. All rights reserved.

Zelda Fitzgerald: The Collected Writings. Copyright © 1991 by
The Trustees under agreement dated July 3, 1975, created by
Frances Scott Fitzgerald Smith. All rights reserved.

Excerpts from THE CRACK-UP, by F. Scott Fitzgerald, are reprinted
by permission of New Directions Publishing Corp. Copyright © 1945
by New Directions Publishing Corp.

Library of Congress Cataloging-in-Publication Data
Names: Brown, David S. (David Scott), 1966– author.
Title: Paradise lost : a life of F. Scott Fitzgerald / David S. Brown.
Description: Cambridge, Massachusetts : The Belknap Press of Harvard
University Press, 2017. | Includes bibliographical references and index.
Identifiers: LCCN 2016048811 | ISBN 9780674504820 (hardcover : alk. paper)
Subjects: LCSH: Fitzgerald, F. Scott (Francis Scott), 1896–1940. | Fitzgerald,
Zelda, 1900–1948. | Nostalgia in literature. | American literature—
20th century—History and criticism.
Classification: LCC PS3511.I9 Z5589 2017 | DDC 813/.52—dc23
LC record available at https://lccn.loc.gov/2016048811

Book design by Dean Bornstein

For Hyun

Like clouds, flowers, and wind

With the end of winter set in another pleasant pumped-dry period and while I took a little time off a fresh picture of life in America began to form before my eyes. The uncertainties of 1919 were over—there seemed little doubt about what was going to happen—America was going on the greatest, gaudiest spree in history and there was going to be plenty to tell about it.

F. Scott Fitzgerald, 1937

CONTENTS

Contents

Illustrations follow page 180.

PARADISE LOST

Introduction — Clio and Scott

I feel that Scott's greatest contribution was the
dramatization of a heart-broken era.

Zelda Fitzgerald, 1947

Scott Fitzgerald once wrote, "There never was a good biography of a good novelist. There couldn't be. He is too many people if he's any good."[1] Despite this preemptory warning, several important Fitzgerald biographies have appeared over the years. Most have emphasized some particular aspect of the man, be it his personality, writings, relationships with women, or battles with the bottle. Each of these studies has benefited from a surplus of primary source material. Fitzgerald was a meticulous self-chronicler, leaving behind a large cache of notes, hundreds of letters, a detailed *Ledger,* and several autobiographical essays. His admonitions notwithstanding, one might fairly argue for his role as a recurrent collaborator with the brotherhood of biographers. He wished to be understood on his own terms, principally as an artist immersed in his times, sensitive to change, and writing for the ages. As a point of departure, that is the premise behind this book.

Within a larger life and work narrative, I treat Fitzgerald as a cultural historian, the annalist as novelist who recorded the wildly fluctuating fortunes of America in the boom twenties and bust thirties. Equal parts author, observer, and participant, he supposed himself uniquely capable of probing below the surface of his society. "I really believe," he once put the matter to the literary critic Edmund Wilson, his old Princeton classmate and an important influence, "that no one else could have written so searchingly the story of the youth of our generation."[2] Certainly he captured its "mood," aspirations, and uncertainties more evocatively than did any writer commenting on the era's strange mingling of ebullience and insecurity, this transformative period pinched between the destabilizing powers of two world wars.

My own training as a historian has shaped how I read Fitzgerald and offers, I trust, a few fresh insights into a much-discussed life. To grasp Fitzgerald's concern in *The Great Gatsby,* for example, that the romantic pioneer promise of America no longer inspired its people is to more broadly recognize his sharp reaction to the death of Victorian idealism that followed the Great War. In this respect, I see Fitzgerald less as a mere and familiar commentator on Gatsby's Jazz Age Manhattan than as a national and even an international interpreter in the company of such contemporaries as Gertrude Stein, John Maynard Keynes, and Pablo Picasso. Alike, they struggled to make sense of the first unsettled decades of the new century—a particularly violent epoch marked by the collapse of several European empires, a severe global economic downturn, and a fierce ideological struggle between democracy, communism, and fascism. It is this linking of the man and his much-mythologized times that I emphasize in these pages.

Like most historians, Fitzgerald approached the past with a point of view. Though pigeonholed in popular memory as a Jazz Age epicurean, he was at heart a moralist struck by the sudden cultural shift in mood and manners that trailed the ill-fated Treaty of Versailles. As he stressed to his daughter, Scottie, in 1938, "my generation of radicals and breakers-down never found anything to take the place of the old virtues of work and courage and the old graces of courtesy and politeness." Deeply suspicious of money's stunning power in industrial America, Fitzgerald possessed a historical sensibility that leaned toward the aristocratic, the premodern, and the romantic. In a youth touched by financial uncertainty, he liked to imagine himself the foundling child of a courageous king; a hungry reader of history, his taste in biography ran to the "great man" school of Caesar and Napoleon. Money, the inevitable "fins and wings" of a restless modern West, meant little to Fitzgerald, except as a long-standing source of resentment. "I have never been able to forgive the rich for being rich," he once confessed, "and it has colored my entire life and works."[3]

With America's landed gentry passing from the scene, Fitzgerald's literary imagination was drawn to the new urban set—the bonds traders and the bootleggers, the Freudians and the flappers—suddenly in saddle. More than agents of affluence, these archetypes of the "Roaring Twenties" now set the cultural tone and tempo, seizing from small-town America the socializing power to shape a civilization. As a popular short-story writer, Fitzgerald enjoyed access to the new money, and it gave him a vantage of cultural insight that would have been otherwise closed. Still, he never thought of himself, even during his peak earning years, as being part of the nouveau riche. His deepest allegiances, rather, were to that rapidly fading complex of courtly antebellum beliefs that he connected with his father's fashionable Chesapeake Bay roots. More specifically, as a midwesterner, as an Irish Catholic, and (despite a steady stream of royalties and advances) as a perpetually in-debt author, he felt every bit the social and economic outsider in the *haute bourgeoisie* haunts— Lake Forest, Princeton, and certain Hollywood enclaves—that had such a prevailing impact on his work. Wilson hit the mark when saying of Fitzgerald, "He casts himself in the role of playboy, yet at the playboy he incessantly mocks."[4]

Fitzgerald's historical awareness was at its core sentimental, nostalgic, and conservative. He never lost his boyish enthusiasm for the valor of Civil War generals or collegiate football heroes, nor did he doubt that the coming world of large-scale bureaucratic structures—whether in the guise of rising capitalist corporations or powerful trade unions—would injure the cause of individual freedom, glory, and ambition. In his everyday life, Fitzgerald held, as this book explores, rather conventional to ultra-conventional views on sex, marriage, and child rearing. His choice in homes reflected further a taste for playing the country squire that time forgot. From 1927 to 1929, the Fitzgeralds leased Ellerslie, a ducal 1842 Greek Revival mansion situated alongside the Delaware River just out-side of Wilmington; in the early 1930s, they moved to La Paix, a rambling Victorian in a wooded area north of Baltimore where Scott completed what some people believe to be his best book, *Tender Is the Night*. He thought of this last address as a return home, of sorts. Though Minnesota born, he descended on his father's side from several pre-Revolutionary

Maryland families. Armed with a patriotic pedigree (he claimed a distant connection to Francis Scott Key), Fitzgerald saw himself as something of an "authentic" aristocrat put out to pasture by the pocket-book power of wealthy arrivistes. "I believe he'd have lived a completely happy life and died a happy death," his good friend John Biggs Jr. told a reporter in the 1970s, "as an Irish landed gentleman of the 17th century."[5]

The solidity of place and station to which Fitzgerald aspired no doubt reflected the ongoing uncertainties of his situation. Put simply, Scott uprooted easily. In some sense, the pretensions of an established Maryland lineage cushioned the reality that he remained throughout his life a restless and somewhat transitory figure. Before the age of thirteen, he had lived in St. Paul (twice), Syracuse, and Buffalo (twice). When he was an adult, this itinerant pattern continued; move followed move, on both sides of the Atlantic—New York gave way to Paris, Paris to Provence, Provence to . . . Perhaps he needed the "landed gentleman" façade to give him a sense of home-groundedness that would lend his writing its unusually assured voice, flair, and perspective. Or, stated slightly differently, perhaps the Maryland strain, both real and magnified, furnished Fitzgerald with a distinct angle of vision.

On a far more private level, however, beyond the reflected glory of a gilded family tree, Fitzgerald saw himself as a fundamentally weak man. His penchant for hero worship—from football players to film producers—can undoubtedly be traced back to seeking in others those particular qualities of self-discipline and self-assurance that he so conspicuously lacked. Fitzgerald worried about his height, his sexuality, and his physical courage on the athletic field. He grew defensive over his drinking and debts and the nearly decade-long pause between the publication of *The Great Gatsby* (1925) and its successor, *Tender Is the Night* (1934). He wanted to be the "whole man" but knew that required a certain emotional sobriety beyond his ken. His, we know from countless reports, was a life of drama and self-destruction; high living and reckless spending, wounding marital battles, and the occasional brawls with bouncers and cabbies form a large part of the eternal Fitzgerald narrative.

If Fitzgerald was anxious and erratic in his private life, he took on a more confident public persona. With the success of his first novel, *This*

Side of Paradise (1920), the then twenty-three-year-old writer suddenly became an authority on, as one reviewer grandly put it, "the intellectual and moral reaction that has set in among the more advanced American circles."[6] From the moment he gained a sizeable audience, in other words, Fitzgerald was being read as an authoritative cultural commentator. Indeed, *Paradise* doubled as a social history of the times, and a great many readers—not just those in "the more advanced . . . circles"—thumbed through its pages in search of clues, observations, and advice on the new world that was coming or had already arrived.

More particularly, *Paradise* touched on the social permissiveness of the era, increasingly candid attitudes toward sexuality, and the general coming down of prewar cultural taboos. As the suddenly anointed interpreter of American youth, Fitzgerald was expected to be an expert on such matters as Prohibition-defying drinking, petting parties, and the bacchanalian side of the collegiate circuit. In this way, very early in his career and not for the better, did the lines separating his personal and public lives blur. Many readers, undoubtedly, wanted to believe that he *lived* his books, and the popular press only encouraged this fantasy. No wonder that he once wrote with some frustration to Max Perkins, his editor at Scribner, "I'm tired of being the author of *This Side of Paradise* and I want to start over."[7]

In a very meaningful way, he never did. For despite the reputation of *Paradise* as a book for the young or the young at heart, it proved to be a template for Fitzgerald's mature works. Whether in the Jazz Age twenties or the Depression thirties, his best novels, short stories, and essays seemed to be of multiple moments, recording both the immediate and the more distant rhythms of capital accumulation, immigration, and sexual politics that were moving America further away from its Protestant agrarian moorings. Today, in a new century, we continue to find his handling of these themes absorbing. The shiny surfaces of his writings—the pitch-perfect cadences, the knowing eye for contemporary color, and the discerning ear for "current" dialogue—are put in the service of a deeper and seemingly timeless historical vision. Fitzgerald's penetrating descriptions of the Western world's leap from feudalism to capitalism, from faith to secularism, and from the tradition oriented to the flux oriented make him one of the more important cultural commentators America has produced.

His truest intellectual contemporaries include the historian Henry Adams (1838–1918) and the German historian/philosopher Oswald Spengler (1880–1936), both of whom are treated in this study. They, along with Fitzgerald, belonged to what we might call the "Decline" school of historical thought. All three doubted whether older pre-Enlightenment notions of art, creativity, paternalism, and worship would survive the onset of what we have since come to call "modernity."

In a sense, we have always understood Fitzgerald to be a student of the past who took up as his special expertise the Jeffersonian "pursuit of happiness" hypothesis known today as the "American Dream." For today's readers, the "Dream" might signify a private, temporal triumph—a good job, a well-furnished home, and a comfortable retirement. To Fitzgerald, however, the promise of America meant something much different. Like the Founders, he saw America as a continent of possibilities, a place to escape the Old World's rigidly enforced class structures and adopt new identities. Put another way, his emphasis was not on the *accumulating* but rather on the *becoming*. He wrote in one short story that "The best of America was the best of the world," and he identified a distinctive "willingness of the heart"—an unquestioning commitment to human freedom—as the special something that had once made Americans a unique, even transcendent people.[8] Fitzgerald thought of these virtues as having largely expired in the decades following the Civil War as the new era—the Gilded Age—underwrote the rise of vast industrial fortunes that blotted out an earlier idealism with a dynamic if, by comparison, soulless materialism. That is why his heroes tend to be tragic figures, romantics destroyed in the end by bureaucrats and "baby vamps," by the idle rich and by fate itself. Disillusioned with a society that offered little more than avenues to make money, their heroic sensibilities were invariably blocked and blunted. Time and again, Fitzgerald relentlessly raised the question from which he himself could not rest: if America was founded on a towering if fragile dream, then what would come to pass when all the dreamers were gone?

Most books can point to a pedigree, and this one is no exception. Fitzgerald's remarkably sensitive historical imagination has long stirred interest among a subset of scholars, even as his popular reputation remained firmly tied to the 1920s. His contemporary, the influential literary critic Malcolm Cowley, got Scott right, I think, when he observed: "Fitzgerald never lost a quality that very few writers are able to acquire: a sense of living in history. Manners and morals were changing all through his life and he set himself the task of recording the changes." Eager to tease out meaning from the everyday, Fitzgerald utilized a kind of page-by-page cultural saturation strategy. His books and stories, essays and articles are filled with news makers, athletes, and entertainers, as well as popular films, music, and books. His reflective 1931 essay "Echoes of the Jazz Age" is scaffolded by the May Day Riots of 1919, the Sacco and Vanzetti case, the Leopold and Loeb trial, Charles Lindbergh, Clara Bow, and Warren G. Harding—all of it textbook material to this day. The following year, his elegiac "My Lost City," written of New York in the high Depression summer of 1932, inventoried the fast-fading world of Jazz Age Manhattan, including references to various period-piece hotels, eateries, and bars (Bustanoby's Café de la Paix, the Club de Vingt on East Fifty-Eighth Street, and "the cool Japanese gardens of the Ritz"). Far from an exercise in nostalgia, however, the essay strives for a broader and more telling point. It closes with Fitzgerald standing on the observation deck of the recently erected Empire State Building, dismayed by the sudden awareness of the central "meaning" of the 1920s: that the City, the nation, and the economy without limits *had* limits. Not for the first time did he link perspective with penance.[9]

Cowley's appreciation of Fitzgerald's historical sensibility anticipated scores of studies assaying this important theme—and many of them inform my own work. They very often and understandably focus their analyses on Fitzgerald's most celebrated books, *The Great Gatsby* and *Tender Is the Night.* An example of the former is Richard Lehan's thoughtful 1995 monograph *The Great Gatsby: The Limits of Wonder.* Lehan persuasively argues that *Gatsby* cannot be properly appraised without taking into account the Western world's erratic course following the Franco-Prussian War (1870–1871). That conflict unified Germany and prefaced the European alliance system that led disastrously to the Continent's collapse in 1914. On a somewhat smaller scale, Lehan looks closely at the 1920s, a decade of deep and irreversible changes in America. Immigration from southern and eastern Europe contrasted with traditional northern European settlement, socialists questioned the country's capitalist orientation, and the 1920 census reported that for the first time there were more Americans living in cities than in the countryside. Scott recognized all of this, and Lehan rightly concludes that to grasp the fundamental ideas and insecurities underpinning *The Great Gatsby,* readers must, like its author, have a working sense of the past.[10]

That resolve holds equally true for *Gatsby's* follow-up, *Tender Is the Night.* In an illuminating 1994 study of that novel, Milton R. Stern emphasizes how the Great War made Scott "aware of the total cultural exhaustion of the Victorian world of his parents." In Stern's reading, Fitzgerald mistrusted the relaxed moral restraints and stock-market materialism of the twenties that had eroded a once-ascendant strain of romantic idealism. Completed in the depths of the Great Depression amid the rising tide of fascism, *Tender* shoulders the weight of its author's concerns that contemporary culture, politics, and economics were running at best to questionable ends. What, then, was the point of urban-industrial America? Would liberal democracies survive the decade? And how could the old ways be reconciled with the new? More than anything Fitzgerald wrote, *Tender* wrestles with the perils of America's stumbling march to modernity, prompting Stern to call it "*the* American historical novel."[11]

Apart from these types of "large" appraisals of Fitzgerald in which he is read as something of a post-Victorian prophet, scholars have also been interested in "smaller" assessments evaluating his relationship to the interwar period (1920–1940). *The Cambridge Companion to F. Scott Fitzgerald,* edited by Ruth Prigozy (2001), and the Kirk Curnutt–edited volume *A Historical Guide to F. Scott Fitzgerald* (2004) offer several fine essays that take up this task. These include studies on the postwar consumer and intellectual environment, the impact of "Flappers and Flapper films" on Fitzgerald's writing, and his relationship to the American publishing industry. Collectively the articles make the case for an interdisciplinary approach to Fitzgerald and his works, one sensitive to the milieu in which he lived and wrote. Tellingly, the Curnutt book includes an illustrated chronology pairing "Fitzgerald's Life" with a proportionate list of "Historical Events"—the Armory Show, the Paris Peace Conference, Lindbergh's transatlantic flight—that shaped his days.[12]

A more recent collection that reads Fitzgerald through his times and vice versa is Bryant Mangum's edited work *F. Scott Fitzgerald in Context* (2013). Indeed, the book's attention to historical setting is such that both Fitzgerald students and those more generally interested in the cultural development of America in the 1920s and 1930s will find it indispensable. Its wide-ranging exploration of more than three-dozen topics—including nuanced looks at class, ethnicity, fashion, and architecture—marks it as the most comprehensive source of its kind and certainly the latest word on Fitzgerald studies.[13]

Perhaps the work with which mine aligns most closely is Robert Sklar's pioneering survey *F. Scott Fitzgerald: The Last Laocoön* (1967). I largely agree with Sklar's contention that Fitzgerald's deepest loyalties were to "the genteel romantic ideals that pervaded late nineteenth-century American culture." These include once firmly rooted conceptions of chivalry and honor, deference and paternalism. Invoking Virgil's *Aeneid,* Sklar compares Fitzgerald to Laocoön, "a priest of Apollo, [who] thrust his spear into the wooden horse to warn his Trojan countrymen against Greek treachery. The Trojans failed to heed him. Then two serpents at Athena's call came up from the sea and destroyed him with his sons."[14] Cautioning readers that the loss of traditional moral codes would harm them, Scott, like Laocoön, was ignored and, in terms of declining book sales/royalties, "killed." So Sklar contends. I believe, in broad terms, this to be a provocative and defendable argument.

Where the present study diverges from Sklar's work is less in its conclusions than in its biographical approach. What I find lacking in *Laocoön* is any substantial discussion of the *personal* dynamics that formed Fitzgerald's thinking on the urban-industrial process. His mother, Mollie McQuillan, and father, Edward Fitzgerald, were, I think, critical in this regard. Though they embodied for Fitzgerald distinct sides of the American experience—the rising immigrant in Mollie's case, the vanishing southern aristocracy in Edward's—they shared a marital life burdened by an inexorable slide into polite poverty. This left an indelible mark on Scott. Attracted to his ineffectual father's courtly if historically spent outlook, he evinced early and for the rest of his life a genuine compassion for those who were plowed under by "progress." Certainly the doomed "heroes" of his novels fit this problematic profile. Thus, his relationship to what Sklar calls the "Apollonian" virtues must, I think, be understood within the context of provincial St. Paul and the ancestral Fitzgeralds in Francis Scott Key's Maryland. Together, Fitzgerald's parents merit but a single citation in Sklar's study, and the Chesapeake/Civil War angle is, considering its vital importance to Fitzgerald's sense of "past," underplayed. I believe that Fitzgerald was able to write as powerfully as he did about historical change in America because he identified with it in such a personal way. He *knew* that his great-grandmother once visited Dolley Madison—and that was important to him.

A second distinction between this study and Sklar's is worth noting. Whereas *Laocoön* traces Fitzgerald to an older tradition of American writers preoccupied with shifting Western beliefs and values—Cooper, Hawthorne, Melville, and James—I see him as far more intellectually in tune with his times and strongly influenced by social critics and historians as well as literary writers. Specifically, he interpreted the great American boom in ways that overlapped with contemporaries Charles Beard and Thorstein Veblen; in ruminating on the meaning of a frontierless America, he echoed the concerns of Frederick Jackson Turner; and in writing on the travails of youth, he can be read profitably alongside Randolph Bourne. That two of these writers were among the most influential historians of the twentieth century should not surprise us; the past never ceased speaking to Scott.

My biography of Fitzgerald is composed of four parts. The first, "Beginnings," explores Fitzgerald's early life from birth (1896) to his marriage in 1920 to the Alabama belle Zelda Sayre. It surveys first loves, writings, and influences while detailing family history and the set of social, economic, and psychological factors that merged to create in Fitzgerald a complex and oversensitive personality. Money, or the lack of it, always teased him. His maternal grandfather had made a small fortune in the wholesale grocery business, and that kept two succeeding generations lingering on the outer edge of well-bred St. Paul, Minnesota, society. Feeling, as he put it late in life, like "a poor boy in a rich town; a poor boy in a rich boy's school," Fitzgerald recognized in his precarious prep-boy status the sharp insecurities that one day underlay Jay Gatsby's tenuous claim to Daisy Fay.[15]

Part 2, "Building Up," assays Fitzgerald's early novels and short stories within the contexts of both his personal circumstances and the broader dimensions of American life. These were, in many respects, triumphant years for Fitzgerald. He forged what proved to be a long-standing relationship with the distinguished house of Scribner, he began making real money by selling his short stories to the *Saturday Evening Post,* and he became a father. His life would never look so promising as it did in 1925 with the publication of *The Great Gatsby,* a remarkable artistic leap beyond his first two books. In later years, he often glanced back on this golden period as the culmination of an early success that had brought him to the summit of American letters.

Part 3, "Breaking Down," the book's longest section, examines the many difficulties that began to close in on Fitzgerald. These were years of increasing alcohol abuse and declining financial fortunes, which coincide with Zelda's institutionalization for what her physicians diagnosed as schizophrenia. Much of this period overlapped the Great Depression, and Fitzgerald, once the embodiment of twenties excess, now styled himself in his writings as a case of thirties contrition. He embellished on these unsettling emotions in his 1934 novel *Tender Is the Night.* His favorite among his own books, *Tender* analyzed within the narrative framework of a dying marriage the collapse of the old Victorian universe and its replacement by a brave new world dominated by hardened "survivors" who had managed to pass through the carnage of the Great War seemingly without regret or reflection. They inherited, Fitzgerald argued, a diminished social order bereft of compassion, sentimentality, or even the comforting consistency of, as he put it, "middle-class love."[16]

This section closes with chapters on Fitzgerald's Hollywood years (1937–1940), the final years of his life. As a screenwriter, he managed some semblance of financial responsibility, found a new golden girl (the syndicated gossip columnist Sheilah Graham), and was deep into a fresh novel at the time of his death, the posthumously published *The Last Tycoon* (1941). Despite such compensations, this late-in-the-game Hollywood turn brought Fitzgerald little peace. A part of him saw these years as a dull aftermath, as a kind of atonement for the high, hard living of the past. The fact that he never liked living in California and found it impossible to mute his deeply ingrained aversion to the business-first mentality of the studio bosses further contributed to his sense of alienation on the West Coast.

Part 4, "Ghosts and Legends," looks briefly at Zelda's life after Scott and the unexpected rise of the Fitzgerald "legend." All but forgotten at the time of his death, Fitzgerald received in his last royalty check a double-unlucky $13.13. And yet within a few years, this all-but-forgotten oracle of the 1920s found in his afterlife new fame as the interpreter of the "American Dream." Even those who were closest to him were amazed at Fitzgerald's growing reputation and the devotion of many of his readers. As Wilson remembered, "I had to recognize that my gifted but all too human old friend had been cast . . . in the role of Attis-Adonis—the fair youth, untimely slain, who is ritually bewailed by women, then resuscitates, as Fitzgerald did, after perishing in the decline of his reputation, when his books were republished and more seriously read than they had usually been during his lifetime and when his legend became full-fledged and beyond his own power to shatter it."[17]

Of course, that legend remains indestructible in our own time, a testimony to the enduring fascination readers have with Fitzgerald's life and books. This biography examines both, reading his relationships and writings alike within the context of the cultural revolution that marked the transition from the genteel world of "morality" to the modern world of "mobility." The latter promised through the miracle of mass production a coming age of endless purchases and personal choices, yet Fitzgerald believed that something profound in the human experience had perished along the way. Expected to be "happy," "productive," and "successful," many of the privileged Americans he wrote about were burdened by the "advantages" of their abundance and unable to develop mature perspectives. As he stated the problem to Scottie, "Once one is caught up into the material world not one person in ten thousand finds time . . . to form what, for lack of a better phrase, I might call the wise and tragic sense of life. By this I mean . . . the sense that life is essentially a cheat and its conditions are those of defeat."[18]

More generally, however, Fitzgerald, for all his wise words on the "tragic sense of life," remained a willing captive to the romantic optimism that shadowed so much of his early work. Even when dogged by a host of personal demons, he never gave up on America, never lost his appreciation for a country that, for all its adventures in postwar escapism, represented, as he once affectionately put it, "the warm center of the world."[19] Neither a skeptic nor a cynic, he struggled until the end of his life to recognize the waning nineteenth-century conventions of his father's generation and to call into question the self-congratulatory spending at the heart of twentieth-century America's rising republic of consumers. It is the tension between these two positions and Fitzgerald's desire to somehow sustain the former and to regain this paradise lost that bring an unusual power, introspection, and pathos to his writing.

ᴄ— PART I —ᴐ

Beginnings, 1896–1920

When I was your age I lived with a great dream.
The dream grew and I learned how to speak of it
and make people listen.

F. Scott Fitzgerald to Scottie Fitzgerald (age sixteen), 1938

ONE

Prince and Pauper

I've been thinking about my father again +
it makes me sad like the past always does.

F. Scott Fitzgerald, 1931

In the spring of 1934, John Jamieson, a Pittsburgher, wrote to Scott Fitzgerald, asking him about the origins of his most iconic character—the "great" Jay Gatsby. In a lettered reply, Fitzgerald explained, "He was perhaps created on the image of some forgotten farm type of Minnesota that I have known and forgotten, and associated at the same moment with some sense of romance." Gatsby's origins have long occasioned debate among literary detectives. In company with Fitzgerald's "forgotten farm type," some have recognized in Gatsby the echoes of John Keats's disillusioned lovers, Henry Adams's mythical medieval "Virgin," or Oswald Spengler's anachronistic Apollonian man—bearer of reason and harmony in an increasingly inharmonious world. In common did these writers confront the modern West's transition from a civilization based on hierarchy, tradition, and cultural "unity" to one increasingly fragmented in the push-pull of the emergent urban-industrial process.[1] They memorialized, in other words, a dying spirit of romantic expression.

Among these "types," one might too include the industrious Philip Francis McQuillan, a romantic in his own right. Fitzgerald's maternal grandfather and resident model of the self-made man rising in America, McQuillan emigrated at the age of eight from County Fermanagh, Ireland, in 1842, settling with his parents and six siblings in Galena, a small upper-Illinois town near the Mississippi River. The hamlet became for

Fitzgerald an idealized place of possibilities, the embodiment of, as he put it in *Gatsby*, "a fresh, green breast of the new world" that once drew Dutch sailors over Atlantic squalls and now called their ancestral sons across a continent. In his 1934 novel *Tender Is the Night*, Fitzgerald described a young and then-obscure Ulysses S. Grant, "lolling in his general store in Galena . . . ready to be called to an intricate destiny."[2] And when fate came knocking in 1861, Grant grew into himself. Rising in rank from colonel of the Twenty-First Illinois Volunteer Infantry Regiment to commander of all Union armies, he led the military charge against the slaveholders' rebellion, claiming key victories at Shiloh and Vicksburg in the war's western theater before bleeding Robert E. Lee's celebrated Army of Northern Virginia and overseeing its surrender at Appomattox Courthouse in the early spring of 1865. From there, his star kept ascending, and Grant served two terms as president (1869–1877). After his death in 1885 at the age of sixty-three, he was interred at the General Grant National Memorial (colloquially known as "Grant's Tomb"), which to this day remains the largest mausoleum in North America. For Scott, Grant's success was a quintessentially American story, literally the stuff that dreams were made of.

Like Grant (and Gatsby), McQuillan discovered in the erratic mobility of America an inexhaustible arena for reinvention. In 1857, he moved to St. Paul, capital city of the Minnesota Territory, and found work as a book-keeper for Beaupre & Temple, a major wholesale grocery establishment; at thirty-eight, he took over the business and soon amassed a fortune. Along the way, McQuillan married Louisa Allen of Galena, and they had eight children, five of whom lived beyond infancy. Like Fitzgerald's, McQuillan's life was marked by a brilliant early success followed by an early exit. Suffering from chronic nephritis compounded by tuberculosis, he died in April 1877, just one week after turning forty-three; he left behind a considerable legacy of some $270,000, a relative value today of about $6 million.

From immigrant poverty to industrial-age prosperity, McQuillan corporealized for many Minnesotans the material side of the American Dream. One obituary called his life "a living romance, for in the brief period of twenty years he passed, by his own unaided exertions, from the humblest beginnings to a place among the merchant princes of the country."[3] Another St. Paul paper evoked the "rising people" theme, celebrated in both Benjamin Franklin's iconic *Autobiography* and Horatio Alger's formulaic *Luck and Pluck* tales, when reviewing McQuillan's splendid ascent: "He came here a poor boy with but a few dollars in his pocket, depending solely on a clear head, sound judgment, good habits, strict honesty and willing hands, with strict integrity his guiding motive. How these qualities have aided him is shown in the immense business he has built up, the acquisition of large property outside, and the universal respect felt for him by the businessmen of the county, among whom probably no man was better known or stood higher."[4] But if McQuillan's commercial kingdom symbolized local capitalist success, it further, and less agreeably, suggested the inevitable eclipse of an older pastoral ideal. One broadsheet described Philip Francis as a "*pioneer* of wholesale grocery," a tribute that blurred the lines between backwoodsman and businessman and thus traded on the public's affection for a fading frontier archetype.[5] Amid a booming urban-industrial backdrop, Americans looked nostalgically on the last open lands as their final link to the old democracy, mobility, and independence. It was this sentiment that informed Frederick Jackson Turner's famous Frontier Thesis and later coaxed Henry Ford to create, in the Detroit suburb of Dearborn, Greenfield Village, a shrine of sorts to the passing age of nineteenth-century American individualism. Filled with workshops, farmhouses, and mills, it embodies to this day the spirit of the old horse-and-buggy Middle West that Ford's automobile empire had, ironically, done so much to obliterate.

McQuillan's surviving children enjoyed all the material, cultural, and educational accoutrements that their affluent father could provide. The family occupied a multistory Victorian in the heart of St. Paul and generously patronized the city's many Catholic appendages. In the words of one appreciative resident archbishop, "none have merited more of the church in this city." Mary (Mollie) McQuillan, Philip Francis's eldest daughter and Fitzgerald's mother, was born in 1860 and bred to expectations of upper-middle-class respectability. She attended Manhattanville College of the Sacred Heart, a Catholic boarding school for girls then located in New York City, and made several trips to Europe; the governor of Minnesota attended her wedding reception.[6]

A distracted, dowdy woman inclined to eccentricities, Mollie Mc-Quillan gave the impression of wanting far more from life than life was willing to give her. Contemporaries, put off by her sometimes-mismatched shoes (a habit of breaking one in at a time), unkempt hair, and habitual umbrella, referred to her unkindly as a witch. One of Scott's schoolteachers remembered her "dressed like the devil, always coming apart." Her tendency to innocently unleash the oddly inappropriate comment—"I'm trying to decide how you'll look in mourning," she once let slip to the wife of a dying man—fueled the casual hostility of the people around her. As one St. Paulian put it, Mollie was "a pathetic, wispy little woman. People were cruel to her and Scott was ashamed of her." This embarrassment can be read in the opening line of Fitzgerald's 1936 story "An Author's Mother": "She was a halting old lady in a black silk dress and a rather preposterously high-crowned hat that some milliner had foisted upon her declining sight." Nearing a then-spinsterish thirty in 1890, Mollie married Edward Fitzgerald, a man whom she had known for several years and who was several years her senior. Scottie Fitzgerald later recounted for a biographer the family gossip regarding their supposedly one-sided courtship: "Daddy said that his father had told him that he was sitting in the parlor one night with Molly . . . and talking about this and that when she called her parents in . . . and announced how wonderful it was that she was engaged to marry Ed; and that he had been too much a gentleman to know how to get out of it." Scottie knew in relating this story that Mollie's father had died several years before his daughter's marriage, but she passed it on nevertheless as she believed, even with the particulars in question, that "it must have had more than a germ of truth." In any case, the Fitzgerald-McQuillan marriage did not produce a meeting of minds, hearts, or bank accounts. Decamping on a European honeymoon, the little-traveled Edward eagerly awaited the Champs-Elysees and requested Mollie's company for a first-day stroll. Her tactless rejoinder—"But I've already seen Paris!"—anticipated decades of marital disconnects.[7]

Though Edward shared Mollie's Irish Catholicism, he brought to their alliance a decidedly different range of references. A southerner born near Rockville, Maryland, in 1853, he was weaned on memories of the Confederate Lost Cause and seemed ill suited to the land of Yankee capitalism, to which—first in Chicago and subsequently in St. Paul—the postwar boom brought him. His maternal roots, the Scott side, ran deep into the American past and gave him a vicarious glory that no amount of McQuillan money could buy. Scott Fitzgerald picked up on these ancestral cues and sported with Philip Francis's "grubby" merchant roots in his first novel, *This Side of Paradise*. In it, a hitherto-admired Princetonian's stock drops after a classmate reveals an ugly secret: "if you want to know the shocking truth, his father was a grocery clerk."[8] The Fitzgeralds, by contrast, could point proudly to generations of civic service in colonial legislatures and governors' assemblies. The most famous branch of the family tree led to Francis Scott Key, the author of "The Star-Spangled Banner" and brother to Edward's great-great-grandfather. And, adding notoriety, the ill-fated Mary Surratt, convicted and hanged in the summer of 1865 for taking part in the conspiracy to assassinate Abraham Lincoln, was mother-in-law to Edward's first cousin.

Edward himself could claim a personal rendezvous with American history, which, if not on the inflated order of Grant, was still worth the making of several stirring bedtime stories. Though border-state Maryland remained in the Union, its loyalties were divided. The southern and eastern parts of the state were tied to a tobacco and slavery economy and favored joining the new Confederate government; the northern and western areas were typically pro-Union. In the 1860 presidential election, Maryland had given its eight electoral votes to Kentucky's John C. Breckenridge, the candidate of the southern Democratic coalition that had formed that summer and split the Democratic Party in half. Lincoln, by contrast, carried less than 3 percent of the state's popular vote. An alleged February 1861 plot to assassinate the president-elect in Baltimore forced Lincoln to take the precautionary measure of traveling through the city unannounced in the dead of night—critics called him a coward. Three months later, a thousand federal soldiers under General Benjamin F. Butler occupied Federal Hill overlooking Baltimore and arrested the city's mayor and police commissioner. Martial law was declared, and by that summer, Union power was asserted throughout the state. Edward's adolescent sympathies, along with much of the Rockville / Montgomery County area, were with the South. At the age of nine, in the first full year of the Civil War, he had rowed Confederate spies across the Potomac. He subsequently helped a member of Mosby's Raiders—the famed Forty-Third Battalion, First Virginia Calvary, led by John Singleton Mosby— avoid arrest. And he cheered on Jubal Early's army as it drove off Union forces at the Battle of Monocacy just outside of Frederick (July 1864) and proceeded to march on nearby Washington before meeting stiff resistance at Fort Stevens and retreating. In weighing this paternal impact, Scott Fitzgerald was later to write, "so many legends of my family went west with father."[9]

Courtly, deferential, and distinguished by a neatly sculpted Vandyke beard, Edward fairly trailed clouds of faded southern glory. A cultural conservative indifferent to the businessman's perspective, he had chivalric manners that were conspicuously dated in the dawning age of machines. Marriage to Mollie inspired no Philip Francis–like success on his part; if anything, Edward seemed silently, stubbornly proud of his inability to make money. Faintly indolent and temperamentally unsuited for St. Paul's bustle and vigor, he tried his luck in upstate New York (1898–1908) before finally falling into a permanent occupational paralysis. Eventually given a sinecure by the McQuillans (an office with no duties), he came to resent his in-laws; humiliated, he chalked up his penury to a superior aristocratic sensibility.

In June 1896, the Fitzgeralds cruelly lost their two young daughters, Mary and Louise, to an epidemic. Heartbroken, Edward wrote his mother, "I wonder sometimes if I will ever have any interest in life again. Perhaps so but certainly the keen zest of enjoyment is gone forever." Three months later, on 24 September, his son, Francis Scott Fitzgerald, was born. The deaths, though never brought up, seemed in some firm if incommunicable way to set in motion the new child's "intricate destiny." Certain suggestions, feelings, and intangibles were conveyed in Mollie's pain. "[Shortly] before I was born," Fitzgerald later recalled, "my mother lost her other two children and I think that came first of all though I don't know how it worked exactly. I think I started then to be a writer."[10]

As if to compensate for both the deaths of Mary and Louise and the embarrassment of Edward's inertia, Mollie lavished a mother's love on her son. Much to Fitzgerald's mortification, she spoiled him so obviously as to be the source of his first youthful shame. Writing from Camp Chatham at Orillia, Ontario, in the summer of 1907, he tried with the fumbling tact of a ten-year-old to dissuade her unwanted visit. "Dear Mother, I received your letter this morning and though I would like very much to have you up here I dont think you would like it as you know no one hear except Mrs. Upton and she is busy most of the time I dont think you would like the accomadations as it is only a small town and no good hotels. There are some very nise boarding houses but about the only fare is lamb and beef." By late adolescence, Fitzgerald had come to see Mollie's persistent petting as the cause of both his sensitive bearing and insecurity-driven snobbishness. In reaction, he idolized football players, war heroes, and business titans—men presumably able to overcome the nursery caresses doled out by doting mothers (or the thin legacy of idle fathers). In later life, Scott blamed Mollie for his brittle ego: "So you see I looked at myself in two ways. There seemed to have been a conspiracy to spoil me and all my inordinate vanity was absorbed from that. All this was on the surface, however, and liable to be toppled over at one blow by an unpleasant remark or a missed tackle; and underneath it, came my own sense of lack of courage and stability."[11]

Scott's distance from Mollie lingers about *This Side of Paradise*. The spirited Beatrice Blaine, Amory Blaine's mother, seems the *parentis maximus* of Scott's dreams. Sophisticated, educated, and privileged, she is everything that Mollie was not. "Her youth passed in renaissance glory"; her "small talk was broadened . . . during a winter in Vienna." Without Mollie, Fitzgerald supposed, he would have been emotionally stronger and better equipped to deal with adversity; he blamed her for lowering his horizons and limiting his opportunities. "Mother and I never had anything in common except a relentless stubborn quality," he once told his sister, Annabel (born in 1901). She embarrassed him, she didn't understand him, and she never encouraged his writing. In what seems a lightly veiled maternal reference, he wrote in one story, "the books by her son were not vivid to her, and while she was proud of him in a way, and was always glad when a librarian mentioned him or when someone asked her if she was his mother, her secret opinion was that such a profession was risky and eccentric."[12]

In 1931, the year Edward died, Scott Fitzgerald transcribed a dream that he believed got to the root of his resentments:

> I am in an upstairs apartment where I live with my mother, old, white haired, clumsy and in mourning, as she is today. On another floor are a group of handsome & rich, young men, whom I seem to have known slightly as a child and now want to know better, but they look at me suspiciously. I talk to one who is agreeable and not at all snobbish, but obviously he does not encourage my acquaintance—whether because he considers me poor, unimportant, ill bred, or of ill renown I don't know, or rather don't think about—only I scent the polite indifference and even understand it.[13]

A quarrel with Mollie ensues in the dream, born largely of Fitzgerald's refusal to be pitied for his tenuous social position. Hurt and frustrated, he arrives at the house of a stronger woman—his Aunt Annabel—only to find that Mollie has followed him there. Hungry, they both order bacon and eggs. Mollie is served only bacon; Scott, only eggs.

Edward left his son with a different if only slightly less difficult mix of childhood memories. In search of work to supplement Mollie's legacy, he moved the family in the spring of 1898 to Buffalo, where, hopelessly chasing Philip Francis's star, he took a position as a salesman with Procter & Gamble. A series of upstate transfers followed until, in March 1908, Edward lost his job at age fifty-five. Scott learned of the blow via an overheard telephone conversation, and from that point on, he considered his father—his favorite parent—irrelevant. "That morning," Fitzgerald told a reporter years later, Edward "had gone out a comparatively young man, a man full of strength, full of confidence. He came home that evening, an old man, a completely broken man. He had lost his essential drive, his immaculateness of purpose. He was a failure the rest of his days." Embarrassed for Edward, and no doubt for himself, Fitzgerald conjured up an alternative backstory. "He once told me his father was an engineer for Jim Hill, the Western railroad builder," remembered a college friend; "it was a lie."[14]

Failure or not, Edward still retained a firm hold on his son's heart. Offsetting Mollie's overindulgence, he established for Scott expectations of conduct and consequences that nourished his moral imagination. Fitzgerald's adult recollection of a youthful indiscretion underline the importance of this paternal influence:

> I ran away when I was seven on the Fourth of July—I spent the day with a friend in a pear orchard and the police were informed that I was missing and on my return my father thrashed me according to the custom of the nineties—on the bottom—and then let me come out and watch the night fireworks from the balcony with my pants still down and my behind smarting and knowing in my heart that he was absolutely right. Afterwards, seeing in his face his regret that it had to happen, I asked him to tell me a story.[15]

Perhaps as important as the occasional whipping, Edward offered Scott an alternative to McQuillan pretension. True, he had failed to secure a fortune, returning from work one day a "broken man," but this vice could be revisited as a real and positive virtue. Lacking the heart of a merchant or the taste for America's great post-Appomattox launch toward materialism, Edward paid tribute to his quasi-patrician roots by emphasizing ease over energy, benevolence over self-interest. In the ancestral contest between Fitzgerald romance and McQuillan verve, Scott's loyalties ran decidedly toward the former. Time and again, Edward's endangered principles appeared in his son's novels, carrying the moral weight of all good fathers everywhere. "In my younger and more vulnerable years," *The Great Gatsby* begins, "my father gave me some advice that I've been turning over in my mind ever since. 'Whenever you feel like criticizing anyone,' he told me, 'just remember that all the people in this world haven't had the advantages that you've had.' He didn't say any more but we've always been unusually communicative in a reserved way and I understood that he meant a great deal more than that." And again, in *Tender Is the Night,* Fitzgerald created a father of aristocratic lineage who stands for an older ethical code: "Dick loved his father—again and again he referred judgments to what his father would probably have thought or done. Dick was born several months after the death of two young sisters and his father, guessing what would be the effect on Dick's mother, had saved him from a spoiling by becoming his moral guide. He was of tired stock yet he raised himself to that effort."[16]

The sea of settlers coming to Victorian St. Paul slackened by 1895. And in its aftermath, the city adopted a civic identity fundamentally averse to neighboring Minneapolis. The former imagined itself a Catholic enclave of solid small banking and mercantile interests pitted against bourgeoning, Protestant, speculative Minneapolis. St. Paul thus became for Fitzgerald the worldly embodiment of his father's values. It bowed, that is, before a more dynamic power yet retained those genteel qualities of taste and grace that make life more than a scrum for money. St. Paul, Fitzgerald once explained, considered itself "a little superior" to the likes of Kansas City, Milwaukee, and Indianapolis precisely because it was "a 'three generation' town." And this perspective opened for him a wide avenue of exploration into the American character and its relationship to place and tradition. Fitzgerald's St. Paul suggested solidity and stability, a city of neighborhood hardware stores, spruced up Main Streets, and a few first families to establish tone. In a 1923 review, he selectively traced its history: "In the fifties the climate of St. Paul was reputed exceptionally healthy. Consequently there arrived an element from the East who had both money and fashionable education. These Easterners mingled with the rising German and Irish stock, whose second generation left the cobbler's last, forgot the steerage, and became passionately 'swell' on its own account. But the pace was set by the tubercular Easterners. Hence the particular social complacency of St. Paul."[17] The Atlantic urban centers, by contrast, with their speed and intensity, never quite seemed real to Fitzgerald. "Even when the East excited me most," he wrote in *Gatsby*, "even when I was most keenly aware of its superiority to the bored, sprawling, swollen towns beyond the Ohio, with their interminable inquisitions which spared only the children and the very old—even then it had always for me a quality of distortion." Perhaps this was so, yet even St. Paul, with its merchant-prince possibilities, teased Scott with dreams of grandeur. There, in reaction to assorted parental shortcomings, the itinerate years in upstate New York, and a wishful urgency for release, he imagined himself the foundling child of a Celtic king, like Grant in Galena waiting in the wings for an imminent deliverance.[18]

Scott's gentry-sounding surname supported this fantasy. The Norman "fiz/filz" is cognate to the Latin *filius,* "son of." Thus, "Fitzgerald" means "son of Gerald." When the suffix is "Roi" (king), the meaning becomes "son of the king." For centuries, the English and British royal families used "Fitz" in surnames, often in cases of illegitimacy. These *nullius filius* children include Matilda FitzRoy (Countess of Perche, died 1120, daughter of Henry I), Henry FitzRoy (first Duke of Richmond and Somerset, 1519–1536, son of Henry VIII), and Lady Anne Palmer (Countess of Sussex, known by the alias "Fitzroy," 1661–1721/1722, daughter of King Charles II). Robert FitzRoy, a fourth-generation grandson of Charles II, captained the HMS *Beagle* during Darwin's famous voyage to the Galapagos Islands. In a retrospective 1936 story, "Author's House," Fitzgerald seeks to explain "the complicated dark mixture" of his youth by recalling how he had desperately imagined for himself a different home, family, and life. Taking the reader through the imagined dwelling, he begins in the basement, leading a startled guest to a tomb in one of its corners. "That," he says, "is where I buried my first childish love of myself, my belief that I would never die like other people, and that I wasn't the son of my parents but a son of a king, a king who ruled the whole world."[19]

But back in the real world, the McQuillan fortune, relatively rapid in its making, had begun to stubbornly ebb away. The Fitzgeralds were eager to maintain appearances, and their descent into genteel poverty resulted in years of nomadic wanderings around the city's fashionable Summit Avenue, brief homesteadings taken up and abandoned in the ongoing pursuit of ever more economical leases. The slide appeared to have little impact on Mollie's social expectations. Despite dwindling resources, she anticipated that Scott and Annabel would occupy a place among the local elite that was once so easily open to her and her siblings. This burden weighed on Scott, imparting a powerful poor-boy-among-rich-boys resentment that fed his "foundling" fantasy. In September 1919, Scott wrote a letter to Alida Bigelow, a St. Paul friend then at Smith College. Scott had just completed his first novel but was unsure of his future, and he sounded every bit the frustrated prisoner of the tower, complaining to Bigelow of his current plight:

> In a house below the average
> Of a street above the average
> In a room below the roof
> With a lot above the ears. . . .[20]

More fruitfully, Fitzgerald formed from the anxieties of adolescence a language and a literary mood that spoke observantly to a nation suddenly "modern" yet inescapably nostalgic for those parts of itself now irretrievably gone. This sense of lost time came straight from the nursery. It bore the burdens of Edward's youthful Confederate sympathies, Mollie's lost children, and the vanishing McQuillan wealth. The foundations of Fitzgerald's writings were laid, in other words, in the hauntedness of home.

TWO

Celtic Blood

There had been a time when his own Celtic traits
were pillars of his personal philosophy.

F. Scott Fitzgerald, This Side of Paradise, *1920*

In the autumn of 1908, twelve-year-old Scott Fitzgerald enrolled in
St. Paul Academy, a private nonsectarian school for boys one block north
of the city's posh Summit Avenue. There, as a Catholic, as the son of an
idle southerner, and as a sojourner in a succession of houses "below the
average," he swam against the tide. Intelligent in a twelve-going-on-
sixteen kind of way, he compensated by overcompensating. At school, he
talked too much, knew—or pretended to know—too much, and routinely
condescended to his peers, who naturally delighted in shearing him down
to size. "If anybody can poison Scotty or stop his mouth in some way,"
one classmate pleaded in the student paper, "the school at large and myself will be obliged." The cut stuck, and Fitzgerald repeated it nearly verbatim in his autobiographical 1928 short story "The Freshest Boy": "If
someone will please poison young Basil, or find some other means to stop
his mouth, the school at large and myself will be much obliged." In Scott's
case, the fresh boy was plainly father to the author.[1]

Despite suffering the occasional pang of unpopularity, Fitzgerald
looked back on St. Paul Academy with some pride as the place where he
first became a published author. His interest in detective novels inspired
"The Mystery of the Raymond Mortgage," a daffy "whodunit" appearing
in the October 1909 edition of *Now and Then,* the student literary magazine. The tale of a missing document, "Mystery" contains a number of

competent passages amid the occasional screamer—there is, after all, no Ithaca-to-Princeton train. Scott later remembered the excitement of seeing his debut in print: "I read my story through at least six times, and all that day I loitered in the corridors and counted the number of men who were reading it, and tried to ask people casually, 'If they had read it?'"[2] Other stories followed. In "Reade, Substitute Right Half," a physically slight second teamer carries his crew to an improbable gridiron victory. If the story instantiates a wish-fulfillment fantasy, Fitzgerald—a boastful but middling athlete relegated to his school football, basketball, and baseball reserve squads—reveals a deeper, instinctual understanding that his best hope for recognition lay in literary achievement rather than athletic prowess. Two additional stories rate mention. Both are Civil War sagas, evidence that Edward's through-a-boy's-eyes remembrances of the rebellion touched his son deeply. "A Debt of Honor" follows a young Confederate sentry, pardoned by General Lee for falling asleep at his post, finding redemption in a heroic death at the battle of Chancellorsville— this the martial equivalent of Reade's special football exploits. In "The Room with the Green Blinds," Fitzgerald wrote a historical fantasy of John Wilkes Booth surviving the Lincoln assassination hidden in a gothic Georgian mansion; not for the last time would the ill-fated Mary Surratt and the shadowy rooming houses of wartime Georgetown occupy his imagination.

Never a strong student, Fitzgerald made poor marks during his three years at St. Paul. One might blame his devotion to extracurricular activities, though these offered to Scott certain insights into the adolescent condition that could hardly be gleaned in an algebra text. Never lazy, he was, in fact, one of the most engaged students in the academy, but he only engaged in what interested him. "I wrote all through every class," he later recalled, "in the back of my geography book and first year Latin and on the margins of themes and declensions and mathematic problems."[3] Concerned with Scott's low scores, Mollie and Edward agreed that he needed a greater academic challenge and more discipline. They were determined, despite the cost (absorbed by Mollie's mother), to send him east to finish school. Fifteen-year-old Scott, already a secret smoker and a connoisseur of kissing games, welcomed the change. Summit Avenue's store of experiences had grown threadbare. His new academic home, the Newman School, resided on the fringes of Hackensack, New Jersey, less than an hour in the underground from New York City.

The Newman School, self-styled as a Catholic Andover, emphasized a lay education that prepared students for entrée to Princeton or Yale rather than "priest-ridden" Georgetown or Boston College. A tiny scholastic village housing but sixty students, Newman nevertheless enjoyed a reputation for quality, drawing its classes, as one prep publication put it, "from the Roman Catholic families of wealth in all parts of the United States."[4] Fitzgerald—anticipating weekend excursions to Broadway musicals, a fresh audience to measure the growth of his emerging talents, and the ever-fleeting promise of football fame—headed east with the hazy sense that an imminent, if not yet defined, glory there awaited his arrival. Years later, he recalled clearly the inventory of assets that he brought to Newman:

> I had a definite philosophy which was a sort of aristocratic egotism. I considered that I was a fortunate youth capable of expansion to any extent for good or evil. I based this, not on latent strength, but upon facility and superior mentality. I thought there was nothing I could not do, except, perhaps, become a mechanical genius; still I traced special lines in which I considered [I] must excel, even in the eyes of others. *First:* Physically—I marked myself handsome; of great athletic *possibilities,* and an extremely good dancer. Here I gave myself about eighty percent. *Second:* Socially—In this respect, my condition was, perhaps, most dangerous, for I was convinced that I had personality, charm, magnetism, poise, and the ability to dominate others. Also I was sure that I exercised a subtle fascination over women. *Third:* Mentally—Here I was sure that I had a clear field in the world. I was vain of having so much, of being so talented, ingenuous [ingenious] and quick to learn.

He then owned up to a host of liabilities:

> To balance this I had several things on the other side. *First:* Morally—I thought I was rather worse than most boys, due to latent unscrupulousness and the desire to influence people in some way, even for evil. I knew I was rather cold; capable of being cruel; lacked a sense of honor, and

was mordantly selfish. *Second:* Psychologically—Much as I influenced others, I was by no means the "Captain of my Fate." I had a curious cross section of weakness running through my character. I was liable to be swept off my poise into a timid stupidity. I knew I was "fresh" and not popular with older boys. I knew I was completely the slave of my own moods, and often dropped into a surly sensitiveness most unprepossessing to others. *Third:* Generally—I knew that at bottom I lacked the essentials. At the last crisis, I knew I had no real courage, perseverance or self-respect.

Taken altogether, Fitzgerald luxuriated in his prospects at Newman, a sunny premonition, perhaps, of the special fate he believed certain to befall him there. "I should say that, underneath the whole thing," he remembered of that pregnant period, "lay a sense of infinite possibilities."[5]

It was only too predictable, however, that the Newman School never equaled Fitzgerald's impossible expectations. His steady diet of literary juvenilia, including the college-life narratives of C. M. Flandrau (*Harvard Episodes*) and W. J. Lynch (*Princeton Stories*), fed an imagination larger than its surroundings. Years later, in what reads like an autobiographical passage, Fitzgerald wrote of one of his characters having "lived with such intensity on so many stories of boarding-school life that, far from being homesick, he had a . . . feeling of recognition and familiarity." To the extent that Scott experienced a similar sensation at Newman, his confidence was qualified by repeating a humbling pattern of bragging to peers and coming up short on the football field. "He was unpopular starting out," recalled his classmate Charles Donahoe, "partly because his good looks promoted classification as a sissy which was reinforced by a lack of physical courage. But he had an insight into character and motive which enabled him to more than hold his own in worldly disputes, and finally, by practice I suppose, he became inured to psychological impacts with either the school authorities or the more important of his fellow students which in time won him a sense of belonging where his talents had some acclaim." G. Ingersoll Lewis, a female childhood friend of Scott's, deepens this portrait, recalling his ability to overcome ostracism through practiced social skills. Such became his habit of exercising good manners as a kind of currency to pry open otherwise closed doors. As a St. Paulian, Lewis explained, Scott "didn't figure at all in the [Summit Avenue] 'gang' one way or another." But going to Newman increased interest all around. "Later he seemed sort of stylish, had been away to boarding school which few others had, he had a 'line' and flattered you and that began to be fun. . . . By then it was something to say 'Scott took me home last night.'"[6] No doubt he brought to these innocently romantic interludes the knowing attitudes, poses, and "lines" that he had lifted off of Flandrau and Lynch. They gave him a pseudosophistication that aroused the envy of more than one Summit schoolboy.

At Newman, Scott stubbornly sought to overcome his fresh-boy reputation by winning recognition on the athletic field. In fact, just the opposite happened. Of slight build, shaky coordination, and, as Donahoe and others have put it, suspect physical courage, he faced tall odds. One autumn afternoon, these liabilities caught up with him in a humiliating way. Playing on the defensive side of the ball, he conspicuously avoided an especially jarring tackle and was promptly accused of cowardice. The charge must have stung given Fitzgerald's reverence for a game he believed telescoped the youth, intensity, and heroism of life.

In our own day, football's massive popularity has given it a special cultural prominence that, recent and growing concerns about head trauma notwithstanding, we take for granted. Yet in Fitzgerald's time, it was still a relatively new sport that was looking to gain traction. The violence of the game worried critics and supporters alike, then as it does now, and one of the latter, President Theodore Roosevelt, called a summit of sorts in October 1905 to discuss ways to make it safer. The gathering was prompted in no small part by the alarming fact that more than a dozen collegiate and amateur footballers had died that year as a result of injuries sustained on the field. The meeting initiated a series of rules changes that fundamentally altered the way the sport was played. "Legitimized" by the presidential-driven improvements, football became increasingly popular on the college circuit and elsewhere. It became the game that Fitzgerald loved.

Ashamed to be labeled a quitter by classmates, Scott responded to his missed-tackle detractors with "FOOTBALL," his first published poem.

Appearing in the *Newman News,* it trafficked in the eminently safe terrain of school spirit:

> There's the goal, now right before you,
> Ten yards, five yards, bless your name!
> Oh! you Newman, 1911,
> You know how to play the game.

The ballad served further to wishfully revise the circumstances of Scott's recent public shame:

> see that halfback
> Gaining up behind him slow.
> Crash! they're down; he threw him nicely,—
> Classy tackle, hard and low.[7]

The poem, or rather the positive attention it aroused, impressed Fitzgerald. For the first time he began to discover social acclaim in an activity for which, unlike either academics or athletics, he demonstrated a blossoming talent. Thus, despite a frustrating first semester of fistfights and cold-shouldering, loneliness, and poor grades, he returned to St. Paul for the holiday with a new and important self-awareness. "When I went home that Christmas vacation," he later remembered, "it was in my mind that if you weren't able to function in action you might at least be able to tell about it, because you felt the same intensity—it was a back-door way out of facing reality."[8] Put another way, Fitzgerald never quite experienced anything fully until he had written about it.

Scott's second and final year at Newman proved less volatile than the first. He began to settle down emotionally, improved academically, and even managed to shine at a track-and-field meet. At five feet, six inches tall and 130 pounds, with stubby limbs and an uncooperative stride, Fitzgerald was far from a natural athlete. What small gridiron success he experienced—and he managed in his second year as a substitute back to receive some modest acclaim in the school paper—came from sheer will. One observer noted that he had "a desperate, bent-forward, short-legged, scuttling way of running with the ball, but somehow it conveyed emotion, and when he was good, it was thrilling and when he was bad (as he often was) you had to look away from his visible shame."[9]

As Scott's illusions of athletic prowess faded, he discovered his first real intellectual guide in Father Sigourney Webster Fay. Father Fay, in his late thirties at the time, gave to Catholicism all the romance and vitality that Fitzgerald had found wanting in black-clad St. Paul. Porcine, perfumed, and something of a dandy, Fay devoted himself to the study of medieval church history, enjoyed a wide circle of Catholic and non-Catholic connections, and lived as much of the life of an aesthete as a priest on a generous private income could. Born in Philadelphia to an Irish American father and a Bucks County mother with ties to the old Delaware Valley landed gentry, Fay graduated from the University of Pennsylvania and the Episcopal Divinity School in Philadelphia. From there, he taught moral theology at an Anglican seminary near Milwaukee, where he joined the Companions of the Holy Savior. This core of ultra-high-church Anglo-Episcopal clergy was attracted to the quasi-monastic culture of vespers and vestments, incense and chants, then so much in vogue among the English Oxford movement. As romantic critics of liberal theology, they called on Anglicanism to recover the sacred ceremonial traditions and rituals of Christianity lost in the Reformation—in effect, to reverse Protestant positivism. In 1908, a concerned General Convention of the Episcopal Church moved to rein in the Companions' activities. In protest, Fay converted to Catholicism.

Ordained in 1910, Fay taught liturgy and Ecclesiastical Greek at Catholic University in Washington, D.C., until the First World War. In November 1912, he was appointed to the Newman board, in which capacity he met Fitzgerald. Fay made a striking, even revelatory impact on the susceptible sixteen-year-old. The dour Minnesota priests and celibate nunnery that constituted Scott's human contact with the church left him completely unprepared for Fay's *bon vivant*. A friend to Henry Adams, a discerning reader of Oscar Wilde's Faustian prose, and a knowledgeable commentator of medieval art, music, and philosophy, Fay gave the impression of effortlessly merging epicurean pleasures with serious intellectual pursuits. "He was a learned man with much of the delightful child about him," recalled Fay's friend Margaret Chanler. "He combined spiritual with temporal gifts, for he preached admirably, and could bring fire from heaven to kindle the hearts of his hearers, but he was no ascetic and clearly loved good company, good food and drink." Donahoe remembered the cleric well and added of his appealing ecumenicalism, "Fr. Fay possessed the unique advantage as a convert and a priest of not being too tightly bound by loyalty to a creed into which he had come voluntarily and yet at the same time able to trace his own convictions with intelligence."[10]

Fay indulged Scott's impulsive moods and literary ambitions while giving a romantic sheen to his Catholic / Celtic identity. Fay flattered his protégé, made him feel part of a bigger world of ideas, and asked for nothing more than friendship. "He took easily to boys of the type of Fitzgerald," recalled one of Scott's Newman companions. "He had too the gift of being as young as several of the boys he especially cared for." Fay's correspondence with Scott grew increasingly intimate, taking on a dramatic, virtually playacting quality. During the First World War, by which time Scott had matriculated to Princeton, Fay encouraged their taking on a secret—and, he claimed, State Department–backed—mission to Russia, where they would work to unite Catholics following the collapse of the tsarist government. "You will have to take plenty of warm clothes as we shall be in a very cold climate most of the time," Fay wrote Scott. "Now, do be discreet about what you say to anybody. If anybody asks you say you are going as secretary to a Red Cross Commission." Scott went so far as to acquire a passport, though the mission predictably never came off. Fay had looked forward to sharing a room in Russia with Fitzgerald ("it will save some money at least and give us a chance to talk the things over which must be strictly confidential between us"), and his contributions to their correspondence might be read as a series of veiled love letters. He thought of their relationship as reciprocal; they shared certain rare and altogether enviable traits—"we're extraordinary, we're clever, we could be said I suppose to be brilliant"—and, Fay liked to presume, a distinct emotional bond: "I never deny that I need you boys— your companionship and all that—but I am also coming to the conclusion that you . . . need a little touch of me, and I do hope if you get leave . . . you will fly to my paternal arms."[11]

Fitzgerald seemed oblivious to the older man's innuendo, and in any case, he detected in Fay the same man-versus-the-modern quality that he admired in his father. For Scott, the few, the well mannered, and the interesting occupied one distinct sphere and were always on the edge of annihilation by the many, the coarse, and the dull. Later, in tracing the roots of this "chip on a shoulder," "pull for the underdog" complex, Fitzgerald recalled his initial childhood brush with injustice:

> First there was a book that was I think one of the big sensations of my life. It was nothing but a nursery book, but it filled me with the saddest and most yearning emotion. . . . It was about a fight that the large animals, like the elephant, had with the small animals, like the fox. The small animals won the first battle; but the elephants and lions and tigers finally overcame them. The author was prejudiced in favor of the large animals, but my sentiment was all with the small ones. I wonder if even then I had a sense of the wearing-down power of big, respectable people. I can almost weep now when I think of that poor fox, the leader—the fox has somehow typified innocence to me ever since.[12]

As a "poor fox," Fitzgerald championed the Jacobites of the world, and Fay helped considerably on this point by placing Catholicism within an idealized historical context that could be liberally interpreted as equal parts Stuart dynasty and Jeb Stuart—the fated makers, that is, of last stands before the looming might of the modern world. A passage in Fitzgerald's first novel spoke plainly to this impulse:

> "I was for Bonnie Prince Charlie," announced Amory.
>
> "Of course you were—and for Hannibal——"
>
> "Yes, and for the Southern Confederacy." He was rather skeptical about being an Irish patriot—he suspected that being Irish was being somewhat common—but Monsignor assured him that Ireland was a romantic lost cause and Irish people quite charming, and that it should, by all means, be one of his principal biasses.[13]

Despite Fitzgerald's aversion to the "wearing-down power" of history's winners, the healthy, happy Anglo-Saxon remained for him always a point of reference and emulation. His Anglo affectations included an Ivy

League turn, a southern-belle spouse, and a long-standing association with the *Saturday Evening Post,* Middle America's magazine of choice. On occasion, he even fudged his ethnicity. In a brief autobiographical piece used to promote *This Side of Paradise,* Scott described himself physically as "somewhat Nordic," a pose later revisited in an essay describing himself and Zelda on a Parisian holiday: "We . . . , blond both of us, cast supercilious Nordic glances at the play of the dark children around us." Fascinated by privilege, Fitzgerald longed to look behind the closed curtains that suggested richer and rarer treasures. "There was a ripe mystery about it," he wrote of Gatsby's infatuation with Daisy's world, "a hint of bedrooms upstairs more beautiful and cool than other bedrooms, of gay and radiant activities taking place through its corridors and of romances that were not musty and laid away already in lavender but fresh and breathing and redolent of this year's shining motor cars and of dances whose flowers were scarcely withered."[14] This foundling child never stopped searching for his true people—even when he knew the uncomfortable truth.

In a 1933 letter to the writer John O'Hara, Scott dissected the origins of his lifelong Celtic complex:

> I am half black Irish and half old American stock with the usual exaggerated ancestral pretensions. The black Irish half of the family had the money and looked down upon the Maryland side of the family who had, and really had, that certain series of reticences and obligations that go under the poor old shattered word "breeding." . . . So being born in that atmosphere of crack, wisecrack and countercrack I developed a two-cylinder inferiority complex. So if I were elected King of Scotland tomorrow after graduating from Eton, Magdalene to Guards, with an embryonic history which tied me to the Plantagenets, I would still be a parvenue.[15]

In fact, Fitzgerald's ethno-religious background presented something of a double bind. St. Paul's old French families, with their grand Québécois past and genteel aspirations, constituted a kind of higher-caste Catholic; the city's Irish, by contrast, were seen as coming straight off the potato farm.[16] Most of the latter were unskilled laborers—household servants and dockworkers—and thus lacking the colorful occupational ancestry of the region's ethnic-French fur traders. By the late nineteenth century, St. Paul's Irish had become a fixture in the city's politics and police force, and though this brought a kind of security and polite middle-class respectability, it held no charm for Fitzgerald. Like Gatsby, he left the Midwest to adopt a series of identities, be they the "shattered" if pedigreed remnants of the gentry-minded Maryland stock, the "metropolitan spirit" of triumph he associated with New York City, or, in a final and less satisfying permutation, the Hollywood screenwriter.

If places shaped Scott's sense of worth, so too did a few of the new acquaintances he made at the Newman School, particularly the English novelist Shane Leslie. Brought to Newman by Fay, Leslie was the first professional writer to read over Fitzgerald's material and offer criticism and support. More personally, he unveiled to Scott an attractive Celtic cosmopolitanism that countered the culture's prevailing Anglocentrism. Though evidence suggests that Leslie thought Fitzgerald a minor talent and merely humored his callow literary ambitions, Scott seemed blind to any doubts. Rather, and in a typical Fitzgerald fashion, he overdramatized the situation, spying in Leslie, a Catholic crossover like Fay, a Byronic figure equal parts adventurer and aristocrat. And to be sure, Leslie brought to the table all of the surnames, schools, and connections certain to impress Fitzgerald. He was a member of the Irish landed gentry, had attended King's College, at Cambridge, and counted Winston Churchill a cousin. Fitzgerald later recalled his meeting Leslie as both revelatory and multilayered in meaning:

> He first came into my life as the most romantic figure I had ever known. He had sat at the feet of Tolstoy, he had gone swimming with Rupert Brooke, he had been a young Englishman of the governing classes when the sense of being one must have been, as [the writer] Compton McKenzie says, like the sense of being a Roman citizen.
>
> Also, he was a convert to the church of my youth, and he and another [Fay] . . . made of that church a dazzling, golden thing, dispelling its oppressive mugginess and giving the succession of days upon gray days, passing under its plaintive ritual, the romantic glamour of an adolescent dream.[17]

Had Fitzgerald first encountered Leslie, say, even a couple of years later, the impact would likely have been considerably less. Entering a Catholic "phase" and grateful to have a serious author speak seriously with him, Fitzgerald absorbed for a period everything Leslie had to offer.

What Scott lacked during this period was the self-awareness to realize that his patrons, despite their show of intimacy, were putting him on. Amused by his youthful conceit and boyish charm, Leslie and Fay lavishly praised his untried literary talents as something of a sport. "The Monsignor and perhaps myself had induced Fitzgerald to believe he was the future Catholic novelist for the United States, a parallel to Mgr. Hugh Benson in this country," Leslie informed the *Times Literary Supplement* several years after Fitzgerald's death. "We encouraged him to believe that he would write the unwritten great Catholic novel . . . of the United States."[18] Easily flattered, Fitzgerald accepted such sweetened dollops as his due—as the "son of a king."

Yet Fitzgerald was also sensitive that his self-absorption put others off, and he often, if not always persuasively, made light of his ambitions. Deep into his first novel, he concluded a letter to Leslie with the following lark: "Did you ever notice that remarkable coincidence.——Bernard Shaw is 61 yrs old, H. G. Wells is 51, G. K. Chesterton 41, you're 31, and I'm 21——all the great authors of the world in arithmetical progression." Despite the jesting tone, Fitzgerald obviously sought the comparison with Shaw and company, even if he had to be the one to make it. There was both an arrogance and innocence to his questing. At college, he had once naïvely confessed to his friend Edmund Wilson, "I want to be one of the greatest writers who ever lived, don't you."[19] Fitzgerald believed in his emerging talents and had no interest in becoming the next (and now forgotten) Robert Hugh Benson—nor would he confine himself to scratching out the great Catholic novel. As he had told Wilson, rather, he wanted nothing less than immortality; he wanted to write the Great American Novel, that secret wish of writers that remained, in Fitzgerald's era, as inviolable an ambition as Gatsby's own.

THREE

Forever Princeton

Though I loved Princeton I often felt that it was a by-water,
that its snobby institutions were easy to beat and to despise
and unless I was a natural steeplechaser or a society groom
I'd have to find my own private intellectual and emotional life.

F. Scott Fitzgerald to Scottie Fitzgerald, 1940

In the spring of 1913, Fitzgerald anxiously faced his collegiate future. A
spinster McQuillan aunt had promised funding on the condition that
Scott have a Catholic, that is, a Georgetown, education. That prospect
left Scott cold. The obvious alternative, enrollment in the local University of Minnesota, was even less appealing. Weaned on Mollie's pampering
and more recently introduced to Fay and Leslie's Celtic cosmopolitanism,
Fitzgerald considered himself special, unique, even fated. And special,
unique, even fated people did not attend provincial state universities. Nor
did they major in geography, chemistry, or accounting.[1] Caught in the
midst of America's evolving cultural apparatus—its shifting sexual mores,
emerging flapper metaphysics, and first restless tremors of Jazz Age
energy—Scott sought to experience this tilt toward modernism from
center rather than circumference. Accordingly, he looked toward the East
Coast, his eye settling on Princeton.

Early that summer, Scott's money crisis suddenly and accommodatingly lifted. The June death of his grandmother McQuillan left Mollie a
substantial legacy—perhaps as much as $125,000, some $3 million in current dollars. At that point, Fitzgerald determined Princeton to be *the*
place. Its proximity to New York, opportunities for literary outlets, and

aristocratic mien were the underlying attractions, even as other and less obvious factors were at work. Known as the Ivy for southern gentlemen, Princeton exuded a gallant, poised, and privileged quality that appealed to Fitzgerald. "[It] drew him most," he wrote of Amory Blaine, "with its atmosphere of bright colors and its alluring reputation as the pleasantest country club in America." Princeton further conveyed to Scott, in a dashing if doomed Lee-versus-Grant kind of way, the faint suggestion of impending capitulation before larger and more powerful forces. Here the lost cause of southern nationalism anticipated the ill-fated Princeton football team. "Yale always seemed to nose them out in the last quarter by superior 'stamina' as the newspapers called it," he later put the matter. "It was to me a repetition of the story of the foxes and the big animals in the child's book. I imagined the Princeton men as slender and keen and romantic, and the Yale men as brawny and brutal and powerful." *Gatsby*'s Tom Buchanan, he of the "hard mouth," "arrogant eyes," and "cruel body," was a Yale product.[2]

Staying with Fitzgerald's terminology, though applying it somewhat differently, one might say that Princeton's African American population—some 15 percent during this period—constituted the city's true "foxes." Many had come up from North Carolina, retaining their traditional rural folkways and building a strong and supportive community based on church and work. They were consigned in this Jim Crow setting to menial jobs, and their children's educational options were limited to a single segregated school that offered instruction only through the eighth grade. Fitzgerald's contemporary Paul Robeson, the great actor, singer, and political radical, grew up in Princeton and in a 1949 interview described the city of his youth as "spiritually located in Dixie," and he remembered its black population as being forced to engage in "bowing and scraping . . . [and] Uncle Tomming to earn enough to lead miserable lives."[3]

Keeping this racialized town-and-gown divide in mind, it is clear that Princeton meant different things to different people, and the university's lazy, privileged pose, combined with its cool indifference, worked on Scott like an aphrodisiac. In May, he took the university's entrance examinations at the New York YMCA and failed—this despite, as he later confided to his *Ledger,* resorting to the crutch of "Cribbing."[4] Like an ardent suitor, he showed up at Princeton in September and sat for reexams with the same result. Desperate but unwilling to concede defeat, Fitzgerald scheduled an appointment with the Admissions Committee to appeal his case. That day, the day of his seventeenth birthday, he talked himself into Princeton. The foundling child had come "home."

One wonders just how this less-than-stellar student sold himself to the university. No doubt its gatekeepers noticed the respect, indeed reverence, he enthused for the school. They may have further been drawn to his articulateness, charisma, and physical beauty—the kind of magnetic properties of persuasion that had drawn Fay and numerous others struck by Fitzgerald's youthful attractiveness. "In appearance, I remember Scott as handsome, keen-looking, rather dependent on charm to entertain people," wrote one classmate, expressing a common conception. "His . . . eyes were green, which may have been one secret of his fascination. His hair was light in shade, . . . neatly parted in the middle."[5] Projecting the image of a healthy, clean-cut collegiate, Fitzgerald looked the part of a Princeton prep, aided in this overall impression by a slight if telling sartorial affectation that he was never to surrender. Even in his final, balmy Hollywood days, he remained uniformed in saddle shoes, oxford shirt, and blazer.

Some critics and readers have seen in Fitzgerald's pursuit of Princeton a broader infatuation with money that negatively shaped both his personal values and his literary imagination. John Peale Bishop, a minor poet and man of letters, befriended Scott at Princeton, and years later, in a notable 1937 essay, "The Missing All," he wrote, "Though love is always in the foreground in the sentimental world of Fitzgerald, no allure is so potent as money. . . . In the Midwest where Fitzgerald grew up, it was the common dream that riches made the superior person. . . . Fitzgerald partakes of that dream and is too intelligent not to know it for what it is worth." Scott took this criticism in stride, writing to yet another Princeton friend, "[Bishop] reproached me with being a suck around the rich. I've had this before."[6]

In fact, wealth interested Fitzgerald primarily as an entry to experiences otherwise denied. One need not read far into the Fitzgerald canon to understand his complex reactions to the leisure class, which might be fairly synopsized as a measured contempt for its inability to make much of its advantages. In effect, he believed that wealth was wasted on the rich. Like Gatsby, Scott regarded money as a means to greater emotional ends rather than an end in itself. He clarified this attitude in "Winter Dreams," a fine 1922 short story whose title serves as a euphemism for the evanescent promises of youth, love, and happiness. In that story, Fitzgerald briefly but pointedly analyzes a posh eastern university's magical hold on one Dexter Green, another September freshman from Minnesota:

> Now, of course, the quality and the seasonability of these winter dreams varied, but the stuff of them remained. They persuaded Dexter several years later to pass up a business course at the State university . . . for the precarious advantage of attending an older and more famous university in the East, where he was bothered by his scanty funds. But do not get the impression, because his winter dreams happened to be concerned at first with musings on the rich, that there was anything merely snobbish in the boy. He wanted not associations with glittering things and glittering people—he wanted the glittering things themselves. Often he reached out for the best without knowing why he wanted it.[7]

In reaching out to Princeton, Fitzgerald took the school only partly on its own terms, romanticizing its gothic façade into a sentimental education distinct from the self-conscious intellectual grind of a Harvard or a Yale. In an almost indolent way, the school refused to acknowledge the world beyond its garden green. Much of the country experienced fierce cultural clashes during these years, pitting metropolitan and rural, ethnic and Anglo, and, on the Prohibition front, wets and drys. The rise of a new United States of America, one distinctly urban, industrial, and more conspicuously tinctured with Slavic, Mediterranean, and Jewish peoples, fueled this friction, but Princeton, as far as the still-in-his-teens Fitzgerald could see, remained detached and indifferent. Its young men basked in the superiority of their superiority. Very much the outsider wanting to be inside, Scott never mastered this passive persona. He operated emotionally close to the surface of things, violating the gentlemen's agreement to exude a practiced poise. Such callow admissions as he made to Wilson about wanting to be "one of the greatest writers who have ever lived" came perilously close, in the parlance of the day, to "running it out." Fitzgerald's response to the reserved Princetonians—and perhaps Wilson—can be read in *This Side of Paradise:* "Well then don't spoil it. If I enjoy going around telling people guilelessly that I think I'm a genius, let me do it."[8]

As to formal instruction, Fitzgerald found little in Princeton's curriculum to fire his imagination. The study of poetry and literature—Fitzgerald's proposed field—belonged to a department anchored in orthodoxy. Robert Browning's verse, Matthew Arnold's criticism, and Charles Dickens's novels passed as "contemporary" writing, while Frank Norris, Jack London, and Joseph Conrad, the emissaries of recent innovations in realism and naturalism, were summarily ignored. Dismayed at the dons' tone deafness, Scott later called the English department "surprisingly pallid, . . . top-heavy, undistinguished and with an uncanny knack of making literature distasteful to young men." He unapologetically ignored them.

As usual, Fitzgerald found it easier to reimagine the surface of his surroundings than to defer to an unpleasant or merely tedious reality. Thus, his "Princeton" radiated a "quieter, mellower and less exigent" mood, one that evoked an autumnal paradise of scented burning leaves drifting over a dreamy college-scape.[9] He affectionately wrote in a 1927 essay of the spell the university had cast on him:

> Princeton is in the flat midlands of New Jersey, rising, a green Phoenix, out of the ugliest country in the world. Sordid Trenton sweats and festers a few miles south; northward are Elizabeth and the Erie Railroad and the suburban slums of New York; westward the dreary upper purlieus of the Delaware River. But around Princeton, shielding her, is a ring of silence—certified milk dairies, great estates with peacocks and deer parks, pleasant farms and woodlands which we paced off and mapped down in the spring of 1917 in preparation for the war. The busy East has already dropped away when the branch train rattles familiarly from the junction. Two tall spires and then suddenly all around you spreads out the loveliest riot of Gothic architecture in America, battlement linked on to battlement, hall to hall, arch-broken, vine-covered—luxuriant and lovely over two square miles of green grass. Here is no monotony, no

feeling that it was all built yesterday at the whim of last week's millionaire; Nassau Hall was already twenty years old when Hessian bullets pierced its sides.[10]

This gilded Princeton portrait is meant to distance the campus from the desultory game of buying and selling, the crimsoned business of birth and dying going on outside its gates. Here is an Edenic vision of an older pastoral America still resonant on the eve of the Great War. Of course, much of it is pure fabrication. The "ancient" architectural structures described by Fitzgerald, including the "two tall spires" dominating the Princeton campus—Holder and Cleveland—were erected, respectively, in 1910 and 1913, the latter being the year Fitzgerald arrived. Most of the university's buildings dated back only one or two generations, the gifts of industrial titans and prosperous bankers. Fitzgerald's unwillingness to think of Princeton as a place that grasped for reputation and respectability is a special case. Note, by comparison, his shrewd observations of Long Island's arrivistes. Jay Gatsby, for one, occupies an impossibly grand Hôtel de Ville knockoff whose thinly ivied exterior hints at its recent construction.

Edmund Wilson returned to Princeton often over the years, immune to its magic and Scott's sentimentality. "By the time I read Fitzgerald's *This Side of Paradise*," he remembered, "his picture of Princeton life had seemed to me more or less preposterous. I told him later that he had never really been to Princeton, that he had always been drunk or deluded, and had lived in a personal fantasy." Precisely. Yet it was this set-to-dreaming sensibility that brought a distinctive voice to Fitzgerald's writing. Thus, Wilson's reproach of his friend for having "made little attempt to learn anything, as far as his courses were concerned," seems distinctly off center.[11] After all, Princeton's real *and imagined* charm, history, and traditions are what moved Scott, who then took what he needed from the extended encounter and castle-built the rest.

The *actual* Princeton of Fitzgerald's day lent itself to a romantic rendering on the grounds that in an age of rampant industrial development, it still retained the ambience of a nineteenth-century village. The student body in 1913 stood at about fifteen hundred, while Nassau Street, Princeton's main thoroughfare, remained unpaved and the near-exclusive province of horses, buggies, and bicycles—only six undergraduates registered automobiles that year. Unsurprisingly, a conservative outlook distinguished the campus. According to a class survey, only slightly more than half of the students in Scott's senior cohort said they had kissed a girl; over 10 percent believed that causal kissing constituted a vice. About 65 percent claimed they did not drink, and nearly 20 percent declared drinking "morally wrong." Students were required to attend chapel through Fitzgerald's sophomore year, and Sunday sporting activities were frowned on. As at other universities, students found security in conformity. Bishop later wrote of Princeton's firm if unstated social code, "Nothing matters much but that a man bear an agreeable person and maintain with slightly mature modifications the standards of prep school. Any extreme in habiliment [clothing], pleasures or opinions . . . is to lose all chance of social distinction."[12]

Academically, Princeton presented Fitzgerald with his greatest collegiate challenge. Admitted with conditions in algebra, Latin, French, and physics, he fell into the habit of failing classes, which were expected to be made up the following semester while carrying the new term's regular load. He did not stand alone in this respect; some two-thirds of his 430 classmates were admitted with conditions; about 10 percent did not complete their first year.[13] Still, Scott begged the point and the patience of his professors, taking forty-nine cuts as a freshman, the allowable limit before penalty. There is evidence that he later regretted his half education and felt a certain intellectual impoverishment because of it. In the late 1930s, he wrote to a college-bound Scottie,

> One time in sophomore year at Princeton, Dean West got up and rolled out the great lines of Horace:
>
> > "Integer Vitae, scelerisque pueris
> > Non eget mauris, facule nec arcu—"
>
> And I knew in my heart that I had missed something by being a poor Latin scholar, like a blessed evening with a lovely girl. It was a great human experience I had rejected through laziness, through having sown no painful seed.[14]

In sum, Scott regarded the lecture hall as but one of many and by no means the most important of collegiate experiences. An apathetic student who left without a degree, he nevertheless made his mark on the school as few of its graduates ever have. His novels, *Post* stories, and autobiographical essays bear the indelible impress of the Princeton years and more broadly his experiences within the privileged world of the Ivy elite. In the best sense, Scott made Princeton pay—and he paid Princeton back. While battling a rearguard action against poor grades, he plied the *Nassau Literary Magazine,* the *Princeton Tiger,* and the *Daily Princetonian* with scraps, doggerel, poems, and ephemera. During sophomore year, he penned "A Cheer for Princeton," the winning lyric in a competition to introduce a new football fight song. Far more than most of his peers, Fitzgerald contributed, and did so gladly, to the mystique of the school—his apprentice writings trickled through the dorms and the dining halls, shaping in their wake the identity of Princeton 1917.

As at many universities, the quickest route to campus immortality still ran through football, and the undersized Fitzgerald (138 pounds) gamely gave the sport one final try. He wired Mollie that first September, "ADMITTED SEND FOOTBALL PADS AND SHOES IMMEDIATELY PLEASE WAIT TRUNK." After a single day of practice, he set his gear aside forever. Triangle Club, a popular theatrical troupe founded in 1891 that in Fitzgerald's day toured during the Christmas holiday as far west as St. Louis, presented a secondary but perfectly respectable path to glory. Indeed, Scott later recounted it as the main reason for his coming to Princeton: "Near the end of my last year at [Newman] I came across a new musical-comedy score lying on top of the piano. It was a show called 'His Honor the Sultan,' and the title furnished the information that it had been presented by the Triangle Club of Princeton University. That was enough for me. From then on the university question was settled. I was bound for Princeton." Though just a freshman, Fitzgerald was determined to write the lyrics for Triangle's 1914–1915 show. Accordingly, he devoted his second semester to the enterprise, cut dozens of classes, and ended the academic year with new conditions. His *Ledger* report for February 1914 reads in part, "Began ▲ play. . . . Failed many exams." Even when accounting for this surfeit of low marks, however, he got what he wanted. His entry to the competition—*Fie! Fie! Fi-Fi!*, the surface-silly tale of an American grifter who becomes prime minister of Monaco—won out. Interestingly, but perhaps not surprisingly, its opening chorus chimed with the themes of place, dispossession, and status that preoccupied its author:

> Cynical, critical, bored and analytical.
> Visitors from ev'ry land that sports a millionaire,
> Nouveau riche, pedigreed, of a high or petty breed,
> Wandering from place to place to get a traveled air.[15]

Poor grades and quashed football fantasies aside, Fitzgerald had made much of his first year at Princeton. Going forward, he would try to rack up as many publications and prizes as he could pack into his collegiate turn before the cycle of failed exams inevitably squeezed him out of the university.

In December of Fitzgerald's sophomore year, *Fie! Fie! Fi-Fi!* premiered at Princeton before setting off on an elaborate Christmas tour that included stops in Chicago and St. Louis. Impressed reviewers singled out Fitzgerald for particular praise. The *Baltimore Sun* said, "Much of the success of the entertainment was due to the clever lyrics of F. S. Fitzgerald, who has written some really excellent 'pater songs.'" The *Louisville Post* insisted, "F. S. Fitzgerald . . . could take his place right now with the brightest writers of witty lyrics in America." That late winter, the accolades continued. Triangle made Fitzgerald its secretary-elect, and he received bids from several university eating clubs (the school banned fraternities from the mid-nineteenth century until the 1980s) before choosing Cottage, one of the "big four" residing on Prospect Avenue. Housed in a ruddy-bricked two-and-a-half-story Georgian Revival building, Cottage was described by Wilson, also a member, as "social and convivial in a lightweight way."[16]

At the election dinner, Fitzgerald got tight, an increasingly common activity noticed by his peers. Some friends believed that his drinking was nothing more than a rite of passage, part of the collegiate experience as much as athletics, course work, and clubs. "Occasionally, I was conscious of his stumbling down the corridor when he came in, or dropping his pencil," recalled Dale Warren, a freshman during Fitzgerald's junior year when the two lived across the hall from each other in Little Hall: "His few hours' sleep seldom refreshed him, and I began to sus-pect that the morning haze might well be due to a beery night at the 'Nass,' Princeton's nearest equivalent to a den of iniquity. Once or twice I found him lying fully or partly clothed on top of the rumpled bed-spread. One morning when he was not there at all I assumed that he was out-of-town, but later learned through the grapevine that he had spent the small hours of the night on the dewy grass somewhere out behind the Peacock Inn."[17] Such sporadic evening siestas combined with an im-pending Triangle Club production and the inevitable campus publications to leave Fitzgerald little time for study. Moreover, the beckoning of major metropolitan centers provided temptations certain to torpedo the scholastically indifferent. Fitzgerald recited his struggles in the *Nassau Literary Magazine:* "Winter muses, unacademic and cloistered by 42nd Street and Broadway, had stolen hours from the dreary stretches of Feb-ruary and March. Later, time had crept insidiously through the lazy April afternoons and seemed so intangible in the long spring twilights. So June found him unprepared." Having made no concessions to the academic calendar, he was required to take postterm makeup exams in coordinate geometry, Latin, and qualitative analysis.[18]

If sophomore year brought to Fitzgerald the promise of prizes, junior year hastened the end of his collegiate career. Fall term found Scott aca-demically ineligible to hold a Triangle Club office, though he remained deeply involved in its upcoming production, all the while plying the *Tiger* with offerings. As usual, his course work suffered. In November, he vis-ited the infirmary on two occasions with an apparently light case of ma-laria; later that month, he withdrew from Princeton and returned to St. Paul. Under the cloak of illness, Fitzgerald managed to avoid taking exams, but the repercussions were ruinous. Hoping to return to campus in February and simply make up a few classes, he learned instead that he would have to repeat his junior year. Christian Gauss, a member of the English department and Fitzgerald's favorite professor, later re-called the circumstances of his withdrawal. "To say Scott left college in 1916 because of illness is a polite fiction. Scott left before the examina-tions, as I recall, because he had been neglecting his work very badly and I know he was failing a course he was taking with me. He knew it too! He had spent most of his time working on the Triangle show and by dropping out before the examinations he saved himself from academic difficulties which were seriously impending." A letter to Fitzgerald from the university made clear that his difficulties at Princeton were due to his poor academic performance. Embarrassed and sensing he had been out-foxed, Fitzgerald moved to alter the historical record and, if possible, salvage his collegiate future. In May, he wheedled from Dean Howard McClenahan a revised statement: "Mr. F. Scott Fitzgerald withdrew from Princeton voluntarily on January third, nineteen hundred and six-teen, because of ill health and he was fully at liberty, at that time, to go on with his class, if his health had permitted." Under separate cover, McClenahan sneered at Fitzgerald's tactical maneuver: "This is for your sensitive feelings. I hope you will find it soothing."[19]

In retrospect, Fitzgerald should never have returned to Princeton. While he managed to salvage a little immediate personal pride, it came at the expense of further humiliations. "I had lost certain offices," he later recalled; "the chief one was the presidency of the Triangle Club . . . and also I dropped back a class. To me college would never be the same. There were to be no badges of pride, no medals after all."[20] Fitzgerald continued to publish in the campus periodicals, but it became increasingly evident that he had passed a point of no return at Princeton—he was now simply marking time. The January 1917 exams nearly finished him off when the impending U.S. entry into the First World War—evident in Germany's resumption that month of unrestricted submarine warfare—changed everything. Scott took advantage of a university program that allowed students who signed up for intensive military training to immediately drop their courses but receive credit for them. In effect, the war gave Fitzgerald an honorable out from his scholastic dead end.

Despite struggling academically, Fitzgerald had made great strides in-tellectually at Princeton. His natural curiosity, combined with a com-petitive desire to be "in the know," inspired a bookishness that had little to do with the curriculum. Like many gifted, high-achieving people who were poor students, Fitzgerald was largely self-taught; his solitary reading, constant writing, and engagement with peers constituted a kind of alternative schooling. Wilson, a year ahead of Fitzgerald, remembered such informal tutorials playing a critical role at Princeton. The men who sought each other out fashioned, he observed years later, "a kind of professional group, now becoming extinct and a legend, in which the practice of letters was a common craft and the belief in its value a common motivation. . . . You read Shakespeare, Shelley, George Meredith, Dostoevsky, Ibsen, and you wanted, however imperfectly and on however infinitesimal a scale, to learn their trade and have the freedom of their company. [When Fitzgerald] got to better writers, his standards and achievements went sharply up, and he would always have pitted himself against the best in his own line that he knew."[21] And perhaps "the best" at Princeton, the man most capable of stimulating Fitzgerald with his own infectious love of literature, was John Peale Bishop.

Bishop entered Princeton in 1913 at the age of twenty-one, following a debilitating illness that had caused him to temporarily lose his sight. Mature, steady, sensitive, and generous, he complemented the spontaneous, surface-unserious Fitzgerald. "Long afterwards," Bishop wrote, "I complained to him that I thought he took seventeen as his norm, making everything later a falling off. For a moment he demurred, then said, 'If you make it fifteen, I will agree with you.'" They met early in their freshmen year, suddenly sitting side by side in a corner table at the Peacock Inn. "So quick to conversation" is how Bishop remembered Fitzgerald. They talked through late afternoon and into the evening; other students joined along, left, joined, and left, the rolling exchange a litany of books, authors, and Fitzgerald's sundry "accomplishments." Bishop's regal manner—one professor said that "John had a self possession and self mastery which gave him the pose and bearing of a young English lord"—no doubt appealed to Scott. More, the two shared both a love of literature and a sense of coming to Princeton as outsiders. Bishop, a West Virginian, was older than his classmates and had arrived in the East after attending Mercersburg Academy, a second-tier prep school in rural south-central Pennsylvania, just north of the Mason-Dixon line.[22]

In the 1920s, Bishop married into wealth—and that bothered Fitzgerald. Scott believed that this union deadened his friend's writing, and he remarked uncharitably to Wilson, "nobody ever sold himself for as little gold as he did."[23] In quieter moments, Fitzgerald could recount with a fair degree of honesty Bishop's special contributions to his literary development. In one 1940 letter to Scottie, then a Vassar junior, he offered the following tutorial: "[Poetry] isn't something easy to get started on by yourself. You need, at the beginning, some enthusiast who also knows his way around—John Peale Bishop performed that service for me at Princeton. I had always dabbled in 'verse' but he made me see, in the course of a couple of months, the difference between poetry and non-poetry. After that one of my first discoveries was that some of the professors who were teaching really hated it and didn't know what it was about."[24]

Bishop's contributions to Fitzgerald's education were real enough, but the relationship was far from one-sided. Scott's alertness to changing cultural attitudes, pitch-perfect ear, and finely honed writing put the friendship on equal grounds. And despite their temperamental differences, both were drawn to the artistic and intellectual possibilities embedded in the beautiful-boy-genius role sometimes played by Scott, who came to embody for Bishop a kind of Grecian ideal. Bishop reflected on this role when he wrote "The Hours," an elegy published in the *New Republic* shortly after Scott's death. It reads in part,

> No promise such as yours when like the spring
> You came, colors of jonquils in your hair,
> Inspired as the wind, when woods are bare
> And every silence is about to sing.
> None had such promise then, and none
> Your scapegrace wit or your disarming grace;
> For you were bold as was Danaë's son,
> Conceived like Perseus in a dream of gold.
> And there was none when you were young, not one,
> So prompt in the reflecting shield to trace
> The glittering aspect of a Gorgon age.[25]

Like Fay, Bishop discovered in Fitzgerald a persistent spirit, oddly infectious. Taken in whole, he received perhaps the best of their bond.

One might say the same of Edmund "Bunny" Wilson, one of the "American Century's" great men of letters. A year older than Fitzgerald, bookish and reserved, "Bunny" (his mother thought he resembled a rabbit) and Scott were friendly if not particularly intimate at Princeton. They collaborated on the 1915–1916 Triangle Club production *The Evil Eye,* with Wilson writing the book and Fitzgerald the lyrics. The former initiated the joint venture after composing a dry draft. "I am sick of it myself," he wrote Scott; "perhaps you can infuse into it some of the fresh effervescence of youth for which you are so justly celebrated."[26] Later, as a distinguished literary critic, Wilson served as editor of Fitzgerald's final and unfinished novel, *The Last Tycoon,* as well as of *The Crack-Up,* a collection of Scott's essays, notes, and letters. In this keeper-of-the-flame capacity, he had a large and not altogether salutary impact on Fitzgerald's reputation into the 1960s.

Despite the collaborative nature of Fitzgerald's relationship with Wilson while at Princeton, Fitzgerald quickly deferred to Bunny, and this set a pattern that followed both men through their lives. Long after their college days, Scott remained sensitive to Wilson's presence, opinions, and judgments. "For twenty years a certain man had been my intellectual conscience," Fitzgerald wrote in a 1936 essay. "That was Edmund Wilson." As one might guess, the returns on such an unbalanced friendship were somewhat mixed. Fitzgerald's infrequent if invaluable communications with Wilson gave him the sense of belonging to a small circle of Americans intensely interested in literary trends. Less constructively, Wilson's habit of slighting Fitzgerald, both in print and in his private writings and comments, denigrated his friend's artistic merits and guided critics for a generation. In an early profile of Scott published in the March 1922 edition of the *Bookman,* Wilson wrote that Fitzgerald "has been given imagination without intellectual control of it; he has been given the desire for beauty without an aesthetic ideal; and he has been given a gift for expression without very many ideas to express."[27] In other words, Scott was something of a clever fool.

Princeton, for its part, also remained an ideal of scholarly erudition and fashionable society that Scott could never shake. As if to keep his ardor fresh, the school stayed always at arm's distance. In April 1920,

Fitzgerald returned to Princeton with his new bride, Zelda Sayre, to serve, incredibly, as chaperones at a weekend house party. Delighting in an audience but as usual exaggerating the moment, Scott introduced Zelda as his mistress and later took a black eye in a small ruckus. Insisting that he had shamed his old club, Cottage briefly suspended Scott's membership. A number of years later, Fitzgerald asked his former teacher Christian Gauss, now dean of the college, if he might offer a lecture series through the English department "on the actual business of creating fiction." Concerned with Scott's drinking, Gauss politely told the author of *The Great Gatsby* and *Tender Is the Night* that he could meet more or less informally—and without financial remuneration—with an undergraduate literary club instead.[28]

Those who knew Fitzgerald agreed that Princeton had done him more harm than good. Sensitive and impressionable, this argument runs, he confused surface for substance, conceptualizing an idealized Anglo-Saxon world. John Biggs, who briefly roomed with Scott in Campbell Hall, recalled, "We were all snobs about something, . . . [and] Fitzgerald was a snob's snob. But I think it was to cover up a sense of inferiority." John D. McMaster, a *Tiger* editor, observed that Scott's Newman School credentials paled in comparison to Princeton's traditional feeders, which included Exeter and Andover, Lawrenceville and St. Georges. "What Fitzgerald really had in mind, what he felt deep in his own heart," McMaster believed, "was the want of full social acceptance in the nest of the Wasps in which he found himself."[29] And not long after Scott's death, Wilson wrote to Gauss that Princeton had poisoned his friend (the Mary that Wilson refers to is his wife, the writer Mary McCarthy): "I have been thinking about the whole group, and I believe that, in certain ways, Princeton did not serve them very well. I said this to Mary, who has had considerable opportunity to observe the men from the various colleges, and she said: 'Yes, Princeton didn't give them quite moral principle enough to be writers.' Instead, it gave you too much respect for money and country-house social prestige. Both Scott and John [Peale Bishop] in their respective ways, I think, fell victim to this."[30] Taken altogether, Biggs's, Wilson's, and McCarthy's insights say much about Fitzgerald's uneven reaction to the rich. He coveted their privileges, ease, and self-confidence, all the while resenting their essentially materialistic worldview. As Morris Dickstein has cogently put the matter, "like Henry James in *The Portrait of a Lady,* [Fitzgerald] sees how leisure and culture are intertwined, though he's hardly convinced that one assures the other."[31]

Outside the Princeton circuit, others took note of Scott's alienation. Marjorie Kinnan Rawlings, author of the Pulitzer Prize–winning novel *The Yearling,* met Fitzgerald in the fall of 1936, and the two subsequently engaged in a brief correspondence. She later remembered that Fitzgerald "talked of the caste system at such places as Princeton and Harvard": "I realized that a great part of Scott's writings and personal difficulties came from a sense of inferiority, in the face of such a collegiate system. My impression of him was of the true artist, who had been conditioned to false values, and that while he understood that the values were spurious, could not disassociate himself from them."[32] True as those words are, they tell only part of Fitzgerald's Princeton story. For although Rawlings correctly identified the university's corrosive influence on Scott, she underestimated the extent to which it armed him with a wealth of material, perspectives, and provocations. A sensitive reading of his books demonstrates both their fealty to the Ivy epitome and their awareness that such devotion ultimately rests on an illusion. He was, after all, in on the joke. Like the golden girls he immortalized, the preps and the Princetons contained below their polished surfaces hidden depths and dangers. Or, put slightly differently, the seeker got what the seeker sought. In a retrospective essay Fitzgerald wrote on his collegiate years, written a decade after his class (but not he) had graduated, he stressed the radiant over the routine, shrewdly dissecting the special magic of America's campus culture: "Looking back over a decade one sees the ideal of a university become a myth, a vision, a meadow lark among the smoke stacks. Yet perhaps it is there at Princeton, only more elusive than under the skies of the Prussian Rhineland or Oxfordshire; or perhaps some men come upon it suddenly and possess it, while others wander forever outside. Even these seek in vain through middle age for any corner of the republic that preserves so much of what is fair, gracious, charming and honorable in American life."[33]

FOUR

Golden Girl

I *know* I am a flirt and I can't stop it. . . . I am pretty
good on the whole, but you know how much alike we are.

Ginevra King to F. Scott Fitzgerald, 1915

Readers and scholars alike have long recognized Fitzgerald's faculty for
capturing in an unusually vivid way the particular hopes and disappointments of youth. His stories and nonfiction pieces are filled with the telling
and retelling of firsts—the long review of early successes, rapidly made
fortunes, and formative loves. Much of what Scott wrote on these themes
he had experienced directly, be it in a larger or smaller scope. As a child,
he could claim a diminishing if still felt connection to the upper-
midwestern gentry, and as an emerging writer in his early twenties, he
knew the pleasure of publishing with both the house of Scribner and the
Saturday Evening Post. He knew, too, the sudden, unexpected alchemy
of boyish romance. His first impressionable flirtation proved to be an
innocent, safe, and altogether affable courtship of Marie Hersey, a
St. Paul neighbor. The new emotion is recorded in Scott's *Ledger* entry
for March 1911 (he was fourteen at the time), reading in part, "Dancing
school. Marie. Love."[1]

As a professional writer, Fitzgerald sometimes drew on his St. Paul
days for material, and Hersey makes an occasional appearance in his work.
One can find her inspiration most distinctly in "The Scandal Detectives,"
a 1928 short story that inaugurated the Basil Duke Lee series, in which
Scott mined from his youthful exploits and remembrances from, say,
ten to seventeen. In one splendid scene, Fitzgerald beautifully captures

the precise moment when a budding sexuality first imposes itself on a boy's will:

> Basil rode over to Imogene Bissel and balanced idly on his wheel before her. Something in his face then must have attracted her, for she looked up at him, looked at him really, and slowly smiled. She was to be a beauty and belle of many proms in a few years. . . . For a moment Basil was granted an insight into the future, and the spell of her vitality crept over him suddenly. For the first time in his life he realized a girl completely as something opposite and complementary to him, and he was subject to a warm chill of mingled pleasure and pain. It was a definite experience and he was immediately conscious of it.[2]

And just as sympathetically did he probe the perishability of young love, writing a few pages later, "After another week [Basil] found that he no longer grieved over losing Imogene. Meeting her, he saw only the familiar little girl he had always known. The ecstatic moment of that afternoon had been a premature birth, an emotion left over from an already fleeting spring." This passage stands as Scott's remembrance of his friendly rival Reuben Warner's superior courting skills and of his own struggles to make sense of his adolescent emotions. He and Hersey remained on good terms, and in 1936, after reading Scott's confessional "Crack-Up" essays in *Esquire* (a not-for-the-faint-of-heart series detailing his struggles with drink and depression), she generously reached out to him. "It was damn nice of you to write me," he replied in a chatty and unreserved letter. "I think of you as about my oldest real friend, certainly my first love."[3] And through this first love, he met his next love—the one that he never quite shook or wanted to.

Halfway through Fitzgerald's sophomore year at Princeton, he made the acquaintance of the beautiful Ginevra King, a Chicago debutante whose family was part of the Windy City's turn-of-the-century banking and brokerage aristocracy. If not quite of Swift, McCormick, or Armour stock, the Kings nevertheless could be counted among a small concentration of first families who migrated to Lake Forest each summer to escape the oppressive city heat in elegant North Shore manors. In the city, the Kings occupied a home on North Astor Street, part of the

"Gold Coast" district developed in the 1880s by the businessman Potter Palmer, who put up a mock Rhenish castle that could easily have rivaled Gatsby's grand mansion. More than a gathering of the local elite, this area contained some of the nation's wealthiest people. As Chicago's central and southern neighborhoods swelled with industry, butchering yards, and immigrants, the well-to-do sought to create peaceful suburban spaces to the north, far from offending noises and smells. These residential areas contained modern amenities including paved streets, sewage lines, and water mains; encounters—and potential clashes—between social classes were unlikely.

Considering the Kings' elevated status, Scott's courtship of Ginevra appears to have been a fool's errand, a case of begging inevitable disappointment. And to be sure, there is something in character in Fitzgerald's quixotic pursuit. A dreamy sympathizer with Confederates and Celts, he leaned easily toward history's beautiful losers; as a lost "foundling child," a failed footballer, and an Ivy outsider, he counted himself among their brave number, always, and unevenly, fighting above his bantam weight. Ginevra represented yet another variation of this theme. What place, aside from an occasional amusing companion, could Fitzgerald have with her?

With Fitzgerald's contact with Ginevra confined to letters and a precious few assignations, he was free to construct the relationship largely in his mind as he turned Ginevra into a muse. In the end, this proved far more valuable than anything she could have directly given him. Ginevra became in his novels and short stories a composite of flapper, flirt, and baby-vamp, the temptress who stands for wealth and irresponsibility in relation to a man situated precariously between his work and his woman. She was, as James L. W. West III, the author of an authoritative study on the Fitzgerald-King romance, has accurately observed, "arguably the most important romance Fitzgerald ever experienced, more than Zelda. He lost her, but his ideal of her remained throughout his life."[4]

Lithe, refined, and crowned with curly dark hair complemented by large brown eyes, Ginevra King—extravagantly named after Leonardo's painting *Ginevra de Benci* (1474)—was sixteen when she met Fitzgerald at a Summit Avenue house party in January 1915. He was on winter break from

Princeton, and she from Westover School in Middlebury, Connecticut. Hersey, her classmate, hosted the gathering. Together with Edith Cummings, Courtney Letts, and Margaret Carry, Ginevra was part of the self-proclaimed "Big Four," a small band of debutantes belonging to wealthy Chicago families. Practiced players of country-club and summerhouse circles, they were noted for their looks, charm, and athleticism. Cummings, a gifted amateur golfer (nicknamed "the Fairway Flapper"), was to appear on the cover of *Time* magazine in 1924—Fitzgerald modeled Jordan Baker after her in *The Great Gatsby*.

Set to return to Princeton later that evening, Scott felt an instant attraction to Ginevra and rearranged his train schedule in order to see her the following day at yet another gathering. Immediately thereafter, he commenced a steady bombardment of letters to Middlebury. These were lengthy dispatches, some too full to fit into a single envelope. Infatuated if not quite in love, Ginevra prized Fitzgerald's communiqués as evidence of her desirability. A popular girl, she could produce (and perhaps read aloud) his letters as trophies of her conquest.

Scott was a collector too, and standing near the shine of Ginevra's North Shore star, he could observe up close the workings of wealth and privilege. These experiences would be transformed in his fiction into the trope of spoiled girl and earnest boy and, still more broadly, into the allegory of corruptive power versus the pure imaginative impulse. If not literal renditions of his Lake Forest interlude, they nevertheless conveyed Fitzgerald's gnawing sense of inferiority. A few years after his death, Ginevra explained to one biographer the lightness in which she approached their relationship and the insecurity that her aloofness inevitably aroused: "I was definitely out for quantity in beaux, and although Scott was top man, I still wasn't serious enough not to want plenty of other attention! . . . Certainly my attitude didn't help an already super-sensitive and sentimental person."[5]

In fact, she and Scott were playing the same game, for he, too, was "out for quantity," although for decidedly different reasons. "I think she told herself that I was hers for the *special* effort," Fitzgerald wrote about the naïve Marie Hersey in a 1940 letter to Scottie. He then advised his daughter that, just as he had refused to indulge in a conventional romance, she might profitably play the field, taking in a wider array of passions and pains than her current admirer, one Bobby Coleman, could offer. "The point is that you have not exhausted any other type at its best except Bobby—you have only examined the second rate unproved man of other species. . . . You should know the young predatory business type, hard as hell, he will lick you maybe but you should know him."[6]

If Ginevra "defeated" Scott, it was a conquest he accepted as payment for proximity. An incorrigible inquisitor, he displayed early the writer's interest in how things worked. Before annoying Hemingway with questions about his premarital sexual experiences and bothering good friends Gerald and Sara Murphy with similar delicate queries, he asked Ginevra for details of her teen conquests. Beyond this vicarious voyeurism, and perhaps most importantly, the relationship allowed Scott to practice, as he was to put it in *Gatsby,* a "romantic readiness," the stimulant state that has forever pushed seekers onward. At times, the intensity of his attentions could be overpowering. "For heaven's sake," Ginevra wrote to him a few months after their first meeting, "D O N T idealize me!"[7] In truth, Fitzgerald gloried in the situation more than in the girl. Where something like love but not love existed, he easily filled in the empty spaces with his own imaginative placement of circumstances and emotions. This had less to do with Ginevra than with Scott's desire to take his writing beyond the *Nassau Literary Magazine.* To do so, he needed to discover a new range of sentiments, sensations, and sufferings. As with Princeton, entry into Ginevra's world offered Fitzgerald such an opportunity—and on both accounts, the clock was ticking.

By the spring, Ginevra's letters to Scott revealed a lessening of interest. Not long after they had met, she had several dreams about him, but now she replied to his probing in a perfunctory manner: "You're so darling and I wish I could see you again as you're so nice and I'd like to talk to you." This cooling may have simply reflected the short shelf life of a teenage crush, though it is possible that Scott's "in a house below the average" status tipped her hand. Just how far, after all, could he take her playful promise to him, to "marry any kind of man under the

sun—'Richman, poorman, beggarman, thief,' etc., if I really loved him."
Fitzgerald had good looks, a quick mind, and a thousand lines; his talent
for expression was already polished. Yet these represented, as he knew,
only secondary virtues, and the gulf between his and Ginevra's socioeconomic circumstances only widened on reflection. In any case, others may
have been eager to make Scott certain of his ancillary status. In the
summer of 1916, on a rare North Shore visit, someone at a party, if
Fitzgerald is to be believed, cruelly cut him down to size with the belit-
tling observation, "poor boys shouldn't think of marrying rich girls." The
line survives in Scott's *Ledger,* alongside other August entries, "Lake
Forrest . . . Petting Party. Ginevra . . . Dissapointment . . . Beautiful Billy
Mitchell" (the new "top man").[8]

Just who may have set Scott in his place remains a matter of conjecture, though one plausible candidate is Ginevra's father, Charles Garfield
King, to whom Gatsby's protagonist, the bullying Tom Buchanan, bears
a striking resemblance. Both attended Yale, both played polo, and both
called Lake Forest home. Buchanan is described in *Gatsby* as having "a
supercilious manner."[9] That King would have spoken such harsh words,
however, seems doubtful, and Fitzgerald may well have recorded them
not as a quote or paraphrase but as a truthful indication of what he felt
in such company. Wounded pride aside, Scott could stake some claim to
superiority in his fleeting association with the Kings. In his eyes, after
all, they had failed to translate their wealth into something finer than the
usual collection of country clubs and lawn parties that seemed to attract
their type. In this way, from the psychology of second best, Fitzgerald
silently struck his own flag, signaling a tentative prestige. For unlike
Ginevra's people, he came from "breeding."

Fitzgerald's romance with Ginevra ended in January 1917, precisely
two years after it began. In total, they had actually seen each other for
perhaps twenty-five or thirty hours spread out over a couple of Princeton-
Yale football games, the occasional house party, a chaperoned day in
New York, and a brief visit to Westover. Hurt, Fitzgerald asked for his
letters back. The full force of Ginevra's studied detachment must have
hit him hard when he received her cool reply:

Dear Scott—

I have destroyed your letters—so you needn't be afraid that they will be held up as incriminating evidence. They were harmless—have you a guilty conscience?

I'm sorry you think that I would hold them up to you as I never did think they meant anything.

If it isn't too much trouble you might destroy mine too.

Sincerely
Ginevra[10]

Fitzgerald complied with Ginevra's request, though not before making duplicates of the letters. In this way, he could literally honor her wish while retaining possession of her words. These transcriptions were subsequently typed and bound, though we don't know when Scott had this done; they come to over two hundred double-spaced pages.[11] Fitzgerald would draw on this private archive over the years as a resource as he tried to recapture in his prose the color and texture of the youthful struggle for love and glory. He used Zelda's diary—which he also had transcribed—for the same purpose.

Fitzgerald's courtship of Ginevra tells us something important about his mixed attitude toward women. Even a cursory perusal of his published writing reveals a penchant for dividing the genders between female realism and male romance. In the Fitzgerald canon, women are often wreckers of men, taking their dignity, extracting their vitality, and dulling their work habits. The classic example is the complex relationship between Nicole Warren and Dick Diver in *Tender Is the Night*. As Nicole's lover, physician, and husband, Diver nurses his most precious patient to health in an exchange of strength for weakness; Nicole's cure is actuated from her "dry suckling at his lean chest." In Fitzgerald's earlier novel *The Beautiful and Damned,* the ultramodern Gloria Gilbert "had been so spoiled—in a rather complete and unusual way. She had been suckled until she was three, for instance, when she could probably have chewed sticks. . . . The Men? Oh, she made them miserable, literally!" And then there is the flirt nonpareil Josephine Baker (née Ginevra King), about whom Fitzgerald wrote five short stories in the early 1930s: "She was manifestly to be the spectacular debutante of Chicago next year, in spite of the fact that she was an egoist who played not for popularity but for individual men. While Josephine always recovered, the men frequently didn't—her mail from Chicago, from New Haven, from the Yale Battery on the border, averaged a dozen letters a day."[12] One could list a good many more examples in the Fitzgerald catalogue.

It is less certain but more intriguing to consider Ginevra's possible impact on *The Great Gatsby*. In February 1916, while on health leave from Princeton, Fitzgerald sent her two stories, including one titled "The Perfect Hour," a phrase Ginevra had used earlier in their correspondence to express her ideal of romantic love. "Honestly and truly," she now wrote Scott upon receipt, "it would be wonderful to have that perfect hour, sometime, someday and somewhere." For a couple communicating essentially through correspondence, their dreamy meeting in a "perfect hour" took on added import. Ginevra replied with her own literary effort. "Enclosed," she wrote Fitzgerald in early March, "you'll find out my idea of what a 'Perfect Hour' is, so you see my idea is quite different from yours."[13] Presumably, Fitzgerald's story—which does not survive—offered a happy ending, for Ginevra's decidedly did not.

Ginevra's story opened with wedding bells: "To-day Ginevra King was to wed the Count Spagettioni. Everyone expected it to be one of the prettiest weddings of the season, and were proud of the Chicago girl who had been won by a titled Russian." As in *Gatsby*, Ginevra's treatment portrayed a romantic disillusioned by a lover's conventionality. Ginevra wrote that the Count "was good but no, he could not give her what she craved—affection—*real deep* sympathy. . . . Something was lacking in her married life." In the novel, this precise marital disenchantment serves as a prologue to Daisy's brief affair with Gatsby. Ginevra's Daisy-like character leaves her gilded cage in a Rolls-Royce "speeding past the beautiful residences of the popular suburb" toward a "Mr. Fitz-Gerald." There her dream is shattered. Instead of finding paradise, she discovers "a thriving business man" who doesn't recall either their initial St. Paul acquaintance or subsequent flirtation. And in this respect, she now takes on the Gatsby role. Her attempt to reunite with a former lover ends in failure. "There she saw, vanishing with the last of her beautiful air-castles, the vision of a perfect hour. . . . [It] was fading away like a spent rose."[14] Anticipating Gatsby, she too had hoped, and failed, to repeat the past.

From Ginevra's perspective, the story may have come from some dawning awareness that no matter how much she wished to think of herself as someone who might "marry any kind of man under the sun," she was, in fact, bound by certain inviolable class restraints. She would have her Count, whether she wanted him or not; money would marry money. In this way, Ginevra may have been as much the prisoner in the tower as Scott was the peasant in the field. Their romance gave to each the opportunity to playact, to class jump, and more generally to experiment with "love" before life intruded. One can well imagine Fitzgerald understanding at the time that, considering their ages, their families, and their futures, nothing more than a largely epistolary relationship was possible. Even if he had wished their connection to continue, could Scott really have envisioned taking Ginevra to that aforementioned "house below the average" to meet Mollie? And would he have been content to work in Chicago, toiling away in a job secured for him by his father-in-law in the city's banking sector? Such speculation is checked by the fact that a family-favored beau was hovering on the horizon ready to whisk Ginevra away to her inevitable destiny.

In July 1918, while stationed at Camp Sheridan near Montgomery, Alabama, Fitzgerald wrote to Ginevra for perhaps the first time in some eighteen months. His letter does not survive; her 15 July reply reads,

Dear Scott:—

I certainly was glad to hear from you and to know that you were still alive. . . . I've got a piece of very wonderful news for you, that I am sure will be a great surprise. I am announcing my engagement to William Mitchell on July 16th.

To say I am the happiest girl on earth would be expressing it mildly and I wish you knew Bill so that you could know how very lucky I am.

The family are all East, but they have been marvelous about the whole thing, and now I am hoping to be able to persuade them that I must be married soon and go to Key West where Bill is stationed as ensign in naval aviation. Pardon the brevity of this but I wanted you to know first!

As Always,
Ginevra.

Fitzgerald rallied for a sporting reply:

Dear Ginev:

This is to congratulate you—I dont know Billy Mitchell but from all I've heard of him he must be one of the best ever—

Doesn't it make you sigh with relief to be settled and think of all the men you escaped marrying?

As Ever
Scott[15]

Ginevra had known William Mitchell for years, and their union could not have come as much of a surprise to Fitzgerald. William's father, John J. Mitchell, had founded and served as president of the Illinois Trust & Savings Bank and was friendly with Ginevra's father; the two financiers had offices in the same downtown Chicago building. A Harvard man, "Billy" was to fulfill his class obligations impressively. He cofounded an investment-banking firm, proved to be a generous benefactor to a number of national organizations including the American Red Cross and the Salvation Army, and served as trustee to several of Chicago's leading educational institutions including Northwestern University and the Field Museum of Natural History. The heading of his 1987 *Chicago Tribune* obituary read, "Banker, Philanthropist."[16] The only thing better than one King-Mitchell union would be two—and indeed Marjorie King, Ginevra's younger sister, later wed William's younger brother, Clarence.

Leonardo's Ginevra (also born into a prominent banking family) was rumored to be an unhappy bride. Married off at sixteen to a widower several years her senior, the Florentine noblewoman found herself in an arranged match that linked wealth to wealth. Her portrait presents an unmistakably dispirited young woman with pallid skin and lifeless eyes.

Scott's Ginevra agreed to her nuptials with far more enthusiasm and expectations for future happiness; she married Mitchell on 4 September 1918. Three days later, according to Fitzgerald's *Ledger*, he celebrated the promise of a new relationship while mourning the death of an old one: "Fell in love on the 7th." It is tempting to speculate that Ginevra's marriage "released" Fitzgerald to fall in love with Zelda Sayre, only eighteen and known in her native Montgomery as a flirt and a free spirit. And yet even with a new girl on his mind, he returned again and again over the years to his romance with Ginevra, magnifying both its promise and its letdown. Scott attached a photograph of Ginevra and a newspaper clipping about her wedding inside his scrapbook. On the bottom of the page containing these precious relics, he wrote, "The End of a Once Poignant Story."[17]

But it was not really the end just yet. For like Gatsby, Fitzgerald tried to repeat the past. Scott and Ginevra's story picked up again in 1933 when Scott arranged for his two golden girls to meet. Zelda, in between sanitarium stays and with a professional caregiver in tow, was visiting the world's fair in Chicago. Perhaps in hopes of restarting an old association or to add Zelda's reaction to his thinning file of Ginevra recollections, Scott called King—Mrs. Mitchell—and asked that she luncheon with his wife. Ginevra politely assented. Considering the circumstances, the request seems, in the least, insensitive. As West writes, "Surely Zelda knew that Ginevra had been Scott's first love, and probably she had some idea of how important Ginevra had been to him in his creative life. Zelda must also have been acutely conscious of how different her own current state was from Ginevra's." Unsurprisingly, the circumstances of their encounter were difficult and the summit unsuccessful. Ginevra recalled in a 1974 interview for the *Princeton Alumni Weekly* that Zelda skipped lunch and went straight to a succession of cocktails. "It was terribly sad," she recollected.[18]

In October 1937, after an interval of twenty-one years, Scott and Ginevra saw each other one final time. Fitzgerald was in Hollywood writing screenplays and learned through a St. Paul friend that Mrs. King was visiting her second son, Charles (called "Buddy"), in Santa Barbara. She had never been far from his thoughts. Just three months earlier, in a letter to Scottie, Fitzgerald had referred to Ginevra as something of an object lesson, noting how his old love's "wild" behavior at Westover—conversing with boys from a dorm window—had nearly gotten her expelled from school. "For premature adventure one pays an atrocious price," he wrote, playing the moralist. "It's in the logic of life that no young person ever 'gets away with anything.' . . . It was in the cards that Ginevra King should get fired from Westover—also that your mother should wear out young."[19] Now, in October, he informed Scottie that Ginevra had wired him.

In truth, it was Scott who initiated this last meeting. No doubt surprised, Ginevra invited Fitzgerald to a dinner at a friend's house. He preferred a luncheon in Hollywood with just the two of them, and she agreed. Scott abstained from alcohol while they ate but then promptly fell off the wagon. "[We] had a much better time than I had anticipated," Ginevra later remembered. "Afterwards . . . he suggested we go to the bar—I settled for a lemonade but he insisted on a series of double Tom Collins. I was heartsick. . . . For the next few days I was besieged with calls." Fitzgerald, for his part, remembered their final hours with regret: "Met the love of my youth. . . . She is still a charming woman and I'm sorry I didn't see more of her." But how could he? The very aristocratic advantages he coveted in her ensured their separation. Like Princeton, she could not love him back. "She enjoyed him and said he was very bright, very witty," Ginevra's daughter, Ginevra Mitchell Hunter, told a reporter in 2003. "She said he was always on the outside looking in."[20]

FIVE

Opposites Alike

When Zelda Sayre and I were young,
the war was in the sky.

F. Scott Fitzgerald, undated

The first months of 1917 brought to Fitzgerald a string of inevitable end-ings. His long-distance flirtation with Ginevra King now over and his Princeton days past, he moved forward toward an uncertain future. For him, the Great War came just in time. Boyishly in search of the next great adventure, he planned to storm the Western Front. Commissioned that fall as a second lieutenant in the infantry, Scott promptly marched off to the Provisional Officers' School at Fort Leavenworth, Kansas, smartly attired in a custom-made Brooks Brothers uniform. By consensus, he proved to be a lousy soldier. Sized up by his fellow officers as a loudmouth and a lightweight, he found himself the frequent object of their ridicule. Among his own troops, he was prone to punish quickly and had a repu-tation for unreliability. One member of his platoon dismissed him as "a hard Drill Master" who "did a lot of drinking." Several times Scott failed to appear at reveille, forcing his first sergeant to step in and report the company "all present or accounted for."[1]

Devereaux Josephs was in Fitzgerald's training company and in the 1940s recalled for a biographer Scott's complicated personality. With Fitzgerald repeating his prep-school and collegiate practice of flashing hot and cold between insecurity and sophistication, he must have been something of an enigma to many of his peers. "He was eager to be liked by his companions and almost vain in seeking praise," Josephs wrote. "At the same time he was unwilling to conform to the various patterns of dullness and majority opinion which would insure popularity. To sum up, I think it might be said that he was superficially quite immature in his relations with other people and the current task of becoming a soldier. Beneath this surface, however, he was wholly different than the other men in his company. He was more sensitive, better read and less influenced by his surroundings—hence at bottom more mature."[2]

Fitzgerald's brief military interlude conformed to the Ginevra/Princeton pattern, one in which Scott willfully reimagined his circumstances to produce a more intense experience. When both love and education fell short of his expectations, he raised them up by romanticizing them—and now did the same with war. If he didn't know what it was, he knew what it *should* be. And he knew that just as the hero got the girl and scored the winning touchdown, he should die heroically in battle. "The youth of me and my generation ends sometime during the present year, rather summarily," he wrote to a cousin in the late spring of 1917. "If we ever get back, and I don't particularly care, we'll be rather aged—in the worst way. After all life hasn't much to offer except youth and I suppose for older people the love of youth in others."[3] There is a casual, conjectural courage in such remarks, the pretending to a war-weary maturity not yet earned and, as things turned out, never to be earned. As a marker of manhood, the Western Front proved indifferent to Fitzgerald's Doughboy fantasies; he never made it to France, never went "over the top," and never got to play Grant. Instead, he wrote a novel.

Originally, Fitzgerald had planned a book of poems. Influenced by Bishop, inspired by Keats, and burning to become the American Rupert Brooke, Scott hoped to meld his Princeton pieces into a definitive statement. "I had decided," he recounted, "that poetry was the only thing worth while, so with my head ringing with the meters of Swinburne and the matters of . . . Brooke, I spent the spring doing sonnets, ballads and rondels into the small hours. I had read somewhere that every great poet had written great poetry before he was twenty-one. I had only a year and, besides, war was impending. I must publish a book of startling verse before I was engulfed." Scott hoped further, and somewhat competitively, to match the output of his friends; the small Boston press

Sherman, French & Company had issued Bishop's poems in 1917 under the title *Green Fruit,* and "Bunny" Wilson was at the time exchanging sonnets with Fitzgerald.[4]

For a brief period, verse writing captured the creative energies of, as Fitzgerald loftily put it, these "Princeton intellectuals." Soon enough, however, he had moved on to a far more substantial project. To Shane Leslie, he pled distraction for his new direction—"I've only got about twenty poems and cant write any more in this atmosphere"—but write he did.[5] And the big idea behind it, a meditation on this last Victorian generation in its last days, stuck. Published in 1920 as *This Side of Paradise,* the novel first took form as "The Romantic Egotist," an army version hastily written in late 1917. Post-Catholic upbringing, post-Ginevra, post-Princeton, Scott hoped to produce a lasting artistic statement before the hourglass emptied. He had never worked so hard or so urgently. With the outcome still in doubt, he wrote his concerns into the manuscript:

> I intended so much when I started, and I'm realizing how impossible it all is. I can't re-write and all I do is form the vague notes for chapters that I have here beside me and the uncertain channels of an uneven memory. I don't seem to be able to trace the skeins of development as I ought. I'm trying to set down the story part of my generation in America and put myself in the middle as a sort of observer and conscious factor.
>
> But I've got to write now, for when the war's over I won't be able to see these things as important—even now they are fading out against the back-ground of the map of Europe. I'll never be able to do it again; well done or poorly. So I'm writing almost desperately—and so futily.[6]

Within three months, he had completed a first draft.

As "The Romantic Egotist" circulated in 1918 from author to friends and finally to publisher, Fitzgerald was transferred from one army base to another. After completing his training at Fort Leavenworth in February, he received a brief leave and then reported to Camp Zachary Taylor outside of Louisville before heading to Camp Gordon, Georgia, and thence to Camp Sheridan near Montgomery, Alabama. There, at this last posting, Scott met Zelda Sayre. Named by her mother for a fictional gypsy queen, Zelda could point to a distinguished lineage every bit as steeped in American history as Fitzgerald's. One great-uncle, John Tyler Morgan, had been a Confederate general and later sat in the U.S. Senate for thirty years. Her maternal grandfather, Willis Benson Machen of Kentucky, served in the first and second Confederate Congresses and, briefly, the United States Senate; Zelda's father, Anthony Dickinson Sayre, was an associate justice on the Alabama Supreme Court from 1909 to 1931. In all, the Sayres must have been somewhat recognizable to the class-sensitive Fitzgerald, who would also have appreciated their particular place in American history. If not quite the McQuillans, they nevertheless kept a small domestic staff and lived in the fashionable west side of Montgomery. Their direct ties to the old Confederacy perhaps brought to Scott's mind the Maryland childhood of his father.

Friends remember Zelda, four years younger than Scott, as an unconventionally attractive woman whose "fine and full hearted selfishness and chill-mindedness," as Fitzgerald once described her to Edmund Wilson, enhanced her beauty.[7] With thin blue eyes, a direct nose, and penciled mouth, she projected a hawkish visage accentuated by short, honey-blond hair. A chameleon-like quality underlined her looks, which seemed to alter from photograph to photograph. Like Scott, Zelda (the fourth and by several years youngest surviving child) won special treatment from her mother, who breast-fed her until the age of four. Indulged by older parents and known as a practiced flirt with a reckless streak, the southerner Zelda Sayre in some ways resembled the Chicago-based Ginevra King, though the Sayres did not come from the same monied class as the Kings.

Legend has it that Scott met Zelda in July at the Country Club of Montgomery, just a month removed from her high school graduation. There, Major Dana Palmer later related, Fitzgerald "saw me dancing with her. After the dance he asked me who she was, and if I would introduce him." Zelda's biographer Sally Cline notes, however, that the two may have crossed paths earlier at a tea party. "In that version," Cline writes, "neither Zelda nor Scott took much notice of the other." That would have been hard to do. For Fitzgerald—like Zelda—possessed a rare physical charm that drew the attention of others. "He had blond hair with a slight wave, a cleft chin and, I think, a bit of a dimple," remembers one officer who served with Fitzgerald in Montgomery. "His most striking features, however, were his eyes which were deeply lashed with black." What we do know with certainty is that over the next few weeks, Scott and Zelda took quite a lot of notice of each other. Scott's charm offensive included daily phone calls, and he gave Zelda his military insignia for her glove box. It was not until September, two months after receiving news of Ginevra's wedding engagement, however, that Fitzgerald declared his love to Zelda. She held back too. Flattered by Scott's interest but used to enjoying the attention of several beaux, she continued to circulate through the late summer. Perhaps most noticeably, she had retained the affections of a small group of aviation officers who cavalierly performed feats of aerial acrobatics above the Sayres' 6 Pleasant Avenue home. Fitzgerald later drew on his southern courtship of Zelda—and reflected on the antics of her army-pilot enthusiasts—in one of his finer *Post* stories, "The Last of the Belles," published in 1929. The solicitations of these officers in 1917 only emboldened Scott, a hopeless collector desperate to win over the best school, best people, and best girl.[8]

In late October, the army sent Fitzgerald to Camp Mills, Long Island, near the point of embarkation at Hoboken. He later wrote that by then, he and Zelda had consummated their relationship; they may very well have understood themselves to be engaged. Scott's description of Gatsby and Daisy's initial coupling (also in October)—"He felt married to her, that was all"—suggests such a possibility. The tenderness of this period never left Zelda, who, more than twenty years later, in what proved to be her final Valentine's Day card to Scott before his death, wrote to him, "'Here is my heart, it's yours for keeps, until we part.' ... The last thing you said to me before you left for the port of embarkation."[9] Shortly after Fitzgerald's arrival at Camp Mills, the war came to an end. Rather than rejoice, Scott was terribly disappointed at having "history" pass him by. One veteran, Sam Broomfield, met Fitzgerald in France in the early 1920s and recalled his curious attitude:

> The war seemed to be an obsession with him or rather the fact that he had missed out in the war and by never having been in active service at the front had missed the greatest experience a man could have in his

generation. It always seemed to me that his reaction was not so much one of morbidity as of regret. When he was with me and Hemingway he would ask questions about our experiences at the front which continued literally for hours. It seemed to me that he felt that he had been living a trivial life during that period . . . and that he would forever be handicapped by having missed the greatest experience of his time.[10]

And Wilson adds,

The truth was that Scott himself felt that he had missed the war. It was as if, when he came later to read books about it, he decided that he had been greatly to blame for not having had any real idea of what had been going on at the time, and he suddenly produced his old French helmet which had never seen the shores of France and hung it up in his bedroom at Wilmington and would surprise his visitors there by showing them, as if it were a revelation, a book of pictures of horribly mutilated soldiers.[11]

Though Fitzgerald never wrote a war novel per se, and never attempted the type of fine battlefield narration that can be found in Hemingway's *A Farewell to Arms*, he saw farther than most writers the long term "meaning" and consequences of the Great War. As a work of cultural history, his knowing and critical appraisal of the timeworn Victorian certainties that many people blamed for provoking the conflict—its self-consciously refined sensibilities, its stifling moralism, and its unreflective confidence in science and technology—reaches for a kind of higher interpretive truth.

Ordered back to Montgomery to await discharge, Fitzgerald, with no money and as yet no book contract, in his personal correspondence exaggerated and performed his anxieties about marriage to Zelda for dramatic effect. In early December 1918, he wrote to a St. Paul friend, "My mind is firmly made up that I will not, shall not, can not, should not, must not marry—still, she *is* remarkable—I'm trying desperately *exire armis* [to exit valorously]."[12] Naturally he pressed for an engagement. In reply, Zelda inserted a condition: if Scott went to New York and succeeded, she would follow him; however, until such time as he demonstrated himself capable of supporting her, she would remain in Alabama as though nothing had changed. In other words, while she considered herself engaged (she accepted Scott's mother's engagement ring), she planned to attend dances and parties with other men. And these things she did. Viewed from Zelda's side, her wait-and-see arrangement made perfect sense. Here was a lowly (if impeccably dressed) infantry officer who had failed to complete his degree at Princeton and now seemed intent on gambling his professional prospects on a long-shot writing career.

To Scott, however, Zelda's delay inserted an early wedge in their relationship, one that he would never forget. He left for New York alone, aware that his fiancée held serious doubts about his prospects. Several years later, in the privacy of a notebook, he wrote with some simmering bitterness, "Except for the sexual recklessness, Zelda was cagey about throwing in her lot with me before I was a money-maker, and I think by temperament she was the most reckless of all. She was young and in a period where any exploiter or middle-man seemed a better risk than a worker in the arts."[13]

With Scott's romance and engagement in limbo, the first half of 1919 rolled on miserably for him. By midyear, "The Romantic Egotist" (now "The Education of a Personage") remained without a publisher, prompting Zelda to break off their engagement in June. For Scott, these matters of art and the heart were unmistakably linked together, a point later confirmed by Charles Lawton Campbell, a friend of both parties: "My impression from what [Zelda] said is something like this: 'If Scott sells the book, I'll marry the man, because he is sweet. Don't you think so?'" And after the book "sold," Scott's prospects did indeed rise considerably. Campbell saw Fitzgerald at the Yale Club in New York and remembered his friend, with a fresh, hopeful urgency, saying, "I phoned her long distance last night. She's still on the fence and I may have to go to Montgomery and get her but I believe this will do the trick."[14]

It did. In November, after Scott had made the promised pilgrimage to Montgomery, he and Zelda resumed their engagement, and that same month, largely on the strength of his forthcoming novel, Fitzgerald sold his first story to the *Saturday Evening Post* ("Head and Shoulders"). In other words, he had now proven himself "a money-maker." Five months later, on 4 April 1920, in a small, rushed ceremony, Scott and Zelda were wed in the rectory of St. Patrick's Cathedral in New York. Just eight days earlier, "Personage," now *This Side of Paradise,* had been published. This combining of professional and personal "conquests" gave its author not simply a book and a wife but another legend that permitted him to indulge his multilayered sense of persecution. For at Montgomery, no less than at Princeton and Lake Forrest, Fitzgerald had faced down a potentially devastating humiliation. "I had . . . over-extended my flank," he later wrote of the machinations that led to his marriage. "It was one of those tragic loves doomed for lack of money, and one day the girl closed it out on the basis of common sense. During a long summer of despair I wrote a novel instead of letters, so it came out all right, but it came out all right for a different person."[15] But had it? Throughout his courtship, Scott stood always on familiar ground. He had made a fantasy of Zelda, amplifying her "sins" and enlarging her eccentricities, which meant that he was also and perhaps primarily commenting on the largeness of his own love—he would take her unconditionally as is.

Weeks before the marriage, Fitzgerald addressed the issue of Zelda's "reckless" behavior to Isabelle Amorous, the sister of a Newman School friend. His letter tells us at least as much about Scott:

> No personality as strong as Zelda's could go without getting critisisms and as you say she is not above reproach. I've always known that. Any girl who gets stewed in public, who frankly enjoys and tells shocking stories, who smokes constantly and makes the remark that she has "kissed thousands of men and intends to kiss thousands more," cannot be considered beyond reproach even if above it. But Isabelle I fell in love with her courage, her sincerity and her flaming self respect and its these things I'd believe in even if the whole world indulged in wild suspicions that she wasn't all that she should be.
>
> But of course the real reason, Isabelle, is that I love her and that's the beginning and end of everything. You're still a Catholic but Zelda's the only God I have left now.[16]

And in worshiping Zelda, Scott worshiped a part of himself. Both were attractive and spoiled—the offspring of older parents who had lost children; some thought them, physically and temperamentally, alike enough to be mistaken for incestuous siblings. Fitzgerald offered an appraisal of their prospects perhaps truer than he knew when he informed his friend Ruth Sturtevant, "She's very beautiful and very wise and very brave as you can imagine—but she's a perfect baby and a more irresponsible pair than we'll be will be hard to imagine."[17]

In fact, Scott and Zelda left little to the imagination. Fitzgerald's friends commented on the chaos that reigned in their New York hotel rooms, collecting places for dirty clothes, crusted dishes, and overflowing ashtrays. The writer Donald Ogden Stewart remembered showing up at the couple's Fifty-Ninth Street apartment expecting a quiet supper with a few friends. Instead, he watched uncomfortably as Scott and Zelda vied for the attention of their several guests:

> I found myself eventually swept along dinnerless with ten or fifteen others to a ball at the Savoy Plaza given by the daughters of the Southern Confederacy. It was not the same Scott I had known in St. Paul, and I wasn't sure that I was as crazy about Zelda as everyone appeared to be. She seemed much more interested in her own conversation than in mine; so did Scott, and I felt like some embarrassed spectator caught by the unexpected rising of the curtain on the stage of a comedy in which the two stars were competing for the spotlight.[18]

Fortuitous timing kept their ball bouncing. The Fitzgeralds' earliest days as a married couple coincided with Scott's rising celebrity, and rather than simply enjoy the moment, they were determined to push it forward, prolonging its intensity and exhausting its possibilities. As if performing, they played up several personalities (the writer, the belle, the flapper, the moralist, the drunkard . . .) before attentive audiences. What they lacked was a stretch of time off the society pages to develop a deeper rapport, though in fact neither seemed to want this. Their mutual "fame" was part of the attraction that had brought them together. From the beginning, their union took on a self-conscious quality, noted by several observers over the years. As James Thurber accurately reported, "In even their most carefree moments and their most abandoned moods there was scarcely ever the casual ring of authentic gaiety. . . . [They] did not know how to invite gaiety. They twisted its arm, got it down, and sat on its chest."[19]

At times, their antics bore the faint scent of premeditation, as though they were auditioning in the papers for the roles of Mr. and Mrs. Jazz Age. The Pulitzer, Union Square, and Washington Square fountains were graced with Zelda's immersions; to enliven a July Fourth party, she called in a fire alarm, beating her chest and explaining to a gathering audience that the fire was "Here!" Over the course of a few desperate honey-mooning weeks, tables were danced on, fistfights broke out, and the Fitzgeralds were told to leave the Biltmore and Commodore Hotels. Babes in the celebrity profession, they met the press more than halfway, excited to see their names in print and not yet conceiving of the bill. "A dive into a civic fountain," Scott later recalled with some derision, "a casual brush with the law, was enough to get us into the gossip columns and we were quoted on a variety of subjects we knew nothing about."[20] Eager to make progress on his new novel, "The Beautiful Lady without Mercy" (later called "The Flight of the Rocket" and still later published under the title *The Beautiful and Damned*), he and Zelda abandoned the city for a quiet Connecticut suburb in what turned out to be yet another restless, impermanent stay.

In many respects, and despite early and evident marital strains, Scott and Zelda formed in their first years together a productive if one-sided partnership. For while Fitzgerald's best work demonstrates a unique, original, and immense talent, he certainly took his inspiration where he could find it. And Zelda, with her unconventional outlook, quotable southern locutions, and endearing Dixie charm, was undeniably inspiring. Her expressions and ideas delighted Scott, who was proudly impressed and occasionally envious of her ability to string together memorable expressions. "She was both his inspiration and anathema," Campbell observed; "she gave him spontaneously much of his material and his dialogue. He would hang on her words and applaud her actions, often repeating them for future reference, often writing them down as they came from the fountain-head."[21]

Zelda's diaries were of particular interest to Scott. They did not survive the Fitzgeralds' constant wanderings, and we do not know when she began keeping them or how often she wrote in them. What we do have are the impressions they made, for Scott liked to show them off. His

Newman and Princeton classmate Stephan Parrott remarked non-committally to Fitzgerald on their stream-of-consciousness quality: "As you say, it is a very human document, but somehow I cannot altogether understand it." George Jean Nathan, a drama critic and coeditor (along with H. L. Mencken) of the *Smart Set,* the Jazz Age's literary magazine of choice, was far more impressed. He proposed publishing them under the title "A Young Girl's Diary," until Fitzgerald quashed the idea. He had other plans for the daybooks. Nathan remembered Fitzgerald saying "he had gained a lot of inspiration from them and wanted to use parts of them in his own novels and short stories."[22] And use he did, though the results were often less than flattering. Most of Fitzgerald's books were peopled with selfish and insensitive females, possessed with great inner strength yet of doubtful integrity. These characters were composites of several women Scott knew, but of course he knew Zelda best. The extent to which she gave him what he wanted—as she gave the press what it wanted—is something of an open question. In the end, perhaps it is enough to say that they were partners, legend makers of a kind who were eventually consumed by the intensity of their celebrity.

— PART II —

Building Up, 1920–1925

The talent that matures early is usually of the poetic,
which mine was in large part.

F. Scott Fitzgerald, 1940

{ SIX }

Trouble in Paradise

As an endless dream it went on: the spirit of the
past brooding over a new generation.

F. Scott Fitzgerald, This Side of Paradise, 1920

In the anxious months that led somewhat circuitously to Fitzgerald's marriage to Zelda Sayre, Scott struggled to find his footing as a professional author. Unable to sell his stories and bored writing bad copy at the Barron Collier advertising agency, he abandoned New York, returning to the Midwest with his confidence shaken. "I retired not on my profits," he later remembered, "but on my liabilities, which included debts, despair and a broken engagement and crept home to St. Paul to 'finish a novel.'" Writing through the summer, he completed a heavily reworked version of "Romantic Egotist," now titled, with a bow to Rupert Brooke, *This Side of Paradise*. When published the following year, it proved a surprising success, going through a dozen printings and reversing Scott's sagging fortunes.[1] It was *almost* as good as scoring the winning touchdown against Yale. With his future on the line, Fitzgerald had banked everything on the book and won . . . this time.

Paradise is admired for its striking portrayal of American youth on the eve of the Great War and remains a readable first novel. Its power comes from its sensitivity to the sexual self-awareness, adolescent unease, and cultural pessimism felt by its author's rising generation. The book bears further the touch of an unusual talent, equal parts amateur anthropologist and fabulist. As if acquainting the Victorian American gerontocracy with a newly discovered people, Fitzgerald reported from the field on the curious phenomenon of the petting party, translated the strange slang practiced by its participants, and confessed the collegiate crowd's edgy suspicion that the faiths and morals, promises and patriotisms of fathers and grandfathers alike were at bottom hollow to their core.

More than an American story, *Paradise* is part of a broader trans-Atlantic rebirth of the coming-of-age novel. In both the United States and particularly in Europe, the travails of youth were then receiving increasing attention. A modest list includes Jack London's *Martin Eden* (1909), D. H. Lawrence's *Sons and Lovers* (1913), James Joyce's *A Portrait of the Artist as a Young Man* (1915), Willa Cather's *The Song of the Lark* (1915), Somerset Maugham's *Of Human Bondage* (1915), and Hermann Hesse's Jungian-inspired *Demian* (1919). These probing works might all be said to reflect in some sense a post-Victorian shift in cultural tone from assurance to anxiety. The Enlightenment heritage passed down by Isaac Newton, John Locke, and Adam Smith—order, reason, and symmetry in the fields of physics, classical liberalism, and economics—was challenged on one side by Einstein's theories on special and general relativity and on another by the Marxian-Socialist critique of capitalism. Nietzsche's epigrammatic promise that "God is dead" coldly questioned the idea of cosmic order, while Darwinism, Freudianism, and Boasianism decentered once-sacred views on humanity, mind, and culture. It was this unprecedented and complicated cosmopolitanism that youth inherited.

One might think that *Paradise*'s time-bound language and attention to period fashion marked it too obviously, and thus fatally, as a relic of the twenties. Yet its enduring interest among readers attests to a vitality larger than the circumstances from which it arrived. Placed in context, its story line—callow boy runs through the gamut of love and war, education and disillusionment before discovering he can trust only in himself—taps into fertile if well-tilled literary soil. It is an old tale dressed up in the two-tone Oxford saddle shoes conspicuous to the era's collegiate crowd. The novel centers on the exploits of Amory Blaine, a young man with literary ambitions who is a prone to "moodiness," "laziness," and "playing the fool." Here Fitzgerald wields a sharp and unsparing pen, for in Amory, of course, do we recognize the particular insecurities of his creator. Like Scott, Amory's prep-school "masters considered him idle, unreliable and superficially clever." The young egotist is not unaware of his shortcomings: "There was . . . a curious strain of weakness running crosswise through his make-up . . . a harsh phrase from the lips of an older boy (older boys usually detested him) was liable to sweep him off his poise into surly sensitiveness or timid stupidity . . . he was a slave to his own moods and he felt that though he was capable of recklessness and audacity, he possessed neither courage, perseverance nor self-respect."[2]

Amory leaves his native Midwest for an eastern prep school, plants himself at Princeton, and promptly falls in love with Isabelle Borge, doing a more than passable "baby vamp" version of Ginevra King. After their predictable breakup—"perhaps all along she had been nothing except what he had read into her"—Amory joins the army and, unlike Fitzgerald, gets into the fight. *Paradise* has appropriately little to say about what he saw or did in France. Upon returning stateside, Amory falls in love with Rosalind Connage—who seems a composite of Zelda and Ginevra—though penury dooms their relationship. Rosalind's mother is made to stand in for old money, calling Amory "a theoretical genius who hasn't a penny to his name, . . . a nice well-born boy, but a dreamer—merely *clever.*" With these puncturing lines, Fitzgerald makes public the accumulated private resentments and humiliations that have shadowed his psyche. The sadness of the romance's inevitable ending combines with Amory's contempt for "this Victorian war," grief over the deaths of several close friends, and general lament against capitalist-bourgeois civilization to provoke a haunting self-awareness. "Here was a new generation," the novel famously proclaimed, "grown up to find all Gods dead, all wars fought, all faiths in man shaken."[3]

In many respects, *Paradise* can be read as a classic quest novel in which the main character achieves a hard-earned insight. Along the complicated path of self-discovery, a host of isms—Catholicism, capitalism, socialism, and militarism—are variously trotted out and summarily discarded. The shadows of these rotting hulks cast an atmosphere of gloom and doubt over the novel, for no love goes unpunished, no creed escapes unscathed. But Amory proves emotionally stronger, more mature, and less tolerant of received wisdom after surviving the "predatory" world of eastern schools and eastern women. In this regard, *Paradise* prefaces *The Great Gatsby*. For in both novels does Fitzgerald ruminate on the corruptions, equal parts petty and large, awaiting young midwestern men in tempting metropolises. Amory's outcome is far better than the fate awaiting Jimmy Gatz, for Amory is ultimately stripped of nothing more than a covey of youthful conceits. Indeed, in a book famous for its precise dissections of period speech, dress, fads, and "philosophies," *Paradise*'s universal theme is the falling away of the ephemeral in the search for the essential. Unlike the romantic Gatsby, reaching out in a fool's hope for a best forgotten dream—"He stretched out his arms toward the dark water in a curious way, and far as I was from him I could have sworn he was trembling"— Amory stargazes no more: "he stretched out his arms to the crystalline, radiant sky," the novel closes; " 'I know myself,' he cried, 'but that is all—' "[4]

Though *Paradise* is remembered chiefly for its heralding of Jazz Age America, it might just as easily be memorialized as a novel of alienation—and we might therefore consider placing Fitzgerald in a line of distinguished Progressive-era (1900–1920) intellectuals, running from the radical economist Thorstein Veblen to the left-leaning social critic Randolph Bourne to the right-leaning cultural critic H. L. Mencken. *Paradise* offered, after all, a penetrating commentary on the American failure to transcend the cash nexus that sustained, as Veblen had put it, the country's peculiar loyalty to its glittering if rapacious "leisure class." As such, Fitzgerald merged the novel's surface plot—a quest for love and money—into a deeper complaint against the nation's pandering to railroad barons and candy-bar kings. "My whole generation is restless," he wrote. "I'm sick of a system where the richest man gets the most beautiful girl if he wants her, where the artist without an income has to sell his talents to a button manufacturer. Even if I had no talents I'd not be content to work ten years, condemned either to celibacy or a furtive indulgence, to give some man's son an automobile." The words are Amory's, but they reflect the acerbity that Fitzgerald then harbored, would always harbor, against the idea that money—more so than courage, talent, or "breeding"—made the man. He had, of course, lost Ginevra to "the richest man" and, as an "artist without an income," had to "sell his talents" to a Manhattan marketing firm.[5] Even with a Cottage Club pin, access to (provincial) country clubs, and a taste for aping the sartorial fashions of the Anglo prep elite, he remained a tourist admiring from afar Lake Forrest's blue, manicured lawns.

If *Paradise* questioned the implications of America's new money mania, it further denounced its abettors and defenders—the lost generation, not Fitzgerald's storied Jazz Age cohort, mind you, but rather its parents. They were the ones, he argued, that allowed the robber barons to rule, that foolishly sent their sons off to fight a "war to end all wars," and that promised purity through Prohibition. Accordingly, Scott dismisses Amory's parents as trivial, unserious people. His father is "an ineffectual, inarticulate man with a taste for Byron and a habit of drowsing over the *Encyclopædia Britannica*"; his mother "absorbed the sort of education that will be quite impossible ever again, a tutelage measured by the number of things and people one could be contemptuous of and charming about, a culture . . . barren of all ideas."[6] What chance did Fitzgerald or his peers have sprouting from such thin topsoil?

Amory, eager to avoid the false promises inherited from his elders, is anything but lost. He is engaged, rather, in deliberate revolt from the set of muggy Victorian social values handed down to him at youth and more or less sustained through a misbegotten education. These Victorian codes, the historian Stanley Coben has noted, commanded a host of exacting expectations:

An analysis of hundreds of statements about character from a great variety of sources indicates that a male or female person of character was dependably self-controlled, punctual, orderly, hardworking, conscientious, sober, respectful of other Victorians' property rights, ready to postpone immediate gratification for long-term goals, pious toward a usually friendly God, a believer in the truth of the Bible, oriented strongly toward home and family, honorable in relations with other Victorians, anxious for self-improvement in a fashion which might appear compulsive to modern observers, and patriotic.[7]

The Victorianism that Fitzgerald wrote against was on its last legs by 1920. It had played a critical role in establishing the standards of a modern industrial society and defining Anglo-American "culture" as normative in a United States with substantial black and ethnic populations. In having Amory denounce American materialism and hypocrisy, Fitzgerald takes his place as part of an emergent and nontraditional intellectual class— including George Santayana and Alain Locke, Alice Paul and Margaret Mead, to name but a few—that pushed for progressive ideas in a more open and pluralistic postwar nation. Scott's particular contribution was holding up the old order for some well-considered ridicule. He probably responded most alertly to generational politics, though under Fay's spell, he readily absorbed the idea of a romantic Celtic civilization struggling for expression before the bland Brahmin cultural standards negatively defined by Santayana as the "Genteel Tradition."[8]

With Victorian-era strictures waning, Amory is for a time cast aimlessly adrift without the cultural resources to find solid ground. He eventually discovers two individuals—Clara Page and Burne Holliday—who, in much different ways, serve him as important models. Clara, his widowed cousin and the mother of two young children, impresses the temperamental Amory with her ability to combine a rich imagination with a hard, smart realism. Sweetly, she knows just how to call him up short: "There you go—running through your catalogue of emotions in five seconds." Naturally he falls in love with her. Burne, a fellow Princetonian, gamely risks "running it out" by backing away from the clubs and honors critical to collegiate popularity. In a similar spirit of revolt, he begins to read outside the curriculum, thus cutting himself free from the confining "truisms" pushed by his professors and preceptors. "Amory was struck by Burne's intense earnestness, a quality he was accustomed to associate only with the dread stupidity, and by the great enthusiasm that struck dead chords in his heart. Burne stood vaguely for a land Amory hoped he was drifting toward."[9] By orbiting around serious personalities, Amory gives evidence that his private upheaval had broader boundaries than himself. Rather than flout convention on a whim, he seeks liberation from a set of codes that no longer work—he seeks out, that is, a new covenant to which he might be bound.

Clara, affectionately modeled after Fitzgerald's favorite cousin, Ce-
cilia "Ceci" Taylor, is also a searcher of sorts, and through her, *Paradise*
makes a surprisingly sensitive argument in favor of female rebellion. For
while Amory and his Princeton peers struggle to discover meaningful
life work—not merely a "job"—the women of their generation are, if anything, facing an even greater challenge. While Amory's male friends feel
trapped within an all-encompassing socioeconomic structure that expects
of them sexual, occupational, and spiritual "regularity," a certain independent male agency—as Burne and later Amory demonstrate—remains
possible. Women, however, are far more confined. The Victorian emphasis
on family, place, and station offered females fewer options, the slender
catalogue typically running from spinsterhood to the acquisition of a
suitable husband.

Edith Wharton had covered similar ground years earlier in *The House
of Mirth* (1905) and *The Custom of the Country* (1913), though both books
traffic in extremes. *Mirth*'s sacrificial Lilly Bart chooses suicide over mat-
rimony; *Custom*'s unstoppable Undine Spragg maneuvers from marriage
to marriage until she resides triumphantly atop New York high society
as a wicked robber bride. The supposedly puerile *Paradise,* by contrast,
offers more subtle assessments. In Isabella—the object of Amory's first
stab at mature love—Fitzgerald pens a frank and thoroughly identifiable
portrait of an upper-class girl unapologetically enamored with a calendar
premised on parties and proms. Isabella is a "speed," likes to be kissed,
and democratically squeezes the hands of all the young men with whom
she dances. Below her ebullient surface, Amory encounters a trivial and
self-absorbed personality: "her coldness piqued him," and in time, "he became aware that he had not an ounce of real affection for Isabelle."[10]

Rosalind, on the other hand, resents her gilded cage. Amory recognizes in her, as Fitzgerald did in Zelda, a kindred spirit, telling her, "You
and I are somewhat alike." Rosalind is bored with the procession of beaux
whom her mother trots before her and goes on strike. To one worshiper,
she explains her newly discovered philosophy: "There used to be two
kinds of kisses: First when girls were kissed and deserted; second, when
they were engaged. Now there's a third kind, where the man is kissed
and deserted. If Mr. Jones of the nineties bragged he'd kissed a girl,

everyone knew he was through with her. If Mr. Jones of 1919 brags the same, everyone knows it's because he can't kiss her any more. Given a decent start any girl can beat a man nowadays." But this isn't quite true, a point that Rosalind proves by inevitably succumbing to the caste system that has shaped her. When the moment for valor arrives, her love for Amory is soundly checked by his problematic bank account. "I don't want to think about pots and kitchens and brooms," she explains; "I want to worry whether my legs will get slick and brown when I swim in the summer." As she prepares to embark on a loveless marriage with a handsome, wealthy, and boring swain, all is not well: "ROSALIND *feels that she has lost something, she knows not what, she knows not why.*"[11]

Rosalind's class-bound conventionality causes Amory great suffering, setting him up for a dangerous autumn relationship with the aptly named Eleanor Savage. Uneasy, atheistic, and joylessly blasphemous, Eleanor has abandoned all notions of progress and morality. She plays for keeps, gives off the atmosphere of a bewitched pagan princess, and declares herself a Nietzschean materialist. Attuned to the "half-sensual, half-neurotic quality" that she radiates, Amory is undeniably enamored. Yet as he observes Eleanor's studied irreligion and faithless march to the grave, he discovers in himself contrasting impulses. Eleanor's rejection of the old cultural signposts exceeds by far Amory's more mild insubordination, reaching an extreme state that threatens to consume her. On their last morning together, Amory and Eleanor ride on horseback into a neighboring wood. When Amory calls her infidelism a pose—"like Napoleon and Oscar Wilde and the rest of your type, you'll yell loudly for a priest on your death bed"—she turns her horse toward a nearby plateau and breaks violently toward it.[12] Feet from the cliff's edge, she throws herself from her mount as the riderless horse plunges to its death. With it perishes Amory's love, for Eleanor's apostasy can only destroy the good along with the bad. Her self-destructive nature finds its strength in a sterile nihilism. She does, however, play a lasting role in Amory's education. For if Isabelle bruises and Rosalind breaks his heart, then Eleanor has shown him what a rebellion without redemption looks like.

While many reviewers hailed *Paradise* as a glimpse into, as one of their number put it, the rollicking "revolt of youth," the novel resists such a pat and superficial reading. Though thoroughly sensitive to Victorianism's hypocrisies, Fitzgerald proved to be no less suspicious of the new sexuality, indulgences, and licenses. In various passages, he sounds far more moralist than modernist. The question of Eleanor's malignant character, for example, is hardly hidden. Fitzgerald writes that she was "the last time that evil crept close to Amory under the mask of beauty," and "[Eleanor cried] there *is* no God, not even a definite abstract goodness." Her hellish connections are also plain to see. One late eve, she is warned by Amory, "you'll get the devil," and he subsequently refers to her as "you little devil."[13]

In fact, Fitzgerald's infatuation with "evil," broadly defined, permeates *Paradise*. Aside from Eleanor, various other characters—typically physically attractive and erotically inclined—are in line to trip up Amory's path from egotist to personage. What stands out in these passages is Fitzgerald's unambiguous elegy for romantic love. In his reckoning, the once-honored "'belle' had become the 'flirt,' and the 'flirt' had become the baby 'vamp.'" This awareness forms the core of Amory's real education and establishes the grounds on which his soul is to be seduced. He demonstrates his moral firmness one evening at a country-club dance on the verge of reconfiguring into a petting party. Like a character in a Hawthorne tale, he is confronted with a fleshy temptation—"Amory found it rather fascinating to feel that any popular girl he met before eight he might quite possibly kiss before twelve." Parked outside the club with one such willing partner, he suddenly opines on the meaninglessness of the moment: "Why on earth are we here?" Her response—"I don't know. I'm just full of the devil"—kills the occasion for Amory and sends the now-alienated couple back inside.[14]

Amory's subsequent branding of the young women who participate with boys in petting parties brings to mind the scarlet letter that must be worn by Hester Prynne. After one party too many, Amory impishly provides the moniker for the sleeveless hand-knit jerseys popular among teenage temptresses: "When the hand-knit sleeveless jerseys were stylish, Amory, in a burst of inspiration, named them 'petting shirts.' The name travelled from coast to coast on the lips of parlor-snakes and P.D.'s."[15] This kind of cultural observation is vital to understanding what Fitzgerald attempted to achieve in his writing, both in *Paradise* and beyond. When commentators explore the sources of his early inspiration, they often point to Compton Mackenzie's coming-of-age novel *Sinister Street* (1914) and Owen Johnson's collegiate tale *Stover at Yale* (1912), the latter of which Scott once called the "textbook" of his generation. Yet in thinking of Fitzgerald within a wider cross-generational literary context, his connections with Hawthorne are perhaps more revealing. Looking back to the Puritan past, Hawthorne helped to distinguish a distinctly American consciousness, then shifting during his lifetime (1804–1864) between the poles of an older agrarian cosmology and a nascent industrialization. His writing often pitted "good" and "evil" in tension over the susceptible soul of an individual, a community, or a country. Fitzgerald also wrote in the midst of an American civilization in flux, one whose stuffy Victorianism he lampooned all the while warming to the code of antebellum honor he associated with his father.

Amory's ethical struggle is further shown in his complex feelings toward Dick Humbird, a parvenu from Tacoma whose place at Princeton was secured by his father's real estate fortune. Humbird had once seemed to Amory "a perfect type of aristocrat, . . . the eternal example of what the upper class tries to be," though after Amory learns of Dick's plebian origins, he considers Dick a fraud. How, after all, can Humbird, like Amory, come to know himself if he swapped his "personage" for the world's approval? In the end, Dick's fate is a cautionary tale. He is killed while driving drunk, and his laid-out body suggests an essential spiritual emptiness. Amory "raised one of the hands and let it fall back inertly. . . . All that remained of the charm and personality of the Dick Humbird he had known—oh, it was all so horrible and unaristocratic and close to the earth. . . . The way animals die."[16]

Not long after Humbird's demise, Amory meets the devil himself. In a supernatural sequence that is part Hawthorne and part Henry James, he falls prey to the questionable temptations of one "Phoebe," in whose flat he contemplates the prospects of a brandy and fizz and, in the spirit of the times, perhaps a quick sexual congress. But as her head rests on his shoulder, he suddenly observes a man, half leaning, half sitting on a corner divan. Only he, however, sees the intruder. Bolting from the apartment, Amory finds himself in a darkened alley with the demon when suddenly a mask flashes before him: *"it was the face of Dick Humbird."* Shaken by this nightmare and more generally disheartened by his empty encounters with various vamps and posers, Amory begins to spiritually distance himself from his peers. "For the first time in his life he rather longed for death to roll over his generation," writes Fitzgerald, "obliterating their petty fevers and struggles and exultations."[17] What has gone wrong? Scott blames the ubiquitous demon next door on his generation's lack of faith—its inability to give the devil his due. Modern, rational, and "sophisticated," the post-Victorians had burned the moral bridge just crossed, thus acquitting themselves of certain painful hypocrisies but also leaving behind their faculty for belief and wonder, optimism and authenticity. For Fitzgerald, beauty without principles, license without control, led to a trivial, superficial civilization that was perhaps more menacing in its Nietzschean pretensions than the one it had replaced.

Ultimately, *Paradise* turns on Amory's transition from a glib egotist to an emotionally mature personage. The two great obstacles to his enlightenment are wealth and charm in their most treacherous forms—extravagance and entitlement. Dick Humbird and Rosalind Connage are the human incarnations of these "sins." The former impresses Amory with his easy, seemingly effortless successes at Princeton; the latter's siren-like beauty conquers all comers. But nothing that easy, that unearned, Fitzgerald seems to say, can bring about growth. The novel ends on this note and in the hope that its hero's moral education has only just begun.

———

Until the Fitzgerald "revival" of the 1950s canonized *The Great Gatsby* and *Tender Is the Night*, *Paradise* outsold them both—combined. It is ironic, then, that it proved so difficult to place with a publisher. Several early readers failed to grasp the book's penetrating social analysis and took it as a barely controlled exercise, imitative of the college-boy genre. Shane Leslie's patronizing reaction is a case in point. Having volunteered to write to Charles Scribner on behalf of Scott, he accurately conveyed in his letter to Scribner *Paradise*'s ability to capture the tone of "American youth" while missing its more mature observations:

I am sending you the MS of a book by a Princeton boy, a friend of mine and a descendant of the author of the Star spangled banner. . . . I have read it through and in spite of its disguises it has given me a vivid picture of the American generation that is hastening to war. I marvel at its crudity and cleverness. It is naive in places, shocking in others, painful to the conventional and not without losing the impression that it is written by an American Rupert Brooke. . . . It interests me as a boys book and I think gives expression to that real American youth that the sentimentalists and super patriots are so anxious to drape behind the canvas of the Y.M.C.A.[18]

Despite this friendly push, Leslie saw little merit in *Paradise,* claiming some years later in a 1966 memoir that he had merely done a favor for a friend: "when I begged Scribner not to return the MS as the author was not likely to return from France, he smiled and kept it in his safe. . . . After some rewriting it appeared as a best seller to my immense surprise." Of course, the manuscript never saw the inside of a safe. It was, rather, read, discussed, and generally loathed in the Scribner offices of Fifth Avenue. As one longtime associate of the house recalled,

An important member of the sales department, . . . often mistrusting his own literary judgment, . . . used to take [books] home to an erudite sister to read. His sister was supposed to be infallible and it was true that many of the novels she had "cried over" sold prodigiously. So when it was known that he had taken *This Side of Paradise* home for the week-end, his colleagues were agog on Monday morning. "And what did your sister say?" they asked in chorus. "She picked it up with the tongs," he replied, "because she wouldn't touch it with her hands after reading it, and put it into the fire."[19]

Apparently a good many others at Scribner were preparing their own pyres. The manuscript was rejected in August 1918 and, after Fitzgerald resubmitted a quick rewrite, rejected again in October. The thirty-four-year-old Maxwell Perkins, one of the house's rising editors, however, saw the project's promise and encouraged its author to keep massaging the material, offering as well the critical suggestion of transposing it from the first person to the third. Asked by an anxious Fitzgerald to shop the manuscript around, Perkins held his breath and did so but found no takers. No one, it seemed, "got" *Paradise*—least of all Scribner. A distinguished publisher with a conservative reputation, its catalogue included a diminishing galaxy of aging and recently perished greats including Edith Wharton, John Galsworthy, and Henry James. Like the fussy Princeton English department, the old guard at Scribner had no immediate connection with the kind of material that moved Fitzgerald and his generation. One among their number, Edward L. Burlingame, undoubtedly spoke for the majority when he declared *Paradise* "hard sledding."[20]

Back in St. Paul, Fitzgerald reworked the manuscript yet again, entrusting this third draft to a friend who, in September 1919, hand delivered it to the Scribner offices. Facing considerable opposition from colleagues who doubted the manuscript's literary merits, Perkins proved a decisive champion of the revised novel. "My feeling," he faced his fellow editors, "is that a publisher's first allegiance is to talent. And if we aren't going to publish a talent like this, it is a very serious thing. Then we might as well go out of business. If we're going to turn down the likes of Fitzgerald, I will lose all interest in publishing books."[21] One of the youngest men in the room, Perkins knew that such contemporary talents as Sinclair Lewis, Sherwood Anderson, and Theodore Dreiser wrote for other publishers. The fate of *Paradise* seemed to offer a referendum of sorts on Scribner's willingness to bank on rising literary voices. A vote on the manuscript only produced a tie that reflected the house's generational divide. The one noneditor at the table, old Charles Scribner himself, would thus cast the deciding ballot—but not that day. Faced with conflicting reports from his staff, he put the decision off, before finally crossing his fingers and saying yes.

Perkins immediately wrote to Scott, declaring victory and sensibly giving no hint of his colleagues' doubts:

> I am very glad, personally, to be able to write to you that we are all for publishing your book, "This Side of Paradise." Viewing it as the same book that was here before, which in a sense it is, though translated into somewhat different terms and extended further, I think that you have improved it enormously. As the first manuscript did, it abounds in energy

and life and it seems to me to be in much better proportion. I was afraid that, when we declined the first manuscript, you might be done with us conservatives. I am glad you are not. The book is so different that it is hard to prophesy how it will sell but we are all for taking a chance and supporting it with vigor.[22]

More than backing a book, Scribner played a critical role in lending Fitzgerald legitimacy as he began to find his authorial voice. A "radical" writer, eager to attack an antiquated Victorianism, he understood that publishing with a conservative and well-established press advanced considerably his chances of success. Scribner, one of the major publishers of the former president Theodore Roosevelt's books, papers, and letters, offered Scott such a respectable platform.

And Scribner offered Perkins, as well. The faith that the young editor showed in Fitzgerald, an unproven writer, was characteristic of the man. Aside from editing Scott's books, he was a critical financial resource over the years, securing Fitzgerald advances on forthcoming novels and even, despite supporting a large family, providing him personal loans. Greater than this, he remained a friend, confidant, and a critical connection to the literary world for Scott in the 1930s when Fitzgerald's life was coming apart. Together, they formed one of the most vital and famous editor/author partnerships of the twentieth century.

Years later, Fitzgerald remembered these anxious summer months of 1919 as the culmination of his youth. They symbolized for him the mountain climbing of many days' labors, marking his own private pathway from egotist to personage. Nothing would be so good again. "When the girl threw me over," he later recalled, "I went home and finished my novel. And then, suddenly everything changed [with] . . . that first wild wind of success and the delicious mist it brings with it. It is a short and precious time—for when the mist rises in a few weeks, or a few months, one finds that the very best is over."[23]

SEVEN

Corruptions—The Early Stories

This is where the United States ends.

F. Scott Fitzgerald, "The Diamond as Big as the Ritz," 1922

Although Fitzgerald earned a small fortune writing short stories, he resented the medium's oppressive pull on his creativity. Pigeonholed as a chronicler of young love, he cycled and recycled plotlines, a convenient "trick," as he occasionally put it, to pay the bills. As time passed and the words no longer came so easily, he adopted something of a Faustian attitude and wondered if he had not betrayed his gift. "I have asked a lot of my emotions—one hundred and twenty stories," he confessed in a notebook. "The price was high, right up with Kipling, because there was one little drop of something not blood, not a tear, not my seed, but me more intimately than these, in every story, it was the extra I had. Now it has gone and I am just like you now."[1]

Though this is an exaggerated statement, it does suggest the insecurities that plagued Fitzgerald, an artist often misread as a popularizer. As we have seen, some peers dismissed Scott as an accomplished amateur, a facile thinker with a talent for mimicry and a flair for creating atmosphere. Too often Fitzgerald internalized these opinions of his "intellectual betters"—Wilson, Bishop, and Leslie—even as they undermined his self-confidence. The truth is, he had few apologies to make. His short stories frequently anticipated the ideas, dialogue, and incidents later to appear in his novels. This is not to imply that Fitzgerald's themes are necessarily better suited to the novel form; his best stories are among the best we have. Rather, his short fiction helped him to understand how to develop and control these themes. A case in point is his writings on youth culture; they are central to his early magazine pieces, are vital to *Paradise,* and contributed immensely to a genre that hardly existed before the twentieth century.

Today only scholars know the name Horace Bushnell, but his 1847 study *Christian Nurture* influenced generations of American Protestants and helped to sustain the Victorian view of childhood that Fitzgerald later wrote against. An ordained minister of the North Congregational church in Hartford, Connecticut, Bushnell (1802–1876) disparaged the evangelical revivals that moved across much of antebellum America. He doubted the emotional immediacy of the tent-meeting conversion experience, arguing instead that closely knit relationships connecting children, family, and community served to nurture the young into a more "natural" and "authentic" conversion. Rather than being given a kind of laissez-faire leave to suffer through a period of religious questioning and rebellion, "the child," Bushnell wrote, is to know seamless, steady direction that he may "grow up in the life of the parent, and be a Christian in Principle, from his earliest years."[2] The well-managed Christian family, in other words, was to be the firm and ordered foundation of American civilization.

But Bushnell's America did not survive the century. The sovereign small-scale organic connections that he regarded as vital to the development of the child—the home, the church, the village—were being challenged in the emerging age of industry and urbanization. Fitzgerald, himself a product of that era, took account of these changes in his writing. His characters have complicated interior lives independent of their parents, and the range of their aspirations and concerns often extend beyond the reach of the "nurturing" culture that Bushnell had prized. These stories take for granted the retreat of family authority along with the corresponding emergence of athletic fields, petting parties, and parked cars as spaces reserved for the young.

The relative permissiveness of the times produced among more urbane adolescents an entirely fresh style of language and humor, dress and dating that began to replace the stiff formalities associated with Victorianism. In these, as in so many other ways, argued the social critic Randolph Bourne (1886–1918), the rising generation believed its ambitions to be more authentic than the quotidian hypocrisies of its parents. "Youth sees with almost passionate despair its plans and dreams and enthusiasms, that it knows so well to be right and true and noble, brushed calmly aside," Bourne explained in his essay "Youth," published in the April 1912 *Atlantic Monthly.* "Not because of any sincere searching into their practicability," he continued, "but because of the timidity and laziness of the old, who sit in the saddle and ride mankind. And nothing torments youth so much as to have this inertia justified on the ground of experience. For youth thinks that it sees through this sophism of 'experience.'"[3] It was precisely this point that Fitzgerald hoped to drive home in *Paradise.* The book opened with two epigraphs, though readers tend to remember only the Rupert Brooke line:

> . . . Well, This side of paradise
> There's little comfort in the wise.

But the other inscription is a better encapsulation of the novel:

> Experience is the name so many people
> give to their mistakes.

Oscar Wilde's teasing statement implied that the older generation's traditional hold on the young was no longer to be indulged.

But that is not to say that youths suddenly felt themselves in charge. Bombarded with a host of recently won liberties and options unimaginable to their parents, teens were eager to locate knowledgeable translators, interpreters, and guides. Did good girls bob their hair and smoke cigarettes? Did bad boys kiss and tell? A load of new protocol suddenly pressed itself on youth, and Fitzgerald, still in his twenties through most of the 1920s, understood well the insecurities of both old and young and sought to portray their inevitable clashes in humane, recognizable, and unpatronizing terms.

Such authorial insights gave to Fitzgerald's work a striking candor that was largely absent from the "awkward age" genre to this point. In Booth Tarkington's best-seller *Seventeen* (1916), for example, the fragility of adolescent love is played for laughs, assuring readers that young hearts heal quickly. Tarkington provided a set of stock characters, from the love-struck William Sylvanus Baxter and his bubbly would-be bride to his wise-acre little sister, Jane. His is a small-town romance, a series of humorous misadventures not to be taken too seriously. When Willie slips a mawkish and grammatically shaky ("my heart is braking") farewell letter into a one-pound box of chocolates, we smile. The book could have been titled "Thirteen." The *New York Times* was impressed with its light touch, calling *Seventeen* "a deliciously funny story" and praising Tarkington's decision to make Willie an object of the reader's amusement: "The picture is carica-tured a little. . . . It would not be nearly so amusing otherwise." William Lyon Phelps, a professor of English at Yale and a reviewer for the *Bookman,* similarly noted *Seventeen*'s ability to conjure "side-splitting mirth."[4]

A novel much nearer to Fitzgerald's fictional terrain—and one that had an influence on *Paradise*—is the already-mentioned Owen Johnson's *Stover at Yale,* the story of a Big Man on Campus. Johnson's prep-school hero, Dink Stover, is everything Amory Blaine is not: chivalrous, athletic, and self-assured. He matures at school, whereas Blaine's college days are a prolonged struggle that forces him to realize how much growth lies be-yond graduation. Stover's major "crisis" is a principled stand against se-cret societies, and this threatens his social success at Yale. "You should be captain [of the football team] and chairman of the Prom," one wooden character explains to Stover, "but you renounce everything—you seem to delight in it. It's too absurd; it's ridiculous."[5] But in the end, it's all right. Stover gets into Skull and Bones, gets the girl, and gets the glory. We know what Scott got—and Amory, too.

In both *Seventeen* and *Stover at Yale,* youth is depicted as a safe phase before the inevitable complexities of life take hold; Baxter and Stover never face real emotional crises, never give the reader reason to doubt their integrity or intentions—they represent youth as parents like to think of the young. And this was par for the course. The older generation, as older generations are wont to do, read its own aspirations, insecurities, and fantasies into its children's generation. Consider Bruce Bliven's con-descending 1925 *New Republic* composite of "Flapper Jane." If Tarkington hoped to amuse his readers, Bliven wished to titillate them. In a few broad strokes, he reduced the New Woman to a factor of "paint, cigarettes, [and] cocktails." His assessment of "Jane's" sartorial tang and boyish bob is voyeuristic and written in a way certain to appeal to the *New Republic*'s decidedly old-boy readership:

> Jane isn't wearing much, this summer. If you'd like to know exactly, it is: one dress, one step-in, two stockings, two shoes. A step-in, if you are 999 and 44/100ths percent ignorant, is underwear—one piece, light, exceedingly brief but roomy. Her dress, as you can't possibly help knowing if you have even one good eye, and get around at all outside the Old People's Home, is also brief. It is cut low where it might be high, and vice versa. The skirt comes just an inch below her knees, overlapping by a faint fraction her rolled and twisted stocking.... The corset is as dead as the dodo's grandfather.... The petticoat is even more defunct.... The brassiere has been abandoned since 1924.[6]

Fitzgerald, too, saw the flapper as a new star in the heavens, though unlike the flippant Bliven, he endowed his "Jane"—*Paradise*'s "Rosalind"—with psychological depth and realism as she makes her way through life as best she can. He understood that she, and her generational sisters, faced a far more challenging and difficult path than the slicks let on.

Scott, of course, knew all about the slicks; between 1920 and 1937, he published sixty-five stories in the *Saturday Evening Post,* then one of the undisputed arbiters of Middle American mores. Founded in the 1820s, the "modern" *Post* began publishing weekly in the 1890s and enticed readers with stories and lavish illustrations along with general-interest articles, cartoons, and editorials. Norman Rockwell, just two years younger than Fitzgerald, submitted his first *Post* cover painting in 1916. The magazine circulated widely, reaching nearly three million readers by the late twenties, while advertising revenues brought in about $50 million a year during the same period. Scott also wrote for more highbrow magazines (including the *Smart Set, Collier's,* and the *American Mercury*), but none of them paid so well. In the depths of the Depression, Fitzgerald was making an incredible $4,000 per *Post* story—some $55,000 in current purchasing power. *The Great Gatsby,* by comparison, sold fewer than five hundred copies in the *entire* decade of the 1930s. Fitzgerald was grateful for the *Post*'s munificence but concerned for his reputation. He had a complex relationship with the magazine and with the *Post* editor George Lorimer. "I am very tired of being Mr. Lorimer's little boy year after year," he once confided to his old Princeton instructor Christian Gauss, yet he acknowledged, "I don't know what I'd do without him."[7]

A perusal of Fitzgerald's early stories reveals an unusually sensitive eye and ear for situational color and language. But more than merely describing the surface of the times, Fitzgerald took its temperature as well, injecting into his more memorable pieces sharp social commentary. Much of this material, including the serious-below-the-surface "Bernice Bobs Her Hair" (May 1920), drew from Scott's private memories. Based on a letter that Fitzgerald wrote to his sister, Annabel, "Bernice" illuminates the punishing rivalry among the young for social success. In it, the smart Marjorie Harvey, she of the "dazzling" tongue and modern outlook, resents having to squire around her wealthy, physically attractive, but "boring" visiting cousin, Bernice. Mostly she chafes at having to beg boys to dance with a wet blanket—"no girl can permanently bolster up a lame-duck visitor, because these days it's every girl for herself."[8] A row between the cousins ensues, followed quickly by Bernice's willful determination to become popular by, in effect, becoming another person. Desperate, restless, and something of an innocent, she allows Marjorie to make her over. Bernice is dead; long live Bernice.

This Pygmalion sequence follows closely Fitzgerald's brotherly advice to Annabel, documented in a circa-1915 sibling-to-sibling letter on such topics as dress, poise, and personality. Bernice's imprisoned dance partner "wondered idly whether she was a poor conversationalist because she got no attention or got no attention because she was a poor conversationalist." Fitzgerald had written to Annabel, "Conversation like grace is a cultivated art. Only to the very few does it come naturally. You are as you know, not a good conversationalist." Marjorie's criticism of her cousin's grooming—"you never take care of your eyebrows. They're black and lustrous, but by leaving them straggly they're a blemish"—follows Fitzgerald's admonition to Annabel: "A girl should always be careful about such things as . . . mussy eyebrows (with such splendid eyebrows as yours you should brush them or wet them and train them every morning and night as I advised you to do long ago.)" And Marjorie's insistence that when dancing Beatrice not "lean on a man [because] . . . it's much harder on the man, and he's the one that counts," hues closely to Fitzgerald's emphasis to Annabel that "in dancing it is very important to hold yourself well. . . . *You can not be lazy.* You should try not to trow a bit of weight on the man."[9]

Marjorie accomplishes her task all too well. Given a new look and new lines, Bernice proceeds to charm her cousin's friends, even threatening to win over Marjorie's main admirer, one Warren McIntyre. Bernice is insouciant in her fresh façade, entertaining but fundamentally distanced from her old self. In her search for popularity, she is little more than a gifted mimic. "I want to be a society vampire," she says, hoping to scandalize one admirer, and she tells another (stealing from Oscar Wilde), "you've either got to amuse people or feed 'em or shock 'em." When Bernice's success begins to upend Marjorie's carefully cultivated hierarchy of friends and admirers, Marjorie strikes back, maneuvering Bernice into a choice of humiliations: she can either publicly acknowledge that her "line" about an impending bob job had been only so much flapper chatter, or she can actually go through with the shearing, losing her cherished Victorian tresses and thus offending respectable society. Bernice, sensing that her newly won acceptance is in danger, gamely chooses the latter—and "it was ugly as sin," Fitzgerald writes of the untested barber's pruning. Bested by Marjorie, Bernice plans to run away in the night, conscious "that her chance at beauty had been sacrificed to the jealous whim of a selfish girl."[10] Then, an inspiration hits. Before leaving for the train station, she stealthily enters her sleeping cousin's room and snips off two long braids: a scalping—and a humiliation—to match her own.

Despite the story's inclusion in the sunny *Post* canon, "Bernice" is a morally ambivalent tale. While Marjorie will presumably realize her comeuppance the moment she wakes up a few pounds lighter, her cousin's fate is less clear. When a prebobbed Bernice is asked if she "believe[s] in bobbed hair"—a question packed with meaning—she replies, "I think it's unmoral." But what would a postbobbed Bernice say? Fitzgerald offers no definitive answer but allows that a threshold has been crossed: Bernice's bob, the source of both her shame and her strength, "was quite a new look . . . and it carried consequences."[11]

Viewed expansively, Bernice's story is the story of a growing number of young American women in the 1920s. She had entered the decade with an unquestioned inheritance, that of the "womanly woman" who aspired to the charm, modesty, and restraint expected of her sex. But when taken out of the matronocracy of her native Eau Clair, Wisconsin, she comes to realize the "error" of her moral education. Born and bred to Victorian virtues, Bernice is shocked to learn that chaste girls are no longer prized and that fast girls like Marjorie are more likely to joy-fully roll their teen triumphs into future glories than to "come to a bad end." Removed from the protection of her parents' money, Bernice begins to understand that she will have to cultivate other resources if she hopes to be popular. In effect, Marjorie shows her how to file her nails and whet her teeth, a suddenly relevant skill set that she might know-ingly share with a select few Wisconsin girlfriends. In any case, she will enter that rustic arena with a distinct advantage. Her bob is a badge; it stands for a newfound hardness, awareness, and wisdom. The twentieth century awaits.

"Bernice" is one of a handful of important Fitzgerald stories that scru-tinized aspects of postwar change. These efforts show Scott's rapidly maturing talents as both a writer and a social observer and give hints of masterworks to come. One of his most striking efforts, "The Diamond as Big as the Ritz," is a powerful condemnation of greed, a direct rebuke to the speculative orgy that was already then coming to grip the 1920s. Catching the faint scent of heresy, the *Post* passed on the story, and it sub-sequently appeared in Mencken's *Smart Set* (June 1922) for a mere $300, quite a comedown from the standard $1,500 he commanded from George Lorimer for a story at this point in his career. Briefly, John Unger leaves Hades, a provincial hamlet on the Mississippi River, to prep in the East. While there, he meets Percy Washington, a direct descendant of George Washington, and is invited to spend the summer at the Washingtons' ranch deep in the Montana Rockies. There, Percy declares, "My father . . . is by far the richest man in the world," a ridiculous-sounding boast that turns out to be true.[12] The family homestead sits hard by a flawless dia-mond the size of a small mountain—or, as the title would have it, the size of the Ritz-Carlton Hotel.

Essentially a state within a state, the Washington compound is distinguished by a grotesque luxury of jeweled, ivoried, and furred elegance; a small army of slaves sees to every need. John falls in love with Kismine, Percy's ungainly named sister, and begins to learn about the hidden horrors of the place—including his own impending execution. The Washingtons, he quickly learns, have kept their wealth a secret through the killing and kidnaping of those who are unfortunate enough to happen upon the secluded compound. Before John can be sacrificed, however, the ranch is suddenly assaulted from the air, its fantastic secret having gotten out. Braddock Washington, Percy's father—with bombs flying, his estate in ruins, and his empire falling—climbs to the top of a summit, where he ascends to a high rock and proceeds, with the aid of a few loyal subjects, to lift a giant diamond toward the heavens. It is a bribe to God. The sky grows dark, the birds cease to sing, and the air becomes still while a deep rumble of angry thunder echoes over the mountains. God had said no. Amid the chaos, John escapes, leaving Hades to return to . . . Hades.

Playing off various episodes in American history, Fitzgerald presents in "Diamond" a nation in danger of losing its soul. George Washington's eighteenth-century efforts to create an empire of liberty in the New World has given way to Braddock Washington's entirely selfish efforts to protect a private empire of wealth. Here as elsewhere, Fitzgerald's preoccupation with ethical bankruptcy underscores the story, as does his habit of viewing the country's past as a morality play in which the greed of the post–Civil War robber barons anticipates the speculative boom of the post–Great War bond kings. Attentive to the historical record, Fitzgerald knew that millions of pioneers had within recent decades pushed into the American West, following the paths of the newly built transcontinental railroads and looking for their own mountains of precious minerals. His reproach of this process questioned the very idea of the American frontier as a source of democratic vitality. Such a view further, if indirectly, took in both the region's Native peoples, for whom the late nineteenth century was a violent era of removal and reservations, and the many non-Natives, for whom westward migration proved to be an endurance test of poverty and isolation, boomtowns and ghost towns. The diamond rejected by God symbolizes the mining culture that placed ruthless extraction at the center of its enterprise. Percy's grandfather Fitz-Norman Culpepper Washington left the Old Dominion after the Civil War and is the actual discoverer of the diamond. He may be thought of as a kind of "founding" capitalist: having crossed a continent, he literally unearths his immense wealth, which he then uses to obtain power. His son, Braddock, by comparison, is nothing more than a glorified bureaucrat. With no more worlds to conquer, he oversees the camp's slave-labor force, tends to its security, and stands despotically for all manor of executive, judicial, and congressional power in its domain. Writ large, Fitzgerald tells us the story of how the age of discovery gave way to the age of incorporation.

Scott's critical account of the colonizing of the American West anticipates a school of historiography that would begin to gain influence in the 1970s and 1980s. Prior to those decades, scholars had come to regard the history of the West as something of an intellectual dead end, the gathering ground of antiquarians absorbed in a long series of cowboy and Indian wars. The combination, however, of the Vietnam conflict and the energy crisis began to encourage some students to delve into the topics of anti-imperialism and environmentalism in ways that connected with the country's problematic history of continental growth. Together, these "new western" historians—among them scholars such as Donald Worster, Patricia Nelson Limerick, William Cronon, and Richard White—reframed the historical significance of the West. Often credited with advancing independence and individualism, the frontier, these scholars argued, had left Americans a far more complex inheritance. As Limerick put it, the westward expansion constituted nothing less than a "conquest" that "shapes the present as dramatically . . . as the old mines shape the mountainsides."[13]

Fitzgerald's inspiration for "Diamond" was a 1915 summer he spent at a ranch near White Sulphur Springs, Montana, owned by the family of his Newman and Princeton friend Charles Donahoe. If not a "scholar" of the region, Fitzgerald perceptively grasped its importance as both a source of wealth and an unvarnished symbol of the American interest in turning a profit from nature. The West, no less than the East, in other words, served self-interests and capitalist aggrandizement.[14]

At the epicenter of said "capitalist aggrandizement" was New York City, having just surpassed London in economic and cultural power in the budding American century. "Diamond's" secreted western setting, however, precluded Fitzgerald from commenting in that story on the impact of such a pivotal historical moment. It is, rather, in his remarkable novella "May Day" that he brilliantly explored the anxieties of the postwar period from its fluid urban focal point. Along with "Diamond," it negatively assays a defined and pronounced period of wealth gathering (1870–1920) that left many Americans doubting the future of democratic government in a robber baron's republic. Published in the July 1920 *Smart Set,* "May Day" centers on the surfacing tensions afflicting American society in the months following the Great War as demobilized troops made their way home. The title refers to International Workers' Day—the first of May—the setting is New York City, the year is 1919. On that date, in several U.S. cities, normally peaceful parades broke into violent clashes between unionists and their critics. Fear and uncertainty fueled the sudden eruption. The recent Bolshevik Revolution in Russia presented fresh challenges to Western capitalism while appealing to an active minority of Americans. This was, after all, the heyday of the collectivist dream in the United States.

Most Americans did not share this radical vision, and the country's defensive reaction was reflected in its treatment of Eugene V. Debs, the five-time Socialist Party of America candidate for the presidency who captured 6 percent of the popular vote in the 1912 election. A critic of the administration of Woodrow Wilson and the war, Debs was imprisoned following a speech he had given in Canton, Ohio, in June 1918 calling for resistance to the military draft. He was charged with multiple counts of sedition. Sentenced to a decade in prison (and disenfranchised for life), Debs was sitting in a jail cell at the Atlanta Federal Penitentiary as Fitzgerald wrote "May Day."

Anarchism was also much on the public mind following the war and probably aroused more raw fear than socialism did. Before the 9/11 attacks on the Twin Towers and the Pentagon building, "terrorism" in American history was largely associated with the anarchist movement that crested in 1919. Between April and June of that year, Galleanists (followers of the anarchist Luigi Galleani, an Italian immigrant deported that summer from the United States) delivered more than three dozen mail bombs to prominent politicians, newspapers, and businessmen (including John D. Rockefeller). This bombing campaign set the nation on edge and fed into the restless momentum that led to the Red Scare (1919–1920).

Fitzgerald scanned this jittery scene with great historical interest. For here was a distinct mingling of cultural anxiety, violence, and energy not seen in America since the Civil War. Fitzgerald would pinpoint May Day 1919 as the birth date of a new era, when for the first time the sheer velocity of the times seemed to be carrying the nation toward an unknown destination—what he called "the general hysteria of that spring which inaugurated the Age of Jazz." Seeking to capture something of its texture and uncertain mood, he focused his "May Day" on three interrelated events: privileged Yale alumni meeting for a dinner dance, the violent reaction to anarchists and socialists by the returning veterans, and a once promising young man's suicide. When the story was republished in his second collection of stories, *Tales of the Jazz Age,* Fitzgerald accurately described it as a "somewhat unpleasant tale."[15]

On more personal grounds, "May Day" tells us something about Fitzgerald's own insecurities in those early months of 1919. One of the characters in the story, the Ivy-educated Gordon Sterrett, bears a resemblance to Scott in that he too is a young and struggling artist looking to make his mark. Several of Gordon's college friends are in New York for a Gamma Psi fraternity dance, and he tracks down his old senior-year roommate (Philip Dean) at the Biltmore Hotel in hopes of managing a quick loan. He makes a desperate plea: "Phil, I can draw like a streak, and you know it. But half the time I haven't had the money to buy decent drawing materials—and I can't draw when I'm tired and discouraged and all in. With a little ready money I can take a few weeks off and get started." Sterrett is both humiliated at having to approach his old friend and envious of Phil's conspicuous good fortune. While Gordon is walking around in a shabby suit, graying shirt, and faded tie, he notices Phil's "family of thick silk shirts, . . . impressive neckties and soft woollen socks" littered about the room.[16] In Gordon's obvious discomfort, we gain insight into Fitzgerald's simmering resentment of the artist having to beg before the man with money in his pocket.

Scott later recalled this period as "the four most impressionable months" of his life.[17] It began in February 1919, when he was discharged from the army, and extended to the early summer, at which time he left New York in defeat and returned to St. Paul to live with his parents and finish his first novel. In between, as noted earlier, he listlessly scratched out copy at the Barron Collier advertising agency, failed to interest publishers in his short stories, and, despite three trips to Alabama, could not stop Zelda from breaking their engagement. For Scott, it was a period of consecutive and unforgettable defeats that he later looked back on with a wizened eye: "I struggled on in a business I detested and all the confidence I had garnered at Princeton and in a haughty career as the army's worst aide-de-camp melted gradually away. Lost and forgotten, I walked quickly from certain places—from the pawn-shop where one left the field glasses, from prosperous friends whom one met when wearing the suit from before the war—from restaurants after tipping with the last nickel, from busy cheerful offices that were saving the jobs for their own boys from the war."[18] For all his postwar New York angst, however, Scott is not Gordon. The latter is a self-imposed prisoner of personal weaknesses that stunt his presumed artistic skills. Fitzgerald believed completely in his talents, put them first, and, though temporarily beaten by circumstances, rallied over the second half of 1919 to reverse them completely.

Another story line in "May Day" involves the superpatriot hostility to socialists that Fitzgerald would have seen during his time in Manhattan. Since a magical night in a Harrisburg country club, Gordon has carried a torch for Edith Bradin, whose brother, Henry, a Cornell-educated socialist, runs a radical weekly newspaper. In the late evening of May Day, a mob of demobilized soldiers break into his offices and bust the place up. Trapped in the surge, one of the rioters is pushed out of an open window and drops to his death. Fitzgerald, stressing the brutality of the mob, is sympathetic to Bradin's labors on behalf of the working class. He always considered himself politically on the left and self-identified as a "Socialist" in *Who's Who in America* when he appeared in its pages for the first time in 1921.[19] Even so, it seems more logical to locate Fitzgerald's critique of capitalism as coming from a primarily conservative impulse. Whereas Marxists looked forward to an age of large-scale labor organization, Scott looked back to a preindustrial era of small-scale localism. Andrew Turnbull, who, as a child, knew Fitzgerald in the early 1930s, later drew an accurate portrait of the writer's historical imagination:

> History for him was chiefly color, personalities, and romance. It was Jackson's Valley Campaign; it was the Gallant Pelham rapid-firing—one cannon against sixteen—at Fredericksburg. The individual meant everything to Fitzgerald. And so he expounded Marxism to my parents as one seeking to *épater le bourgeois* [shock the bourgeois], the self-made man in him being mildly contemptuous of us as privileged, protected folk who did not know what the real rough-and-tumble was all about. Despite his claims to "unflinching rationality," Fitzgerald's political thought, like all his thought, was emotional and impulsive, general ideas being for him little more than a backdrop to his fiction.[20]

Ideology aside, in "May Day," Fitzgerald appeared to be more of a debunker than a socialist. Under the spell at that time of the influential editor and critic of American culture H. L. Mencken, Fitzgerald was unwilling to invest his faith in "the people." Bradin may be sensitive to the miseries caused by capitalism, but he is also a highly educated economist who cannot really connect with the masses. He's an intellectual and above them—as Phil, with his class privilege, would always be above Gordon.

"May Day" concludes with a much-smaller riot in a diner on West Fifty-Ninth Street, at the southwest corner of Columbus Circle. The choice of eatery—Childs—again underlines Fitzgerald's attention to the "sense of living history" that made his work an accurate register of so much of the music and sports, architecture and popular entertainment of the era. Childs was a national chain, and the West Fifty-Ninth Street store referenced by Fitzgerald opened in 1911 and closed in 1953. There, in the early-morning hours of the day after May Day, Gordon and Jewel Hudson, a lower-class woman he has been involved with and who is now blackmailing him, inadvertently run into a stewed Phil, accompanied by an equally tight Ivy undergraduate. Gordon had earlier confided to his old roommate about his girl troubles, and Phil now derisively shakes his finger at Gordon. Harsh words are exchanged, after which Gordon and the girl leave, but Phil and his friend remain and threaten to beat up a waiter before being chased out of the establishment. Really no worse for the wear (bad things simply do not happen to healthy young Yalies in easy possession of a "family of thick silk shirts"), they set off, amiably enough, in search of "breakfast and liquor." Gordon, however, wakes with a hangover to find that in his sorrow and inebriation, he has married Jewell. Creeping out of their hotel room, he buys a revolver, returns to his own apartment, and there kills himself.

It seems fitting that Fitzgerald brought several of "May Day's" principal characters to Columbus Circle, whose towering Gaetano Russo statue was erected in 1892 to commemorate the four hundredth anniversary of Columbus's voyage to the New World. Here, Scott seems to be saying, one era had unquestionably ended, and another was just coming to life: "Dawn had come up in Columbus Circle, magical, breathless dawn, silhouetting the great statue of the immortal Christopher."[21] In this new morning, new light, matters suddenly appeared different, less assured than they had before the confusion and violence of the previous evening. A phase of American development had now passed. The long era of discovery—over oceans, mountains, and prairies—was complete. The sphinxlike Columbus, looking over "his" disordered city, must have wondered if the best was yet to come or had already run its course.

"May Day" joins "Diamond" and "Bernice" as one of Fitzgerald's most important early short fictions. Together they constitute a powerful triumvirate, smart, absorbing, and true to the mood from which they were conceived. They are the work of an inspired writer, just beginning to master his trade. Their value today remains twofold, reaching the reader as both entertainment and as surprisingly effective meditations on cultural and economic change. Here, Fitzgerald began to hone a capacious and, in American terms, altogether comprehensive historical vision. He draws on Columbus, Washington, and quite appropriately Bernice to tell the story of a new people tempted by the trappings of wealth and mocked by the mixed blessings of eternal youth. These are defiant, oppositional exercises, written in a critical key for a country perpetually in search of its next new self.

EIGHT

The Knock-Off Artist

Like so many alcoholics, he has a certain charm.

F. Scott Fitzgerald, "A New Leaf," 1931

Excessive drinking is a perennial if overplayed feature of the Fitzgerald legend, threatening at times to reduce the writer of the Great American Novel to something of a sad clown. Mindful of Scott's punishing cycle of drunkard's holidays and drying-out periods, crack-ups and breakdowns, Hemingway believed his friend had carelessly squandered, as he put it to a biographer in 1950, "his lovely, golden . . . talent." Although this is certainly true to a point, one can make too much of this important but not artistically decisive fact, missing, so to speak, the books for the beer. This biography does not seek to hide or to minimize the impact of Fitzgerald's alcoholism; it negatively affected his personal relationships, his ability to work, and even his judgment concerning hiring decisions. Frances Kroll, Scott's last secretary, won the job in part because, after being asked during her interview with Fitzgerald to open a bottom bureau drawer filled with empty gin bottles, she didn't blink. Others were only too happy to notice. In 1936, a *New York Evening Post* reporter interviewed Scott on his fortieth birthday and made his subject's tippling the centerpiece of the story. Its last, maleficent line—"He stumbled over to the highboy and poured himself another drink"—may have been excessive, but it played to type.[1] Beautiful and gifted, Scott attracted a host of envious predators eager to slight his accomplishments and prey on his flaws. Some of these men he counted among his friends.

Drawn to "heroes," Fitzgerald idolized generals and football players, but in the arts, Edmund Wilson and Ernest Hemingway set for him a different kind of standard. The latter he first met at the Dingo Bar, on the Rue Delambre in Paris in April 1925, and, outside of James Boswell and Samuel Johnson's friendship, theirs is perhaps literary history's most colorful and famous. Having written three novels and two books of short stories at the time, Fitzgerald was the senior partner in their Paris days. Eager to advance talent, Scott paternally shepherded Hemingway toward Scribner, under whose imprint two of the century's most important novels, *The Sun Also Rises* and *A Farewell to Arms,* were to appear before the end of the decade. "He's the real thing," Scott promised Max Perkins.[2] Aside from mastering a stoic prose style, Hemingway's conspicuous show of presuccess penury, taste for boxing and bull fighting, and Italian Front war wounds all appealed to Fitzgerald. Though occasionally Scott's champion, Hemingway—and Wilson—not infrequently undermined his confidence with the random cutting review, the unsatisfying conversation, or the long silence. Alcoholics too, they never allowed strong drink to reduce their reputations. Fitzgerald's brave if somewhat incautious tilt toward confessional writing in the thirties, on the other hand, gave detractors an easy target.

Privately, he resented the bull's-eye on his back. An early salvo arrived in 1922 when Wilson sent Scott a draft of an essay he was then preparing for the *Bookman.* In it, Wilson had identified three influences on Fitzgerald's writing: St. Paul, Irish ancestry, and alcohol. The reference to drinking caused Scott to pause:

> Now as to the liquor thing—it's true, but nevertheless I'm going to ask you take it out. It leaves a loophole through which I can be attacked and discredited by every moralist who reads the article. Wasn't it Bernard Shaw who said that you've either got to be conventional in your work or in your private life or get into trouble? Anyway the legend about my liquoring is terribly widespread and this thing would hurt me more than you could imagine—both in my contact with the people with whom I'm thrown—relatives and respectable friends—and, what is much more important, financially.
>
> So I'm asking you to cut.[3]

And cut Wilson did. The published article claimed that only two influences—the urban, country-club Midwest and a romantic Celtic quality—informed Scott's writing. As far as the drinking "factor," Fitzgerald, sensing its value among a readership eager to live vicariously on the edge of the Eighteenth Amendment, wanted not so much to excise it as to own it, control it, and make use of it. Indeed, Fitzgerald "outed" himself in print on several occasions, though typically with a wink and a nod that came off as harmless Prohibition-era fun.[4]

The same month that Wilson's *Bookman* essay appeared, Scott's St. Paul friend the writer Thomas Alexander Boyd published an interview with Fitzgerald in the *St. Paul Daily News.* The two men were only recently acquainted but had developed something of a mutual admiration (felt more strongly on Boyd's side) based on their shared love of literature and their World War I service records. Boyd had seen active duty in the marines and wrote about it in a manuscript that Scribner initially rejected before Scott interceded and helped to see it published in 1923. "When Scribner's turned down *Through the Wheat* I cried on reading the letter of rejection," Boyd wrote Scott in gratitude. "I feel quite aware that it is only through you and your inexhaustible exuberance that Scribner's took the book." Fitzgerald first mentioned Boyd to Max Perkins a month before the *Daily News* interview appeared. That conversation—tellingly titled "Literary Libels"—seemed calculated to counteract the stories about Scott's reckless drinking, then beginning to draw attention. In one section, Boyd wrote, "The various rumors that I had heard concerning Fitzgerald came to my mind. I judged that if they were true he would appear rather dissipated. No one could drink a thousand bottles of liquor in one year without having a red nose and a blue-veined face!" He happily reported that Fitzgerald's "eyes were blue and clear." And later on, he quoted Scott's pious claim, "For me, narcotics are deadening to work. I can understand anyone drinking coffee to get a stimulating effect, but whisky—oh, no."[5]

Other times, Fitzgerald owned up to a bit of boozing, but again, it was all in good fun. In the comedic "A Short Autobiography" published in the 25 May 1929 *New Yorker,* he ascribed a particular drink to a particular year:

1922

Kaly's crème de cacao cocktails in St. Paul. My own first and last manufacture of gin.

1923

Oceans of Canadian Ale with R. Lardner in Great Neck, Long Island.

1924

Champagne cocktails on the *Minnewaska* and apologizing to the old lady we kept awake.[6]

And so on.

Scott's earliest memories of alcohol began at home. Edward's quiet condemnation of Yankee capitalism and Calvinist morality offered cover for a range of weaknesses, including a distinct taste for getting tight. Scott remembered well the chance childhood embarrassments this prompted. An entry in his *Ledger* for the age of ten reads, "[My] father used to Drink too much and then play baseball in the backyard."[7] Excepting the occasional St. Paul dip into sweet sherry, Scott's own experiments with alcohol began during his time at the Newman School, which he used as an outpost to explore New York's off-Broadway dives. He had also begun at this time to sneak the random cigarette, from then on a lifelong habit. Princeton's genial drinking culture reinforced Fitzgerald's intake, which increased with his marriage. Zelda drank too but didn't *need* it the way Scott did. The writer Louis Bromfield, a Paris expat like the Fitzgeralds, later observed,

> Scott, like many others who got the name of being drunkards, simply couldn't drink. One cocktail and he was always off. . . . Immediately he was out of control and there was only one end, . . . that he became thoroughly drunk, and like many Irishmen when he became drunk he usually became very disagreeable and rude and quarrelsome, as if all his resentments were released at once. I always cleared out when I saw it coming, because the end was always the same. Of the two Zelda drank better and had, I think, the stronger character, and I have sometimes thought that she could have given it up without any great difficulty.[8]

In Fitzgerald's case, a certain degree of self-abasement and self-punishment accompanied his drinking. Simple gaiety rarely entered into the picture. He typically threw drinks back, got high as quickly as possible, and proceeded to engage, as Bromfield noted, in a haze of bad and boorish behavior. Was he self-medicating to ease his guilt for the "mishandling" of his talents? Had he bought into the belief that he required alcohol to write? Scott told Laura Guthrie Hearne, a palmist he had met while staying in Asheville, North Carolina, in 1935, "Drink heightens feeling. When I drink it heightens my emotions and I put it in a story. But then it becomes hard to keep reason and emotion in balance."[9] In *The Real Scott Fitzgerald,* one of a handful of books written by the Hollywood gossip columnist Sheilah Graham that reviewed her three-and-a-half-year relationship with Fitzgerald, she recalled the constant artistic pressures Fitzgerald faced:

> Scott . . . was a famous author before he had done much living. To fill his books, he had to create his life, to make it as fascinating as possible. The drinking heightened his experience—as Rimbaud did with drugs—and yielded material for fiction. It was then almost impossible for Scott to stop, even when he realized his health was being damaged. . . . He told me of the searching deep within himself to come up with something new, something that had not been said before. He drank, he said, to escape from the strain of this extraordinary effort and perhaps to give himself the courage to make it once again.[10]

Fitzgerald's claim that alcohol facilitated writing offered a ready reply to moralizers, killjoys, and critics. His cavalier (if correct) premonition of an early death further argued against caution. In his second novel, *The Beautiful and Damned,* Fitzgerald, then twenty-five, wrote the following exchange between the story's main characters: "'You drink all the time, don't you?' she said suddenly. . . . 'You have something to drink every day and you're only twenty-five. Haven't you any ambition? Think what you'll be at forty?' 'I sincerely trust that I won't live that long.'"[11] Scott did, of course, live that long, but he never saw forty-five.

Prognostications of an early death aside, Fitzgerald recognized drinking to be an almost indispensable part of the writer's world. Occasions on which to discuss books, publishing, and composing were invariably occasions to drink. It was easy to blur the lines between leisure and labor to the extent that cocktails or fifths of gin could be subscribed to for emotional preparation prior to work, stimulant to work, and easing off work.

Like many alcoholics, Fitzgerald trafficked in both deception and self-deception, a punishing strategy facilitated by the widespread cultural ignorance of the illness. For most Americans at this time, "alcoholism" was not yet regarded as a disease, and Fitzgerald tended to diagnose his drinking (when not deflecting it) as a private weakness. To one of Zelda's physicians, Dr. Oscar Forel, he described his use of hard spirits as controlled and negligible: "During the first seven years of our marriage it was she who wanted to drink while I worked. . . . I assure you of my intention to help her, to permanently give up all liquors and strong drink as I have this summer." And to Zelda's sister Rosalind, he defensively compared his reliance on the bottle to that of General Grant, who, in the course of closing the Mississippi to Rebel forces, defeating Lee, and saving the Union, "needed stimulant and used it." In more reflective moments, however, Scott coldly and critically reflected on his relationship to alcohol. In the 1931 story "A New Leaf," he wrote of an American playboy chronically in his cups. The description, if not precisely autobiography, nonetheless taps into his understanding of alcohol's appeal: "I found that with a few drinks I got Irish and expansive and somehow had the ability to please people, and the idea turned my head. Then I began to take a whole lot of drinks to keep going and have everybody think I was wonderful. Well, I got plastered a lot and quarreled with most of my friends."[12]

Many of Fitzgerald's characters are drinkers, casual or otherwise, and the presence of the latter offered a stratagem to pursue a favorite Fitzgerald theme: dissipation. His books and stories are filled with would-be heroes who, through ill luck, personal weakness, changing times, or some combination of the three, fail to become the "whole man." The extent to which he counted himself among this tormented contingent is an open question. It is more certain that when he wrote about alcoholism, he did so from a personal perspective. This is not to suggest that these writings are extensively autobiographical but rather that they exploited his firsthand knowledge of what it meant to lose control of one's drinking. Fitzgerald was never one to waste material—or to let it grow cold on him. If alcohol is ever present in his writings, it nevertheless remains an evolving subject, one that he became increasingly knowledgeable about. As noted earlier, a young Fitzgerald often played up drinking for laughs; for much of the twenties, it fit his mood and that of the times. As he grew older, however, he adopted a more serious and searching attitude toward alcoholism. In "Echoes of the Jazz Age," Scott noted that several "contemporaries" of his had come to premature ends; he drew up a brief catalogue of casualties that included one unfortunate "killed in a speak-easy in Chicago."[13]

A good example of Fitzgerald's mature writing on drinking can be found in his 1937 short story "An Alcoholic Case," published in *Esquire*. A short piece, it is filled with conspicuous Fitzgerald signage—the main character, an unnamed alcoholic, is an artist (a "well-known" cartoonist) interested in the Yale-Dartmouth football game and currently residing at the "Forest-Park Inn" (Scott had stayed at the Grove Park Inn just outside Asheville, North Carolina, during the summers of 1935 and '36). The plot concerns a young nurse's decision to remain on her "alcoholic case," even as it threatens to turn violent. But the real point of the story comes at the end, when said nurse reflects to her superior, "It's not like anything you can beat—no matter how hard you try. . . . It's just that you can't really help them and it's so discouraging—it's all for nothing."[14] Here, as clearly as anything Fitzgerald would ever write, is his admission that alcohol had gotten the better of him. But it hadn't gotten everything. He was a "functioning alcoholic" who continued to write, publish, and plan for the next novel, literally until the day he died.

By the 1930s, Fitzgerald was hoping to taper his intake. He switched a number of times from hard liquor to beer and occasionally checked himself into hospitals for "rest" and water cures. In a confessional moment, he wrote to Max Perkins of the dead weight that drinking had been on his writing:

It has become increasingly plain to me that the very excellent organization of a long book or the finest perceptions and judgment in time of revision do not go well with liquor. A short story can be written on a bottle, but for a novel you need the mental speed that enables you to keep the whole pattern in your head and ruthlessly sacrifice the sideshows as Ernest did in "A Farewell to Arms." If a mind is slowed up ever so little it lives in the individual part of a book rather than in a book as a whole; memory is dulled. I would give anything if I hadn't had to write Part III of "Tender is the Night" entirely on stimulant. If I had one more crack at it cold sober I believe it might have made a great difference.[15]

In the end, however, the disease was bigger than he was. Taking "one more crack" at writing a novel "cold sober" (*The Last Tycoon*, unfinished at the time of his death), he found he couldn't. Scott's secretary at that time, the aforementioned Frances Kroll, later wrote of his final struggle with alcohol, "Drink in small quantities acted as a stimulus and did not affect the quality of his writing, although he continued to write when he was roaring drunk, as well, most of the effort had, in the long run, to be discarded. . . . The only time he really stopped drinking was after the first heart attack. . . . He took precautions, remained in bed a good deal of time and buckled down to real work on the Last Tycoon. I feel he wanted desperately to finish it before anything might happen to his life."[16] Only three weeks of sobriety passed between the first attack noted by Kroll and the fatal second attack.

Long before that, Fitzgerald's reputation as a drinker had rivaled his standing as an author. Newspapers were eager to conflate his literary world of flappers, romancers, and boozers with the man himself. With an eye to please, Scott often played along. In his first major interview, a May 1920 sit-down with the *New York Tribune*'s Heywood Broun, he breezily described writing as "sort of a substitute form of dissipation"—a line he had used in print to promote *This Side of Paradise*. A couple of years later, he obligingly fashioned himself for the readers of the *New York Evening World* as the Emily Post of Prohibition-era etiquette: "Possessing liquor is a proof of respectability, of social position. You can't go anywhere without having your host bring out his bottle and offer you a drink. He displays his liquor as he used to display his new car or his wife's jewels." And still later, Zelda confirmed Scott's (and her own) eagerness to oblige the press when she wrote with hindsight to Scottie, "Daddy loved glamour and so I also had a great respect for popular acclaim."[17]

The cumulative impact of these print "portraits" diminished Fitzgerald's literary credibility and gave credence to critics' assertions that his work was essentially trivial and superficial. As previously noted, some of the most damning dismissals came from friends—Bishop, Wilson, and Hemingway. In this, they joined Shane Leslie as a Fitzgerald confidant surprised at Scott's sudden success and unsure of what to make of it. Bishop never developed into a major American poet, and his single novel, *Act of Darkness* (1935), failed to find a readership; Wilson's most ambitious novel, *Memoirs of Hecate County* (1946), is remembered less for its artistic merits than for its racy contents, which got it banned in New York and all but killed its distribution elsewhere. Max Perkins once observed from a front-row seat that "Edmund Wilson would give his eyeteeth to have half the reputation as a novelist that Scott Fitzgerald has."[18] At bottom, Wilson failed to appreciate Scott's keen historical sensitivity and ability to capture in a thimbleful of evocative words the pulse of his times. A year after *Paradise* appeared, he wrote to Fitzgerald to set him straight: "The truth is that you are so saturated with twentieth-century America, bad as well as good—you are so used to hotels, plumbing, drugstores, aesthetic ideals, and [the] vast commercial prosperity of the country—that you can't appreciate those institutions of France, for example, which are really superior to American ones. . . . Settle down and learn French and apply a little French leisure and measure to that restless and jumpy nervous system. It would be a service to American letters: your novels would never be the same afterwards."[19] Never the same perhaps—but his novels would have been awful had he followed this prescription. It was, after all, precisely Fitzgerald's knowledge of "hotels," "drugstores," and the "commercial prosperity of the country" that enlivened his stories and made *The Great Gatsby* both a contemporary document and a lasting masterwork. That novel offered readers a peek into the imposing Plaza Hotel, informed them that pharmacies were excellent places to buy illegal hootch, and effectively contrasted the nation's new wealth gathering with its older and presumably less material-minded ideals.

As one of the doyens of twentieth-century American literary criticism, Wilson articulated views on Fitzgerald that carried substantial weight. Indeed, the fact that he was Scott's old college classmate gave a kind proprietary heft to his analysis. For years, his stood as both the first and final "informed" word on Fitzgerald. One has only to read the opening sentences of the formerly mentioned *Bookman* essay to see the extent of Wilson's dismissiveness:

> It has been said by a celebrated person [Edna St. Vincent Millay] that to meet F. Scott Fitzgerald is to think of a stupid old woman with whom someone has left a diamond; she is extremely proud of the diamond and shows it to everyone who comes by, and everyone is surprised that such an ignorant old woman should possess so valuable a jewel. . . . Scott Fitzgerald is, in fact, no old woman, but a very good-looking young man, nor is he in the least stupid, but, on the contrary, exhilaratingly clever. Yet there *is* a symbolic truth in the description quoted above: it is true that Fitzgerald has been left with a jewel which he doesn't know quite what to do with.[20]

"Good-looking," "young," "clever"—in a word, superficial. With the deferential tone of Fitzgerald's relationship with Wilson set forever at Princeton, Scott more or less accepted Bunny's from-on-high observations, an outcome that ultimately satisfied neither man. A 1933 argument between the two offered an air clearing of sorts, and Wilson took the initiative: "I'm sorry about the other day, but you are sometimes a hard guy to get along with and I'm told I'm not wonderful in this respect either. What I object to precisely is the 'scholar and vulgarian,' 'you helped me more than I helped you' business. I know that this isn't entirely a role you've foisted on me: I've partly created it myself. But don't you think at our present time of life we might dispense with this high school (Princeton University) stuff?"[21]

But there could be no "dispensing" on Fitzgerald's part. Wilson's encyclopedic knowledge, monastic work habits, and genteel poverty impressed Scott as the attributes of a "purer" imaginative conscience. Even as Fitzgerald marshaled the creative resources to write a novel as aesthetically sophisticated and historically complex as *Tender Is the Night,* he remained intellectually insecure—more the self-professed "feeler" than the analytical "thinker." In one of his final letters to Wilson, sent after a fall 1938 reunion at Wilson's Stamford, Connecticut, home, Fitzgerald remained unable to reach out to his old friend as an equal. "Believe me, Bunny, it meant more to me than it could possibly have meant to you to see you that evening. It seemed to renew old times learning about Franz Kafka and latter things that are going on in the world of poetry, because I am still the ignoramus that you and John Bishop wrote about at Princeton."[22]

NINE

Rich Boy, Poor Boy

Why, it was impossible that I should be poor!
I was living at the best hotel in New York!

F. Scott Fitzgerald, "How to Live on $36,000 a Year," 1924

The old McQuillan fortune may have dwindled, but it had once opened, and in some ways would always open, certain doors for Fitzgerald. Under its not-always-beneficent influence, he discovered what it meant to be a poor boy at a series of rich-boy schools and how to entertain a moneyed hostess while serving as a clever guest among the Lake Forest elite. Such lessons were not to be forgotten or, in Scott's case, ever to be settled. As a down-on-his-luck Hollywood screenwriter, he swallowed a high rent in hopes of appearing prosperous—a revisitation of the barbed verse—"In a house below the average . . . On a street above the average"—he had sent to Alida Bigelow twenty years earlier. In various ways, these were bruising, humiliating encounters, and yet they brought Scott an understanding of the involved workings of wealth that was more developed and *felt* than he could have otherwise attained.

Even during those periods when Fitzgerald's pockets were full, he thought that mere wealth held little promise as a creative force in American life. Still, its power as a historical player could not be ignored. Strategically, he placed the rising cash nexus in relation to what he often described in his writing as a declining tradition of honest work, personal independence, and social responsibility—Edward's world, at its best, as imagined by Scott. Fitzgerald prized, in other words, the now-passing small-town civilities that he believed were once the cornerstone of the presidencies of Thomas Jefferson and Andrew Jackson. Enemies of the country's First (1791–1811) and Second (1816–1836) National Banks, these frontier aristocrats envisioned a national economy free from the virtue-depleting evils of greed, corruption, and speculation. Fitzgerald used Jackson in particular as a point of cultural reference in his final novel, *The Last Tycoon*. Jackson's Nashville plantation, the Hermitage, is visited early one morning by a small group of Hollywooders connected to the film industry. "We crossed a brook over an old rattly iron bridge laid with planks," one of them describes their trip back in time. "Now there were roosters crowing and blue-green shadows stirring every time we passed a farm house." Here were the new powerbrokers visiting the shattered grounds of the old.[1]

If Scott was something of a Jeffersonian of the heart, however, the *promise* of the rich never ceased to attract him. Here, after all, stood a class capable of turning money into rare and precious experiences that others could only dream of. Undoubtedly a certain snobbery underlined his wealth watching, though it was, in the main, an elitism anchored in abstraction. He was more taken, that is, by the storybook concept of aristocracy than by its reality—yet another example of Scott's romantic sensibility enlarging on the actual. As an "idea," affluence suggested to Fitzgerald the possibility of days more sparkling, intense, and imaginative than the working and middle classes could ever know. That he literally trusted in this chimera is doubtful—anymore than he trusted in Ginevra's everlasting love, Princeton's handsome pose, or the imperishability of his youth or his talent. Each and all were talismans, symbols of things not to be. He wrote less about the "Beautiful People," after all, than he did about the "Beautiful and Damned."

Fitzgerald's mixed mindedness on the "wealth" question is compellingly captured in the iconic Jay Gatsby. As a poor boy from the provinces, Gatsby learns the painful lesson that no matter how much money he makes, he can never cross the carefully guarded border into "respectable" society. "Wealth," in other words, is more than money; it is the right schools, right Manhattan telephone exchanges, and right marriages. But for all the elegant mansions atop freshly manicured lawns, none among Gatsby's Long Island neighbors could match his romantic vision, his freedom *from* the right schools, right Manhattan telephone exchanges, and right marriages. And it is this roughneck, this arriviste, who exposes the empty heart of the modern plutocracy.

More generally, Jay Gatsby stands in a long line of Fitzgerald types— flawed heroes, poor boys—who smash against the collective might of their well-to-do tormentors. In *Tender Is the Night,* Dick Diver, a talented psychiatrist on the verge of publishing a "big book," succumbs to a life of privilege that compromises his talents, distorts his perspective, and undermines his self-respect. In *The Last Tycoon,* the Hollywood producer Monroe Stahr engages in a losing battle with the big studio impresarios to create films of lasting depth and quality. In these and many other Fitzgerald works lies a patent sympathy for the imperfect dreamer, healer, and craftsman. In Gatsby, Diver, and Stahr, Fitzgerald invested a part of himself—or self-image—into their tragic circumstances. Accordingly, he measured the value of their character by the quality of their quests. Like him, they were "old" Americans, the spiritual children of Puritans, cava- liers, and cowboys who suddenly found themselves on the outside. And like him, they too harbored an underlying and deep-seated resentment toward a myopic American gentry that seemed to have all the opportu- nities in the world but little idea of what to do with them.

As a bankable writer, Fitzgerald cleared rather princely sums for many years, earning ever-increasing royalties for his short stories in the 1920s and early '30s. Altogether, his career income totaled some $300,000— over $4 million in current dollars or, spread out over the twenty years that he wrote professionally, roughly $200,000 a year, again in current dollars. Outside of a prized life-insurance policy, Fitzgerald showed re- markably little interest in investments, be they stocks, bonds, homes, or real estate. He and Zelda were perpetual renters; they rang up high hotel bills, kept cooks and nannies, and treated friends and hangers-on alike to generous Prohibition-era parties fueled by forbidden alcohol. Actually *having* money meant little to Fitzgerald; he sought, rather, its immediate exchange into something tangible and pleasurable. He wished not to count but to experience. In a never-sent 1939 letter to Fitzgerald, Harold

Ober, his literary agent and banker of sorts (advancing Scott cash on the basis of future story sales), sought to dispense some well-meaning financial advice: "I notice that both Scottie and you would always rather send a telegram or make an expensive telephone call than send a letter for three cents. You give tips four and five times as large as you need to. . . . I am sure that if you could look back over the years with some kind of a celestial bookkeeper to note down your expenses, you would find that a large part of the money you have earned has gone for things that brought you no return."[2] Had the letter gone out, it might have drawn from Fitzgerald a defense similar to the one that he had given to his mother in 1930, after she had questioned his large lifestyle: "All big men have spent money freely. I hate avarice or even caution."[3] Casual and careless with his finances, Fitzgerald paid willingly for his indulgences and delighted that he possessed the high-wire writing skills to escape looming financial peril. He became the true heir of the conflicting economic personalities of his parentage: a McQuillan made money; a Fitzgerald spent money.

Though dismissive of wealth, Fitzgerald understood its power only too well because it had injured him so often. He never forgot Edward's ancient business misfortunes, his futile Lake Forest social climbing, or the fact that Zelda had refused to marry him until assured of his ability to support her lifestyle. When the money did begin to roll in, he naturally viewed it with suspicion. Eager to assert his independence, he dispensed hard-earned bank notes with surprising ease. He seemed less interested in owning things than in demonstrating that things did not own him. As Ober noticed, he gave outlandishly generous tips, contemptuously carried huge sums in his pockets, and excused the occasional drunken antic by throwing dollars at the indiscretion. By willfully wasting money, he denied its power over him. But in never developing a mature attitude toward finances, by failing, that is, to regulate his spending or to put money aside, Fitzgerald resigned himself—and his family—to living on whatever immediate income, credit, or compassion he could secure. It proved to be a precarious and, at times, humiliating feast-or-famine existence.[4]

In trying so hard to deny wealth's reach, Fitzgerald tacitly acknowledged his failure to escape its hold. In one of his favorite short stories, "The Offshore Pirate" (1920), he brought these unsettled emotions into the open. The story's protagonist is a Fitzgeraldesque playboy in pursuit of a moneyed-up golden girl named Ardita. Because of the golden girl's desire to have her dollars attended with romance and adventure, he is forced to assume a new identity. This he does, as a faux pirate/band leader. He further concocts an elaborate personal history of hating the rich that he details for the golden girl:

> Half a dozen times they played at private dances at three thousand dollars a night, and it seemed as if these crystallized all his distaste for his mode of livelihood. They took place in clubs and houses that he couldn't have gone into in the daytime. After all, he was merely playing the rôle of the eternal monkey, a sort of sublimated chorus man. He was sick of the very smell of the theatre, of powder and rouge and the chatter of the greenroom and the patronizing approval of the boxes. He couldn't put his heart into it any more.[5]

Our "pirate" sees beyond the bottom line of a bank statement, valuing money not for its own sake but rather for the episodes and relationships it could generate. Assuming the role of an outcast, he articulates for Ardita an attitude toward spending in which he demonstrates an understanding of wealth's "true" value: "He wanted to have a lot of money and time, and opportunity to read and play, and the sort of men and women round him that he could never have—the kind who, if they thought of him at all, would have considered him rather contemptible; in short he wanted all those things which he was beginning to lump under the general head of aristocracy, an aristocracy which it seemed almost any money could buy except money made as he was making it."[6]

But our protagonist is, after all, pedigreed and only plays at being a pirate, and so his talk of smashing on the shore of class snobbery—Gatsby's fate—is an empty anxiety. Accordingly, "Offshore Pirate" ends on a typically softened note for readers of the *Saturday Evening Post*. In a moment of winking self-regard in the story, Fitzgerald gently mocks his war on the rich: "Sometimes when you're round," the heroine coos, "I've been tempted to kiss you suddenly and tell you that you were just an idealistic boy with a lot of caste nonsense in his head."[7] Below the surface of a saleable story, however, Fitzgerald knew that it was not all nonsense.

The country had relegated an older vision of republican self-sufficiency (the agrarian republic of Jefferson and Jackson) to the history books while forging a new identity as a republic of consumers (the republic of *Tender Is the Night*'s Nicole Diver).

Fitzgerald wrestled with this change in much of his work. At times, as with the darkly brilliant short story "The Rich Boy" (1926), he penetrates deep into the pernicious impact of money on imagination. The story contemplates the lonely life of Anson Hunter, whose privileged upbringing elicits in others deference to his judgments and talents. Constantly suspicious of his peers' motives and never fully trusting anyone, he becomes an isolate. Hunter is modeled after Ludlow Fowler, a school friend of Scott's who served as the best man at his wedding. "I have written a . . . story about you called *The Rich Boy*," Fitzgerald wrote to Fowler in advance of the story's publication in the January and February 1926 issues of *Redbook* magazine. Fitzgerald assured Fowler that few readers would see it as anything more than fiction: "It is so disguised that no one except you and me and maybe two of the girls concerned would recognize, unless you give it away, but it is in a large measure the story of your life, toned down here and there and symplified. Also many gaps had to come out of my imagination. It is frank, unsparing but sympathetic and I think you will like it—it is one of the best things I have ever [d]one."[8]

After reading the story, Fowler asked Fitzgerald to cut two brief passages before it appeared in print. One of them told of a "pretty debutante" whom Hunter "knew in his car"; the other related how Hunter taught a Sunday-school class after a night of carousing, and "by some mutual instinct several children" in the room moved to the back row. Fitzgerald agreed to the cuts and notified Ober: "Too bad about the Fowler changes. . . . It is the story of his life—he's an old friend—we went to Princeton together + he told me those things in confidence."[9] Fitzgerald failed, however, to identify for Ober the exact passages to be excised, perhaps assuming that Fowler would himself get in touch with the agent. He did not, and the material appeared in the magazine version of "The Rich Boy." Fitzgerald later made the cuts himself while reading proofs of the story in preparation for its appearance in *All the Sad Young Men* (1926), his third collection of short fiction.

"The Rich Boy" opens with one of Fitzgerald's most quoted epigrams:

> Let me tell you about the very rich. They are different from you and me. They possess and enjoy early, and it does something to them, makes them soft where we are hard and cynical where we are trustful, in a way that, unless you were born rich, it is very difficult to understand. They think, deep in their hearts, that they are better than we are because we had to discover the compensations and refuges of life for ourselves. Even when they enter deep into our world or sink below us, they still think that they are better than we are. They are different.[10]

In describing a pathology of mistrust among "the very rich" for any but their own, Fitzgerald revealed his doubts about the leisure class. Of course he had constantly sought to put himself in its path.

In a Darwinian world, Anson Hunter, as his surname suggests, sits at the top of the food chain. Wealthy and emotionally aloof, he establishes his own rules and expects others to defer. Without the quaint middle-class ceilings on sex and drinking to work as regulators, the New York–based Anson indulges himself, living the life of an urban prince with a Yale pedigree. But if wealth has blessed Anson, it has also wrecked him. Given so much, so early, he is unfit for marriage. He falls in love with a beautiful young woman named Paula Legendre, but when the relationship progresses toward marriage and threatens to disturb his cynical reserve and sense of superiority, he withdraws. He suffers from a kind of emotional paralysis: "He need say no more, commit their destinies to no practical enigma. Why should he, when he might hold her so, biding his own time, for another year—forever?"[11] Never having given anything of himself, he begins to dimly understand how little he has to offer.

After Paula's rebound marriage to another man, Anson comes close to a nervous breakdown. To salve his unacknowledged wound, he takes up with Dolly Karger, a woman he has never been able to take entirely seriously because she has come from recent money—"only a few old families like the Hunters could question whether or not she 'belonged.'"[12]

Tired of Anson's distance, Dolly tries to make him jealous by hinting at her interest in a certain Perry Hull from Chicago. Anson, a master of extrication himself, sees through the ruse immediately. But rather than simply let Dolly go, he now maneuvers to obliterate completely this assault on his position. To do this, he sets about winning Dolly over again. One night, after an evening designed, so she is led to believe, to culminate in the consummation of their relationship, Anson cruelly leaves her bedside as she begs him to tell her that he loves her. Once assured of his advantage, he takes no further interest in her. Like Paula, Dolly quickly marries.

And then as Anson approaches middle age, a strange thing happens to him: he begins to find himself abandoned. His once-wide circle of chums has narrowed to nil as the combination of weddings and work, growing up and growing old, cuts his old collegiate connections one by one. The death of his mother brings to light yet another disquieting realization: with New York's influx of new money, the Hunters' nineteenth-century fortune no longer commands its old respect. One day, as Anson looks upward into a window of a club to which he belongs but scarcely visits any longer, he sees "a grey man with watery eyes star[ing] down at him."[13] A sudden shock of recognition takes hold of Anson: is this to be *his* future? With mounting anxiety, he realizes that for the first time in his life, he has no place to go and no one to see. If he is not the "rich boy" whom other men admire and all single women desire, who is he?

Taking a long rest from work, Anson books passage on a cruise ship sailing for Europe. On it, he meets a pretty girl in a smart red tam whom he instantly, instinctively begins to charm. In winning her over, he stands to regain his sense of supremacy, to know that any woman that he desires would at his slight signaling give the best she had—in years, love, and loyalty—just to be with him. For Anson, in other words, arrested development remains the order of the day. For him, there will be no emotional strengthening, no adult maturity, and no domestic happiness. "Life," he astutely complains, amid a backdrop of privilege, "has made a cynic of me."[14]

If Fitzgerald played up Lud Fowler's pathos in "The Rich Boy," he turned to his own experiences among the affluent in "How to Live on $36,000 a Year" (1924), a comedic essay with a sharp edge. It details a disastrous financial year endured by Scott and Zelda while living in a well-to-do neighborhood on Long Island. With *This Side of Paradise* trailing clouds of glory, Fitzgerald admits that he lost sight of economic reality and became credit dependent. At first, it all seemed a bit of a lark—"when successful authors ran out of money all they had to do was to sign checks." But when the bills came due, he discovered there was no cash to cover the claims. Where had the $36,000 gone? Into a lavish lifestyle, Fitzgerald complains, and one that the wealthy encouraged precisely to keep gate-crashers at bay. Tongue only partly in cheek, he hints at a conspiracy of grocers and servants, nannies and lawn keepers to drain his funds. Astonished at the high price of food, he ponders the advantages of a community co-op, only to quickly drop the subject: "It would absolutely ruin us with our neighbors, who would suspect that we actually cared about our money."[15]

With debt mounting, Fitzgerald had to break ranks, demonstrating in the process that, pride aside, he did indeed care about money—but not the money of the rich, not, that is, the easy credit, the large inheritance, or the cashing in of so many gifted stocks and bonds. Fitzgerald, rather, rolled up his sleeves and went to work: "Over our garage is a large bare room wither I now retired with pencil, paper and the oil stove, emerging the next afternoon at five o'clock with a 7000-word story. That was something; it would pay the rent and last month's overdue bills. It took twelve hours a day for five weeks to rise from abject poverty back into the middle class, but within that time we had paid our debts, and the cause for immediate worry was over."[16] More or less, he wrote the truth. Over a disagreeable four-month period during the winter of 1923–1924, Fitzgerald composed eleven short stories, earning him a face-saving $17,000. The effort left him exhausted and somewhat bitter—he knew debt had gotten the better of him, had drawn him away from "serious" writing. He subsequently complained to Wilson, "I really worked hard as hell last winter—but it was all trash and it nearly broke my heart as well as my iron constitution."[17] Shortly after penning the last of these stories, Scott, Zelda, and Scottie traded Long Island's entrapments for a nearly three-year European sojourn. The exchange rate was favorable; they hoped to economize.

Considering Fitzgerald's caustic literary references to various "rich boys" and girls, it seems fair to ask why he believed in the possibilities of wealth to promote refinement and taste rather than mere diversion. Certainly his romantic conception of the old southern quasi-aristocracy played a role here, as did his dreamy emotional investment in Princeton and Lake Forest. But these youthful conceits would have to be supplemented if they were to survive. And they were—by the Murphys.

Gerald and Sara Murphy, an expatriate couple first introduced to the Fitzgeralds at Cap d'Antibes near Cannes in 1924, embodied the elegant art of turning money into amity, leisure, and adventure. Sara, grandniece to William Tecumseh Sherman, was the daughter of the ink manufacturer Frank Wiborg, a self-made millionaire. The Murphy family owned the Mark Cross Company, sellers of fine leather goods. Neither Gerald nor Sara was interested in making money. Gerald in particular considered himself an aesthete, and with his appreciation for the various arts and his own ample talents as a painter in the precisionist style, a European encampment called. As their daughter, Honoria, explained, "My parents' chief reason for leaving the U.S. was to seek cultural nourishment, but there were other factors—negative factors, if you will. There was . . . a reaction to American social and business customs. . . . Their discontent had to do with an absence of cultural stimulation in America, a philistine attitude."[18]

From the Murphys' Mediterranean chalet—christened "Villa America" by Gerald—the couple engaged in what Fitzgerald later and appreciatively called an "inventive life." Costumes, children's parties, and picnics on the shore were part of a routine that pulled in a sweet confusion of creative personalities charmed and inspired by their host's *bons vivant*. Visitors to Villa America included Hemingway, Dorothy Parker, Pablo Picasso, Archibald MacLeish, John Dos Passos, Fernand Léger, and Gerald's Yale classmate Cole Porter. "It wasn't the parties that made it such a gay time," Sara later observed. "There was such affection between everybody. You loved your friends and wanted to see them every day, and usually you did see them every day. It was like a great fair, and everybody was so young."[19]

The Murphy model both enchanted and haunted Fitzgerald. In creating a cloudland on the Riviera, Gerald and Sara had for a brief time made real the good life once described by Scott, in another context, as "the eternal Carnival by the Sea."[20] Yet Fitzgerald also understood that there was a great gulf that separated him from Gerald. Whereas Scott led with ambition, nerves, and emotion, Gerald projected poise and self-control. Everything Gerald did seemed natural and right; Fitzgerald typically found such peace only in his writing. Scott and Zelda were competitive with each other and often at cross-purposes, while Gerald and Sara, by contrast, worked in tandem. The Murphys' dignity as a couple was never so impressively apparent as when they suffered the early deaths of their two sons, a cruel twin affliction that resonated deeply with Fitzgerald. His sensitive interest in the temporal nature of youth gave him an involved perspective on the losses. Following the unexpected passing of Baoth Murphy in 1935, a casualty of meningitis exasperated by measles, Gerald marveled at Scott's compassion:

> Of all our friends, it seems to me that you alone knew how we felt these days. . . . You are the only person to whom I can ever tell the bleak truth of what I feel. Sara's courage and the amazing job which she is doing for Patrick [their youngest son, who was to succumb to tuberculosis in 1937] make unbearably poignant the tragedy of what has happened—what life has tried to do to her. I know now that what you said in *Tender Is the Night* is true. Only the invented part of our life—the unreal part—has had any scheme any beauty. Life itself has stepped in now and blundered, scarred and destroyed. In my heart I dreaded the moment when our youth and invention would be attacked in our only vulnerable spot—the children, their growth, their heath, their future. How ugly and blasting it can be, and how idly ruthless.[21]

Gerald's finding comfort in *Tender Is the Night* is fitting given how much of "the invented part of our life," the picturesque part of the Murphys, made it into Fitzgerald's novel. The book opens with a beautiful description of an enchanted slice of the Mediterranean world as seen from the Villa America point of view: "On the pleasant shore of the

French Riviera, about half way between Marseilles and the Italian border, stands a large, proud, rose-colored hotel. Deferential palms cool its flushed façade, and before it stretches a short dazzling beach. . . . The hotel and its bright tan prayer rug of a beach were one. In the early morning the distant image of Cannes, the pink and cream of old fortifications, the purple Alp that bounded Italy, were cast across the water and lay quavering in the ripples and rings sent up by sea-plants through the clear shallows."[22]

The Murphys and their circle offered an outstanding example of the fatherly financial advice that Edward had once whimsically bestowed on a then-twelve-year-old Scott, away at summer camp: "I enclose $1.00. Spend it liberally, generously, carefully, judiciously, sensibly. Get from it pleasure, wisdom, health and experience."[23] Blessed with abundant resources, Gerald and Sara spent wisely on friends, family, amusements, and the arts. Hemingway, so dismissive of Fitzgerald's interest in the rich, also fell under their spell. In person and as a "type," the Murphys left an indelible imprint on Fitzgerald and his writing. For in them did Scott discover an altogether convincing complement to the absorbed, adrift "rich boy" who had gained the world but lost his soul.

TEN

The Wages of Sin—
The Beautiful and Damned

There's the philosophy of ever so many young people to-day.
They don't believe in the old standards and authorities, and they're
not intelligent enough, many of them, to put a code of morals and
conduct in place of the sanctions that have been destroyed for
them. They drift. Their attitude toward life might be summed up:
'This is ALL. Then what does it matter? We don't care! Let's GO!'

F. Scott Fitzgerald, 1922

In March 1922, Scribner released Fitzgerald's second novel, *The Beautiful
and Damned*. Written at the height of the Jazz Age, it cut against the era's
surface shimmer by offering a remarkably bleak social portrait under-
pinned by generational drift and the restless search for meaningful as
opposed to merely remunerative work. Something of an afterthought at
the time of Fitzgerald's death, the book failed to connect with those many
readers looking for yet another Jazz Age story about flappers, prohibi-
tionists, and Princetonians. To be sure, these former headliners make an
appearance, but the tone is different. Informed by the young author's
critical reflections on the postwar West, the novel wrestled a bit clumsily if intuitively with materialism's recent and striking ascent. As a kind
of sweeping civilizational commentary, it might plausibly be paired with
the politically tinted poetry of contemporaries T. S. Eliot and Allen Tate
or the slightly more distant observations of Henrys James and Adams,

discontents alike of modernism's triumph over tradition, Cassandras of a new money-centric world rising.

One might also see in the novel's scaffolding the acidic influence of H. L. Mencken. Notorious in the twenties for his draw-blood diatribes against evangelicals, superpatriots, and the "boobsoisie," Mencken was an early if fleeting influence on Fitzgerald and in particular an influence on *The Beautiful and Damned*. His favorable *Smart Set* review of *This Side of Paradise*—he called it "the best American novel that I have seen of late"—sparked a largely letter-writing acquaintance with Fitzgerald. Sixteen years older than Scott, Mencken briefly (1920–1922) took over the mentor-as-artistic-conscience role once played by the recently deceased Father Fay and then more fully by Bunny Wilson. During this period, Mencken encouraged the young writer, by his own pungent example, to show the philistines no quarter. The bitter charisma of his more corrosive portraits fairly jumped off the pages. In one such offering, a pitiless ridiculing of the followers of the Nebraska-based political fundamentalist William Jennings Bryan, Mencken cracked, "Wherever the flambeaux of Chautauqua smoked and guttered, and the bilge of idealism ran in the veins, and Baptist pastors dammed the brooks with the sanctified, and men gathered who were weary and heavy laden, and their wives who were fully of Peruna and as fecund as the shad . . . there the indefatigable Jennings set up his traps and spread his bait." If never quite matching Mencken's gift for turning the harangue into an extravagant, witty work of art, Scott did introduce an unmistakable if somewhat forced Menckenese into *The Beautiful and Damned*. Accordingly, the Bible thumpers and the business class alike are held up for burlesque. Fitzgerald writes of missionaries "converting the heathen of China or America to a nebulous protestantism," while one doubtful Harvard product understands that "to succeed [on Wall Street] the idea of success must grasp and limit his mind."[1]

Despite the novel's deft handling of several familiar Fitzgerald themes—namely, the struggle between prewar convention and postwar flux—*The Beautiful and Damned* has long battled a kind of literary inferiority complex. One might gather a glimpse of its secondary status in Scott's obvious pleasure at receiving a telegram from his friend the writer and photographer Carl Van Vechten praising the book. "I'm always glad when anyone likes *The Beautiful and Damned*," he wrote in reply. "Most people prefer *This Side of Paradise* and while I do myself I hate to see one child preferred above another." Among critics, the artistically superior duo of *The Great Gatsby* (1925) and *Tender Is the Night* (1934) understandably overshadow *This Side of Paradise* (1920) and *The Beautiful and Damned* (1922)—and of the latter two, it is *Paradise*'s expressive portrait of youth, its quixotic coming-of-age quest, that has struck the more resonant chord among readers. *The Beautiful and Damned,* by contrast, finds Fitzgerald experimenting with naturalism, a literary style at odds with Romanticism and thus alien to his strongest artistic sensibilities. Much taken at the time by the works of Frank Norris and Theodore Dreiser, he sought to imitate their approach to tragedy, which involved a fatalistic outcome determined by hereditary or social environment that left little room for human agency, let alone heroes. As one scholar has argued, this "doctrine of the meaningless of life was a denial of everything [Fitzgerald] really believed in, and frustrated what was perhaps his truest impulse—his sense of wonder at the inexhaustible possibilities of existence." Certainly the artistically evolving Scott never attempted to repeat his mixed-results adventures in Dreiserism. While deep into the writing of *Gatsby,* he informed one correspondent of his movement toward a more atmospheric and less empirical approach: "I am so anxious for people to see my new novel which is a new thinking out of the idea of illusion (an idea which I suppose will dominate my more serious stuff) much more mature and much more romantic than This Side of Paradise. The B & D was a better book than the first but it was a false lead, . . . a concession to Mencken. . . . The business of creating illusion is much more to my taste and my talent."[2]

And make no mistake, *The Beautiful and Damned* is a work of unrelieved disillusionment; its lead, Anthony Patch, is paralyzed by privilege and an ennui inducing lack of vocation. As the anxiously awaiting heir to a Wall Street fortune, he feels little compulsion to do anything finer with his post-Harvard prospects than to live—or at least affect—the life of an aesthete. His studied detachment becomes dangerously paralytic when, unexpectedly cut out of his grandfather's will, he cannot muster the emotional resources to make a fresh start. Instead, he dabbles in short-story writing and invests a humiliating (and alcohol-fueled) afternoon as the door-to-door foot soldier of a minor Ponzi scheme. Still, Fitzgerald is not without sympathy for Anthony or his wife, Gloria. Surveying their limited options, he condemns modern America's dry industrial sameness, business-booster mentality, and puritanical mores (Grandfather Patch found Jesus at fifty-seven and became "a reformer among reformers"). Presumably this material hit close to home for Fitzgerald. Just three years earlier, he had angered his parents by turning down a position as advertising manager for the St. Paul wholesaler Griggs Cooper & Co. Instead of producing ad copy, he wrote his first novel. One finds an echo of this rebellion in *The Beautiful and Damned* in Gloria's acquiescence to Anthony's unwillingness to sit in an office all day: "She would never blame him for being the ineffectual idler so long as he did it sincerely, from the attitude that nothing much was worth doing."[3]

Together, Anthony and Gloria's marriage is a perfect disaster. The hardest of partiers, the most beautifully useless of human décor, they race across the continent in a frantic pursuit of diversion and pleasure. Think Tom and Daisy Buchanan in a lesser key. The elder Patch, by contrast, represents the now-passing generation shaped by the fire of Civil War and the dynamic industrial process that followed. Heeding Lincoln's call for volunteers to put down the slaveholders' rebellion, old Adam left his father's Tarrytown farm in 1861 to join a hastily assembled New York cavalry unit. Discharged from service as a major, he then tackled Wall Street and, "amid much fuss, fume, applause, and ill will," laid claim to a staggering fortune.[4] A conventional capitalist, Adam absorbed Benjamin Franklin's catechism of hard work and public piety, these the practical complements to the rocket ride of wishing and willing that, at a deeper level, drove his dream. And it is precisely this fierce and full journey that Anthony can now never make. With the greatest war already won and the most spectacular stock market already cornered, life offered a kind of "is that all?" aftermath. The buccaneering temperament remained, but its opportunity for actualization now slowed considerably. In desperation, Anthony, like his younger brother, Gatsby, sought to anchor his remaining romantic instincts on the transitory promise of a woman's beauty—with predictably ruinous results.

Gloria, the handsome woman in question, bears enough resemblance to Zelda to give *The Beautiful and Damned* a voyeuristic quality, a feeling of easy intimacy turned into public property. Little in Fitzgerald's own life, and certainly not his marriage, was off-limits as material for his novel. Anthony and Gloria's alarm at "hear[ing] rumors about themselves from all quarters, rumors founded usually on a soupçon of truth, but overlaid with preposterous and sinister detail" memorialized the toxic gossip circulating about Scott and Zelda.[5] And from this indelicate airing of dirty laundry, the novel embarked unpleasantly on a series of spouse baitings, sexual insecurities, and petty postnuptial skirmishes. Gloria's childlike whining for a fashionable new fur coat—over Anthony's economizing objection—hints at Fitzgerald's reaction to a similar plea; and Gloria's concern that Anthony's drinking endangers both his health and their budget plays on Zelda's grievances.

Fitzgerald's uneasy reflections on Anthony and Gloria undoubtedly emerged from the circumstances of his own recent nuptials. Scott's friends worrisomely remembered the domestic Sturm und Drang that ruled the couple's early years of marriage. Alexander McKaig, formerly editor of the *Daily Princetonian* and a part of the Fitzgeralds' earliest New York "group," thought their union doomed. "Called on Scott Fitz and his bride," he confided in a diary. "[Zelda] temperamental small-town Southern belle. Chews gum. Shows knees. I don't think marriage can succeed. Both drinking heavily. Think they will be divorced in three years." And Lawton Campbell recalled finding Scott and Zelda holed up in the bedroom of their small West Fifty-Ninth Street apartment, "a breakfast tray perched on the unmade bed and vestiges of the previous evening were everywhere: half-empty glasses, ashtrays overflowing with cigarette butts and manuscript pages scattered around the room."[6]

Such marital theatrics were liberally mined for Scott's new novel. On Anthony and Gloria's six-month West Coast honeymoon, the couple engaged in a petty but depleting conjugal cold war over who bore responsibility for sending out their dirty laundry. Gloria's insouciance carried the campaign but at a cost. For "there were days," wrote Fitzgerald, "when they hurt each other purposely—taking almost a delight in the thrust." In later years, he would look back on the novel as an incomplete yet telling documentation of their first and lasting troubles. "I wish the Beautiful and Damned had been a maturely written book," he told Zelda in 1930, "because it was all true." Well, perhaps it was not all true, as Scott well knew, but the novel accurately enough captured Fitzgerald's self-doubts as a young husband; he loved Zelda's boldness, her dance-at-any-time-of-the-day irreverence, yet recognized her power to consume his writing hours and deplete his creative energy. In light of their subsequent troubled history—Zelda's deteriorating mental health, their unfriendly competition, and Fitzgerald's sexual anxieties—Anthony's marital misgivings take on an eerie, prophetic quality. One wonders about the degree of personal history embedded in Fitzgerald's ugly claim that Anthony's "wild thoughts varied between a passionate desire for [Gloria's] kisses and an equally passionate craving to hurt and mar her. . . . She was beautiful—but especially she was without mercy. He must own that strength that could send him away."[7]

Several years later, in the summer of 1940, Fitzgerald denied in a letter to his daughter the autobiographical nature of many of the less elegant details packed into *The Beautiful and Damned*. The letter suggests that Scottie, now eighteen and perhaps having recently read the book, had pressed her father for an explanation after making a number of uncomfortable connections. In reply, Scott gamely if carefully defended both Zelda and their marriage: "Gloria was a much more trivial and vulgar person than your mother. I can't really say there was any resemblance except in the beauty and certain terms of expression she used, and also I naturally used many circumstantial events of our early married life. However the emphases were entirely different. We had a much better time than Anthony and Gloria had."[8] If illuminating, the letter also sought to shield and is perhaps best approached as a combination of selective memory and a father's right to revision.

Aside from detailing the Fitzgeralds' marital squabbles, *The Beautiful and Damned* took on a deeper confessional quality for its author. Under Anthony's shadow, Scott wrote of his increasing reliance on alcohol, inability to live without debt, and fear of atrophy: "I am essentially weak," Anthony recognized; "I need work to do, work to do." Anthony in this underscored last point voices the concerns of a generation, for in Mencken's

America, it appeared that the age of heroic labor had passed, to be replaced instead by unrewarding toil in a tangle of real estate, booze, and bonds markets. Fitzgerald almost assuredly knew a series of Anthonys—boys at prep school, young men at Princeton, dilettantes in New York—idling away the years until the expected legacy arrived. "What chance have they," he complained in an April 1922 *New York Evening World* interview, "these men and women of my generation who come from families with some money!" Here teetered a leisure class in its least impressive incarnation. Though educated in the better academies and given all the advantages of place and station that their powerful families could provide, many in fact followed Anthony's aimless course. In "Echoes of the Jazz Age," Fitzgerald recalled how no fewer than six of his Princeton classmates met early and violent deaths due in part to alcohol and depression. He found the commonplace of this collective tragedy striking: "These are not catastrophes that I went out of my way to look for—these were my friends."[9]

Anthony and Gloria thought themselves financially set and so became wastrels. Living off the sweat equity earned by previous generations, they could find no continents of their own to conquer, no higher purpose to life than expensive clothing, a trip or three to Europe, and a tasteful brownstone. Anthony dreamily, or perhaps desperately, hangs onto the notion that he will one day write a grand history of the Middle Ages—or perhaps the Renaissance popes. One subject is as good as another, of course, because he has nothing to say. Later, he tries his hand at short fiction. Removed from the hustle and strain of daily existence, he can only halfheartedly engage in literary efforts that are slack and derivative. Too late does he discover that the inability to give run to one's resources, valor, and empathy is itself a form of death before death. Without purpose, Fitzgerald suggests, there can be no passion. "Work is the one salvation for all of us," he remarked in the press blitz leading up to the publication of *The Beautiful and Damned*, "even if we must work to forget there's nothing worth while to work for, even if the work we turn out—books, for example—doesn't satisfy us. The young man must work. His wife must work."[10]

But Gloria Patch does not work, and thus her fate is sealed. Fitzgerald (with headline-grabbing hyperbole) described "our American women" to one interviewer at this time as "an utterly useless fourth generation trading on the accomplishment of their pioneer great-grandmothers."[11] Coconspirators in the great rush to civilize the frontier, women of an earlier generation took a second seat to no man, including Adam Patch, in their efforts to build a nation. But with the frontier's closing and industrialization's demand for predictability, coercion, and docility, Gloria has no place to go and nothing to do. The irony is obvious. Possessed of beauty, brains, and a modest sinecure, she would appear to have all that her society could offer—as that society reckoned the things a woman should want. But Gloria's unhappiness is the most evident thing about her. She is channeled into the same encumbering lifestyle that drags Anthony down, and her world contracts to a trivial, restless interest in travel, parties, and a twitchy consumerism. She seeks neither truth nor justice but would sell her soul for a gray-squirrel fur coat.

Gloria's inherent tenacity and enduring pride mark her as the novel's true tragedian. Late in the book, she contacts an old beau, now a big shot in the rising movie industry. Aware that her looks are in a slow fade but not yet gone, she bravely asks for and subsequently endures a nerve-wracking audition before the camera. More than a mere paycheck rests on the outcome, for Gloria's sense of self-worth is tied up in her looks and the power of her beauty to conquer all worlds. Her friend's charity only deepens the cut: "*My dear Gloria: We had the test run off yesterday afternoon, and [the director] seemed to think that for the part he had in mind he needed a younger woman. He said that the acting was not bad, and that there was a small character part supposed to be a very haughty rich widow that he thought you might—.*"We like Gloria better for this humiliation. Whereas Anthony casually drops his never-very-serious writing ambitions, Gloria is devastated in defeat. And if there should come a time when life on her own terms proves impossible, she hopes to exit on her own terms. Gloria counsels Anthony that if he loses his inheritance, they should cash in their last bearing bonds, go to Italy and live a few wild years, "and then just die." But here, too, a confused Anthony demurs.[12]

In fact, neither Anthony nor society, as it is depicted in the novel, quite knows what to make of Gloria. Society had once encouraged the country's "pioneer great-grandmothers" to help settle a continent, but now long after the closure of the frontier, it has burdened women with the twin obsessions of youth and beauty. Throughout the novel, Gloria's preoccupation with these perishable variables suggests a certain shallowness—her screen-test failure induces the pathetic cry of "oh, my pretty face!" But on this day, the day of her twenty-ninth birthday, her last year of relative youth, Gloria realizes that "the world was melting away before her eyes." And she is right. Her "radical" revolt from the middle-class matronocracy owes much to her "pretty face" and to the illusion of a perpetual juvenescence that it inspires. Not really in a position so different from her corseted Victorian mother, Gloria has before her a limited range of marital and vocational possibilities. She may, as Fitzgerald writes, take "all she can get!" but only until the clock strikes midnight.[13]

As a social history, *The Beautiful and Damned* offered caustic appraisals of many American institutions, none more so than higher education. Unlike Fitzgerald, Anthony goes on to collect his Ivy League degree—but it's a nugatory difference. Fitzgerald portrays Anthony's alma mater, Harvard, as a place that indulges rather than challenges an embedded sense of privilege—and one is none too lightly reminded here of certain passages in *Paradise* that emphasize the country-club aspects of Princeton life. In both books, Fitzgerald questions the gentry's preference for a dilettantish education that teaches its children to congregate by class, segregate by connection, and love too much their material possessions. Rather than assume the responsibilities of noblesse oblige, Anthony and his well-tailored, book-smart Harvard classmates graduate into decades of idle days. Injured by snobbery and lacking an appetite for "purposeful" work, they accrue legacies made by other men and for which they have scant ideas how to manage, excepting the daily and empty diversionary spending.[14]

In sum, education has reinforced rather than shaken Anthony's twenty-something cynicism. What, after all, does life have to offer beyond money and youth? He's punched the academic clock at Cambridge, sniffed around Wall Street, and taken a turn as a wartime soldier who, like Fitzgerald, never experienced war. In his stale security, he sees no higher purpose in life, no urgency to draw him out. Though Amory Blaine flirted with a like conclusion, he nevertheless fought against the framework of his constraints and began taking the first tentative steps toward a life that he might call his own. Anthony and Gloria can see no such escape. Their vague goal is to create through their freshness, charm, and declining capital all the intensity and scope of experience that can be mustered in Warren G. Harding's America. But the expiration date on these passing assets is clear and nonnegotiable. Hence Gloria's preference for a spectacular, explosive exit—a few high-flying years in Europe, then death—to a long and quiet retreat. Given the culture's intense infatuation with the temporary and the ephemeral, their decision is perhaps not quite so grotesque as it may appear on the surface. Both Anthony and Gloria are, after all, bereft of vocations, strong moral judgments, and the resolve to create productive lives. With nothing more than the fleeting virtues of youth and beauty to rest on, they quite obviously lack the emotional resources to emulate Amory's determination.

This begs the question, where does Fitzgerald stand on the problem of where responsibility begins and ends? The fatalistic logic of *The Beautiful and Damned* and its Dreiser-like pessimism about modern life suggests that for all his romantic instincts, Scott thought the individual had little chance against the historical weight of twentieth-century capitalism. Indeed, the arresting idealism that shapes his most memorable characters—Jay Gatsby, Dick Diver, and Monroe Stahr—is powerfully connected to their doomed struggles against stronger forces that lack their imaginative visions but are far more in tune to the materialistic side of life.

The supremacy of this money-oriented society is perhaps most plainly on display in the artistic seduction of Richard Caramel, Anthony's friend and Gloria's cousin. Caramel has the makings of a serious writer, but after his first book—"The Demon Lover," an obvious parody of *Paradise*—succeeds, he begins writing down for money. In these scenes, Fitzgerald reflects on his own insecurities as a man of undeniable literary talent faced with the temptation to trade debt for *Saturday Evening Post* dollars. It is little wonder that his second novel laments the fate of writing in

America. The poor author found himself, after all, at the not-so-tender mercies of a tooth-and-claw economy. If he published, he ate, if not . . . Without a salary or sinecure, a pension plan or union, a writer could claim only the most tangential connection to an organized "profession." For the nine-to-five business of merely generating, say, advertising copy, that might be fine, but for the invention of genuine artistic work, the want of a guild to provide fellowship and financial relief often derailed Caramel's real-life counterparts. Fitzgerald takes an insider swipe at the state of American publishing when he notes that after composing a popular first novel, Caramel finds that he must "write trash" for a steady paycheck. In an obvious autobiographical passage, Caramel complains, "I don't suppose I'm being so careful. I'm certainly writing faster and I don't seem to be thinking as much as I used to."[15] So even though Caramel is "successful," he has no more been able to evade the coercive power of the "free market" than Anthony or Gloria have.

Thinking over such stern subject matter, one is tempted to see in *The Beautiful and Damned* the outline of a Puritan jeremiad. Here, the materially ascendant postwar United States is arraigned for lacking the redeeming qualities of discipline, sympathy, and meaning. The wheels are spinning, but to what effect? Motion is coveted, but no one can say why. Anthony's alcoholism, Gloria's self-centeredness, and the corruption of Caramel's talent are destructive reactions to easy money and the promise of easy money. While many of the era's popular commentators celebrated the presumed lightness of the twenties, Fitzgerald offered instead a stark portrait of what we might call Jazz Age grief. Consider: one evening a bored Anthony and Gloria drift into a "cabaret"; its atmosphere vibrates a kind of raucous, unconscious distress: "There on Sunday nights gather the credulous, sentimental, underpaid, overworked people with hyphenated occupations: book-keepers, ticket-sellers, office-managers, salesmen, and, most of all, clerks—clerks of the express, of the mail, of the grocery, of the brokerage, of the bank. With them are their giggling, over-gestured, pathetically pretentious women, who grow fat with them, bear them too many babies, and float helpless and uncontent in a colorless sea of drudgery and broken hopes."[16] This human pell-mell is what Gloria has in mind when she advocates a brisk and bright European end to a slow American suicide.

———

In April 1921, Fitzgerald completed an early draft of *The Beautiful and Damned,* which, even in embryo, he sensed would be something of an unloved child: "After the ten months I have been working on it it has turned out as I expected—and rather dreaded—a bitter and insolent book that I fear will never be popular and that will undoubtedly offend a lot of people." Doubtful of its future as a moneymaker, Fitzgerald clung instead to its prospects as a reputation maker. "My one hope," he wrote to Max Perkins, "is to be endorsed by the intellectually élite & thus be *forced* on to people as Conrad has." And by being forced onto that elusive if much-sought-after general readership and by "assuming," he continued to Perkins, that his "work grows in sincerity and proficiency from year to year as it has so far," Fitzgerald saw a clear path ahead.[17] Critical success meant canonization, and canonization meant that while he might "undoubtedly offend a lot of people," he might also, over the long haul, realize a steady stream of income.

Commercial prospects aside, Perkins thought *The Beautiful and Damned* a striking artistic statement. In a word, he *got* the book. He recognized its expansive cultural appraisal, its strong moral/satiric tone, and its sensitivity to American class structure. A few months before the novel appeared in print, Perkins wrote enthusiastically to Scott:

> There is especially in this country, a rootless class of society into which Gloria and Anthony drifted,—a large class and one which has an important effect on society in general. It is certainly worth presenting in a novel. I know that you did not deliberately undertake to do this but I think "The Beautiful and Damned" has in effect, done this; and that this makes it a valuable as well as brilliant commentary upon American society. Perhaps you have never even formulated the idea that it does do this thing, but don't you think it is true? The book is not written according to the usual conventions of the novel, and its greatest interest is not that of

the usual novel. Its satire will not of itself be understood by the great simple minded public without a little help. For instance, in talking to one man about the book, I received the comment that Anthony was unscathed; that he came through with his millions, and thinking well of himself. This man completely missed the extraordinarily effective irony of the last few paragraphs.[18]

These "last few paragraphs" conclude with Anthony and Gloria—the Patch fortune now safely theirs—sailing to Europe. Any suggestion of a happy ending is quashed by Fitzgerald's harrowing description of Anthony, now confined to a wheelchair, his private physician close at hand. Gloria sports a fashionable Russian-sable coat yet strikes one passenger as *"unclean."*[19]

Despite the book's Faustian presumptions, the media remained wedded to a vision of Fitzgerald that began with *This Side of Paradise* and ended somewhere near "The Offshore Pirate," one of Scott's lighter *Saturday Evening Post* offerings. *Metropolitan Magazine*'s serialization of *The Beautiful and Damned* is a case in point. Promising readers "a novel of the Revolt of American Youth," *Metropolitan* editor Carl Hovey proceeded to cut some forty thousand words from Fitzgerald's manuscript, presumably in a hope-against-hope attempt to make the story read, well, like the revolt of American youth. He cut, for example, this unsettling observation about Anthony's decline: "He turned his blood-shot eyes on her reproachfully—eyes that had once been a deep, clear blue, that were weak now, strained, and half-ruined from reading when he was drunk." Similarly, he spared readers from descriptions of Gloria's misery: "Finishing her first drink, Gloria got herself a second. After slipping on a negligée and making herself comfortable on the lounge, she became conscious that she was miserable and that the tears were rolling down her cheeks." More generally, as James West has written, 'Anthony's dissolute behavior was removed, . . . and Gloria, though still beautiful and unconventional, has little sexual allure in the serial. Much of the satire was blunted, and the criticisms of religiosity in the sections dealing with Anthony's grandfather, the reformer Adam Patch, were lost." Hovey's unreflective response to the book irritated Fitzgerald, though it would be fair to say that Scott had willingly entered his own Faustian bargain. *Metropolitan,* after all, had paid him $7,000 for the serial rights, while Warner Brothers gave $2,500 for the screen rights; neither, however, was eager to embrace the work as is. For this among other reasons, Scott looked forward to burying a part of his literary past: "the flapper idea," he wrote Perkins, "God knows I am indebted to it but . . . its time to let it go."[20]

Perkins shared Fitzgerald's concerns and took care that Scribner marketed *The Beautiful and Damned* appropriately. Promotional copy affixed on the book's back cover—written, Scott believed, by Perkins—avoided the "flapper," "youth revolt" signage to stress the novel's morality-play approach. It reads in part,

> The appearance of "This Side of Paradise" infused a new vitality into American fiction. . . . It became a chief topic of discussion and a "best seller." "The Beautiful and Damned" will certainly not cause less of a stir. In relating the story of the love and marriage of Anthony Patch and the vivid beauty, Gloria, it reveals with devastating satire a section of American society which has never before been recognized as an entity—that wealthy, floating population which throngs the restaurants, cabarets, theatres, and hotels of our great cities—people adrift on a sea of luxury, without the anchors of homes and the rudders of responsibilities—people without roots or backgrounds. . . . Through the medium of a fascinating story [Fitzgerald] reveals a significant phase of modern life hitherto unrealized.

Scott praised the back-cover copy, hoping it might cut short critics eager to denounce the book's "immorality," which, he knew, would damage sales. Perkins assured him on this front that for certain authors, Scribner looked beyond the bottom line. With some thirty-three thousand copies sold in the first month, he granted to Fitzgerald that the book would not be "an overwhelming success now" but trusted that an important corner had been turned: "I think the book has consolidated your position. . . . Of course I wanted it to sell a hundred thousand or more and I hoped that the extraordinary exhilaration of your style from paragraph to paragraph might make it do so in spite of the fact that it was a tragedy and necessarily unpleasant because of its nature. . . . It has, [however], made a stir among the discriminating and has therefore been all to the good except from the most purely commercial viewpoint." In any event, Perkins concluded, Scribner's support was unconditional and not, like the flapper theme, of the moment. "For our part," he wrote Scott, "we are backing you for a long race and are more than ever convinced that you will win it."[21]

Others were convinced of Fitzgerald's talent too, though not every reader appreciated *The Beautiful and Damned.* One London editor, wishing for a happier ending, called for Fitzgerald's speedy return to the more *Post*-friendly material of earlier days: "I can quite understand your wanting to write a study in degeneration and, as one of the rebels against materialism, it is natural that you should attack it fiercely. At the same time, I think your touch in some such stories as The Offshore Pirates is so beautifully light and amusing that I am sure you have a future as a writer of less harsh books than The Beautiful and Damned."[22] In all, the novel received a mixed critical reception. The *Chicago Sunday Tribune*'s reviewer, Fanny Butcher, chided it for "technical faults," while the *New York Globe* writer N. P. Dawson thought it the worse for certain "defects and extravagances." More positively, John Peale Bishop wrote in a *New York Herald* commentary that "the book represents both in plan and execution an advance on *This Side of Paradise,*" while Henry Seidel Canby understood perfectly the kind of moral questions Fitzgerald hoped to provoke. Canby's *Literary Review of the New York Evening Post* review reads,

> Scott Fitzgerald, rather surprisingly, has written a tragedy. An almost uncompromising tragedy, which is more than their critics have led us to expect from one of the younger generation. He has felt the implications of a rudderless society steering gayly for nowhere and has followed them down the rapids to final catastrophe. Not, of course, in any Puritan fashion nor with an Ibsen view of the sins of the race, but simply because his story led him that way; and defiantly scoffing at lessons, joyously dwelling upon the life that leads his friends to perdition, he follows. I admire him for it; and if *This Side of Paradise* showed in certain passages and in the essential energy of the whole that he had glimpses of a genius for sheer writing, this book proves that he has the artist's conscience and

enough intellect to learn how to control the life that fascinates him. . . . He will write better novels, but he will probably never give us better documents of distraught and abandoned but intensely living youth.[23]

Fitzgerald did, of course, write better novels, but he never recovered his first and largest market, the readership awaiting *Paradise Part II*. Descending into debt as sales of *The Beautiful and Damned* slowed, he followed his own advice, the advice that Caramel gave Anthony: "You say you need money right away? . . . Try some popular short stories. And, by the way, unless they're exceptionally brilliant they have to be cheerful and on the side of the heaviest artillery to make you any money."[24]

These "cheerful" contributions to the flapper idiom marked Fitzgerald in the public mind as a kind of Jazz Age laureate. But his early books might be better understood as explorations of more conventional themes—wealth, marriage, education, and vocation—under modern pressures. His mature writing continued to wrestle with these topics, though with a firmer command of their meanings and messages. In this way, *The Beautiful and Damned* marked a passing phase in Fitzgerald's development. Only twenty-five, he left his experiments in naturalism, Menckenism, and bildungsromanism behind.

ELEVEN

Exile in Great Neck

In Great Neck there was always disorder and quarrels.

Zelda Fitzgerald, 1930

In youth, Fitzgerald learned to uproot easily. After a few colorless years bouncing about upstate New York "in one town or another," he returned at the age of eleven to the McQuillan matriarchy in St. Paul, living in a succession of Summit Avenue residences. Marriage brought no end to this congenital bedouinism. During Scott and Zelda's first exhausting eighteen months together, the couple colonized Connecticut, New York, Europe, Alabama, and Minnesota. In need of a more permanent encampment, Fitzgerald took his small family—a daughter, Scottie, arrived in 1921—and rented a house on Long Island's Great Neck peninsula, a thick finger of land situated across the Manhasset Bay from Sands Point, the fashionable summer sanctum occupied by the industrial kings of the late last century. Settled in their "nifty-little Babbitt house" from October 1922 to April 1924, the new tenants watched the nouveau riche swamp the island's North Shore. Theater and film stars, musicians and songwriters commuted into the city each day; rumors of the inevitable bootlegger next door added a certain scandalous excitement to the scenery. Drawn to the special energy that seemed to envelope the rich and famous, Fitzgerald appreciated the uncommon amenities of his new home: "Great Neck is a great place for celebrities," he wrote a cousin. "It is most amusing after the dull healthy middle west." Zelda called their boom village "razzle-dazzle a hundred fold" and, espying its prohibition against prohibition, laughed, "All [its] pools and even the Sound reek of gin whisky and beer to say nothing of light wines. I am afraid we have moved to a place of very ill repute."[1]

During much of this Long Island layover, Fitzgerald worked on revisions to *The Vegetable,* a full-length play he hoped might serve as something of a cash cow. Its failure—the production closed after a single staging—intensified his desire to write novels of both artistic distinction and popular appeal. And judged by these criteria, the New York experiment might appear to be, aside from a handful of strong stories, creatively barren. Rather than produce a quick follow-up to *The Beautiful and Damned*—as *The Beautiful and Damned* had quickly followed *This Side of Paradise*—Fitzgerald spent his days on the Long Island Express traveling to countless *Vegetable* rehearsals; an endless succession of parties claimed his nights. But below the surface of this anxious wheel spinning, Great Neck proved to be immensely valuable to the writer. For here, as on the Princeton campus, the outsider Fitzgerald was a keen observer of life—in this case of a strange amalgamation of rich and poor, famous and notorious. The volatile pulse of the City and its island satellite nourished his imagination, suggesting new ways to write about the postwar American condition. From the telling vantage of a rattling commuter car, Fitzgerald took in the expensive village groceries and shops, the expansive green lawns of shaded estates, and the built environment that separated classes. He saw too the sprawling Corona ash dumps of Queens, a tremendous rat-infested rubbish ground nestled between Great Neck and the City that resided incongruously on the edge of opulence. This striking juxtaposition of Babylon and wasteland played on Fitzgerald's imagination, and before settling on the title *The Great Gatsby,* he briefly toyed with calling his New York novel "Among Ash-Heaps and Millionaires."

After leaving St. Paul in the early autumn of 1922, Fitzgerald never returned to the Midwest. The last eighteen years of his life were spent migrantly in Long Island and Europe, Towson and Baltimore, and finally Appalachian North Carolina and Hollywood. Despite these many wanderings, Fitzgerald remains associated in the popular imagination primarily with New York. This has everything to do with Gatsby's West Egg mansion, his incomparable parties, and the mesmeric green light at the end of the Buchanans' dock. Yet for all these evocations, Fitzgerald's observations of the City and its bedroom communities remain those of an outsider. He lived in Manhattan/Long Island all told a mere two years. His values and judgments were inextricably tied up with the late-Victorian attitudes of Mollie's upper Middle West and the chivalric pretenses of Edward's border-state South. An astute critic of the petty hypocrisies and bland cultural life of these regions, he saw too their still-enduring relationships with an older America rooted in discipline, achievement, and solidity.

New York, however, could not be denied. As the center of American art, finance, and ideas, the bustling city was for Fitzgerald equal parts trip wire and tremor. Attracted to its energy, he studied its recent past, and his reading brought him into contact with another New York landscape of which he was also a keen observer: Edith Wharton's Manhattan trilogy, *The House of Mirth* (1905), *The Custom of the Country* (1913), and *The Age of Innocence* (1920). Wharton wrote about an earlier generation of the same moneyed New York class that Fitzgerald would satirize in his fiction. The chief difference is that Wharton was decidedly *not* an outsider to moneyed New York society. In certain respects, including shifting attitudes toward love and money, Wharton's books serve as something of a prologue to both *The Beautiful and Damned* and *The Great Gatsby*. Consider, for example, *Mirth*'s Lily Bart and Fitzgerald's equally desperate Gloria Gilbert, soul sisters reduced to commodities for men who might graciously relieve them of their impending spinsterhood. Beautiful, intelligent, and lively, they nevertheless are socialized into spending a great deal of time contemplating their looks and fretting over the occasional blemish; both reach the age of twenty-nine in quiet turmoil. Wharton's description of Lily's evening devotion—"As she sat before the mirror brushing her hair, her face looked hollow and pale, and she was frightened by two little lines near her mouth, faint flaws in the smooth curve of the cheek"—anticipates Fitzgerald's eulogy to Gloria's youth: "She walked into the bedroom . . . and sank down upon her knees before the long mirror on the wardrobe floor. . . . She strained to see until she could feel the flesh on her temples pull forward. Yes—the cheeks were ever so faintly thin, the corners of the eyes were lined with tiny wrinkles. The eyes were different. Why, they were different! . . . And then suddenly she knew how tired her eyes were."[2] Neither Lily nor Gloria is able to translate her looks or charm into productive and fulfilling relationships. And once age, despondency, and competition have eroded the women's advantages, they fall to earth.

In *The Custom of the Country*, Gatsby's ill-starred relationship with Daisy Fay is prefigured in Ralph Marvell's doomed marriage to Undine Spragg. Wharton's vanilla Marvell, scion of crusty Knickerbocker respectability, falls for the frighteningly ambitious Spragg, a class jumper par excellence. Courting her, he idolizes the act of love itself, blind to Spragg's true character. Ignorant of his intended's less-than-respectable past (notably a secret marriage/secret divorce), Marvell comically revels in her "virgin innocence." Unfortunately for him, a certain "cheaply fashionable" Mr. Van Degen also covets Spragg, and Marvell ratchets up his wooing with the sober intensity of a comic-book crusader about to slay the dragon and win the princess: "To save her from Van Degen and Van Degenism: was that really to be his mission—the 'call' for which his life had obscurely waited?" Of course it is. The old-moneyed Marvell was educated to respect gentility, integrity, and honor—the blue-blooded knot of virtues that Gatsby seeks to assimilate into his less impressive pedigree. But more than love for love's sake drives these men. They believe, rather, in the higher aspirations of their emotions and invest romantically in women incapable of reciprocating their feelings. When Wharton writes, "It was this faith [in a perfect love] that made [Marvell] so easy a victim when love had at last appeared clad in the attributes of romance; the imaginative man's indestructible dream of a rounded passion," she might be describing the questing psychology of the grand lover's illusion that breathes fire into *Gatsby*.[3]

Finally, Wharton's take on the "new woman" can lay some claim to anticipating Fitzgerald's golden girls. Seven years before *This Side of Paradise*'s largely unflattering queue of emancipated females graced the literary landscape, Wharton had unveiled Spragg to American readers. Willful, opinionated, and sexually liberated, Undine is impatient with the fusty platitudes and attitudes clumsily employed to clip her wings. When Marvell attempts to play the gentleman—"You know nothing of this society you're in; of its antecedents, its rules, its conventions; and it's my

affair to look after you, and warn you when you're on the wrong track"—
Spragg cuts him off: "Mercy, what a solemn speech! . . . I don't believe an
American woman needs to know such a lot about their old rules. They
can see I mean to follow my own, and if they don't like it they needn't go
with me."[4] Here we have, in prewar 1913, before the age of jazz and gin,
a true-blue American flapper.

Fitzgerald first met Wharton in 1920 when both were in the Scribner
Building the same day; he hunted her down in Charles Scribner's office
and, in typical Scott fashion, literally knelt at her feet in a showy adulation
that must have embarrassed Wharton, if not Scribner. In June 1925, while
in France, Scott sent Wharton a copy of *Gatsby*. In a playful "thank you"
note, she assumed the role of elder stateswoman: "To your generation,
which has taken such a flying leap into the future, I must represent the
literary equivalent of tufted furniture and gas chandeliers." She invited the
Fitzgeralds to luncheon. This, Fitzgerald and Wharton's second meeting,
proved even more awkward than the first. With a hesitant Zelda opting
out, Scott sought company for the occasion, but just who is a matter of
some mystery. Biographers Andrew Turnbull and Matthew Bruccoli insist
that the young American composer Theodore Chanler accompanied Scott,
while yet another biographer, André La Vot, has written that Gerald Murphy's sister, Esther, told him that "she was the one who rode in the Renault
with Fitzgerald to show him the way." There is less confusion regarding
Scott's behavior that day. He fortified his courage along the route with
alcohol and showed up late at Wharton's eighteenth-century château de
Saint-Brice. Nervous and maybe a little tight, he ventured to tell, after
asking for Wharton's permission, a "rough story" about an American couple
in Paris who spent three days in what they thought was a hotel before real-
izing, after encountering a host of luggageless guests, that it was a brothel.
Perhaps missing the intended humor, Wharton responded laconically that
the story lacked details. Having bombed, Scott retreated into an awkward
silence. "Horrible," Wharton remembered the day to her diary.[5]

Fitzgerald's best New York friendship, and one that tells us something of
his artistic direction and emotional makeup during this period, was with

his Great Neck neighbor and drinking buddy Ring Lardner. A nationally known sports columnist and writer of satirical short stories, Lardner shared with Fitzgerald a sense of exile on Long Island's gold coast. Hailing from tiny Niles, Michigan, Lardner endorsed Fitzgerald's suspicions about the "anarchic" drift of postwar life, and in a series of sardonic newspaper and magazine articles, several published in the *Saturday Evening Post,* he spoofed the new acquisitiveness. Quietly subversive in his observations, he struck contemporaries as a deeply reflective figure, solitary and inscrutable. John Dos Passos remembered Lardner as "a tall sallow mournful man with a higharched nose, . . . dark hollow eyes, [and] hollow cheeks." Fitzgerald memorialized Lardner in *Tender Is the Night* as the disillusioned musician Abe North: "His voice was slow and shy; he had one of the saddest faces Rosemary had ever seen, the high cheek-bones of an Indian, a long upper lip, and enormous deep-set dark golden eyes."[6] Both Dos Passos and Fitzgerald inevitably remarked on Lardner's alcoholism. Possessed of a memorably droll delivery, Lardner heightened the effect of his irony-based humor by playing his own stoic straight man; his "sad face" brought to mind the deadpan genius of a Buster Keaton.

One of Lardner's more pointed attacks on middle-class pretensions, the *Gullible's Travels* stories (published in 1915–1916), trafficked in the kind of material soon to attract Fitzgerald. Briefly, the South Side Chicago everyman "Joe Gullible" has a problem: his poor wife has caught "the society bacillus"—she wants, that is, to rub shoulders with the snobs. But Joe is the "wise boob"—more concerned with the perils of overtipping than with catching a glimpse of Emily Vanderbilt, he regards opera nights, fine dress, and expensive restaurants as putting on airs.[7] Still, vanity must be served. While on a Palm Beach social-climbing excursion, Joe's wife is crushingly mistaken by a Chicago grande dame for a chambermaid. In defeat, the Gullibles make a hasty retreat back home. All this is handled rather sweetly by Lardner, whose no ordinary Joe responds sensitively to his wife's humiliation. And in her failed conquest, Lardner offers a satire of suburban aspirations along with the observation that high society's trivial, condescending ways were in fact unworthy of the Gullibles' emulation.

Eleven years older than Fitzgerald, the laconic Lardner served as a sober sounding board for his friend's critical judgments. A seasoned professional writer, well traveled, and several years married with four boys, Lardner had a wealth of experience to impart to his younger, still-stuck-on-Princeton friend. The question is, what brought them together? Aside from the difference in their ages, a host of personality distinctions argued for distance: Lardner's self-control, stoicism, and cynicism clashed with Fitzgerald's lack of restraint, boyish enthusiasm, and appetite for the elegiac. Physically, they made for an odd couple in Great Neck. Lardner stood tall, dark, and worn; Fitzgerald was on the short side, light, and fresh. One biographer has argued that "a brotherhood of the intemperate . . . helps to explain the bond," though more important variables must be accounted for. Like the "wise boob" Joe Gullible, both nestled near money even while recognizing that their upbringings, their comparative poverty, and their own attitudes kept them at arm's length from New York's "real" society. Parvenus at heart, they watched the new wealth wash ashore. They were no Long Island escapists, and Great Neck stirred from them dry and wry appraisals grounded in mutual suspicion that sometimes spilled over into barely concealed alienation. Lardner took to calling his estate "The Mange," while Fitzgerald described the peninsula as an elaborate fleecing station, a kind of pre–Las Vegas, Vegas by the Manhasset Bay: "It is one of those little towns springing up on all sides of New York which are built especially for those who have made money suddenly but have never had money before."[8]

Beyond the Great Neck bubble, Lardner and Fitzgerald were united by shared illness and anxiety. Both were alcoholics, were dependent on the middlebrow magazine market, and feared the erosion of their talents. In "Ring," a moving 1933 *New Republic* essay mourning Lardner's death, Fitzgerald wrote, "It was obvious that he felt his work to be directionless, merely 'copy'. . . . He was a faithful and conscientious workman to the end, but he had stopped finding any fun in his work ten years before he died." This heartsick sentiment suggests something of Scott's own mounting struggles at the time, to complete his problematic *Gatsby* follow-up, to make sense of Zelda's descent into mental illness, and to stay solvent. Many years later, Lardner's son, Ring Lardner Jr., wrote, "I think one of the things about Ring that fascinated Scott in the Great Neck days was the image he saw of his own future. He probably felt satisfaction that he could sleep off a drunk and get back to work with much more ease than his older friend, but he must have known he was heading in the same direction."[9]

Several months after "Ring" appeared, Scribner published *Tender Is the Night,* in which Fitzgerald drew on Lardner's difficult last years, alive to their fearful, premonitory power to insinuate his own fate. The rapidly declining Abe North, dissipating on the French Riviera and having gone several years since his last musical composition, is modeled in part on Lardner and is Scott's depiction of an artist who has squandered his talent and grown tired of life: "They stood in an uncomfortable little group weighted down by Abe's gigantic presence: he lay athwart them like the wreck of a galleon, dominating with his presence his own weakness and self-indulgence, his narrowness and bitterness. All of them were conscious of the solemn dignity that flowed from him, of his achievement, fragmentary, suggestive and surpassed. But they were frightened at his survivant will, once a will to live, now become a will to die."[10] With Lardner's passing squarely in mind, Fitzgerald wrote this passage when he had less than seven years of his own life to live.

———

Creatively, Fitzgerald passed his first Great Neck year working on *The Vegetable,* a play he had written in St. Paul. He saw the venture principally as a moneymaker, a way to alleviate the constant pressure of having to crank out short stories. In a boyish note to Perkins, he described the object of his labor: "[It's] an awfully funny play that's going to make me rich forever. It really is. I'm so damned tired of the feeling that I'm living up to my income." In another communication, Fitzgerald called the first and third acts of the show "probably the best pieces of dramatic comedy written in English in the last 5 years."[11] In fact, the project proved a bust. Prewar productions typically traveled off Broadway to recoup investment in the midwestern market, and these shows pandered to certain regional prejudices, accenting, say, the "Heartland's" presumed moral superiority.

But in the war's aftermath, the theater scene changed considerably. Mounting touring costs kept productions in the East, and story lines catered increasingly to more urbane New York audiences. Sophistication replaced sentiment; sharp wit superseded cornpone humor. *The Vegetable,* a lampoon of America's get-ahead mania, lacked the subtlety that the new theater required, relying, as it did, on constant sideshows, burlesques, and an awkwardly unfunny fantasy sequence.

Already the impresario of several well-received St. Paul and Princeton productions, Fitzgerald had good reason to believe that he could pull off yet another success. Aside from these teen triumphs, his first two novels included dramatic dialogue set (oddly) in stage direction that evoked the earlier works. He seemed unaware until *The Vegetable*'s failure that these strategies detracted from the books. The four producers who turned *The Vegetable* down no doubt spotted such deficiencies, but Sam Harris—a longtime partner of George M. Cohan—was willing to take a chance on the project. Earnest Truex, Fitzgerald's Great Neck neighbor, played the lead.

The production's unappetizing title probably came from Mencken. In his 1922 essay "On Being an American," the Bard of Baltimore sniggered, "here is a country in which it is an axiom that a business man shall be a member of the Chamber of Commerce, an admirer of Charles M. Schwab, a reader of the *Saturday Evening Post,* a golfer—in brief, a vegetable."[12] The plant in question in Fitzgerald's play is one Jerry Frost, a railroad clerk—as per his wife's orders—who pines to be a postman. Bullied into confusion, he gets tight one night on bootleg liquor and dreams he is president of the United States. The social commentary here is plain: Frost is a simple man who simply wants to be left alone, but the culture's obsession with money and mobility trivializes his modest but perfectly respectable aspirations to carry the mail. He no more wants to be president than he wants to be a poodle; he just thinks he *should* want to be president. And why not? In 1920, the country sent the affable Ohioan Warren G. Harding to the White House. Though his résumé presumably ran a few pages longer than Frost's, Harding won over voters as a good-looking lightweight who promised to restore "normalcy" to America. His stunning electoral success (his 60 percent of the popular vote was the highest in a century) demonstrated that one need not be a Founding Father, a Civil War hero, or even particularly competent to rise to the highest office in the land. In other words, Frost's presidential fantasies were met more than halfway by the democratic age—thus increasing the pressure of Frosts everywhere, under the influence or not, to dream bigger still.

Fitzgerald's skeptical reflections on the American dream in *The Great Gatsby* have inspired countless commentaries, and yet it is *The Vegetable,* dismissed as an artistic failure, that anticipates the celebrated novel's primary concerns. In both works, the prizes their heroes are pursuing are shown to be illusions. The presidency? Daisy Fay? In the end, these fantasies of power and elusive love that are so commonly sold in magazines and movies remain, as they must, beyond reach. In a perverse way, to stay true to one's private if modest American dreams—in Frost's case, to become a postman—is to cut against the national neuroses.

The Vegetable, the stardust hopes of Fitzgerald's financial future, opened in Atlantic City's Apollo Theater in November 1923—and died there in a single, dispiriting performance. "In brief," Zelda reported to a friend, "the show flopped as flat as one of Aunt Jemima's famous pancakes. . . . Ernest says he has *never* had an experience on the stage like the second [act]. . . . People were so obviously bored!" Charitably overlooking the production's weaknesses, she pinned its failure on the audience's icy reception to Scott's unsparing dissection of the American system. "It was all very well done, so there was no use trying to fix it up. The idea was what people didn't like—just hopeless!" A few months after the debacle, Fitzgerald looked back on *The Vegetable* with a game gallows humor, detailing for laughs his agonies in a *Saturday Evening Post* piece. Finding the perfect pun, he called the play "a colossal frost" and detailed the creative and financial misery still then shaking his self-confidence: "To my profound astonishment the year, the great year, was almost over. I was $5000 in debt, and my one idea was to get in touch with a reliable poorhouse where we could hire a room and bath for nothing a week." Matters were not quite so grim, however, as Scott let on. Published by Scribner several months before bombing onstage, *The Vegetable* sold nearly eight thousand copies, a more-than-respectable number, particularly for a rookie playwright. Yet for the year and some of labor and faith that Fitzgerald had invested in the project, he could justify nothing less than a spectacular success. Lingering over his career in a 1937 letter to a former lover, he called *The Vegetable* his "only serious flop."[13]

At bottom, the play called for artistic resources beyond Fitzgerald's grasp. His teen theater successes demonstrated a shrewd talent for word-smithery and a sensitive ear for dialogue, though neither of these could make up for other deficiencies in plot and stage direction. Sustaining three acts essentially through conversation—even with strong material, which *The Vegetable* lacked—would tax any audience. Perhaps it is too obvious to say that the play suffered for not being a novel. Fitzgerald's best work relied on a strong authorial voice creating mood, tension, and presence. The "atmosphere" he wove into his books required the kind of subtle imagery and foreshadowing that was not easily transferred from page to stage. Fitzgerald inadvertently identified the trouble himself when, prior to opening night, he informed Perkins that he wished *The Vegetable* "to be advertised" by Scribner "rather as a book of humor . . . than like a play—because of course it is written to be read."[14]

More remarkable than *The Vegetable*'s artistic failure, however, is its political prescience. Three months before the play opened, Harding died of congestive heart failure, and not long after, a string of scandals attached to his administration were brought to light. Here, we learned, once reigned a real Jerry Frost, a man grossly elevated beyond his capabilities, a figure soon to be ridiculed by press and public for his epic ineptitude, one who might well have been better off as, if not a postal carrier, then perhaps a schoolteacher, an insurance salesman, or the publisher of the *Marion Daily Star*—all of which Harding had once been.

Of Fitzgerald's own politics at this time, there is little to say. His correspondence scarcely mentioned public officials or pressing national issues; nowhere does one find reflections on the infamous Sacco and Vanzetti case or the notorious Scopes Monkey Trial. Not until the Great Depression and the rise of German militarism did Fitzgerald—who spent half of the twenties abroad—begin to self-consciously engage with contemporary political issues. Thus, his surprising grasp of modern American democracy in *The Vegetable* might come off as an extraordinary guess. But this would miss the point. His *feel* for the deep rhythms of a fluid and increasingly consumer-oriented society opened avenues of insight that his play intuitively exploited. Not merely a conspicuous "flop," it may be read with reward alongside, and as an extension of, the critique of national life begun in his first novels. Amory Blaine, Anthony Patch, *and* Jerry Frost all encounter pressures of wealth and status that might, and certainly do in Anthony's case, end badly. Rather than indict the country's political parties, however, Fitzgerald calls into question the underlying cultural apparatus that made and moved them. In other words, he didn't bother with mere "Democrats" or "Republicans"; he followed something far more powerful: he followed the money.

{ TWELVE }

After the Gold Rush—
The Great Gatsby

Well, I shall write a novel better than
any novel ever written in America.

F. Scott Fitzgerald, 1924

In May 1924, Scott, Zelda, and Scottie boarded the SS *Minnewaska* in New York bound for Cherbourg, France. More of a financial exile than a culture-seeking expat, Fitzgerald, with money finally in pocket, hoped to work on a new novel minus the multiple distractions of short-story writing. Eyeing an advantageous exchange rate of some twenty francs to the dollar, he considered a lengthy stay. Locating variously in Paris and the Riviera, with a four-month Italian holiday to break up the Gallic monopoly, the Fitzgeralds remained abroad until Christmas 1926. Overseas, Scott encountered a cultural mood distinctly different from New York's. Europe was still reeling from the recent war; its self-confidence had been shaken on the Western Front and in the commensurate collapse of its once-solid Victorian certainties. Here, amid the Old World's unease, thousands of miles from home, Fitzgerald wrote *The Great Gatsby*.

Just two years earlier, in the summer of 1922, Fitzgerald, perhaps under the influence of Wharton's Manhattan trilogy, had informed Perkins of his interest in writing a new novel: "Its locale will be the middle west and New York of 1885 I think." But in Europe, Fitzgerald decided to write a different book. With the twenties boom under way, the opportunity for contemporary social criticism proved too tempting to pass by. Why write of the old Gilded Age when one could draw on the new? Accordingly, he composed eye-candy descriptions of the sun-kissed Queensboro Bridge, the glittering Long Island parties, and the rising sugar-cube city that paid tribute to the modern metropolitan spirit that emerged from the war. Despite *The Great Gatsby*'s urban setting, however, the book is, as Fitzgerald tells us, "a story of the West, after all."[1] Its narrator, Nick Carraway, arrives from the upper Middle West, Daisy Fay Buchanan is a Louisville flirt, and long before the novel's action begins, a young Gatsby broke away from the inevitable limitations of his native rural North Dakota. They all meet up in New York, though none has a vital connection to the city or—with the grim exception of Gatsby, buried somewhere in the vicinity of West Egg—remains there. Their journeys, Fitzgerald makes clear, are each born of some singular desperation that hints at a larger collective truth about the dwindling promise of American life.

Self-conscious of recently acquired wealth, these arrivistes pose as aristocrats. Their marriages united first families (connecting the Louisville Fays with the Chicago Buchanans), their sons acquired Ivy League pedigrees (Nick and Tom dock at Yale), and their houses affect Old World dignity (Gatsby's mansion resembles a sprawling Normandy hostelry; the Buchanans hold court in a mock Georgian Colonial). In a socially fluid America, however, such prizes were by no means permanent and needed to be guarded against the next wave of gate-crashers. Tom's paramour, the impoverished Myrtle Wilson, hopes to bag a Buchanan. The upstart Gatsby pursues his Daisy. And Meyer Wolfsheim, the Jewish racketeer, stands in for the nation's non-Anglo discontents who found their path to prosperity compromised by Wasp privilege. Tom's complaint that "civilization's going to pieces. . . . If we don't look out the white race will be—will be utterly submerged," sounds very much like the frightened whine of an insecure parvenu.[2]

Fitzgerald portrays Buchanan wealth as the worst possible kind, for it comes without the mutual marshaling of lord-to-peasant/peasant-to-lord debts, obligations, and duties that Scott thought distinguished the old money from the new. The latter showed a marked deficit of ease, compassion, or benevolence; it owed little to genealogy or gentility and nearly everything to the brute business of dollar making. In a particularly striking passage from *Gatsby* that concerns the West Egg mansion, Fitzgerald reflects on the odd efforts of the profiteers to assert their assumed baronial privileges in a messy democracy: "A brewer had built [Gatsby's ostentatious house] early in the 'period' craze, a decade before, and there was a story that he'd agreed to pay five years' taxes on all the neighboring cottages if the owners would have their roofs thatched with straw. Perhaps their refusal took the heart out of his plan to Found a Family—he went into an immediate decline. His children sold his house with the black wreath still on the door. Americans, while occasionally willing to be serfs, have always been obstinate about being peasantry."[3] Gatsby keeps his house in order by employing a retinue of "serfs" (gardeners, cooks, and housekeepers), filling his library with tasteful (if unread) editions, and favoring Savile Row over Sears ("I've got a man in England who buys me clothes"). Like a time traveler, he leads Daisy "through Marie Antoinette music rooms, . . . Restoration salons, . . . [and] period bedrooms." The extraordinary tour, Fitzgerald writes, conjures the impression of a "feudal silhouette," a fantasy moment of romantic promise both set against and inspired by the prevailing materialism of America.[4]

It is in such passages that Fitzgerald plays once again on the "conspicuous consumption" idea advanced by the economist Thorstein Veblen (1857–1929). The son of Norwegian immigrants, Veblen, like Scott, was born and raised in the upper Midwest. A caustic Progressive-era critic of capitalism, he studied consumer habits, arguing that lavish purchases were often demonstrations of power, and in that regard, the mere exhibition of an expensive item might be its greatest utility. In his classic work on economics and social stratification, *The Theory of the Leisure Class* (1899), Veblen sought to explain the kind of vulgar display of wealth that was later described by Fitzgerald when he writes about Gatsby's "period craze" mansion, his "swollen . . . rich cream color" car, and his striking sartorial extravagance, tilting in the direction of pink suits and gold-colored ties. Gilded Age apologists, Veblen observed, believed that in a Darwinian world, riches inevitably flowed to the most "capable"—the rich, the argument ran, unavoidably got richer through their everyday virtues, while the poor just as inescapably became needier through their everyday vices. Apportioning blame to this "natural" process, its advocates persisted, would do nothing but harm society as a whole. For society as a whole surely advanced, did it not, by the heroic efforts of the "fittest"? The meager benefited too, from the charity, improvements, inventions, and "power" generated from the elites.[5]

But Veblen argued that social-class consumerism told a much different story. New money was insecure with its recent gains and so sought to stifle its critics with ostentatious purchases that suggested a puffed-up genealogy dating back to some hazy European royalty. *Gatsby* comes so near to this view that only the fact that Fitzgerald almost certainly never read Veblen prohibits us from seeing the novel as a parody of Veblen's ideas. *Gatsby*, after all, is replete with excessive, to the point of comical, examples of conspicuous wealth: Gatsby's books are housed in a room made to look like an Oxford University college library; his house parties are enlivened by bright lights, an orchestra, and a tempting buffet of ham, turkey, pastry pigs, and "salads of harlequin designs" that soon gives way to multiple suppers.[6] The Buchanans, moreover, are part of a wastage class—they produce nothing; they consume extravagantly—outfitted with a slew of cars, homes, and polo ponies to mark them as worthy of emulation in an increasingly money-sensitive society. It is this false faith in wealth that Fitzgerald attacks. A $350,000 pearl necklace (a dowry and perhaps a bribe of sorts) does not bring Daisy marital happiness, nor does it make Tom a generous husband; Gatsby's gold rushing, of course, leads to his disillusionment and finally death. The tragedy is that Gatsby has far more appealing attributes—say, courage, idealism, and the capacity for friendship—to offer, but as a form of currency in East Egg, they can purchase very little.

Fitzgerald appeared to be working out his ideas on the American leisure class in a syndicated article authored in the spring of 1924 and published under various titles including "Our Irresponsible Rich." In it, he criticized America's attraction to conspicuous consumption: "at no period in the world's history, perhaps, has a larger proportion of the family income been spent upon display." He also condemned snobbery: "the American 'leisure class' . . . has frequently no consciousness that leisure is a privilege, not a right, and that a privilege always implies a responsibility." And he further touted the virtues of the impoverished: "Look at the American leisure class and note that it has produced—well, two Presidents out of twenty-seven! The greatest Americans have come almost invariably from the very poor class—Lincoln, Edison, Whitman, Ford, Mark Twain."[7] Like those great Americans, Gatsby too comes from a humble background. To call him "great," as Fitzgerald does, is an ironic assertion meant to emphasize not the height to which he ascends but the distance from which he falls. Eager to ape the leisure class, Gatsby betrays his better instincts in pursuit of an unworthy prize. In the land of the rising dollar, his is a cautionary tale.

The Great Gatsby's climax comes when Daisy, apprised of Gatsby's bootlegging, abandons her lover. In choosing Tom, she remains loyal instead to her class privilege. By dint of circumstances rather than talent and hard work, Tom enjoys a head start over his rival. And yet the secret of his success—inheritance embellished by a number of convenient connections—places him not so far from Gatsby's "drug store" and gaming "gonnegtions," as Wolfsheim might say. This is emphasized when Gatsby, put on the spot by Tom's accusations, digs at his inquisitor: "What about it? . . . I guess your friend Walter Chase wasn't too proud to come in on it. . . . He came to us dead broke. He was very glad to pick up some money, old sport." Fitzgerald's linking Tom and Gatsby in this way is effective, for what does their striving and posturing amount to in the end? Both men chase dollars or the things they thought dollars could buy; neither possesses the solidity, character, and cultural awareness to form a true aristocratic ideal.[8]

Nick Carraway, by contrast, comes closest in the novel to Fitzgerald's notion of a "noble" personage. Carraway's great-uncle, we learn, abandoned Europe after its feudal traditions fell before a rising urban-industrial middle class. Presumably untainted by capitalist association, he left a legacy of "good breeding" to his heirs. Carraway's modest West Egg address compares favorably to the absurd imitation palaces dotting Long Island Sound; his courtly manners, quiet rejection of the bond trade, and loyalty to Gatsby all speak to his good character. Looking deeply into the man, the literary critic Maureen Corrigan has identified, behind a layer of middle-western reticence, "the secret soul of a poet." But his virtues are increasingly out of fashion. For if Tom and Daisy lack the once-binding moral restraints that still matter to Nick, they nevertheless constitute a type that is now too powerful to ignore. To say, as Fitzgerald does of Gatsby's murder, "the holocaust was complete" is an indictment of a culture that gives Daisy's doomed lover both wealth and death. A holocaust is a sacrifice, and Gatsby—a romantic, an idealist, and a star-crossed symbol of America's transcendent possibilities—represents the failure of his civilization to create a higher purpose. Modern man's search, as Fitzgerald eloquently puts it, for "something commensurate to his capacity for wonder" is finally and inevitably an empty pursuit.[9] The Promised Land remains a burning if distant constellation, ever in sight, ever out of reach.

Fitzgerald underlines this last point—the star too far—in a handful of passages connecting Gatsby's hopeless pursuit of Daisy to the lambent green light that adorns the Buchanans' dock. Generations of readers have since enlarged on the significance of this light, regarding it in some sense as a symbol of national identity and, more troubling, as an emblem of the romantic promise of the country in eclipse. This has led to a seemingly inexhaustible cottage industry dedicated to dissecting the theme of the "American Dream" in *Gatsby*.

Rooted in the high hopes of the New World to produce, as the French writer J. Hector St. John de Crèvecoeur put it in 1781, "this new man," the American Dream is based on the presumption that liberty, opportunity, and equality should be a matter of right rather than privilege. For Puritans, Quakers, and other religious reformers, the North American continent represented a place to freely practice their faith; for the signatories of the Declaration of Independence, it literally provided the grounds on which to break from aristocracy and priest craft. Late in life, Thomas Jefferson stressed what he took to be the universal message of the document: "May it be to the world, what I believe it will be, (to some parts sooner, to others later, but finally to all,) the signal of arousing men to burst the chains under which monkish ignorance and superstition had persuaded them to bind themselves, and to assume the blessings and security of self-government." Two generations later, Abraham Lincoln, himself a symbol of the "self-made man," declared that "the progress by which the poor, honest, industrious, and resolute man raises himself . . . is the great principle for which this government was formed."[10] The elasticity of the American Dream theme is such that it captured the imaginations of both a highborn Virginia plantation owner and a lowborn Illinois rail-splitter. More to the point, it is this shared Jeffersonian and Lincolnian vision of human advancement that Fitzgerald adheres to in *Gatsby*. Jimmy Gatz, after all, is another "self-made man," really a romantic nineteenth-century figure who aspires to surpass his modest origins. But the power of wealth has compromised his quest. With the American Dream in transition—emphasizing now the consumer creed of "having" rather than the old promise of "becoming"—Jay Gatsby has no place.

Fitzgerald was not the only writer of his era to remark on the suddenly strong association of success with materialism. Both Sinclair Lewis's satiric *Babbitt* (1922) and Theodore Dreiser's massive *An American Tragedy* (1925) made sharp and unsparing criticisms of this cultural development. Lewis's model of middle-class conformity, George Babbitt, finds affirmation in ownership—he is delighted to be woken each morning by the fine "cathedral chime" of a fancy "modern" alarm clock, after which he puts on a well-cut gray suit and drives to work in an automobile that exemplifies his ideal of "poetry and tragedy, love and heroism." Dreiser's doomed Clyde Griffiths is, like Gatsby, eager to jump class and falls for the fetching Sondra, a rich girl, a "goddess in her shrine of gilt and tinsel so utterly enticing to him." In trying to secure a place in Sondra's world, Clyde commits a brutal murder and is caught, convicted, and executed. Before this violent cycle began, Clyde's jealous cousin Gilbert, educated at Princeton and wise to the ways of the leisure class, could see the calamity coming: "He hasn't any money . . . and he's hanging on here by the skin of his teeth as it is. And for what? If he's taken up by these people [Sondra's family and friends], what can he do? He certainly hasn't the money to do as they do, and he can't get it."[11]

Within a few years, the troubling association of materialism with "success" that was remarked on by Dreiser, Lewis, and Fitzgerald found its way into a major work of popular history. In 1931, the Pulitzer Prize–winning historian James Truslow Adams coined the expression "American Dream" in his book *The Epic of America*. As much as *Gatsby* had, this work cautioned against defining a "richer" life largely in economic terms. "The American Dream," Adams maintained, "has not been a dream of merely material plenty. . . . It has been much more than that. It has been a dream of being able to grow to fullest development as man and woman, unhampered by the barriers which had slowly been erected in older civilizations, unrepressed by social orders which had developed for the benefit of classes rather than for the simple human being of any and every class." Adams wrote in the depths of the Great Depression, whose severity no doubt colored his commentary. Interestingly, Fitzgerald did just the opposite, drafting *Gatsby,* his elegy for the American Dream, in an era that was warmly enshrined in popular memory as the "Roaring Twenties." In this respect, he wrote against the culture—and the politicians. In an October 1928 speech in New York, the presidential candidate Herbert Hoover, on the cusp of winning a landslide election, insisted that "the American system . . . [of] liberty, freedom and equal opportunity" was a welcome feature of the new stock-market capitalism that, he argued, had brought the nation "nearer today to the ideal of the abolition of poverty and fear from the lives of men and women than ever before in any land."[12] Unlike Adams, Fitzgerald did not need the market crash, the migrant mothers, or the suited apple sellers to prompt his admonishing observations. These came from a number of pre–Black Thursday sources including Edward's reminiscences of the ill-fated antebellum South, the striking uptick in consumerism that followed the Great War, and, more generally, Scott's sensitive ear for cultural change in Greater New York.

About a year before beginning *Gatsby,* Fitzgerald informed a St. Paul friend, "I shall never write another document-novel. I have decided to be a pure artist + experiment in form and emotion." He decided, that is, to be an American Joseph Conrad. With a tragic sensibility and engagement with large philosophical themes, Conrad's novels appealed to a still relatively young writer who wished to move beyond what he described in 1923 as "those annoying novels of American manners." He called Conrad's *Nostromo* (1904) "the greatest novel since 'Vanity Fair'" and incorporated certain of its premises and characterizations into *Gatsby.* A meditation on corruption and colonialism in the Latin American nation of "Costaguana," *Nostromo* explores the poisoning impact of the "San Tome" silver mine on individuals, corporations, and countries. Charles Gould, a native Costaguanero of English ancestry, believes the mine can bring peace to the faction-torn republic. Like Gatsby's vision, his is transcendent and agonizingly elusive. "He cannot act or exist without idealizing every simple feeling, desire, or achievement," Conrad writes. "He could not believe his own motives if he did not make them first a part of some fairy tale. The earth is not quite good enough for him."[13] In the end, the extraction of silver only heightens the country's unrest, destroying Gould as assuredly as the pursuit of a "fairy tale" love dooms Gatsby.

The influence of Conrad's short story "Youth" (1902) was just as pronounced. The story employs a participant narrator, Charles Marlow, who foreshadows Fitzgerald's use of Nick Carraway for the same purpose. Both men are innocents of a kind, make perilous journeys "east" (to the Indian Ocean in Marlow's case), and undergo transformative experiences that force them to put away their youthful conceits. Scott was struck by Conrad's true and still-fresh memories of adolescence in the way he handled Marlow's ill-fated voyage as a second mate aboard a coal-transport ship that spontaneously combusts off the western coast of Australia. Marlow's insistence, "I remember my youth and the feeling that will never come back any more—the feeling that I could last for ever, outlast the sea, the earth, and all men," serves as something of a model for Gatsby's pining away for a timeless if never to be reprised love. Fitzgerald, to his credit, did not shy away from acknowledging Conrad's influence. In a 1925 letter to Mencken, he unabashedly called himself one of Conrad's "imitators" and said in regard to the Polish-British writer's impact on *Gatsby,* "God! I've learned a lot from him."[14]

"Youth's" effect on *Gatsby* is further reflected in the latter's celebrated and much-studied ending. Fitzgerald writes, "I became aware of the old island here that flowered once for Dutch sailors' eyes—a fresh, green breast of the new world. Its vanished trees, the trees that had made way for Gatsby's house, had once pandered in whispers to the last and greatest of all human dreams; for a transitory enchanted moment man must have held his breath in the presence of this continent, compelled into an æsthetic contemplation he neither understood nor desired, face to face for the last time in history with something commensurate to his capacity for wonder."[15] Conrad's story concludes on an equally elegiac note that mourns the death of idealism: "our weary eyes looking still, looking always, looking anxiously for something out of life, that while it is expected is already gone—has passed unseen, in a sigh, in a flash—together with the youth, with the strength, with the romance of illusions." In a 1925 review of Francis Brett Young's *Sea Horses,* Mencken called this dramatic manner of ending a story or a novel one "of the familiar Conradian devices." It consists, he explained, "of building up a smashing suspense and then releasing it with a few unexpected words." Fitzgerald once told John Peale Bishop, "I believe it was Ernest Hemingway who developed to me, in conversation, that the dying fall was preferable to the dramatic ending under certain conditions, and I think we both got the germ of the idea from Conrad." *Gatsby*'s iconic last words—"So we beat on, boats against the current, borne back ceaselessly into the past"—offers the quiet coda, the "dying fall," that gives the novel its enduring valediction.[16]

The impact of Fitzgerald's expressive prose would be less than it is without a compelling story or vision to hang the words on. He achieved this with a stunning interpretation of historical progression, commencing with the age of European discovery and concluding with the closing of the American frontier. In place of the virgin land that once attracted European settlers stood a nation whose grandest dreams had run to a dull materialism. In the day of the dynamo, Tom Buchanan's destruction of Gatsby ("broken up like glass against Tom's hard malice") suggested the conquest of empiricism over imagination, machine over garden, Carnegie over Columbus.[17] What, after all, had the promise of 1492 come to? Here culminated the various campaigns of American-led redemption— to export the pure faith from Europe, to throw off divine-right kingships in the name of a people's revolution, to ensure the equality of mankind in a great civil war, and to gift that equality back to Europe in a war to end all wars. Then reality intruded, and just as Gatsby searched in vain for paradise, so perhaps did America. Appomattox gave way to Jim Crow, Lincoln's republic of free labor bowed to industrial autocracy, and Versailles exhausted the idealism of a generation.

History, it seemed, smiled on the exploiters, after all. The cynical golf cheat Jordan Baker moves coolly from country club to country club, while Daisy and Tom retreat safely to Europe following the deaths of Myrtle and Gatsby. The only manor-born son among these vulgarians is Nick. His openness and generosity of spirit are attractive and widen his circle of intimates. Unlike the occupants of Long Island's ersatz estates, he avoids talk of money, shuns conspicuous consumption, and determines to give the slain Gatsby a decent burial. If Tom is a false patriarch, bullying his wife and breaking Myrtle's nose, Nick shows a more gallant side, evident in his principled break with Jordan. Her apathy to Gatsby's fate and underlying indifference to anything but her immediate concerns prompt the loss of Nick's love. Rather than simply walking away, however, as Wolfsheim, Tom, and Daisy do in difficult times, Nick faces up to his responsibilities. "I wanted," he explains, "to leave things in order and not just trust that obliging and indifferent sea to sweep my refuse away."[18]

Gatsby, inspired by an enduring devotion to Daisy, also shows a fierce but ultimately misguided sense of duty. It warps his values and makes him the novel's greatest sham aristocrat. His too-big, too-bright car, his pretend Oxford pedigree, and his line about living as "a young rajah in all the capitals of Europe" are absurd. They are also, in a manner of speaking, unnecessary. His real story, after all, is far more impressive than his Long Island reincarnation. In youth, Gatsby had penned a daily schedule designed for self-improvement, modeled after the "Scheme of Employment" drawn up by Benjamin Franklin, the American high priest of social mobility. Boston born, Franklin left parochial Puritan New England early in life for the more metropolitan Philadelphia. Two centuries later, Gatsby did much the same. His pursuit of Daisy brings to mind the discoverers of old, the adventurers who sailed the seas, scaled the mountains, and crossed the prairies. More than wealth's lure urged them—urges him—on. The possibility of an enduring passion eclipsed the transitory joy of mere possession. "No amount of fire or freshness," Fitzgerald writes, "can challenge what a man will store up in his ghostly heart."[19]

Gatsby, left to his dreams, wills his way to a (short-lived) fortune in the East. Annihilating his better self, he plays Tom's game, impressing

Daisy with lush summer landscaping, piles of monogramed shirts, and a Midas-like gold hairbrush. These commodities of privilege symbolized for Fitzgerald a greater spoilage, casting doubt on the American experiment in self-government by raising the question of whether liberal democracies, wedded to a consumer-oriented industrial capitalism, could survive. T. S. Eliot had this crisis of confidence in mind when he asks in *The Idea of a Christian Society* (1939), "Was our society, which had always been so assured of its superiority and rectitude, so confident of its unexamined premises, assembled round anything more permanent than a congeries of banks, insurance companies and industries, and had it any beliefs more essential than a belief in compound interest and the maintenance of dividends?"[20] He thought not—and Fitzgerald had his doubts as well.

The world that Fitzgerald and Eliot describe, respectively, in *Gatsby* and *Christian Society,* is one bereft of its once-solid religious center. The "Catholic element," so evident in *This Side of Paradise,* makes a less conspicuous but more suggestive appearance in *Gatsby.* The latter, after all, is a parable of Elysian loss and spiritual decline, and the reader is right to ask when this process of internal decay commenced. It is important to note in this regard that while preparing the novel, Fitzgerald appears to have been influenced by Oswald Spengler's sweeping two-volume *The Decline of the West* (volume 1 published in 1918, volume 2 in 1923). Though not translated until the year following *Gatsby*'s publication, *Decline* was the object of numerous English-language reviews and essays available to Fitzgerald as he composed the book. W. K. Stewart's long September 1924 article "Oswald Spengler's 'Downfall of Western Civilization' Explained" filled the pages of the *Century Magazine* with *Gatsby* well under way and stands as perhaps the most conspicuous popular American treatment of *Decline* to that time. Years later, Fitzgerald thought back on the German philosopher's impact on his work, writing to Perkins, "Did you ever read Spengler? . . . I read him the same summer I was writing 'The Great Gatsby' and I don't think I ever quite recovered from him."[21]

According to Spengler, the peoples of the West—once the builders of cathedrals and colonies, the believers in crown and cross—had lost their way. Now, raised in the shadow of Enlightenment rationalism, they worshiped science and technology, leading to their inevitable abandonment of the "authentic" countryside for the "inauthentic" city. Uprooted from long-standing forms of church, community, and economy, they struggled to find meaning in the modern metropolis. Spengler writes that this historical process irrevocably divided past from present: "Two centuries after Puritanism the mechanistic conception of the world stands at its zenith. It is the effective religion of the time. Even those who still thought themselves to be religious in the old sense, to be 'believers in God,' were only mistaking the world in which their waking-consciousness was mirroring itself." In *Gatsby*, it is the ghostly George Wilson, the pallid tender of the hellish valley of ashes, whose tortured soul remains unredeemed. After Wilson's wife is brutally killed, Michaelis, a concerned neighbor, asks, "Have you got a church you go to sometimes, George? Maybe even if you haven't been there for a long time?" And George's deadened reply, "Don't belong to any," spoke to a dawning age of disbelief.[22]

Gatsby, by contrast, is compelled by faith and thus bears more than a passing resemblance to Spengler's modern Faustian man in his final days. A scholar dissatisfied with intellectual limitations, Faust, the old German legend goes, made a deal with the devil, exchanging his soul for ultimate knowledge and worldly pleasure. To Spengler, Western modernization, culminating in the horror of the First World War, epitomized the "Faustian" bargain that European civilization had made, selling the Continent's soul and millions of its sons lives for Eliot's "congeries of banks, insurance companies, and industries." Afflicted with a countinghouse mentality, the West could no longer will itself to sustained sacrifice and great achievement. In the end, Tom and Gatsby, for all their differences, are both products of this bleak historical moment. The former has money but lacks depth, insight, or courage; the latter, an ill-fated Great Neck Faust, is reduced to an impotent last man, a relic of an older romanticism that is now headed to the grave.

This epitaphic tone fostered by Spengler would likely have meant less to Fitzgerald had he not located its American counterpart of a kind in the classical frontier process that shaped so much of the country's thinking during the Progressive era. The key figure here is Frederick Jackson Turner (1861–1932), a historian who, in 1893, wrote one of the seminal documents in Western historiography, "The Significance of the Frontier in American History." The tie-in with Fitzgerald is not direct per se (Fitzgerald never met or appears to have read Turner) but involves rather a linking of common concerns regarding the "closing" of the American borderland. Both men were motivated by romantic impulses, and each observed the settlement of once-open territory as an enclosure of imagination as well as property. Writing in the wake of the 1890 census, which declared that an American frontier no longer existed, Turner startled historians by raising the germane question: if the unsettled lands had created a "democratic" personality type—independent, inventive, egalitarian—then what was the future of an America without frontiers?

Turner's essay was prompted by a host of concerns that extended beyond census statistics. He came of age in a revolutionary period as the nation began to move beyond its rural, agrarian, Wasp roots toward a far more complex multiethnic identity. These late nineteenth-century decades saw populations gravitate to the cities, experienced an explosion of monopolization in the "free" market, and were witness to some seventeen million immigrants entering the country between 1880 and 1910. The ethnic composition of this migration was not of the old Nordic, northern European kind but, rather, ran decidedly more Slavic, Mediterranean, and Jewish—precisely the groups that frightened Tom Buchanan. Like Fitzgerald, Turner hailed from the upper Midwest (Wisconsin), carried about him a light, genteel anti-Semitism, and presumed that America's best days might well be in the past.

Turner reserved his most striking passage in "Significance of the Frontier" for the very end. To read it today is to recall the melancholic cadences employed by Fitzgerald in the final sentences of Gatsby—particularly the nautical acoustic of a "shadowy . . . ferryboat across the Sound," that helps to put Nick in a meditative mood, in which he sees Long Island as if for the first time and experiences the continent as a new frontier with all hopes and dreams, fears and fantasies not yet tested, not yet spoiled. Turner evoked a similarly mournful beat in writing of the Mediterranean Sea and following the circuitous path of history connecting the Ancient Greeks to the modern Americans who now were apparently to be locked on that once-mysterious continent. Uncertain if the United States could thrive without a borderland, he predicted the dawn of a new historical era:

> In spite of environment, and in spite of custom, each frontier did indeed furnish a new field of opportunity, a gate of escape from the bondage of the past; and freshness, and confidence, and scorn of older society, impatience of its restraints and its ideas, and indifference to its lessons, have accompanied the frontier. What the Mediterranean Sea was to the Greeks, breaking the bond of custom, offering new experiences, calling out new institutions and activities, that, and more, the ever retreating frontier has been to the United States directly, and to the nations of Europe more remotely. And now, four centuries from the discovery of America, at the end of a hundred years of life under the Constitution, the frontier has gone, and with its going has closed the first period of American history.[23]

Gatsby is a postfrontier personality type, but his instincts still operate on frontier "time." Like the pioneers of old, he believes it is his prerogative to remake himself. But with the western lands no longer amendable to such magic, he must invert the process and come east. There he discovers a new kind of "wild West." It too is a place of sporadic violence where the occasional fortune might be made. It lacks, however, the emphasis on human freedom that Fitzgerald—and Turner—believed distinguished the long rush westward. Combined, theirs are frankly romantic and selective approaches to reckoning with the industrial process's impact on America. Neither man, for example, gave much consideration to the indigenous peoples living on the continent. Turner's is a classic Western-centric vision of national (and racial) development, drawing a too-fine line connecting classical Greek law, philosophy, and democracy with their putative American successor. Fitzgerald, in turn, would have us suppose that Long Island was virgin territory before the arrival of the Dutch.

Caveats aside, we can read in both Fitzgerald and Turner a shared historical vision. On the surface, such a comparison between the two—the novelist and the academic—may seem unlikely. Turner, after all, pursued rigorous professional training as a graduate student at the relatively new

Johns Hopkins University and proudly counted himself among the first generation of historians to take PhDs. He regarded himself as a social scientist, impartial and influenced by such "indisputable" evidence as statistics, scholarly monographs, and primary source material. Writing in an era much influenced by Darwinism, he spiced his essay on the frontier with such words as "evolution" and "environment," terms meant to link his work with the academic cutting edge. But a closer reading of Turner suggests that, like Fitzgerald, he was a romantic at heart. If he aspired to a scientific language, his narrative was nevertheless driven by a far more conventional set of ideas—as when he described the frontier as "the meeting point between savagery and civilization."[24] Under the cloak of empiricism, he offered something rather different—a philosophy, a meditation, a pleading, and perhaps, at bottom, a lamentation.

If Turner's particular interpretation of the frontier no longer holds currency (no later than the 1930s did he strike most historians as something of a geographic determinist who underestimated the influence of nonenvironmental factors to advance democracy), his essay still retains a certain power. It adopts a peculiar Anglo-Saxon approach to the past, one that associated the urban, immigrant, industrial turn as driving the broader Western world away from "itself." Is this not what Gatsby experienced in a minor but telling key? With the enclosure of the Trans-Mississippi frontier, this child of the West turned east, looking to give shape and substance to something essential within him. But the golden days of Greek and Dutch exploration had passed, not to return—and not to be confused with the errant mission that brought Gatsby to the lonely North Shore of Long Island.

As Fitzgerald put the finishing touches on *Gatsby*, he knew the novel signified a great artistic advance of his talents. "It represents about a year's work and I think it's about ten years better than anything I've done," he informed the writer Ernest Boyd. "All my harsh smartness has been kept ruthlessly out of it—it's the greatest weakness in my work, distracting and disfiguring it even when it calls up an isolated sardonic laugh. I don't think this has a touch left." Notwithstanding the novel's polish and pre-

cision, *Gatsby,* published in April 1925, proved to be a commercial disappointment, selling only some twenty-two thousand copies and thus doing
little more financially then expunging its author's advances for the novel,
which had totaled a little over $4,000. Fitzgerald presumed that the thin
volume—a svelte 218 pages—put book buyers off; he believed as well that
without an appealing female character, women shied away from the novel.
Perkins disagreed, insisting instead that Scott's creative development had
simply outpaced many of his original readers. "It does seem to me . . . that
it is over the heads of more people than you would probably suppose,"
Perkins told him.[25] In any case, sales were not Perkins's top consideration,
and after going over an early draft of *Gatsby,* he knew its author had struck
gold. In a letter dated 20 November 1924, he assured Scott that he had
written something special:

> The amount of meaning you get into a sentence, the dimensions and in-
> tensity of the impression you make a paragraph carry, are most extraor-
> dinary. The manuscript is full of phrases which make a scene blaze with
> life. If one enjoyed a rapid railroad journey I would compare the number
> and vividness of pictures your living words suggest, to the living scenes
> disclosed in that way. It seems in reading a much shorter book than it is,
> but it carries the mind through a series of experiences that one would
> think would require a book of three times its length.
>
> The presentation of Tom, his place, Daisy and Jordan, and the un-
> folding of their characters is unequalled so far as I know. The description
> of the valley of ashes adjacent to the lovely country, the conversation and
> the action in Myrtle's apartment, the marvelous catalogue of those who
> came to Gatsby's house,—these are such things as make a man famous.
> And all these things, the whole pathetic episode, you have given a place
> in time and space, for with the help of T. J. Eckleberg and by an occa-
> sional glance at the sky, or the sea, or the city, you have imparted a sort
> of sense of eternity.[26]

Perkins, as we know, proved correct, for beyond the temporal boundaries of the 1920s, *Gatsby* reads as a timeless work. Too often regarded as
merely an American story, the book trades in more expansive themes.
Gatsby's tragedy, after all, is the tragedy of all romantics; his pursuit for

a cause bigger than himself addresses the restless nature of the human spirit in tension with a taming "civilization"—a subject much on the minds of contemporary thinkers including Sigmund Freud, whose *Civilization and Its Discontents* (1930) shrewdly assayed the inherent clash between the instinctive needs of individuals and society's demand for order, regimentation, and repression. Fitzgerald joined Freud, Conrad, Adams, Spengler, Turner, and Eliot in trying to make sense of the modern age. In humanizing the "problem" of the present, he offered Gatsby, a child of both Faust and Columbus who was destined to an ignoble death in a civilization that no longer recognized him as its own.

Fitzgerald at fifteen, a socially alert and scholastically indifferent student at the Newman School in Hackensack, New Jersey.

Photograph courtesy of F. Scott Fitzgerald Papers (C0187), Manuscripts Division, Department of Rare Books and Special Collections, Princeton University Library.

National Society
OF THE
Children of the American Revolution.

Washington, D.C. Feb 4 190 3

F. Scott Key Fitzgerald

You are hereby informed that your application for membership in the National Society of the Children of the American Revolution has been accepted, and that your name has been placed upon the list of members.

Very respectfully, yours,

Harriet Eldon Seeck
Registrar National Society Children
of the American Revolution.

National No. 5688

Fitzgerald's "Children of the American Revolution" membership card (1903) — tangible proof of young Scott's connection to the country's patriot past.

Photograph courtesy of F. Scott Fitzgerald Papers, Princeton University Library.

Statue Commemorating the Inception of the W
Student Christian Federation Movement
Princeton University

Princeton offered Fitzgerald an inside view of the East Coast haute bourgeoisie and suggested further the gilded pedigree he wished for himself.

Photograph courtesy of Seeley G. Mudd Manuscript Library (AC045), Department of Rare Books and Special Collections, Princeton University Library.

While a sophomore at Princeton, Fitzgerald met his first great love, Ginevra King, the daughter of a prominent Chicago banker—she inspired several of his female characters including Daisy Buchanan in *The Great Gatsby*.

Photograph courtesy of F. Scott Fitzgerald Papers, Princeton University Library.

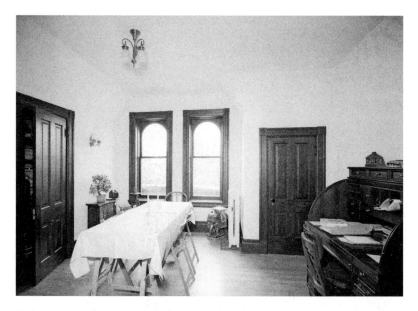

In the summer of 1919 Fitzgerald, having quit his advertising job in New York, returned to his parents' St. Paul home and in an upstairs room completed *This Side of Paradise*.

Photograph courtesy of Library of Congress Prints and Photographs Division, HABS MINN, 62-SAIPA, 27-4.

Fitzgerald met Zelda Sayre at the Country Club of Montgomery in July 1918, the month she turned eighteen—her popularity among southern beaux heightened his interest.

Photograph courtesy of Zelda Fitzgerald Papers (C0183), Manuscript Division, Department of Rare Books and Special Collections, Princeton University Library.

Following a broken engagement, Scott and Zelda were married on April 3, 1920, in the vestry of St. Patrick's Cathedral.

Photograph courtesy of F. Scott Fitzgerald Papers, Princeton University Library.

A Young Novelist Defies Tradition

F. Scott Fitzgerald

In 1920 Fitzgerald published his first novel and sold his first *Saturday Evening Post* stories. At twenty-four he had reached an emotional peak never, he knew, to be surpassed.

Photograph courtesy of F. Scott Fitzgerald Papers, Princeton University Library.

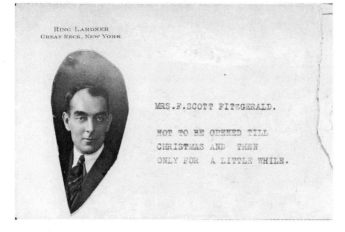

The columnist, satirist, and short-story writer Ring Lardner was Fitzgerald's neighbor in Great Neck on the Long Island North Shore; he was further a dear friend and a fellow drinker.

Photograph courtesy of Zelda Fitzgerald Papers, Princeton University Library.

More than Fitzgerald's editor, Maxwell Perkins of Scribner's proved to be his confidant, occasional banker, and, most importantly, loyal friend.

Photograph courtesy of Archives of Charles Scribner's Sons (C0101), Manuscripts Division, Department of Rare Books and Special Collections, Princeton University Library. Reprinted with the permission of Scribner, a division of Simon & Schuster.

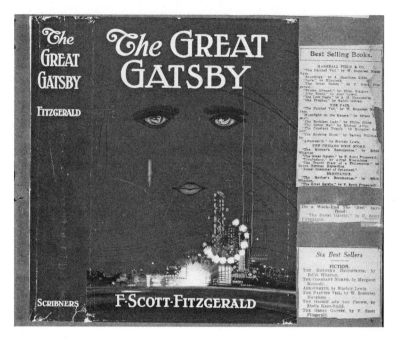

Written and revised in Europe, *The Great Gatsby* is regarded by many as the Great American Novel.

Photograph courtesy of Archives of Charles Scribner's Sons, Princeton University Library. Reprinted with the permission of Scribner, a division of Simon & Schuster, Inc. from *The Great Gatsby* by F. Scott Fitzgerald, © 1925 by Charles Scribner's Sons, © 1953 (renewed) by Frances Scott Fitzgerald Lanahan.

While living in Great Neck, Fitzgerald was taken by the sprawling ash dumps of Corona, Queens, and wrote it into *The Great Gatsby*.

Photograph courtesy of New York City Parks Photo Archive, Negative 13047.

Communications

FALSE AND EXTREMELY UNWISE TRADITION

Graduate Finds Cause for Fear in Advertisement of Erroneous "Sacred Old Football Tradition."

To the Editor of the Princetonian:

Sir:—I see that the fact of a lineman being elected Football Captain is still being sent out to the papers as a "sacred old tradition." As the present writer pointed out in the *Alumni Weekly* last winter, there is no such tradition—Ralph Gilroy was Captain-elect in 1922—and the report serves merely to fill two lines of space for unimaginative Press Club members each year. The point is that I believe it directly responsible for the fact that no first class backs have entered Princeton for four years; where Roper used to make tacklers out of extra halfbacks he is now compelled to make fullbacks out of guards and quarterbacks out of air. If anyone believes that rival colleges don't make full use of this alleged discrimination in winning over prospective triple threats, he is simply an innocent; for American boys have a pretty highly developed desire for glory.

It will take five years to kill this rumor, but the Athletic Association has obviously done nothing—and no matter what steps are taken now we can scarcely expect any more Slagles, Miles, Wittmers and Caulkins until 1940.

"Seventeen."

Paris, January 24, 1930.

JAZZ AGE WRITER MAKES HOME HERE

F. Scott Fitzgerald to Live Near Edge Moor to Finish His Novel.

F. Scott Fitzgerald, novelist and playwright, has made his home in the old Bradford mansion, "Ellerslie," on the banks of the Delaware river, near Edge Moor.

He moves here with his wife and four-year-old daughter, Frances, and will live here for about two years. For the past few years, Mr. Fitzgerald has been "making the grand tour," living in various places in Europe, particularly in France and Italy.

He chose the site near Wilmington particularly because he is a personal friend of John Biggs, Jr., lawyer, of this city, and because he wanted a quiet place to finish a novel. The new novel will be a picaresque one, different from his others, which have been emphasizing the current jazz age.

The Bradford house is a spacious Colonial building, with an expansive view of the river.

Mr. Fitzgerald left Princeton University in 1917 to join the army as an officer. His first novel was "This Side of Paradise," published in 1920. This was followed by "The Beautiful and Damned," issued in 1921; "Tales of Jazz Age," 1922; "The Great Gatsby," in 1925; "All the Sad Young Men," 1926.

His play, "The Vegetable," written in 1923, had its premier in Wilmington.

THE COPLEY-PLAZA, BOSTON.
THE GREENBRIER, WHITE SULPHUR SPRINGS, W. VA.

CABLE ADDRESS, "PLAZA, NEW YORK"
TELEPHONE, PLAZA 1740

NEW YORK   JUN 1 - 1927   192

THE PLAZA

FIFTH AVENUE AT CENTRAL PARK
58TH TO 59TH STREETS

Mr. F. Scott Fitzgerald,

Ellerslie, Edgemoor, Del.

To THE PLAZA Dr.

ROOM NO. 1662

FRED STERRY, PRESIDENT.   JOHN D. OWEN, MANAGER.

ACCT. NO. E5903   RATE 11.00

May 1927

DATE	ITEM	AMOUNT	TOTAL	DATE	ITEM	AMOUNT	TOTAL
23	Rooms	11.00		26	Telephone	.10	
	Cash Advance	10.00	21.00		Hair Dresser	4.25	
					Waiter's Fee	.60	
24	Rooms	11.00			Room Service	4.05	9.00
	Telephone	1.00					
	Tel. Suburb.	.30					275.70
	Cash Adv. Taxi	29.80		24	Cash, Galvin		8.00
	Waiter Fee	3.00					
	Cash Advance	25.00					267.70
		100.00					
	Florist	4.00					
	Cigars	.20					
	Restaurant	16.60					
	Room Service	1.50	192.40				
25	Rooms	11.00					
	Telephone	.90					
	Tel. Long D.	1.55					
	Dr Fee	10.00					
	News	2.35					
	Valet	6.50					
	Florist	4.00					
	Waiter's Fee	.50					
		.60					
		.40					
		2.00					
	Room Service	.45					
		3.35					
		1.85					
		2.20					
		5.65	53.30				

THE PLAZA
PAID
JUN - 6 1927
TREASURER'S OFFICE

Gilbert's address
2 Beekman
Place

Fitzgerald regarded The Plaza hotel as a symbol of American wealth and aristocratic pretention. Its role in *The Great Gatsby* is as central as the valley of ashes.

Photograph courtesy of F. Scott Fitzgerald Papers, Princeton University Library.

(45)

And as I sat there, brooding on the old unknown world I thought of gatsby ~~wonder~~ when he picked out the green light at the end of Daisy's dock. He had come a long way to this blue lawn but now his dream must have seemed so close that he could hardly fail to grasp it. He did not know that ~~he had left it behind long before, I lay~~ ~~somew~~ it was all behind him, ~~day somewhere~~ back in that vast obscurity on the other side of the city, where the dark fields of the republic rolled on under the night.

He believed in the green glimmer, in the orgastic future that year by year recedes before us. It eluded us then but never mind — tomorrow we will run faster, stretch out our arms farther. And one fine morning —

So we beat on, a boat against the current, borne back ceaselessly into the past

The final page of *The Great Gatsby*, perhaps the most famous single sheet of prose, images, and allusions in American literature.

Photograph courtesy of F. Scott Fitzgerald Papers, Princeton University Library.

Sara and Gerald Murphy, an expatriate couple situated on the French Riviera, offered Fitzgerald a model for a cultured, gracious, and ultimately elusive kind of living. He dedicated *Tender Is the Night* to them and invested the novel's protagonists, Dick and Nicole Diver, with their golden charm.

Photograph courtesy of Sara and Gerald Murphy Papers, Box 23, Folder 411, Beinecke Rare Book and Manuscript Library, Yale University. Photo © Estate of Honoria Murphy Donnelly/Licensed by VAGA, New York, NY.

In January 1927, Fitzgerald went to Hollywood to work on a screenplay. There he met the young actress Lois Moran, who became the inspiration for Rosemary Hoyt in *Tender Is the Night*.

Photograph courtesy of Hulton Archive/Stringer/Getty Images.

In April 1931, while in Paris, Zelda suffered her first breakdown; much of her subsequent correspondence with Scott traced the troubled history of their complex marriage.

Photograph courtesy of Sara and Gerald Murphy Papers, Box 29, Folder 572, Beinecke Rare Book and Manuscript Library, Yale University. Photograph © Estate of Honoria Murphy Donnelly/VAGA.

After spending most of the previous seven years abroad, the Fitzgeralds returned to a Depression-mired America in September 1931. Reflecting on the economic collapse, Fitzgerald wrote "My Lost City," an elegy of misplaced American aspirations.

Photograph courtesy of Oversnap/Vetta/Getty Images.

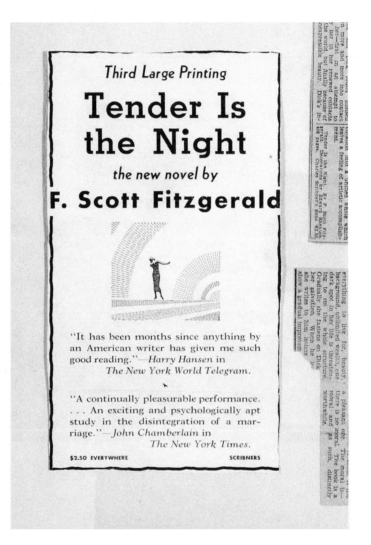

After a frustrating series of false starts, Fitzgerald published his fourth and most personal novel, *Tender Is the Night*, in April 1934.

Photograph courtesy of F. Scott Fitzgerald Papers, Princeton University Library.

Charles and Mary Beard's popular and influential history textbooks questioned the money-centric civilization taking hold in America. Fitzgerald offered a similar regret for his country, which he sometimes portrayed as a market-driven mirage that could not last.

Photograph courtesy of Walter Sanders/The LIFE Picture Collection/ Getty Images.

Fitzgerald, Spenglerian

Youthful Novelist Sees Only Doom For Civilization America Typifies

By Harry Salpeter

F. SCOTT FITZGERALD is a Nietzschean, F. Scott Fitzgerald is a Spenglerian, F. Scott Fitzgerald is in a state of cosmic despair. From within his slightly shuttered eyes, F. Scott Fitzgerald looks out upon a world which is doomed, in his sight, to destruction; from his unbearded lips comes conviction of America that is as final As the sentence is harsh. Rumination of the evidence and conviction came in such a rush of words, in such a tumbling of phrase upon phrase that neither objection nor appeal was possible. It was a rush of words which only powerful feeling could dictate. Here was I interviewing the author of "This Side of Paradise," the voice and embodiment of the jazz age, its product and its beneficiary, a popular novelist, a movie scenarist, a dweller in the gilded palaces, a master of servants, only to find F. Scott Fitzgerald, himself, shorn of these associations, forecasting doom, death and damnation to his generation, in the spirit, if not in the rhetoric, of your typical epithron philosopher. In a pleasant corner of the Plaza tea garden he sounded like an intellectual Samson prophesying the crumbling of its marble columns. He looks like a candid, serious youth. His blue eyes, fair hair and clear-cut profile, no less than his reputation, give the lie to the mind of F. Scott Fitzgerald.

I had caught Fitzgerald at the Plaza, a midway stop between Hollywood where, after much travail, he had completed a scenario for Constance Talmadge, and Brandywine Hundred, Del., an address which tickles him. There he will make his home for the next two years and there he will complete his next novel. This, he said, had been vaguely suggested by the Loeb-Leopold case and in the tragic moments of this novel will be mirrored some of the cosmic despair under the burden of which Fitzgerald manages, somehow, to maintain a resilient step. And after this novel—on which he has already worked three years—is completed? . . .

Why, what is there left to do?, Go to pieces. Or write another novel. A writer is good only for writing and showing off. Then people find him out as he runs out of money and then he goes and writes another novel.

Fitzgerald was drawn to the German philosopher-historian Oswald Spengler's idea that modern Western Civilization was on a course of inevitable decline. Its twilight mood crept into his work.

Photograph courtesy of F. Scott Fitzgerald Papers, Princeton University Library.

The sociologist Thorstein Veblen coined the phrase "conspicuous consumption" to characterize the elaborate spending habits of America's new industrial elite. Fitzgerald satirized this "predatory culture" in *Gatsby*, noting the garish mansions, swollen chrome cars, and elaborate parties that distinguish the floating world in Gatsby's West Egg.

Photograph courtesy of Eva Watson-Schutze/George Eastman House/Getty Images.

Fitzgerald insisted that he had met Henry Adams, the grandson and great-grandson of presidents, as a prep school student while visiting Washington. Adams's pessimistic view of American progress in his classic study *The Education of Henry Adams* (1918)—"As he came up the bay, November 5, 1904 . . . [t]he city had the air and movement of hysteria, and the citizens were crying, in every accent of anger and alarm . . ."—anticipated Fitzgerald's critique of the same in "My Lost City."

Photograph courtesy of Culture Club/Hulton Archive/ Getty Images.

You cannot write about such things dully and Fitzgerald has absolutely no affiliations with dullness. In the second installment his design has begun to unfold and already one's pity is deeply and sincerely engaged.

• • •

Great Verbal Facility
Marks Work of Author.
THERE HAS ALWAYS been the quality of the baroque to Scott Fitzgerald's style. He has a great verbal facility which results in all sorts of ingenious little inspirations, decorations to his prose which in themselves have real charm. The difficulty with elaborate ornament is that it tends to obscure the pattern as a whole. In the writing of "The Great Gatsby" Fitzgerald seemed to be animated by a passion for self-discipline. Quite ruthlessly he cut away the artificial and extraneous. By limiting his interests very strictly, he was able to spend all of his skill on the interpretation of his story. From it emanated a sort of compassion that was the more intense for being expressed with the most sparing economy of means.

Here he has let himself go once more. He sets down all the clever observations that occur to him. He seems to be indulging in a kind of orgy of perception. Just as a verbal exercise this is usually pleasing. One remembers with admiration his

still this side of Paradise

Francis Scott Key Fitzgerald (post-War apostle of the younger generation) and Frances Scott, his

Scottie Fitzgerald (1921–1986) was Scott and Zelda's only child. Taking into account his drinking and Zelda's illness, Fitzgerald sought to protect his daughter from the "weaknesses" of her parents.

Photograph courtesy of F. Scott Fitzgerald Papers, Princeton University Library.

SCREEN WRITERS' GUILD INC.
(Affiliated with the Author's League of America, Inc.)

Membership Card
ACTIVE

F. SCOTT FITZGERALD

Member

Issued SEP 23 1938 193

51

Fitzgerald's final years (1937–1940) were spent in Hollywood. The West Coast offered him a much-needed break from the East, which he had come to associate with debt and illness. Creatively, however, he detested the "factory-like" culture of the film colony.

Photograph courtesy of F. Scott Fitzgerald Papers, Princeton University Library.

In Hollywood, Fitzgerald met the gossip columnist Sheilah Graham—born Lily Sheil in Leeds before moving as an infant to London's East End. She provided him with much needed stability and is commemorated as "Kathleen Moore" in his final, unfinished novel, *The Last Tycoon*.

Photograph courtesy of Pictorial Parade/Archive Photos/Getty Images.

On December 21, 1940, Fitzgerald died of a heart attack in Hollywood. Probably fewer than fifteen copies of *The Great Gatsby* were sold that year. Within a decade, the "Fitzgerald Revival" began to bring him into the American literary canon.

Photograph courtesy of Carl Van Vechten Photograph Collection, Library of Congress Prints and Photographs Division, Washington DC, LC-USZ62-88500.

I feel something fermenting in me or the times that
I can't express and I dont yet know what lights or how strong
will be thrown on it. I don't know, even, whether
I shall be the man to do it. Perhaps the talent,
too long neglected, has passed its prime.

F. Scott Fitzgerald, 1937

THIRTEEN

Adrift Abroad

God, how much I've learned in these two and a half years in
Europe. It seems like a decade & I feel pretty old but I wouldn't
have missed it, even its most unpleasant & painful aspects.

F. Scott Fitzgerald to Max Perkins, 1926

Writing *The Great Gatsby* marked the high point of Fitzgerald's restive
years abroad. In Europe, no less than in America, a host of financial, artistic, and marital concerns preyed on his always surface-close insecurities. In a ranking of recriminations, Zelda's brief 1924 flirtation with
the young French aviator Edouard Jozan presented the chief impasse.
More than a spur-of-the-summer infatuation, it actually had roots across
the Atlantic. A cherished youngest daughter accustomed to the generous
attentions of solicitous southern beaux, Zelda struggled to carve out an
independent identity as Scott's spouse. Lingering dutifully but pointlessly
on the Riviera, she felt neglected. With her husband preoccupied with
Gatsby, she spent long sun-drenched days playing tennis, swimming, and
browning on the St. Raphael beach near Antibes. It was perhaps there
that she met Jozan, stationed at nearby Frejus. The nature of their relationship remains a matter of conjecture, and Jozan, when queried some
years later, denied anything more than a romance of words. With more
certainty, we know that Scott presumed the worst and that "The Big
crisis," as he cryptically put it in his *Ledger,* caused a permanent unsettling in his marriage. "That September 1924," he later recalled, "I knew
something had happened that could never be repaired."[1]

Though hurt by Zelda's involvement with Jozan, Fitzgerald quickly grasped its impressionistic possibilities for his new novel, letting it haunt *The Great Gatsby* as it haunted him. The extent to which the relationship made its way into Fitzgerald's writing can only be guessed at, yet just as fragments of Zelda's journals appeared in *The Beautiful and Damned*—and pieces of her medical record would later materialize in *Tender Is the Night*—something of that summer's twilight mood crept into *Gatsby*. On Zelda's side, the flirtation bore unmistakable evidence of her growing discontent. By turns upset and embarrassed by Scott's drinking and pushed into a world of writers, artists, and actors as something of a marital appendage, she sought to recover her once-strong sense of identity. Whether this struggle anticipated the mental illness that overtook her in 1930 is a much-debated point, though it seems likely that the severe colitis flare-up that troubled her a few months after her break with Jozan owed something to the emotional stress of that crowded summer. Fitzgerald showed little sensitivity to her situation, believing he was the injured party in the "Big crisis." While his novels stressed the virtues of vocation, he failed to recognize that his wife's often-desperate unhappiness, sense of displacement, and need for productive work may well have contributed to her deteriorating health.

Shortly after the Jozan "affair," Fitzgerald entered into what turned out to be a cagey and psychologically complex friendship with Ernest Hemingway. Alerted by Edmund Wilson's recent praise of Hemingway's poems and short stories in the October edition of the *Dial,* Fitzgerald promptly, as noted earlier, informed Perkins "about a young man named . . . Hemmingway who . . . has a brilliant future." Three years Fitzgerald's junior with only a few Parisian-published verses and a thirty-two-page book to his credit (*in our time*), Hemingway stood on the threshold of his own celebrated early success. Through him, Scott could experience again the feelings of that magical autumn of 1919 when Scribner accepted *This Side of Paradise.* "I can't tell you how much your friendship has meant to me during this year and a half," he wrote Hemingway in December 1926; "it is the brightest thing in our trip . . . for me."[2]

Soon thereafter, Fitzgerald endangered that amity by offering criticism of Hemingway's first novel, *The Sun Also Rises,* then in manuscript. "You've . . . got to *not-do* what anyone can do," he warned Hemingway, "and I think that there are about 24 sneers, superiorities, and nose-thumbings-at-nothing that mar the whole narrative up to p. 29 where . . . it really gets going." In contrast to Scott, Zelda never took to Hemingway, whom she saw as something of a "nobody could be *that* macho" poser. When asked by her Alabama friend Sarah Mayfield what *The Sun Also Rises* was about, she replied, "Bullfighting, bullslinging, and bull. . . ." Hemingway returned the compliment and more. In his posthumous score-settling memoir, *A Moveable Feast,* he named Zelda's jealousy as a de-structive, negating influence on Fitzgerald. "Scott did not write anything [after *Gatsby*] that was good," he meanly opined, "until after he knew that she was insane."[3] In retrospect, Zelda and Scott were both correct; Hemingway no doubt indulged in bluster and machismo, but he also pro-duced lasting literature. In fact, it was the marriage of the two that most attracted Fitzgerald.

Ever the romantic, Scott happily bought into the Hemingway myth: a war hero, sportsman, and "starving" artist—a Byronic ideal. As with Wilson, Fitzgerald quickly deferred to Hemingway's presumably "purer" dedication to his craft, a case of the "artiste" and the "knock-off artist" that both kept and cankered their relations. Hemingway repaid Fitzger-ald's admiration by reprising in *Moveable Feast* Edna St. Vincent Millay's unpleasant claim that Scott was gifted but dim. "His talent was as natural as the pattern that was made by the dust on a butterfly's wings," he wrote. "At one time he understood it no more than the butterfly did." And from there, Hemingway provocatively questioned Fitzgerald's masculinity. He remembered that Scott had "a face between handsome and pretty. He had a delicate long-lipped Irish mouth that, on a girl, would have been the mouth of a beauty. . . . The mouth worried you until you knew him and then it worried you more."[4] Still, they maintained contact until Fitzger-ald's death—a rarity for Hemingway, who habitually shed those who had helped advance his career. The assumption between the two, of Heming-way's superiority and Fitzgerald's inferiority, met certain psychological if not particularly healthy needs in both men and thus served as a common bond.

A further and related condition of their relationship involved Hemingway's insistence that he, rather than Fitzgerald, exemplified the expatriate experience—the sensitive American, that is, in search of cultural nourishment abroad. Malcolm Cowley observed in his classic study of the Lost Generation, *Exile's Return,* "to young writers like ourselves, a long sojourn in France was almost a pilgrimage to the Holy Land." The great boom market of the twenties alienated many intellectuals who felt themselves temperamentally out of touch with America. Uprooted from home but also from older prewar traditions and values, many of these expats wrote nostalgically of the past, as did Fitzgerald in *Gatsby.* In comparison to Hemingway, however, Scott rarely regarded the Continent as a source of artistic inspiration; his outlook remained quintessentially "American."[5]

When the European context arises in his work, as it does so powerfully in *Tender Is the Night,* it is often contrasted negatively to the United States. Europe, Fitzgerald believes, is for Americans a place of dissipation. In his 1929 story "The Swimmers," Scott writes of an American—Henry Clay Marston—living in France with his philandering spouse, Choupette. Contrasting New World idealism with Old World cynicism (and no doubt troubled still by the memory of Jozan), Fitzgerald brings the marriage to a crisis, at which time Henry begins to comprehend the true significance of his heritage and makes a final, necessary marital break. In a deft concluding passage that evokes Lincoln's eloquent description of the United States as "the last best, hope of earth," Fitzgerald expressed his belief in American exceptionalism. "The best of America was the best of the world," he wrote. "France was a land, England was a people, but America, having about it still that quality of the idea, was harder to utter—it was the graves at Shiloh and the tired, drawn, nervous faces of its great men, and the country boys dying in the Argonne for a phrase that was empty before their bodies withered. It was a willingness of the heart."[6]

So captivated was Fitzgerald by "the best of America" that he seemed essentially uninterested in discovering what a European perspective had to offer his point of view. Despite his living abroad for nearly six years, the exposure failed to leave a deep impress. No doubt this had much to do with Fitzgerald's personality: a case of carrying one's tightly held insularity across the Atlantic. He frequented American cafés, stayed in hotels that catered to an American clientele, and largely confined his circle of intimates to fellow expats. In one 1931 story, he wrote of an American businessman's disappointment at discovering that the Depression had left Paris "empty," bereft, that is, of his countrymen. Retracing his old haunts, he noticed that the Ritz bar "was not an American bar any more—he felt polite in it, and not as if he owned it. It had gone back into France." Jabbing at Fitzgerald's provincialism, Wilson wrote a little cruelly if amusingly of his friend, "The lower animals frequently die when transplanted."[7]

The writer Louis Bromfield, winner of a 1927 Pulitzer Prize for his novel *Early Autumn,* socialized with Scott and Zelda during their first trip abroad. He later recalled their avoidance of Paris's bohemian Left Bank for a more conventional setting:

> He and Zelda . . . lived on the Right Bank but in the oddest kind of place. I think it was on the Rue Tilsitt and it represented to some degree the old aspirations and a yearning for stability, but somehow it got only halfway and was neither one thing or the other. It was a large flat just off Etoile which must have been expensive but inside it was characterless and almost sordid. The furniture was gilt Louis XVI [straight] from the Galeries Lafayette [department store]. The wall paper was the usual striped stuff in dull colors that went with that sort of flat. It was all rather like a furniture shop window and I always had the impression that the Fitzgeralds were camping out there between two worlds.[8]

The between-worlds metaphor works on a number of levels. First, we see the artistic-minded Fitzgerald settling into the conservative Right Bank; next we note this well-paid American short-story writer trying to economize in Europe; and finally we observe Scott, always on the lookout for inspiration, contrarily taking the Continent on anything but its own terms. While it is true that *Tender Is the Night* unfolds against a European backdrop, the major characters and themes are classically American—a

Hollywood starlet, a Chicago pork heiress, and an idealistic doctor from Buffalo. The only European "types" to appear are essentially inessential. While the Continent had opened for Henry James vast and profitable vistas from which to reflect on the uneven progress of American civilization, Fitzgerald seemed uninterested in this kind of searching cross-cultural comparison. His oeuvre centered on the American scene, its faltering promise, and its representation as the "last best hope" of a romantic ideal.

It is perhaps for this reason that when Fitzgerald wrote about his country's waning Wasp aristocracy, he, unlike, say, Gertrude Stein, E. E. Cummings, or Henry Miller, steered clear of the bohemian sphere. Nor did he desire to imitate Hemingway and portray himself as a starving artist. Such a performance, in any case, would have belied the reality of his financial circumstances. During several trips abroad, the Fitzgeralds traveled in style. Expensive hotels, governesses, cooks, and clothing were the order of the day. More than simply representing a taste for luxury, this expat elegance brought Fitzgerald into closer connection with a world he wished to write about—a world of once firmly fastened upper-middle-class virtues and values giving way to a new economic and cultural elite.

On reflection, one is tempted to see Fitzgerald's years abroad as part of a deeper migratory pattern. He wasn't really Princeton or New York or Hollywood—any more than he was Europe. These were outposts, centers of scenes, moods, and attitudes to be captured, copied, and placed in stories and novels. The Continental experience interested him to the extent that it offered a civilizational contrast to America: the former he characterized as beggarly, statued, and worn; the latter he summed up in terms of dollars, youth, and vitality. As he put the matter in "The Swimmers," "Americans . . . should be born with fins, and perhaps they were—perhaps money was a form of fin. In England property begot a strong place sense, but Americans, restless and with shallow roots, needed fins and wings."[9]

This division—between the winged and the grounded—Fitzgerald attempted to play for laughs in his 1924 *Saturday Evening Post* essay "How to Live on Practically Nothing a Year." A slightly less successful companion piece to "How to Live on $36,000 a Year," it gave evidence of both its author's boorish response to Europe and his pretense to banknote nobility. Even after taking into account Fitzgerald's obvious intent to write a humor piece, shards of the ugly American still shine through. Off to the Riviera, Scott is forewarned to guard against "a number of dark men and women who mean [him] no good." And indeed, he soon runs into a gaggle of porters, domestics, taxi drivers, and rental agents looking to fleece the innocent abroad of his hard-earned money. When a concierge comes to the rescue and smashes an overinsistent cabbie to the ground, Fitzgerald channels his inner Tom Buchanan. "I tossed several nickels—or rather francs—upon the prostrate . . . man," he wrote. From there, the atmosphere turns positively menacing. Scott encounters "two scanty, hungry women" eyeing his baggage; "dark faces," consistent with the Mediterranean's "Arab streak," fill the streets, while Senegalese waiters offer the rich tourists exotic drinks as they shoo away the local "children of the poor." While Fitzgerald takes care to burlesque his own behavior in the essay, lines such as "I felt very American and superior" cut two ways.[10] In the essay, he portrays himself as a rising American prince even as he fails to hide fundamental insecurities. Yet it was precisely this complex amalgamation, of the confident climber and the habitual self-doubter, that gave him such insight into the boom/bust American character, a personality type conditioned to fluctuate like a trembling stock ticker.

In "How to Live," Fitzgerald tells about his having approached an Englishman to inquire about accommodations in a nearby town, only to watch in astonishment as the man suddenly flees from the room. After espying a second Englishman, he repeats the question, only to be rudely rebuffed: "'Don't know any at all,' [the Brit] said coldly. 'And I wouldn't tell *you* if I did.'" Fitzgerald's social striving lent itself to such glancing and occasionally bruising exchanges. The gentry reigned above all, looked down on all, and a part of Scott wanted to look down, too. In fact, "How to Live" and very many of Fitzgerald's other essays and stories contain a fairly broad range of ethnic slurs, graceless assumptions, and unpleasant racial stereotypes. Writing sarcastically to one friend about "all these 'marvelous' places" in the Mediterranean, he coarsely identifies

Spanish Majorca as a breeding ground of "bugs, lepers, Jews [and] consumptives."[11]

For Fitzgerald and many thousands more in America, such casual ethnological typecasting was reinforced by the reigning historical interpretations of the day, which tended to focus on the actions of white elites and diminished black agency. In the United States at this time, a number of leading scholars who had been shaken by the Great War, including James G. Randall, Avery Craven, and E. M. Coulter, went so far as to argue that the American Civil War was a "repressible" conflict caused by a "blundering generation" of high-placed politicians who had failed to uphold the nation's long-standing compromise tradition. Embedded in this argument is the denial of slavery as a cause of the war or, as Lincoln had more generally recognized, a moral crisis in American history. The leading interpreter of plantation slavery in the United States at this time, the Georgia-born U. B. Phillips (1877–1934), had argued that black servitude was a paternalistic, even benign enterprise in which Africans were "civilized" under the tutelage of their masters. They came to America, he assured readers, fundamentally "ignorant," "unenterprising," and "barbaric." Laboring in the fields under the overseer's watchful eye, slaves, Phillips insisted, were introduced to "the most efficient method ever devised for the use of stupid labor in agriculture on a large scale."[12]

Under such cultural and interpretive influences, Fitzgerald's southern sympathies collected around the notion of an idealized "Dixie" (chivalric, refined, and "cavalier") that converged with family history as well as his own romantic sensibility. Like most Americans of his day, Scott never really considered the question of slavery and its aftermath as anything more than an abstraction, and thus he never wrestled with its deep ethical implications. Consequently, he handled somewhat clumsily the few black Americans and Europeans who turn up in his novels and stories. Today, one peruses his depictions, which typically use the then-accepted word "negro" though occasionally descend to "darkie," "coon," and "Sambo," with a certain embarrassment.

There were, of course, contemporary readers who were offended by Fitzgerald's racial characterizations as well, and one, a Mr. Earl Wilkins of Mount Vernon, Missouri, wrote to him directly on the subject in the summer of 1934. "Must all the male Negroes in your books and stories be called 'bucks'?" he asked. "Some time during the past week I read in the then current issue of *The Saturday Evening Post* your 'No Flowers' in which you referred to 'Jim Europe and his bucks.' In *The Great Gatsby* you made a similar reference to a Negro buck. There are indubitably caribou, deer, antelope, elk and other animal bucks, but is there any excuse other than an unworthy and possibly unconscious desire to indicate inferiority to make animal-like bucks out of Negroes?" Wilkins accurately identified Fitzgerald's genteel racism, though he perhaps misread its source. He thought it came from privilege, when actually it reflected a relative poverty. Wilkins's characterizations of Fitzgerald as "reared in an exclusive district of St. Paul and educated at Princeton" were surface observations.[13] For Scott, St. Paul conjured up images of a nomadic existence, a case of the poor relations hanging on in a smart neighborhood. And Princeton had shown him a class-bound license, ease, and security that he might covet but could never claim. Still, Wilkins's letter may well have brought Fitzgerald a soupçon of satisfaction—he had, after all, been confused for one of the beautiful people.

<hr />

Interwar Europe's diverse collection of cultures only magnified Fitzgerald's longing for a lost and presumably more cohesive Faustian world. This he seemed to find both emotionally and intellectually in the chivalry, paternalism, and Catholic sensibility of the Middle Ages—a period that had, a generation earlier, attracted the attention of Henry Adams for perhaps similar reasons. In the mid-1930s, Scott sought to explore this side of European history in the never-completed Philippe series. A poorly conceived mishmash of popular feudal themes—kings, damsels, and witch cults—the stories were contrived, and Fitzgerald's attempts to meld what he took to be ninth-century dialogue with the hard-boiled diction that was fast coming into Hollywood vogue fell flat. "Call me Sire!" Philip demands, and though armed with a sword rather than a tommy gun, he warns his enemies (sounding more than a little like the movie "tough guy" James Cagney), "I'll be back you rats. . . . I'll let daylight through you."[14] If anything, the Philippe stories demonstrated how much Scott's historical imagination was tied to his own times. He needed America—its energy, aspirations, and insecurities—to put together a strong narrative. *Redbook Magazine* published three of the Philippe stories before begging off, and Scott's plans to include them in a novel never came to fruition. His agent, Harold Ober, knew the project would be problematic and doubted its success. In a communication to Scott, he tried to explain the troubles he faced selling the stories to skeptical editors: "I think we have to remember that you have made a reputation for writing a very modern story. If an editor wants an authoritative story about modern society, you are one of the first authors that would come to his mind. The result is that when a reader picks up a magazine with one of your stories in it and finds a story about the ninth century he is going to be shocked. You will remember that I approached several magazines about this series and that is what every editor said."[15]

Fitzgerald's interest in the medieval world suggests the depth of his regret for America's inability to replicate the more rooted and culturally rich history of European civilization. "I don't know what it is," he once told a reporter. "Perhaps America just came too late. . . . The country seems like warmed over hash—warmed over from the day before. America is the place where everybody is always going to have a good time tomorrow. There is nothing, no tradition, no background, that you can summon when you say you are an American, as you can if you could say you were an Englishman, or even a Frenchman."[16] In some sense, these remarks reflected Scott's own struggles to reconcile with family history. The "fins" and "wings" of McQuillan money paled, in his estimation, in comparison to the echoes of Old World romance that he never stopped associating with the Chesapeake Fitzgeralds.

Returning to America in December 1926, Scott and Zelda needed a new home, and Max Perkins knew Fitzgerald well enough to recommend Wilmington, Delaware, as a location that would appeal to his friend. "There's a kind of feudalism," he explained. "The DuPonts, an immense family, mostly female, dominate the town. They marry whom they will. A strong, practical race of vast wealth. We went to a DuPont wedding and saw most of them. . . . The talk is always of the doing of one or another. They have the eccentricity and independence—not arrogance for they are simple and natural—that comes from their position, and offer a most interesting subject for conversation."[17]

This recommendation, along with the encouragement of John Biggs Jr., a Princeton friend and Delaware native, eventuated in the Fitzgeralds' relocation to "Ellerslie," a rambling early nineteenth-century Greek Revival manor just north of Wilmington. As Zelda later wrote, "We leased a very big old mansion on the Delaware River. The squareness of the rooms and the sweep of the columns were to bring us a judicious tranquility. There were sombre horse chestnuts in the yard and a white pine bending as graciously as a Japanese brush drawing."[18] Life in the land of the DuPonts, however, did not go quite as Perkins had imagined—or as languorously as Zelda let on. Biggs recalled some years later that the Fitzgeralds were frequently bored in their new digs and occasionally went slumming in search of excitement:

> There was a bad area near Wilmington known as "Bloodfield," where all kinds of shootings and stabbings took place. The police wouldn't go in except in pairs. Sometimes, Scotty and Zelda would go in there and start drinking. They raised so much hell that residents would call police. The Wilmington police considered them a lady and a gentleman and refused to place them in a cell. They kept them in a gymnasium until I came to get them. But they were rough on Fitzgerald's bodyguard and manservant. He was a former Le Havre taxi driver and boxer whom Fitzgerald had persuaded to come to the US with him in 1927.[19]

Rather than making Wilmington a real or restful home, Scott and Zelda often commuted to New York, moving impatiently about the city from party to party. At one such affair, Fitzgerald met the heavyweight champion Gene Tunney and stayed near him throughout the evening. "I found that every time I came to town," he later wrote, "I was caught up into a complication of events that deposited me a few days later in a somewhat exhausted state on the train for Delaware."[20] When not in Manhattan, the Fitzgeralds' frequent travels—to Virginia Beach, Long Island, the Hudson Valley, Quebec, and several months in Paris—kept them away from Ellerslie. And when at Ellerslie, they often turned on each other. One argument—in front of Zelda's visiting sister Rosalind and her husband, Newman Smith—literally drew blood. Scott's baiting of Zelda led to her calling Scott's father an Irish cop, which led to his slapping her hard on the face. After Zelda asserted to Rosalind her "right" to be hit, the sisters broke into a fierce quarrel. The Smiths, appalled by the behavior of their hosts, retreated from Ellerslie the next morning. When the Fitzgeralds' lease expired in March 1929, they, in a manner of speaking, did the same, returning to Europe. Nine years into their marriage, they remained unsettled, far from peace, far from home.

FOURTEEN

Emotional Bankruptcy

There is something very special to be written about the
psychology of pretty girls. . . . Life promises so very much
to a pretty girl between the ages of sixteen and twenty-five
that she never quite recovers from it.

F. Scott Fitzgerald to Pete and Margaret Finney, 1938

Whether in America or abroad, Fitzgerald failed for several years to find
a suitable subject for a longer work of fiction. After publishing three
novels between 1920 and 1925, this still-young man appeared to have exhausted his storehouse of ideas. Not until 1934 did his next book, *Tender
Is the Night,* appear, and it was a much-different project than the weighty
social novel—à la Zola's *Germinal* and Dostoyevsky's *Crime and Punish-
ment*—he had outlined in the late 1920s. Scott was able to write only
four chapters of this unfinished work. At its center was to be a murder—a
matricide. A young American man, Francis Melarky, twenty-one and
touring the Riviera, quick tempered and baited by his manipulating
mother for a string of failures, plots her death. A number of recent and
well-publicized crimes suggested this narrative. The famous Leopold
and Loeb case (1924) involved the Chicago murder of a little boy by two
adolescents and briefly dominated the headlines; the following year, a
sixteen-year-old San Francisco girl killed her mother during an argument
over the former's persistent partying, and Dreiser's epic *American Tragedy*
(1925), itself based on a notorious criminal case, offered additional
momentum.

Several factors held up progress on the new work—variously called "The Boy Who Killed His Mother," "The World's Fair," and "Our Type." Ever-present financial needs forced Fitzgerald to return to short-story writing; Zelda's deteriorating health, leading to her April 1930 breakdown in Paris, created new conditions in which each now lived; and perhaps most important, Scott proved creatively incapable of pulling off a dense, complicated narrative. He had it right when he moved away from the conspicuous social commentary that weighted down *The Beautiful and Damned* to sketch the compact *Gatsby*. His particular poetics worked much better in an economized format than in a grand Dostoyevskian sweep. Writing against himself, a prolonged block on the project resulted. Having gone through the mass of drafts for the four extant chapters, the literary scholar Henry Dan Piper concluded in 1965 that "Fitzgerald finally abandoned the novel on which he had been at work so long, simply because he no longer knew precisely what it was he wanted to say."[1]

In 1929, Fitzgerald briefly reconceptualized the novel, now focusing on Lew Kelly, a young, brilliant, but disaffected American filmmaker prone to drink. Kelly (probably modeled after the Irish director Rex Ingram) has left Hollywood and seeks a different and presumably more settled life in Europe. Shipboard, he meets Rosemary, an aspiring actress based on the film star Lois Moran, whom Scott had met in Hollywood in 1927. Kelly's jealous wife, Nicole, and a Yale beau add tension to the voyage, but the narrative never gained traction. Frustrated, Fitzgerald shelved this permutation and returned to the Melarky story line, but Zelda's hospitalization put a permanent end to his ambitious "intellectual murder." He began instead to focus on her illness, what it meant to him, and what extrapolations he might make of her "highly nervous state" as a metaphor for the greater "sickness" afflicting Depression-era Western society.[2] This "version" became *Tender Is the Night,* but it did not come for a few more years.

As the Jazz Age came to an end, Fitzgerald faced an artistic future that looked to him as uncertain as the nation's own future in the wake of the stock-market crash of October 1929. Unable to complete his novel in progress and resentful of the time and energy it took to churn out formulaic flapper scenarios, he struggled to open a fresh creative vein. In search of new inspiration, he revisited his past: the difficult years of prep-school unpopularity, the delight of Princeton football weekends, and the half-dreamt hours spent with Ginevra King. Between April 1928 and August 1931, Fitzgerald published thirteen stories in two separate *Saturday Evening Post* series; the first introduced readers to his alter ego, Basil Duke Lee, and the second profiled Basil's female counterpart, the Chicago socialite Josephine Perry. They are of uneven quality, but at their best, the cumulative portrait is compelling.

While the stories bear evidence of their author's usual fascination with youthful precedents—first love, first loss, and, in Fitzgerald's description of Josephine's awakening, feral beauty, "first blood"—they more broadly seek to understand modern America through the choices it presents its children. Unprepared by unearned wealth and unexamined privilege to face life's challenges, Josephine, in particular, is a casualty of her era's moral laxity. Socialized into the sorority of "baby vamps," she can understand no limits until a lack of license itself robs her of the ability to feel deeply about anything. As Fitzgerald says of her fate in the final Perry story, "One cannot both spend and have."[3] Depression-era readers, many presuming that a contrite 1930s would now have to pay off the previous decade's staggering summit of bills, could be excused for reading the series as a moral judgment on bad times.

And on a personal level, perhaps Scott saw the stories similarly. The Basil and Josephine cycle helped him to make sense of the confused circumstances that had seemingly so casually brought him to the point of crisis. Unable to control either his drinking or his escalating expenses, Fitzgerald looked on powerlessly as his life began to spiral out of control. The 1930s were to be a difficult decade for Fitzgerald, but these troubles had little to do with the nation's economic collapse. His worries had begun before, and he wanted to trace them to their more obscure roots. Why had he, like Josephine, exhausted his emotional resources so early in life? Why had he spent recklessly during the very time he should have been saving?

As cultural statements, the Basil and Josephine stories offered a more so-phisticated handling of American youth than popular fiction had previously allowed. The reigning books on the topic, Booth Tarkington's comic Penrod Schofield series, centered on the misadventures of an eleven-year-old boy growing up in the pre–Great War Midwest. Tarkington, as observed earlier, had satirized first love in *Seventeen* (1916), and this work, along with the Penrod sequence, caught Fitzgerald's eye. In a 1917 *Nassau Literary Magazine* review, he praised Tarkington for addressing adolescence in more complete and complex terms than previous writers dared. The adult sins of conceit and arrogance, Tarkington revealed, were rooted in status distinctions that the young took note of, practiced among their own, and were determined to maintain. "Mr. Tarkington has done what so many authors of juvenile books fail to do," wrote Fitzgerald; "he has admitted the unequaled snobbishness of boyhood and has traced the neighborhood social system [where some unfortunates are] . . . never quite admitted as an equal." Though Fitzgerald's observation is true as far as it goes, it is equally so that Tarkington—who later won a Pulitzer Prize for *The Magnificent Ambersons,* a "serious" novel on the decline of a once prominent family—never really put his boys in danger, never fol-lowed the "unequaled snobbishness of boyhood" to its petty cruelties and humiliations. His plots were fundamentally sentimental, with an under-lying hilarity waiting to escape. The reader is meant to laugh, guilt-free, for the problems that Tarkington's children face are never so large, never so insurmountable that they command a deeper sympathy. Youth's prob-lems are minor—adulthood is where danger begins. Basil's and Josephine's uphill marches through adolescence, by contrast, are of an entirely dif-ferent emotional depth. They might more profitably be seen less as Pen-rod's peers than as part of a cross-generational community of searching teens connecting Mark Twain's remarkable Huckleberry Finn to J. D. Sa-linger's alienated Holden Caulfield.[4]

The underlying challenges faced by Basil and Josephine are wealth and entitlement. If America conspicuously celebrates the virtues of discipline, generosity, and compassion, it less loudly offers its advantaged a number of shortcuts, compromises, and moral evasions. Every benefit, if it is boundless, can be a terrible disservice to the beneficiary. Unlike Basil, whose life is marked by a series of character-building opportunities, the far more privileged Josephine has few such chances within the confines of her golden cage. She is mobile only to the extent that she remains loyal to Lake Forest circles, sons, and sisterhoods; she is encouraged to lack a discerning point of view. Never having faced any serious trials, she has channeled all her energies, rather, into different tributaries. Vacations and celebrations, fantasies and flirtations are the sum of stars that fill her adolescent sky—a youth ill served by a surplus of trivial endeavors. Fitzgerald believed that the teen years were a precious, critical, and fleeting period in which character was fixed forever. To abuse these years with slight ambitions, to come out on the other side of pubescence absent the moxie-making trials of unpopularity, athletic defeat, or academic struggles, doomed one to a perpetual unseriousness. It constituted a tragic squandering of emotional capital never to be reinvested, never to stand in reserve.

The Basil series details its protagonist's emotional growth from boyhood to the age of seventeen as a rising freshman at Yale. When we meet Basil, he is callow, conceited, and known among his peers, as one story tells us, for being "the freshest boy" in his prep school. But he matures over the years into a reflective and considerate young man, disciplined by his missteps and careful not to repeat them. The series culminates with "Basil and Cleopatra," whose title alludes to the ill-fated bond between Mark Antony and Cleopatra that tore the Second Triumvirate apart and led to the collapse of the Roman Republic. Fitzgerald's hero, by contrast, loses the girl but keeps his soul. Briefly, Basil's teen crush for Minnie Bibble (née Ginevra King?) comes crashing down after she discovers the sweet-talking, panama-hatted Littleboy Le Moyne—a composite of Zelda's southern loyalists. Basil exacts his revenge while deftly quarterbacking the Yale freshman football team to a closely contested victory over Le Moyne's Princeton squad. Walking off the field that same afternoon, however, he realizes that the triumph means little while the girl remains lost. Later that night, Minnie shows up at a postgame party with yet another admirer, as a distraught Le Moyne crashes the dance in a drunken rage. Basil compassionately observes his former nemesis's downfall and questions his own heart. Taking a step toward adulthood, he realizes "he had made all his mistakes for this time." Going outside, he pensively scans an expressive sky bearing both an early snow and a blazing heaven of cold stars. Instinctively, Fitzgerald writes, Basil knows that his world has slightly, but significantly, changed: "He saw that they were his stars as always—symbols of ambition, struggle and glory. The wind blew through them, trumpeting that high white note for which he always listened, and the thin-blown clouds, stripped for battle, passed in review. The scene was of an unparalleled brightness and magnificence, and only the practiced eye of the commander saw that one star was no longer there."[5] That missing star, representing Basil's weakness for the ephemeral and impressionistic, for his susceptibility to the world's Minnies, had flickered out.

If the Basil and Josephine stories are "do-over" fantasies, they also suggest some sober self-reflection on the part of the author. Distanced now from Ginevra King by some dozen years, Fitzgerald revisited that relationship with growing self-awareness. To be sure, the chip remained on his shoulder, but he now acknowledged some responsibility for its weight. In writing in one of the Josephine stories of the Princetonian Paul Dempster's devotion "to Josephine for a year—long after her own interest had waned" and of Josephine's becoming "simply a projection of [Paul's] own dreams," Fitzgerald acknowledges with a sharp candor the myth he had made of Ginevra.[6]

Beyond dispelling the ghosts of golden girls past, the Basil and Josephine stories continued Fitzgerald's by now de rigueur attack on snobbery. Basil—like Scott—"knew that he was one of the poorest boys in a rich boys' school," and one of Josephine's literally outclassed would-be lovers "knew in his heart he was better than [the Perrys], and he couldn't bear that they should not know it." Her cool elusiveness owed little to imagination or effort but rested, rather, on the advantage of being born into the right family. "The wealth that rolls by in limousines," Fitzgerald writes of Josephine's North Shore world, "is less glamorous than embittering to those on the sidewalk." In recovering the slights and shames of youth, Fitzgerald may well have sought to diminish their lingering hold on him. And in recording Basil's march to manhood, he made for himself a map back to a moment when all paths looked possible. If Fitzgerald still lacked the practiced eye of the commander, he might nevertheless claim some small control of his future by first resetting the past. "His life had been confused and disordered," he had written of Gatsby and perhaps of himself, "but if he could once return to a certain starting place and go over it all slowly, he could find out what that thing was."[7]

Thinking over the principal protagonists in Fitzgerald's work, one is struck by their collective "failure." Only *Paradise*'s Amory Blaine and Basil Lee show signs of developing into mature adults free from the temptations of money and power. In Anthony Patch and Jay Gatsby, Dick Diver and Monroe Stahr, the reader encounters a series of ill-fated characters unable to overcome personal weaknesses. Basil, the youngest of the lot, retains an attractive resiliency and growing sense of integrity that shields him from even the faint suggestion of moral decay. Most important, he learns from his mistakes. Invited in one of the stories by the popular Minnie to accompany her on a family vacation, a self-absorbed Basil talks himself out of the holiday. Chatting alone with Mr. Bibble, Basil falls back on an old habit of discussing his school grades and his likes and dislikes and more generally displaying an inattention to the interests of others—a fault he recognized only too late: "Good-bye. I hope I didn't talk too much." He is promptly disinvited. Yet Basil is neither defeated by the situation nor lightly dismissive of what happened. The lesson becomes, rather, part of his developing social apparatus, a sting but also a springboard to a more controlled and mature outlook. "He lay on his bed, baffled, mistaken, miserable but not beaten," Fitzgerald writes, reflecting perhaps on his various difficulties at Newman, Princeton, and Lake Forest. "Time after time, the same vitality that had led his spirit to a scourging made him able to shake off the blood like water, not to forget, but to carry his wounds with him to new disasters and new atonements—toward his unknown destiny."[8]

Just what that destiny is remains appropriately unclear—this is a series about a boy, after all. Fitzgerald does, however, offer clues to Basil's progress. We see him kiss a less attractive girl to salve her self-respect, overcome a painful prep-school unpopularity by sheer discipline, and take a punch-the-time-clock railroad job to help pay his way through Yale. Confronted with a number of temptations and obstacles that might easily impede or even wreck his future, Basil is saved through self-awareness. Once "the freshest boy" in school, he undergoes a hard hazing culminating in the realization that what he presumed to be his private struggle to make sense of the world, to fight through the cultural malaise in search of an island of ambition and success, is in fact a contest for self-respect enjoined by others. This essential step toward growing up—the replacement of the baby "I" with the adult "we"—is a lesson Basil grasps during a Manhattan excursion, when he secretly observes the Yale football captain, Ted Fay, abruptly dismissed by his beautiful teen intended. For Basil, the universe has suddenly become larger and more mysterious, and in trying to make sense of the moment, he discovers within himself a new emotion: pity for a fallen superman whose troubles are evidently greater than his own. Chaperoned in the city by his "hard specimen" history teacher, Mr. Rooney, Basil is baited by the older man: "Lee ... why don't you get wise to yourself?" But after Basil witnesses his idol's disgrace, he now needs no such instruction; he has decided to repair his reputation at school. Determined to return to campus immediately, he finds the irresponsible Rooney in a drunken torpor. Walking "past the quizzical eyes of the bartender," Basil again hears the rhythmic slur "G'wise to yourself. . . . G'wise to yourself an' let me alone." But this time it has no effect. Preparing to clean up Rooney in the bathroom before the silent train ride home, he says simply, honestly, "I am wise to myself."⁹

As a point of comparison, the Josephine sequence nicely negates the moral accent of the Basil stories. Instead of progressing toward a greater wisdom, Josephine heads in the opposite direction, finding, after endless proms, parties, and pettings, that she is unable to engage in a meaningful relationship. Her queue of would-be lovers has culminated in a kind of relationship stasis—one kiss, one caress is suddenly indistinguishable from another.¹⁰ In this way, though the Basil and Josephine stories are not strictly speaking a companion series, a harmony of mood, tone, and moral shading unites them. Basil remains a searcher, informed but not jaded, wizened but still eager. Josephine, just eighteen, has already "spent" her youth consuming steadies and swains at an alarming rate. She is unable to conceive of, let alone construct, a responsible life out of the materials left to her. Her looks will go, her popularity will dwindle, but even more crushingly momentous than these, she will be incapable of building lasting emotional connections with family, friends, or lovers. The trivial investments she has made up to this point—risky speculations encouraged by the *encumbrances* of wealth and beauty—have failed to pan out. In this sense, Josephine stands as perhaps one of Fitzgerald's truest examples of an "American tragedy." She is spoiled by the very advantages supposed to provide independence and options.

Certainly Josephine has little hope of emulating Basil's success. If he gets it right, if he develops through discipline and perseverance into a curious, sensitive, and strong adult, he has a bright future. Josephine's prospects are decidedly less heroic. She is, after all, expected to do little more than replicate the early-marriage, early-childbirth, and early-middle-age pattern still very much in vogue. Accordingly, one might say that her extravagant expenditure of emotional capital—a party in every port—is merely Josephine's taking of her culture's gendered truisms to heart. Her meter is running, and she has a limited time to squeeze in a hurried adolescence before losing her liberty. At that point, she will presumably live off her husband's workday triumphs, tragedies, and, of course, salary while passing on to her own daughters the time-tested strategies for claiming their share in the marital sweepstakes.

All this begs the question, to what extent had the Victorian restraints on the "fairer sex" truly been brushed aside? Among flapperdom's faithful, one could be excused for thinking such an inquiry silly. The war, female suffrage, and more knowing attitudes toward birth control had produced a "new woman," no? Yet Josephine, even in an age of increased options, seems ultimately not so far removed from her mother's generation. She too conforms to a culture that had yet to make economic, artistic, or educational space equivalent to that offered the Basils of the world. Her scope of conquest, rather, finds nothing more inspiring than a competition for mates. And though she is something of a virtuoso in this game, the hunt hardly brings to mind a higher state of self-realization. "Josephine loved to dance," Fitzgerald writes, "but the field of feminine glory, the ballroom floor, was something you slipped away from—with a man." And from the man came Josephine's impending postmarital value. Is it any wonder that she plays the dating game so hard? She has but two precious years to try out her girlish powers before they are to be forever entombed in a bridal contract. Before Basil looms the purposeful adventures of college, war, and career to test and retest his mettle. Josephine has before her a few seasonal collegiate social-calendar campaigns; in these, her benchmarks are fellow golden girls also trying to claim and be claimed from among a "men of the better schools" lineup of parentally approved gallants.[11]

The biting irony of Josephine's predicament is that her strengths and weaknesses are invariably conjoined. Beauty, charm, and popularity are supposed to guarantee a certain degree of autonomy, and yet without limit, they distort reality and warp personality. In "A Woman with a Past," a double drama is set up pairing the "bad" Josephine and the "good" Adel, a classmate who, despite thick ankles and a less-than-perfect complexion, has managed a romantic understanding with the coveted Dudley Knowleton. What is the secret of Adel's success? She's a female Basil on the road to personage-hood. Josephine's unforeseen defeat produces a minor and all-to-the-good upheaval in her thinking—she realizes now, "There were two kinds of men, those you played with and those you might marry." The epiphany, her "first mature thought," Fitzgerald tells us, can unfortunately gain no footing against the cultural forces arrayed against her, and Josephine quickly falls back into the same old debilitating pattern—trying to both spend and have.[12]

―――

Despite the obvious merits of the Basil and Josephine series, they were dismissed as lesser Fitzgerald until Scribner put out a single-volume edition of the stories in 1973. It was a long time coming, for Scott had once contemplated, only to discard, various strategies to bring his popular adolescent creations together. In the summer of 1928 (pre-Perry), an enthusiastic Fitzgerald wrote to Max Perkins of a proposal: "I plan to publish a book of those Basil Lee stories . . . if you'd want them. . . . [They] would make a nice *light* novel. . . . It would run to perhaps 50 or 60 thousand words." But the following year, a few months after the last Basil essay appeared in the *Post,* he expressed a change of heart. "The Basil Lee stories were a mistake," he wrote one correspondent; "it was too much good material being shoved into a lousy form." In fact, by the spring of 1930, Fitzgerald had grown concerned that the release of a Basil book might undermine his reputation as a "serious" novelist, and despite persistent financial worries, he informed Perkins of his unwillingness to see the stories appear in a collected edition. His 1928 opinion still carried— he thought the stories "would make a nice *light* novel"—but believed his next book must make an unequivocal artistic statement. "I know too well by whom reputations are made and broken to ruin myself completely by such a move—I've seen . . . too many others fall through the eternal trapdoor of trying to cheat the public, no matter what their public is, with substitutes—better to let four years [between books] go by."[13]

Fitzgerald offered to his literary agent, Harold Ober, a still more detailed explanation of his unwillingness to resurrect the Basil stories:

> I know you're losing faith in me + Max too but God knows one has to rely in the end on one's own judgment. I could have published four lowsy, half baked books in the last five years + people would have thought I was at least a worthy young man not drinking myself to pieces in the south seas—but I'd be dead as . . . the others who think they can trick the world with the hurried and the second rate. These *Post* stories *in* the *Post* are at least not any spot on me—they're honest and if their *form* is stereotyped people know what to expect when they pick up the *Post.* The novel is another thing—if, after four years I published the Basil Lee stories as a book I might as well get tickets for Hollywood immediately.[14]

And then four more years went by. In April 1934, Fitzgerald's master-work, *Tender Is the Night,* was published. Now, with a "real" novel just out, he again lingered over the possibility of preparing the "light novel." Indeed, it might now be not quite so light after all, for the addition of the Josephine stories delivered a distinctly fateful tone. Scott wrote to Perkins in May of several publishing plans, the second of which would combine the existing Basil and Josephine stories with one or two additional stories, the last to bring Basil and Josephine together. Fitzgerald remained sensitive, however, to the perils of such a project and told Perkins so:

"This would in some ways look like the best commercial bet because it might be taken . . . almost as a novel, *and the most dangerous artistically for the same reason*—for the people who buy my books might think that I was stringing them by selling them watered goods under a false name." In reply, Perkins informed Scott of Scribner's enthusiastic support for "plan 2."[15] He personally enjoyed the stories, and their popularity among *Post* readers hinted at a perhaps-modest but much-needed financial success for their author. Still, Fitzgerald's proposed ending—to "bring Basil and Josephine together"—would have presented a tremendous challenge. They represented, after all, two distinctly different personality types. What could Josephine be for Basil other than perhaps another temptation to overcome? And what could he be for her? A savior to show her the proper path to maturation? In the arc of the other, each loses his or her distinct character. The faint aroma of tragedy hangs about Josephine just as the strong scent of hope accompanies Basil; the contrast in their conditions—the dichotomy of upper class versus middle class, female versus male, and physical beauty versus personal integrity—produces a persuasive tension that works better from a perspectival distance. Basil and Josephine no more belong together than . . . Fitzgerald and Ginevra King.

Finally, in late May, Scott scrapped the idea of a Basil and Josephine book altogether. Again, artistic doubts took precedence. Perhaps the mixed critical response to *Tender Is the Night* ate away at his wavering willingness to release the "light novel." He now wrote conclusively to Perkins, telling him, "On thinking it over and in going over the Basil and Josephine stories the business seems impossible. They are not as good as I thought." And beyond this question of quality, the idea of passing off the stories as an integrated volume rather than a book of short stories had never ceased to bother Fitzgerald. He raised this concern again, underlining his fear of what such a project might do to his teetering reputation:

> I have not quite enough faith in the [Scribner] Business Department to believe that they would not exploit it to some extent as a novel . . . and any such misconception would just ruin what position I have reconsti-

tuted with the critics. The ones who like "Tender" would be disgusted; the ones who were baffled by it or dislike my work would take full advantage to goose-pile on me. It's too damn risky and I am too old for such a chance and the penalty might be too high. What it amounts to is that if it is presented as a novel it wrecks me and if it were presented as short stories then what is the advantage of it over a better collection of short stories?[16]

Fitzgerald soon answered his own question but in such a way as to leave the impression that he longed to unite Basil and Josephine after all. His volume of short stories *Taps at Reveille* was published in March 1935, and this "better collection" included five Basil and three Josephine tales, nearly half the book. Even as he dismissed these stories to Perkins and Ober as "second rate," Scott never lost sight of their compelling blend of innocence and pathos.

Aside from the two series' bright if brief *Post* life and partial appearance in *Taps,* their relative "remoteness" might be inferred from Ginevra King's ignorance of their existence. It was not until the late 1940s, after two scholars separately brought the stories to her attention, that she first surveyed them. "[I] read with shame the very true portrait of myself in my youth in the Josephine stories," King candidly reported to one. And to the other, she acknowledged, "I was too thoughtless in those days & too much in love with love to think of consequences. These things he emphasized—and over-emphasized in the Josephine stories, but it is only fair to say I asked for some of them."[17]

At heart and particularly in tandem, the Basil and Josephine stories offer a sensitive, selective history assaying the occasional minefield of American adolescence. Thumbing through them today, readers of a certain age might be reminded of Paul Goodman's classic 1960 study *Growing Up Absurd.* Both Fitzgerald and Goodman were, after all, concerned with rising postwar generations finding their places in a self-satisfied nation that hid its assorted anxieties behind a veil of affluence. The dust jacket of *Growing Up Absurd* encapsulates Goodman's view that the young's discontent

reflected a broader cultural angst: "We find frustrating contradictions between what we are told about America and what we discover as we live in
it, what we desire and what we may achieve, what we know our society
can be and what it actually is. Why, in a rich country, where everything is
possible and everything looks so easy, does everything turn out to be so
hard? Why does so much fail?"[18] Some thirty years earlier, Fitzgerald anticipated Goodman's censor in a memorable passage having to do with
Basil's disillusionment upon learning the truth about, broadly speaking,
America's faint interest in advancing heroic ambitions. Following Basil's
triumph of producing his own play, his surface euphoria quickly gives way
to an unsettling discovery, captured in a late-night conversation with his
mother: "He was almost the last to leave, mounting to the stage for a moment and looking around the deserted hall. His mother was waiting and
they strolled home together through the first cool night of the year. 'Well,
I thought it went very well indeed. Were you satisfied?' He didn't answer
for a moment. 'Weren't you satisfied with the way it went?' 'Yes.' He
turned his head away. 'What's the matter?' 'Nothing.' And then, 'Nobody
really cares, do they?' 'About what?' 'About anything.'"[19]

FIFTEEN

Penance

Why do I have to go backwards when everybody else who can goes on? Why does my husband and other people find that what was so satisfactory for them is not the thing for me. And if you do cure me what's going to happen to all the bitterness and unhappiness in my heart. It seems to me a sort of castration, but since I am powerless I suppose I will have to submit though I am neither young enough nor credulous enough to think that you can manufacture out of nothing something to replace the song I had.

Zelda Fitzgerald to Dr. Oscar Forel, 1930

Among Fitzgerald's admirers, the disordered marriage of Scott and Zelda raises a host of troubling questions. By far, the most delicate concern boils down to blame. Put plainly, to what extent did Fitzgerald's alcoholism and its attendant confusions, anxieties, and insecurities contribute to Zelda's declining health? Scott habitually deflected such accusations, elevating his wife's breakdown to a grand morality play on par with the collapse of the country's financial markets. Depression took on a dual meaning for Fitzgerald, whose *Ledger* entry above the calendar year September 1929–September 1930 read, "The Crash! Zelda + America."[1] Sensing history in the making and seeing himself on its front line, Scott interpreted his wife's hospitalization as part of a broader neurosis afflicting the New Woman. This idea, reading Zelda's and his private misfortunes as symptomatic of a larger cultural ailment, appealed to Fitzgerald's tragic sensibility and became an increasingly prominent feature in his writing.

Even under the best of circumstances, the Fitzgerald marriage typically encountered turbulence. Though attracted to Zelda's unconventionality, Scott resented her inability to provide a conventional home life. In time, they began to express their spousal frustrations by showing interest in others. Zelda's Mediterranean flirtation with Jozan is a case in point; so, too, is Scott's attention to the Hollywood starlet Lois Moran, whom he met in January 1927 while working on the United Artists project *Lipstick*. Scott took an immediate liking to the then-seventeen-year-old actress, whose youth, unaffectedness, and charm deeply impressed him. Immortalized as Rosemary Hoyt in *Tender Is the Night*, Moran was embraced by Fitzgerald as a kindred artistic spirit who shared his appreciation for professionalism and getting the work out. He favorably contrasted her discipline with Zelda's "dabbling" in various arts but mastering none. Humiliated by Scott's fawning behavior—"you . . . engaged in flagrantly sentimental relations with a child"—Zelda burned her clothes in the bathtub of their Hollywood hotel room and shortly thereafter, on their return journey home, threw out of a train window the expensive platinum watch that Scott had given to her as an engagement present.[2]

A few months later, Moran, with mother in tow, briefly reentered the couple's lives. The Fitzgeralds were now living at Ellerslie, and during a house party there, Scott conspicuously "courted" the young actress, again undermining Zelda's self-esteem. In response, she determined to make a name for herself. Having studied dance in her teens, she now began commuting to Philadelphia for ballet lessons. Zelda appeared to have accepted Scott's indictment of her "dabbling" and sought to excel in an artistic endeavor like her "rival," though this new course proved to be the source of fresh tensions. For along with ballet, she began to write, and this kindled a latent and fierce competitiveness in the Fitzgeralds' relationship that remained until she agreed, after much bullying, to retreat from Scott's creative terrain.

In all, Zelda published one novel, nearly a dozen stories, and about an equal number of articles. That magazines insisted on using either Fitzgerald's name or a shared byline on her stories attests to the extent to which Scott's authorship cast a shadow over her own work. One of her stories, "A Millionaire's Girl" (1930), earned $4,000 from the *Saturday*

Evening Post—Scott's going rate, but that sum for Zelda was contingent on the condition that her name did not appear in the magazine. After selling the piece, Fitzgerald's agent, Harold Ober, acknowledged the shaky ethics of the appropriation: "I really felt a little guilty about dropping Zelda's name from that story."[3]

As Zelda tried to develop professionally as an author, she faced another and more daunting obstacle than Scott's disapproval: the mental illness that ran in her family and that she inherited. Zelda's maternal grandmother, an aunt, and her brother were all suicides; one sister, Marjorie, suffered from anxiety, while her father experienced bouts of severe depression. Zelda's first breakdown occurred in April 1930 while the Fitzgeralds were in Europe. It followed a period of intense dedication to ballet under the tutelage of Lubov Egorova, a Russian prima ballerina. Briefly taken to Malmaison Hospital, west of Paris, and then to Valmont Clinic near Montreaux, Switzerland, Zelda subsequently received some fifteen months of treatment at the elegant Les Rives des Prangins in Nyon, north of Geneva. Patients were called "guests," and with music and billiard rooms, tennis courts, a riding stable, and bathing beach, Prangins affected the look of an exclusive resort.

Zelda's second collapse occurred in America in February 1932, three months after her father's death. Scottie, visiting her mother at the Henry Phipps Psychiatric Clinic of Johns Hopkins University Hospital, recalled this dark period with a dolorous candor: "We went to see her often. It was a strain, and so sad . . . because she began to look different—as most people with mental illness do. I suppose you are under such a strain that you begin to show the intense fatigue in your face. Mother was not pretty anymore. Sometimes she would seem very normal, but her mind would drift away into some world of her own and we'd all feel the tension." Discharged after four months, Zelda suffered a third breakdown in January 1934 and remained, excepting brief holidays, institutionalized until April 1940. These years were spent mainly at Sheppard Pratt Hospital in Towson, Maryland, and at Highland Hospital in Asheville, North Carolina. Working in Hollywood since July 1937, Fitzgerald returned east on a handful of occasions to visit Zelda. These were typically difficult encounters—as Scott wrote to Zelda's physician Dr. Robert Carroll in the late winter of 1938, "There is simply too much of the past between us."[4] The last time the couple saw each other, a disastrous April 1939 trip to Cuba, a soused Scott received a street beating for trying to stop a cockfight in Havana. Returning to America with Zelda, he registered at the Algonquin Hotel and continued drinking before finally checking himself into Doctors Hospital to dry out. Left alone, Zelda contacted her sister and brother-in-law in Larchmont, and they helped her return to Asheville.

The unorthodox working of Zelda's mind invited the memoirish commentary of numerous acquaintances, though in light of the circulation of stories about Scott's "mad" wife, these should be approached carefully. The silent-screen star Lillian Gish remembered Zelda as something of a careless child, innocently unconcerned with her actions: "[She] could do outlandish things—say anything. It was never offensive when Zelda did it, as you felt she couldn't help it, and was not doing it for effect." The novelist John Dos Passos spent a day with the Fitzgeralds at a carnival and later recalled a few fitful moments sitting next to Zelda on a wobbly Ferris wheel: "The gulf that opened between Zelda and me . . . was something I couldn't explain. It was only looking back at it years later that it occurred to me that, even the first day we knew each other, I had come up against that basic fissure in her mental processes that was to have such tragic consequences." And the English writer Rebecca West offered an uncharitable appraisal of Zelda following their 1923 introduction at Great Neck:

> I knew Zelda was very clever but from the first moment I saw her I knew she was mad. There was this smooth, shining hair and the carefully chosen wild-twenties dress. . . . There was this large, craggy face—a handsome face—but when one got the after-image it always showed a desolate country without frontiers. It is not quite easy to get on good terms with a man if you think his wife whom he is very fond of is mad as a hatter. And I remember once Scott Fitzgerald saying something about Zelda having done something odd, and I had to check the words on my lips, "But surely you realize she's insane?"[5]

Exactly what Fitzgerald realized—and when—are matters of conjecture. His letters suggest that not until the late 1920s, with Zelda's intense devotion to ballet and to Madame Egorova, did he show concern. He more typically regarded Zelda as a distinct, impulsive, and unstructured personality—qualities he found by turns charming and irritating. Her compositional verve delighted his imagination, and as noted earlier, fragments of it found their way into his work. Edmund Wilson exhibited a similar appreciation when he wrote of Zelda, "She talked with so spontaneous a color and wit—almost exactly in the way she wrote—that I very soon ceased to be troubled by the fact that the conversation was in the nature of a 'free association' of ideas and one could never follow up anything."[6]

Zelda's family was decidedly less charmed by her postmarital exhibitions of "free association," believing them by-products of a destructive lifestyle. This allowed the Sayres to blame Scott for her hospitalization. "I would almost rather she die now than escape only to go back to the mad world you and she have created for yourselves," Rosalind Sayre Smith wrote Fitzgerald shortly after her sister's spring 1930 collapse. In a subsequent communication, she quizzed Scott on the external stimuli ("unhappy incidents") that she believed germane to Zelda's condition. Had he gotten interested in another girl? Enough to make Zelda "seriously annoyed"? Scottie Fitzgerald accepted a variation of this argument, writing in 1950 to her father's biographer Arthur Mizener, "Daddy knew he hadn't *caused* it, and that no events after the age of twelve could have possibly *caused* it, but he felt a sense of guilt at having led exactly the wrong kind of life for a person with such a tendency."[7]

Fitzgerald's "guilt" appears to have been one of the underlying assumptions in his story "Two Wrongs," published in the 18 January 1930 *Saturday Evening Post*. In it, he wrestles with the two great factors then confronting him—his increasing reliance on alcohol and Zelda's extraordinary commitment to ballet. Written in Paris in the autumn of 1929, the story preceded Zelda's breakdown by just a few months. "Two Wrongs" involves a successful young theater producer who marries a beautiful southern girl—and then allows his drinking to damage their life together. Bill McChesney is of Irish background, Harvard educated, popular, good-looking, and talented. He also drinks too much and saves too little.

Emmy Pinkard dreams of dancing in the Russian ballet one day, but she's fiercely loyal to Bill and provides him with a good home.

This scenario begins to change some three years into the couple's marriage. Too many highballs have sapped Bill's creative resources, and after two flops in New York, he and Emmy move to London, where he can recycle his old stuff. Impressed by "a lot of dukes," he spends his evenings out, carries on an affair with one Lady Sybil Combrinck, and more generally neglects his wife. This all catches up with Bill when, after a particularly boozy night on the town, he staggers home to discover that a pregnant Emmy has been taken to the hospital, where she has delivered a stillborn child. "This time she hated him," Fitzgerald writes. "She could feel him slipping out of her heart, feel the space he left, and all at once he was gone."[8]

Recovered, Emmy revives her old adolescent dream of becoming a ballerina, and back in New York, she practices hours each day. Fitzgerald writes, perhaps thinking of Zelda's sudden dedication, that dancing "became the realest part of her life." This causes Bill to reflect on his own circumstances. Accustomed to being in control of any situation, he unexpectedly realizes that he now envies Emmy's passion and commitment. His work, by contrast, has come to a standstill, money is more difficult to come by, and he grows sensitive to whispers that drinking has taken his talent. One can only suppose the degree to which autobiography motivated Fitzgerald to write of Bill, "he had begun to pay a price for his irregular life."[9]

The plot turns on Bill's bad health. Like Scott, Bill has a tubercular condition, and when it becomes active, he has to go to Denver. At the same time, Emmy's hard work has paid off handsomely, and she is invited to debut abroad. The couple's futures suddenly at odds, both try to take the high road. Bill insists that Emmy not give up her dream, while Emmy just as firmly promises to stay with her sick husband. In the end, the first wrong—Bill's neglect of Emmy—leads to the second: her decision, after much back-and-forth, not to go to Denver. "He knew then that he had lost her," Fitzgerald writes of Bill, now alone on his westbound train. "He realized perfectly that he had brought all this on himself and that there was some law of compensation involved."[10]

Despite the deep sense of atonement that runs through "Two Wrongs," the story comes down harder on Emmy than it does on Bill. True, Bill has wronged her in London, but his drinking is partly to blame; Emmy has no such excuse for leaving a sick husband, and this is an important difference between Emmy and Zelda. Though Emmy is filled with an "incessant idea . . . to dance," she does not suffer from mental illness. With a clear eye, she coldly lets Bill go. Fitzgerald further tips the scales in Bill's favor—and gives run, perhaps, to his resentment that Zelda's expensive ballet lessons played a part in his inability to set money aside to write—by making Emmy dependent on Bill's earnings. A grateful Emmy apologizes to Bill when she tells him, "You work so hard, and here I've been spending two hundred dollars a week for just my dancing lessons alone—more than I'll be able to earn for years."[11]

When read through the lens of the Fitzgeralds' marriage, "Two Wrongs" is a story of mixed meanings. There is an attractive objective quality to the piece that gives it both valor and pathos, as when Bill realizes "that he had brought all this on himself." But this evenhandedness is undermined to an extent by Fitzgerald's contrasting instinct to make Bill an object of pity. For, even though the story suggests that both Bill and Emmy are to blame for their situation, only she possesses the ability to make things right—and this she refuses to do.

Interestingly, Emmy's contempt for Bill begins the night she gives birth to their stillborn baby. According to Sara Mayfield, a longtime friend of Zelda's who published a book on the Fitzgeralds in the early 1970s, Zelda terminated three pregnancies while married to Scott. Zelda's feelings about these abortions can only be guessed, though she definitely resisted on one occasion, when, a month before their marriage, Fitzgerald brought her pills to induce menstruation:

I wanted to for your sake, because I know what a mess I'm making and how inconvenient it's all going to be—but I simply *can't* and *won't* take those awful pills—so I've thrown them away. I'd rather take carbolic acid. You see, as long as I feel that I had the right, I don't much mind what happens—and besides, I'd rather have a *whole family* than sacrifice my self-respect. They just seem to place everything on the wrong basis—and

I'd feel like a damned whore if I took even one, so you'll try to understand, please Scott—and do what you think best—but don't do *anything* till we *know* because God—or something—has always made things right, and maybe this will be.[12]

In this case, it was "right," though a number of unwanted pregnancies followed. After Zelda's first collapse, her sister Rosalind wrote Fitzgerald, "do you think Zelda's abortions could have had anything to do with her illness?"[13]

In fact, Fitzgerald thought it far more likely that Zelda's obsessive dedication to dance in her approaching middle age brought on her sickness. He seemed unable to recognize or accept that ballet had become for Zelda both a symbol of personal independence and a means by which she might win her husband's respect. He wrote, Moran acted, and what did Zelda have? Consequently she attacked ballet with an intensity that he believed bordered on desperation. In June 1930, Fitzgerald posed a series of questions to Madame Egorova, obviously hoping her responses might convince Zelda, now in the hospital, to give up her danseuse dreams. "Are there things such as balance, etc. that she will never achieve because of her age and because she started too late?" he asked. "Have you ever thought that, lately, Zelda was working too much for someone her age?" Egorova's reply credited Zelda with a talent unseen by Scott: "I am quite certain that in the [Leonide] Massine ballets, without being the star, Zelda could perform with success some important roles. . . . She could possibly become a good dancer." When asked if Zelda could rise to the top of her field, however, Egorova acknowledged, "Zelda will not be able to become a first-class dancer; she started too late to succeed in it." These words, and Scott's siege on Zelda's self-confidence, had both intended and unintended consequences. Zelda was embarrassed by what she called the "disgraceful mess" of her hospitalization and indicated to Scott in an August letter that she would no longer dance. Rather, she looked forward to a quiet marital life in their own home with neighbor children to play with Scottie, where "there will be Sundays and Mondays again which are different from each other." Importantly, she believed Scott was also a casualty of their chaotic marriage, writing pointedly to him about a future, different environment, "my life won't be up the back-stairs of music halls, and yours won't keep trailing down the gutters of Paris."[14] But in wanting a more quiet life, Zelda by no means wished to accept a creatively barren life. No longer able to practice ballet, she moved decisively to write a novel, to occupy, that is, the same artistic space as her husband.

While in treatment at Phipps Clinic during the late winter and early spring of 1932, Zelda wrote *Save Me the Waltz*. "I am proud of my novel," she informed Scott, "but I can hardly restrain myself enough to get it written. You will like it—It is distinctly École Fitzgerald, though more ecstatic than yours—Perhaps too much so."[15] Actually, at the time she wrote to Scott, Zelda had already sent what she considered a more or less finished draft to Max Perkins at Scribner. The work is autobiographical and, despite being subsequently and heavily edited by Fitzgerald, used episodes from the Fitzgeralds' marriage that Scott, as the greater and more bankable writer, considered his. Counseled to quit ballet, separated from her husband and daughter, grieving over the recent death of her father, and depressed with the austere and isolating surroundings at Phipps, Zelda sought in *Save Me the Waltz* to retrace the past in order to understand her current crisis. More generally, the novel portrayed its author's search for self-expression and attempted to satisfy Zelda's obviously large need for creative achievement.

Save Me the Waltz records the marriage of the southern belle Alabama Beggs (Zelda) and her artist beau, David Knight (Fitzgerald). The main outline of the Fitzgerald story—the early success, the Riviera interlude, and the unstable nature of their relationship—is prominently featured. The book captures the free association of thought that was so marked, and remarked on, in Zelda's conversation, which on the page at times brilliantly conveys a mood or emotion. Too often, however, her lush, elaborate wordplay threatens to obscure the plot itself, leaving readers to contend with a coil of fantastic images, sounds, and circumstances. A New England summer "hurls its thesis and bursts against our dignity explosively as the back of a Japanese kimono"; a young man's hair "is like nacre cornucopias"; and Americans in Paris "suspended themselves on costly eccentricities like Saturday's servants on a broken Ferris wheel and made so many readjustments that a constant addenda went on about them like the clang of a Potin cash register."[16] In one passage, Alabama takes in a surreal New York street scene whose twilight tone is suggested by the melodic music of the Broadway composer Vincent Youmans:

> Through the gloom, the whole world went to tea. Girls in short amor‐ phous capes and long flowing skirts and hats like straw bathtubs waited for taxis in front of the Plaza Grill; girls in long satin coats and colored shoes and hats like straw manhole covers tapped the tune of a cataract on the dance floors of the Lorraine and the St. Regis. Under the somber ironic parrots of the Biltmore a halo of golden bobs disintegrated into black lace and shoulder bouquets between the pale hours of tea and dinner that sealed the princely windows; the clank of lank contempora‐ neous silhouettes drowned the clatter of teacups at the Ritz.[17]

Fitzgerald's more candid estimations of Zelda's writing acknowledged both its manifest strengths—he called her "a great original in her way, with perhaps a more intense flame at its highest than I ever had"—and obvious limitations: "She isn't a 'natural story-teller' . . . and unless a story comes to her fully developed and crying to be told she's liable to flounder around rather unsuccessfully among problems of construction."[18] He believed that, as with dancing, Zelda came to writing too late, and he fa‐ vorably contrasted his youthful apprenticeship—teenage playwright at St. Paul, contributor to various Princeton publications, sufferer of count‐ less rejections—with her, by his reckoning, sudden and casual interest in serious composition.

If *Save Me the Waltz* is something less than an artistic success, it earns a certain distinction as a Sayre bildungsroman filled with personal reflec‐ tions, assessments, and suspicions. Zelda drew on her prenuptial value among southern beaux and called Alabama a "thoroughbred!"—meaning, as stated by Alabama, "that I never let them down on the dramatic pos‐ sibilities of a scene—I give a damned good show." Zelda recalls in the novel her early days with Fitzgerald by poking at his inflated ego and failure to register her true worth. She writes that David belittles Alabama as "Miss Alabama Nobody" while talking constantly of his imminent fame. Zelda also writes of her attraction to Jozan (Jacques) and the differences between her Mediterranean lover and her romantic-minded if physically distant husband: "He looks like you," Alabama teases David, "except that he is full of the sun, whereas you are a moon person." Interestingly, she uses a similar corporeal description for both men. On meeting David, Alabama notices that "there seemed to be some heavenly support beneath his shoulder blades that lifted his feet from the ground in ecstatic suspension." And on being with Jacques: "He drew her body against him till she felt the blades of his bones carving her own." There is no description of Alabama's sexual relations with David (her "blond lieutenant"), although there is for Jacques (her "French aviator"): "He was bronze and smelled of the sand and sun; she felt him naked underneath the starched linen. She didn't think of David."[19]

Following the liaison with Jacques, Alabama searches fruitlessly for creative activity to bring independence to her life. Circling back to Madame Egorova's painful admission—"she started too late to succeed in it"—Zelda has Alabama face her own Russian Madame's sharp evaluation: "You are too old. It is a beautiful ballet. Why have you come to me so late?" By contrast, David's artistic ascent has been achieved, and this allows him to occupy the marital high ground; he works, while she merely plays. "He had earned his right to be critical," Zelda writes, but "Alabama felt that she had nothing to give to the world and no way to dispose of what she took away."[20]

Perhaps not so ironically, Zelda initially named her male lead Amory Blaine. Fitzgerald was not amused. Writing to Dr. Mildred Squires, a young resident at Phipps Clinic who had encouraged Zelda's work on the novel (and to whom it is dedicated), he complained that this direct reference to his work—and the rather dyspeptic depiction of Amory/David/Scott—made a mockery of his life, his writing, and his marriage:

> Do you realize that "Amory Blaine" was the name of the character in my first novel to which I attached my adventures and opinions, in effect my autobiography? Do you think that his turning up in a novel signed by my wife as a somewhat aenemic portrait painter with a few ideas lifted

from Clive Bell, Leger, etc. could pass unnoticed? In short it puts me in an absurd and Zelda in a rediculous position. . . . This mixture of fact and fiction is simply calculated to ruin us both, or what is left of us, and I can't let it stand. . . . My God, my books made her a legend and her single intention in this somewhat thin portrait is to make me a non-entity.[21]

Fitzgerald indicated elsewhere in the letter that although he loathed *Save Me the Waltz*'s treatment of his image and reputation, he regarded other autobiographical facets of the novel, including the Jozan affair, as properly belonging to Zelda. This attempt by Scott to neatly divide the couple's experiences introduced yet another complication into their marriage and culminated, after a desperate series of campaigns, in Zelda's acquiescing to Scott's wishes. In this first skirmish, Fitzgerald marked out his wife's artistic terrain: "her own material—her youth, her love for Josaune, her dancing, her observation of Americans in Paris, the fine passages about the death of her father—my critisisms of that will be simply impersonal and professional."[22]

And offer criticisms he did, going over the manuscript thoroughly before sending a revised version to Scribner. "Zelda's novel is now good, improved in every way," he wrote Perkins, whom he also advised to go light on any compliments he might wish to convey. Kind words, after all, would only encourage Zelda. "If you like it please *don't* wire her congratulations, and please keep whatever praise you may see fit to give *on the staid side*—I mean, *as you naturally would,* rather than yield to a tendency one has with invalids to be extra nice to cheer them up. . . . She is not twenty-one and she is not strong, and she must not try to follow the pattern of my trail which is of course blazed distinctly on her mind." Perkins agreed to publish the book, but he drew up a contract for *Save Me the Waltz* that linked Fitzgerald's financial debt to Scribner with his wife's royalty income from sales of the novel, effectively treating Zelda as a dependent: "it is further understood and agreed that one-half of said royalties shall be retained by said Publishers up to a total of Five Thousand Dollars ($5000), said royalties to be credited against the indebtedness of F. Scott Fitzgerald."[23] Scribner printed 3,010 copies and sold 1,392, and Zelda earned $120.73.

Reviewers tended to pan the book. Geoffrey Hellman's negative appraisal in the *Saturday Review of Literature*—denouncing *Save Me the Waltz*'s "steady stream of strained metaphor" and Zelda's "general inability to create full-bodied figures"—stands as something of a representative evaluation. Ironically, Hellman also rejected as unrealistic the fundamental premise of the novel, Alabama's search for meaningful activity. He thought Zelda's protagonist had it all (i.e., spouse and child) and thus dismissed her ennui as "implausible": "The desperation which prompts Alabama to turn to ballet-dancing with a group of dingy, impoverished people in Paris is anything but convincing on the part of a healthy young woman . . . who has a husband whom she loves and a young daughter she adores. In short, Alabama is a poor vehicle for the neuroticism and dissatisfaction which she is suddenly called upon to exemplify." More positively, the *New York Sun*'s William McFee wrote of Zelda, "Here is a peculiar talent, and connoisseurs of style will have a wonderful time. . . . There is the promise of a new and vigorous personality in fiction."[24]

Years later, with Fitzgerald's postmortem reputation on the rise, a fresh evaluation of Zelda's work followed. Along the way, the Scribner editor Donald Hutter offered a politely negative appraisal of *Save Me the Waltz,* in the process shedding light on why a Zelda literary revival never occurred. In a 1960 letter to one researcher, Hutter wrote, "In the course of these reissues and new editions [of Fitzgerald's books] we have considered including SAVE ME THE WALTZ. . . . [One] way to publish it again would be on the basis of its intrinsic qualities, but there the book doesn't seem to us to be quite good enough. It has severe faults . . . and is in many ways badly dated." In 1991, however, Scribner did release *Zelda Fitzgerald: The Collected Writings,* which included *Save Me the Waltz.* On balance, the evaluation of the Fitzgerald scholar Ruth Prigozy seems sound: "It is . . . accurate to state that there are passages of brilliant writing in her stories and her novel, but that she is finally a highly gifted amateur who would not have received the recognition now accorded her had she not first been married to F. Scott Fitzgerald."[25]

Zelda's breakdowns put Fitzgerald on the defensive, and he sought to control how others understood her illness much as he had taken control of *Save Me the Waltz*. A volatile mix of compassion and resentment, affection and frustration colored his feelings for Zelda from this point onward. To their mutual friend Sara Murphy, he suggested that Zelda's "deficient" emotional equipment—perhaps the result of a spoiled upbringing—had doomed her from the beginning. "In an odd way . . . she was always my child, . . . my child in a sense that Scottie isn't, because I've brought Scottie up hard as nails. . . . Outside of the realm of what you called Zelda's 'terribly dangerous secret thoughts' I was her great reality, often the only liaison agent who could make the world tangible to her."[26]

Shortly after Zelda's first hospitalization, in the spring of 1930, Scott began to engage her physician, Dr. Oscar Forel, in a protracted correspondence. He agonized over Zelda's health and wished to provide information that might aid in her treatment, though the letters often took a self-justifying turn, and whether intentionally or not, he frequently denigrated his wife. When informed that his drinking may have aggravated Zelda's condition, he fought back with a combination of selective memory and self-justification, leading to the impression that she, not he, abused alcohol. "The second time I encountered my wife she was, at the age of eighteen so intoxicated on a semi-public dance floor as to be a subject of comment," he appealed to Forel. "During the first seven years of our marriage it was she who wanted to drink while I worked. . . . I am even willing to give up wine for a certain time. But to take any pledges to give up wine forever—that would be an admission to her and her family that I accepted full blame for this catastrophe."[27]

Throughout 1930, Fitzgerald immersed himself in medical literature and began to pester Forel with amateur diagnoses of Zelda's condition. He loathed when readers wrote to him directly offering suggestions for improving a particular book or story yet seemed unaware of the irony in his now playing doctor. He possessed a natural tendency toward overbearance, which at this moment asserted itself. "After this afternoon I am all the more interested in my own theory," he wrote Forel, several months into Zelda's stay at the Prangins clinic. "I hope you will be patient about this letter. A first year medical student could phrase it better than I, who am not sure what a nerve or a gland looks like. But despite my terminological ignorance I think you'll see I'm really not just guessing." Fitzgerald proceeded to speculate on the causes for Zelda's "homosexual" behavior and recent outbreak of eczema. He then drew up a calendar of her "irrational acts" in an attempt to chart the origins of these afflictions before offering his "conclusions," which included "renewal of full physical relations with husband, a thing to be enormously aided by an actual timing of the visits to the periods just before and after menstruation, and avoiding visits in the middle of such times or in the exact centre of the interval."[28]

Aside from the question of Zelda's recovery, Fitzgerald's communications to Prangins emphasized the toll her condition was taking on his writing. Forel quickly grew familiar with Scott, referred to him in correspondence as "My Dear Friend," and seemed sympathetic to his concerns. This may have simply reflected Forel's genial approach to patrons, allowing a patient's well-paying husband to unburden himself. In their correspondence, however, Forel seemed at times to lean in Scott's direction, seeing the point of Zelda's institutionalization as perhaps beneficial for both spouses. Not long after Zelda's second breakdown, Forel suggested her return to Prangins in words that seem calculated to soothe Scott's professional anxieties. "I perfectly understand that you *must* carry on in the best possible conditions. If you are perpetually hampered by the worries that your wife creates for you, the great task of your life will never be completed—and the contrary is what your wife wishes: That your artistic realizations should be brought to the point of perfection. Why would she not accept, on that very ground, to stay in a clinic? I am practically certain that she will immediately catch the point—and go."[29]

Two years later, with "the great task of [Fitzgerald's] life" furthered by the publication of *Tender Is the Night,* he believed its insights illuminated Zelda's case. "I am not sure whether or not I sent you a copy of my book," he wrote her then physician, Dr. Clarence Slocum, of Craig House in Beacon, New York, "with what indirect light it may throw on my wife's problem." Presumably Fitzgerald referred to *Tender*'s inclusion of Zelda's eczema, samples of her letters, and sketches of her symptoms. Yet the book's broader message—the disintegration of one individual before the growing strength of another—lingered over his own insecurities. Prior to *Tender*'s appearance, he had complained to Dr. Thomas Rennie, yet another of Zelda's caregivers, of his frustration at producing hack work in order that his institutionalized wife might therapeutically amuse herself in the arts. "Now for the last five years," he wrote Rennie, "she has come to regard me as the work horse and herself as the artist—the producer of the finer things such as painting, uncommercial literature, ballet, etc., such as I have not been able to mix with the damn Post story writing." He referred in a number of letters to Zelda as "the patient" or "my invalid" yet frequently imagined himself and her conjoined in a misery whose outcome remained shrouded in doubt. "The situation," he ominously reported to Rennie, "has reduced itself in my mind to a rather clear-cut struggle of egos between Zelda and myself."[30]

This "struggle" both predated and survived Zelda's hospitalization. At its worst, not even personal safety was spared. One night on the Riviera, Zelda dared Scott to follow her in a succession of risky high dives into the sea; another time, while dining out with the Murphys, she reacted to the dancer Isadora Duncan's quite obvious come-ons to Scott by throwing herself down a flight of stone steps, from which she emerged cut and bleeding. With the publication of *Save Me the Waltz*, Zelda looked now to even at least one score. A newspaper headline pasted into her scrapbook suggests a desire to fulfill a long-standing fantasy: "Mrs. Fitzgerald's First Novel Places Her on Scott's Level."[31]

But if Fitzgerald interpreted his wife's "obsession" with art as symptomatic of a broader marital cold war, one might just as easily say that dance and writing offered her a sense of security after years of personal and marital drift. The Fitzgeralds' brief but destructive 1927 stay in Hollywood provides some insight into Zelda's shame. Suddenly thrown into this intensely competitive colony of stars, writers, and directors, she suffered a striking loss of confidence. "Everybody here is very clever and can nearly all dance and sing and play and I feel very stupid," she perhaps incautiously wrote to a then five-year-old Scottie. To her daughter's nanny, she admitted, "We have had a very interesting time but I *hate* this country and keep longing to be home."[32] It was a few weeks after returning east that Zelda threw herself into ballet. In search of constructive activity, alarmed by Scott's drinking, and troubled by the absence of fraternal and sexual intimacy, she took flight to the arts, first dance and then, ultimately and disastrously, into his literary métier.

Save Me the Waltz's October 1932 publication encouraged Zelda to write a follow-up, and that decision nearly destroyed her marriage. Like Scott, who was finishing *Tender Is the Night,* she planned to write a novel about mental illness. He was furious and complained to Dr. Rennie:

> Whole fragments of my scenes and cadences come out in her work, which she admits. One is flattered—it is only when she aims to use the materials of our common life, the only fact material that I have (heaven knows there's no possible harm in using her own youth, her dancing, etc.) that she becomes a danger to my life and to us. She knows that my novel is almost entirely concerned with the Riviera and the two years we spent there, and I have continually asked her to keep away from it and she agrees in theory, yet . . . her agitation to begin another novel increases in intensity—I know there will be whole sections of it that are simply muddy transcriptions of things in my current novel—things we both observed and have a right to, but that under the present circumstances I have all rights to.[33]

For several months, the "rights to" battle consumed the Fitzgeralds. Both, it seems fair to say, faced enormous pressures. For Zelda, writing now occupied the place of ballet; she found composition to be a kind of medicine in the great struggle to preserve both her sanity and her self-worth. More, it perhaps promised, in her mind, to once and for all obliterate Scott's suspicion that she lacked substance.

Fitzgerald understood this motivation of Zelda's and even took some responsibility for running down her ego. Still, his strongest instinct was to protect his writing. His reasoning cut in two directions: First, he, Zelda, and Scottie lived off *his* publications, and the impending *Tender Is the Night* represented their best chance for future solvency. Second, he believed unreservedly in his talent, considered it to be the "purest" part of himself, and refused now to compromise it in any way. These concerns he expressed in an April 1933 letter to Dr. Adolf Meyer, director of the Phipps Clinic:

> [Zelda's] inferiority complex [is] caused by a lack of adaptation to the fact that she is working under a greenhouse which is my money and my name and my love. This is my fault—years ago I reproached her for doing nothing and she never got over it. So she is mixed up—she is willing to use the greenhouse to protect her in every way, to nourish every sprout of talent and to exhibit it—and at the same time she feels no responsibility about the greenhouse and feels that she can reach up and knock a piece of glass out of the roof at any moment, yet she is shrewd to cringe when I open the door of the greenhouse and tell her to behave or go.[34]

The following month, Zelda and Scott sat down with Dr. Rennie and a stenographer at the couple's "La Paix" residence outside Baltimore to discuss their "rights to" dispute. It proved to be a long afternoon filled with anger, mistrust, and mutual accusations. Fitzgerald remained committed to Zelda's deference to him and thus the scuttling of her novel. He opened the meeting on a pugilistic note—"I am paid for an enormous fight and struggle that I can carry on"—that anticipated the bruising course of their conversation. From there, Scott proceeded to make his case at Zelda's expense:

> I began that struggle early. That struggle began when I was a boy. When Zelda was seventeen she was just boy-crazy. When I was seventeen I was writing Princeton Triangle Club shows. The whole equipment of my life is to be a novelist. And that is attained with tremendous struggle, that is attained with a tremendous sacrifice which you make to lead in any profession. It was done because I was equipped for it. I was equipped for it as a little boy. I began at age ten when I wrote my first story. My whole life is a professional line towards that. . . . I say I am a different sort of person than Zelda, that my equippment for being a writer, for being an artist, is a different equippment from hers. Her theory is that anything is possible, and that a girl has just got to get along, and so she has the right, therefore, to destroy me completely in order to satisfy herself.[35]

Zelda interjected to defend herself—"That is completely unfair. . . . I have considered you first in everything I have tried to do in my life"—but

Fitzgerald claimed the artistic high ground by contrasting his talent and literary vision with hers. "Now, why did she want to be a novelist?" he asked Dr. Rennie. "Did she have anything to say? No, she has not anything to say. She has certain experiences to report but she has nothing essentially to say. To have something to say is a question of sleepless nights and worry and endless ratiocination of a subject, and the endless trying to dig out the essential truth, the essential justice."[36]

As the proceedings continued, Fitzgerald inevitably drew blood. Zelda's 1924 "affair," he insisted, justified his own. "She went around and flirted with a naval officer, a French naval officer. She did the thing again and again. So I thought I will have some fun, and I began to have some. . . . I got interested in a girl out there [Moran in Hollywood] because the girl seemed to me to be more honest and direct than Zelda." And for a man to whom youth mattered much, Moran had that, too. When Zelda turned twenty-five, Fitzgerald cruelly continued, "she ceased to have that special, that fresh bloom of life." Becoming increasingly emotional, he proceeded to denounce *Save Me the Waltz*: "a dirty, backsided attack on me"; to belittle Zelda's creative efforts: "you are a third-rate writer and a third-rate ballet dancer"; and to inflate his own: "I am a professional writer with a huge following. I am the highest paid short story writer in the world. I have at various times dominated." At this point, Zelda cut in: "it seems to me you are making a rather violent attack on a third-rate talent then."[37]

There followed from Fitzgerald an even broader assault on his wife's self-esteem. "Why do you think you were in the Russian Ballet?" he taunted her. "Why do you think that the Johns Hopkins Clinic got us? . . . It was on my back." And forgetting his occasional rummaging through Zelda's diaries and letters for piquant items to garnish his writing, he accused her, "You pick up the crumbs I drop at the dinner table and stick them into your books." Returning to the issue of whether Zelda could continue her novel, Scott offered no compromise. "It has got," he insisted, "to be an unconditional surrender on her part." Utterly defeated on this front, Zelda at least wanted to make clear for the record her own view of their years together, though even here she met objection. "What is our marriage anyway?" she asked. "It has been nothing but a long battle ever since I can remember." Fitzgerald refused to let this stand: "I don't know about that. We were about the most envied couple in about 1921, in America." "I guess so," Zelda countered. "We were awfully good showmen." Scott gave no ground: "we were awfully happy."[38]

The intensity of Fitzgerald's attack easily eclipsed, at least for that day, the focus on Zelda. So obviously exposed were Scott's anxieties that H. L. Mencken, a sometime dinner companion during this difficult period, took for granted the unsoundness of Scott's mind. A March 1933 entry in his diary reads in part, "Last night Sara [Haardt, Mencken's wife and a Montgomery acquaintance of Zelda's] and I dined with F. Scott Fitzgerald and his wife, Zelda. It was a somewhat weird evening. . . . The fact that Zelda is somewhat abnormal is instantly evident. She occupies herself largely in painting, and her paintings are full of grotesque exaggerations and fantastic ideas. Scott himself also begins to show signs of a disordered mind. . . . Considering his life during the past few years it is no wonder that he has begun to break up."[39]

It was also at this time that Dr. Meyer referred to Fitzgerald as "a potential but unwilling patient." Fitzgerald was sensitive about both his drinking and his mental state and feared that treatment for either might diminish his artistic skill by turning him from an essentially "feeling" personality into a fundamentally "analytical" personality. He accepted hard spirits as the due of an Irish novelist and once explained to a Baltimore neighbor that many great writers were alcoholics. In his view, getting tight served as a necessary precondition to composition. In the early days of Zelda's institutionalization, he had staked out his position on the subject: "Give up strong drink permanently I will" (though in fact he did not). "Bind myself to forswear wine forever I cannot. My vision of the world at its brightest is such that life without the use of its amenities is impossible."[40] Fitzgerald subsequently checked into Johns Hopkins on eight separate occasions for water cures.

Scott was no more interested in discussing his sexuality than he was in talking about his alcoholism. While hospitalized, Zelda had complained of his waning interest in her. This protest may have been linked to an episode a few years earlier when Fitzgerald returned home after a drunken evening carousing with Hemingway. Before passing out, he said, "no more baby," which Zelda inferred to mean that the two men were having an affair. At Prangins, she wrote to Scott about that period in their lives, telling him, "You did not want me. Twice you left my bed saying 'I can't. Don't you understand'—I didn't." The sting of these accusations might be measured in Fitzgerald's insistence to Zelda, "The nearest I ever came to leaving you was when you told me you thot I was a fairy in the Rue Palatine."[41]

Scott routinely deflected questions about his sexuality and drinking, believing that neither Zelda nor her physicians were able to appreciate the true heart of the matter: his considerable literary skills. Immersed in his craft and desperate to produce a lasting follow-up to *Gatsby,* he lost perspective, failing to understand just how enmeshed the issues of Zelda's health and his writing had become. Neither could he grasp that nearly everyone around him considered her illness, not his publishing, the primary fact. He complained in 1934 of Dr. Meyer, "He could never seem to appreciate that my writing was more important than [Zelda's] by a large margin because of the years of preparation for it, and the professional experience, and because my writing kept the mare going, while Zelda's belongs to the luxury trade. In other words, he encouraged the damn women's desire to express herself as if she hadn't broken down on that point twice before." In the end, he remembered Meyer less as Zelda's physician then as his nemesis: "He never really *believed* that I worked very hard, had a serious reputation or made money."[42]

Fitzgerald was certain that his talents were under attack by amateurs and so demeaned Zelda's writing and defended his right to "his" material. He developed this point in a 1934 letter to Dr. Slocum in which he acknowledged Zelda's particular flair for "metaphor and simile" but disparaged what he considered her shallow efforts to create art:

> She can write in the sense that all non-professionals who have a gift for words can write. Somebody once said that every intelligent American thought that they could always sell a plot of land, make a good speech and write a play. Her equipment is better than that but it does boil down to the slang phrase that she can't take it. She can't stand criticism; she hasn't the patience to revise; she has no conception of how fast the world slips from under one's feet and her getting up sophomoric Arostotliana

in a few months cannot bridge the gaps in her education; nonetheless she can write. She writes a brilliant letter and has made marked successes in short character studies and has an extraordinary talent for metaphor and simile. Along that line, with the realism of having to write her stuff to sell she could be, say, a regular contributor to the *New Yorker* and such magazines as publish short pieces. . . . When fronted with the *fait accompli* [of a finished novel] she is impressed as any yokel, and as a yokel she clings to the idea that the thing has all been done with a beautiful intention rather than with a dirty, sweating, heart-breaking effort extending over a long period of time when enthusiasm and all the other flowers have wilted.[43]

Mistrusting the "fait accompli" of his wife's work, Fitzgerald contrasted his efforts to create art with Zelda's more limited possibilities as a commercial writer. He drew a line between these two forms of composition, much as he denigrated his own *Post* stories as literary fodder.

In the question of what came first to Fitzgerald, his marriage or his writing, perhaps it is enough to say that his loyalties remained divided and that despite tremendous difficulties, he stuck with Zelda and she with him. The 1930s brought to the couple severe financial strains, mental illness, and alcoholism but no divorce. Scott returned to Hollywood in the summer of 1937, by which time Zelda was receiving care at the Highland Hospital in Asheville, North Carolina. Their correspondence never faltered, and Fitzgerald came to see their union with the kind of retrospective melancholy characteristic of his better work. Sheilah Graham, his companion in these final years, speculated, "Scott to the end was more bound to Zelda—dependent on her just as he claimed that she was dependent on him—than he ever acknowledged to me. They had leaned against each other and both had fallen down." These words seem right as recognition of the couple's mutual frailties and ongoing fidelity, of a kind. In this sense, they remained opposites alike, or as Fitzgerald wrote to Zelda from a distant California, "Once we were one person and always it will be a little that way."[44]

SIXTEEN

Far from Home

How long are you staying in Europe?

F. Scott Fitzgerald, "One Trip Abroad," 1930

During the difficult period of Zelda's first breakdown, while the Fitzgeralds were living abroad for a second time (March 1929–September 1931), Scott came to believe that having cut himself off from the nourishment of his native soil, he had both morally and artistically lost sight of the American shore. In Paris and the Riviera, he encountered a well-oiled expatriate industry that provided all manner of drink and drugs to thousands of tourists in hundreds of fleshpots and fleecing points. No longer such a young man, he recognized the toxicity of these temptations and thought that in writing about them, he might exorcise their hold over him. Never before, not even in the sad summer days of 1919 after Zelda had closed out their engagement, had he paid such a high price for inspiration. A time of belt-tightening had arrived, and this meant reckoning with the fair years of drifting and dissipation just passed.

Fitzgerald's anxieties about the American expatriate experience need to be seen within the context of an already long and pedigreed trans-Atlantic argument about whether Europe or North America offered the better habitat for political, economic, social, and cultural development. In the eighteenth century, the French naturalist Georges Louis Leclerc, Comte de Buffon (1707–1788), raised the flag for Europe when he argued that the presumably inferior North American environment produced comparatively regressive species of plants, animals, and humans. In one volume of his *Histoire Naturelle* (1766), he claimed, "In America . . .

animated Nature is weaker, less active, and more circumscribed in the variety of her productions; for we perceive, from the enumeration of the American animals, that the number of species is not only fewer, but that, in general, all the animals are much smaller than those of the Old Continent." In the same text, he portrayed the continent's Indigenous peoples as backward and indolent: "His sensations are less acute; and yet he is more timid and cowardly. He has no vivacity, no activity of mind."[1] Buffon suggested that those who immigrated to America would in time decline as well, weakening in a climate that was inhospitable to human progress.

Buffon's theory of degeneracy naturally aroused skepticism among the so-called degenerates. There is a famous story in which Benjamin Franklin addressed the question at a dinner party in Passy, in what is today the sixteenth arrondissement of Paris. Thomas Jefferson was in attendance and reported that during the meal, one of Franklin's French guests, Abbé Raynal, "got on his favorite theory of the degeneracy of animals, and even of man, in America, and urged it with his usual eloquence." A playful Franklin quickly scanned the guests at the table and said, "Come, M[onsieur] l'Abbé, let us try this question by the fact before us. We are here one half Americans, and one half French, and it happens that the Americans have placed themselves at one side of the table, and our French friends on the other. Let both parties rise, and we will see on which side nature has degenerated." Both parties did rise and the Americans, as Franklin had anticipated, towered over the French—"the Abbé himself particularly," Jefferson smiled, "was a mere shrimp."[2]

Eager to more formally acquit America, Jefferson himself had entered the degeneracy debate in his only book, *Notes on the State of Virginia* (1785). As a child of the Enlightenment, he presumed to write a natural and cultural history of the Old Dominion along strictly scientific lines; his study is animated, however, by patriotic fervor: he uses nature—the plants and animals, rivers, mountains, and seaports—to promote the superiority of America. Here was a continent where Europeans came to build a better statecraft, a better economy, and a better world. To refute Buffon and his followers, Jefferson listed the abundance of plant and animal life in Virginia, and he collected fossils and skeletons of impressively large mammals such as cougars, elk, and moose, to name but a few. He hoped someday that a live woolly mammoth might be discovered in the unexplored reaches of the West. Turning Buffon on his head, he insisted that an unusually healthy environment in North America produced superior species in the air, on the land, and in the water. The Natives, he argued, mercifully lacked Europe's penchant for "too much law" and thus constituted a kind of original republican, "happier of themselves" for organizing in small governing societies. Going beyond issues related to political and administrative development, Jefferson offered up a lawyerly defense of the continent that boasted of the remarkable achievements made by a trinity of distinguished former colonials: "In war we have produced a Washington. . . . In physics we have produced a Franklin. . . . [And] we have supposed Mr. [David] Rittenhouse second to no astronomer living."[3] The future, in other words, belonged to America.

Jefferson's special pleading aside, the question of the New World's contribution to global civilization continued to attract attention. In one way or another, a number of notable public thinkers, writers, and statesmen, including Thomas Paine, Ralph Waldo Emerson, and Abraham Lincoln, took up the topic. They agreed on republican America's altogether salutary impact on a world that was too influenced by priest craft and divine-right kingships. Paine called "the cause of America . . . the cause of all mankind," while Emerson confidently announced in his "American Scholar" address, "Our day of dependence, our long apprenticeship to the learning of other lands, draws to a close." Lincoln described the Civil War as "a people's contest," by which he meant, "it is a struggle for maintaining in the world, that form, and substance of government, whose leading object is, to elevate the condition of men."[4] Combined, such lofty eighteenth- and nineteenth-century sentiments advanced the argument that America's democratic institutions had created a more "free" and self-governing civilization than any on earth.

One of the cardinal presumptions of American "exceptionalism" is that it would one day lead to the New World's ascendancy in a number of fields, including the arts. By the time of Fitzgerald's birth, however, in an age of extensive industrial development, this hope began to fade. Moving to the pulse of mass production, the United States came increasingly to be recognized as the land of Ford and Carnegie, with neither a

Shakespeare nor a Cervantes in sight. One school of thought presumed that if the peoples living in America had avoided Buffon's dystopic predictions of physical deterioration, they nevertheless had failed to rival Europe's cultural achievements. Brahmin critics such as Henry James, Isabella Stewart Gardner, Charles Eliot Norton, and Henry Adams thought too many of their compatriots provincial and materialistic. Adams once complained from London to his brother Charles Francis Adams Jr., "what we want, my dear boy, is a *school*. We want a national set of . . . men like ourselves or better, to start new influences not only in politics, but in literature, in law, in society, and throughout the whole social organism of the country. A national school of our own generation. And that is what America has no power to create."[5] James ruminated more extensively on the cultural "impoverishment" theme in his 1903 novel *The Ambassadors*. The novel follows Lambert Strether, an American sent to Paris by a Mrs. Newsome to retrieve her son, Chadwick (Chad), heir to the Newsome Mills in Wollett, Massachusetts. Mrs. Newsome wants Chad at home, in harness and safely married. But to Strether's surprise, he begins, while in Paris, to understand Chad's attraction to the city and comes to the conclusion that the young man is better off on the Continent. It has, in every meaningful respect, "improved" him. Chad has a lover—Madame de Vionnet—whom, due to her religion and social position, he will never be able to marry, and by not returning, he stands to lose a fortune. James suggests, however, that this high (by Yankee standards) price for Chad's permanent expatriation is worth every penny.

James lived outside London for much of his adult life, and Adams, an inveterate traveler, began in the late 1890s to spend half the year in Paris. Years before Fitzgerald set foot on the Continent, other writers—including Edith Wharton, Gertrude Stein, T. S. Eliot, and Ezra Pound—established themselves in England and Europe. Hemingway, John Dos Passos, and E. E. Cummings also arrived for vital if less lengthy immersions, serving in various American ambulance corps during the First World War. Cummings was the son of a Harvard professor who was later ordained minister of Boston's South Congregational Church; once he was freed from his native puritanism, he found Paris a revelation. He remembered with a special joy his first visit to the City of Light: "I participated in an actual marriage of material with immaterial things; I celebrated an immediate reconciling of spirit and flesh, forever and now, heaven and earth. Paris was for me precisely and complexly this homogeneous duality: This accepting transcendence; this living and dying more than death or life. Whereas—by the very act of becoming its improbably gigantic self—New York had reduced mankind to a tribe of pygmies, Paris (in each shape and gesture and avenue and cranny of her being) was continuously expressing the humanness of humanity."[6]

Fitzgerald, by contrast, approached the Continent with less edifying expectations. He came to regard "his" Europe—primarily Paris and the Riviera—as a land that catered to the baser tastes of its American visitors. His conservative perspective developed from two separate instincts. First, there was a chauvinistic side to his Americanness—he favorably compared the rich United States to a devastated post-Versailles Europe. To Fitzgerald, the Continent offered a Prohibition-free place to party, to stretch the dollar, and to take in the castles, cathedrals, statues, and cemeteries of glory gone by. And second, his sense of superiority began to wane the longer he remained on the Continent. There, Fitzgerald's behavior became less controlled and more erratic; Zelda's collapse must in some respects have confirmed his opinion that Europe had been a terrible influence all along. Perhaps the Murphys might manage to thrive in their colorful enclave by the sea (appropriately named Villa America), but not everyone was so lucky.

Though almost certainly unacquainted with Buffon's arguments on environment, Fitzgerald developed his own ideas on degeneracy. Americans were injured, Scott thought, but not by staying in America. Overseas, they tended to adopt superior and snobbish attitudes, socialized with other "drifters," and found themselves steered by the locals into a thicket of bars, casinos, and cabarets. Yet even as he critiqued this glistening floating world, he could not deny its real appeal. Such mixed emotions opened up an altogether fresh creative vein for Fitzgerald and resulted in a number of thematically unified stories tracing the temptations that Americans face in Europe. The most penetrating of them—"The

Swimmers," "One Trip Abroad," and "Babylon Revisited"—helped Scott to clarify his response to the past few years, a necessary reckoning that allowed him to write *Tender Is the Night*.

Though "The Swimmers" is of interest for its cross-cultural comparison, it is not a particularly strong story and may be accurately enough labeled as a marital melodrama. The protagonist, Henry Clay Marston, is an American banker working in Paris. He comes from several generations of Virginia gentlemen, and his name summons the memory of the venerable Kentucky senator Henry Clay (1777–1852). One might guess that Scott supplied Marston with the kind of Chesapeake family tree—a grandfather "freed his slaves in '58, fought from Manassas to Appomattox"—that he wished for himself. Henry met his French wife, Choupette, while stationed in Europe during the war; they have two sons, and he believes himself happily married until discovering Choupette's infidelity. The shock to his system brings about a collapse, and Henry spends several weeks in the hospital. While recuperating on the beach at Saint Jean de Luz, he meets an American girl who offers him a kind of independence—she will teach him how to swim.

For Henry, the girl (a strong suggestion of Lois Moran) quickly becomes a substitute for his native land. With Choupette's philandering standing in for a questionable European morality, the American embodies a freshness and liveliness that he has been missing. When he asks her why she swims, she answers simply, "To get clean."[7] The same impulse leads Henry back to America. Tired of living Choupette's life, which he considers fundamentally snobbish and trivial, he wishes now to live his own and to have his sons absorb a Marston pedigree of southern discretion and politeness. This is a mature decision on Henry's part. As a young, impressionable Doughboy, he uncritically accepts the notion of French superiority, but his marital crisis awakens him to the uncertainty of his situation abroad.

Now, three years later, Henry is living in Virginia with his family and confronts yet another marital crisis—this time Choupette has taken up with Charles Wiese, a parvenu or, as Fitzgerald writes, "a cross between carpetbagger and poor white." Henry is eager to give her a divorce, though both desire custody of their children; Choupette merely wants to keep up appearances, but Henry is deeply disturbed at the thought of his boys aping their mother's cynicism. At an impasse, he goes swimming to clear his head and to his surprise sees the girl he had met on the beach in France years earlier. She turns out to be a kind of female Henry—a Virginian from a good Eastern Shore family who also unsuccessfully married a European (a Spaniard). Soon after, Wiese proposes that he, Choupette, and Henry negotiate a settlement aboard his motorboat. As the three cruise in Hampton Roads half a mile from the shore, Wiese produces a purchased letter from Henry's French physician indicating Henry's post-breakdown unfitness to parent his children. He then crows in apparent victory, "Money is power. . . . It's money that harnesses the forces of nature." This passage both conjures up the white South's perspective of Reconstruction—the rich carpetbagger who can dominate the impoverished genteel southerner—and plays on the idea of money as an instrument of distortion. One is reminded in Wiese's pathetic belief that he can control nature of Braddock Washington's futile effort in "The Diamond as Big as the Ritz" to bribe God. Wiese's end is more or less the same. As if in mockery of his alleged omnipotence, his motorboat shuts off, and "the forces of nature" begin to slowly pull the craft out to sea. A frightened Choupette and Wiese beg Henry to swim to a distant lighthouse for help, which he will do for a price, the custody of his sons. Having that assurance in the form of a sealed confession, he dives into the water and finds it "warm and friendly."[8]

"The Swimmers" appeared in the 19 October 1929 *Saturday Evening Post*—just days, that is, before the market crash. That somber fact no doubt contributed to the less hopeful account of Americans in Europe portrayed in "One Trip Abroad," which *Post* readers perused almost exactly one year later. Its darkening mood anticipates *Tender Is the Night*, which it prefaced to the extent that Fitzgerald later refused to reproduce it in the aforementioned *Taps at Reveille,* his final collection of short stories. Written not long after Zelda's first breakdown, "One Trip Abroad" bore further the special emotional burden of its author's insecurities. If Henry Marston had come to embrace his American heritage and learned to put Europe in perspective, Nicole and Nelson Kelly, the young, attractive couple at the center of "One Trip Abroad," could claim no such mastery. The story is a selectively autobiographical account of the Fitzgeralds' experiences overseas. It opens with the recently wedded Kellys sightseeing in North Africa (a trip that Scott and Zelda had taken earlier in the year). There, the Mileses, a well-traveled, sophisticated, and snooty American couple, approach Nicole and Nelson. The Mileses are bored with themselves and their Euro-Mediterranean routine, and they sense a freshness in the Kellys that they hope to latch onto. The Mileses are, of course, a corruptive influence. The Kellys also see that day another young and attractive couple, much like themselves. Here Fitzgerald uses a double doppelgänger effect—if the Kellys are not careful, the Mileses are their future; the vitality of the other young couple seems invariably tied to their own.

Like so many of Fitzgerald's characters, Nicole and Nelson are unexpectedly but inevitably injured by wealth. Nelson has inherited a large sum, and the couple plans to stay in Europe—he to paint, she to sing. A rift between the newlyweds occurs early in the trip when the Mileses coax them to a café whose Berber girls dance "Oriental style"—in jewelry and little else. Nicole leaves, Nelson stays, and, Fitzgerald writes, "something was harmed." Over the next three years, they drift from Sorrento to Monte Carlo, count among their acquaintants a cloud of restless people like themselves, and drink too much. They also begin to incautiously fill their empty hours with flirtations and philandering, which deepens the breach in their relationship. Determined to pull themselves together, they leave the Riviera and head to Paris—armed with a list of people, bars, and nightclubs they will now avoid. "They did this not in snobbishness," Fitzgerald tells us, "but for self-preservation."[9]

With a fresh resolve, the Kellys return to their painting and singing, make more conservative friends, and decide to have a baby. But their well-intentioned resolution lacks depth and conviction. And here, Fitzgerald may well have been reflecting on his own scattered intentions. He might *want* to cut back on his drinking, he might *wish* to finish his novel, and he might *yearn* to use his American strength to fend off a cloying European dissipation, but these things never happened. Neither do they happen for the Kellys, who fall back into the same debilitating lifestyle. They take up with an impoverished Count ("an attractive relic of the Austrian Court") who couches his parasitic objectives in a fawning courtesy.[10] Staying with the Kellys, he plays on their pretensions with the promise of invitations to an exclusive canal-boat party. Having recently experienced complications in childbirth, Nicole is ordered by her physician to skip the celebration, but vanity prods her on. At the affair, the Kellys realize that it is nothing more than a gathering of the debauched. Nicole, taken ill, returns home to find that both her jewel box and the Count are missing.

"One Trip Abroad" concludes in Switzerland, perhaps appropriately so considering that Zelda was at that time a patient at Dr. Forel's clinic, Le Rives de Prangins, on Lake Geneva. "Switzerland is a country," the most famous line in the story goes, "where very few things begin, but many things end." There, the exhausted Kellys have traded in the casino and café tour for the sanitarium and rest-hotel circuit. And there they encounter once again the now-not-so-young couple that they had seen years before in North Africa. With their hardened faces, they look into the equally hardened faces of their suffering opposites only to recognize themselves. What went wrong? How could so much money, love, and confidence have so steadily eroded? Nicole makes the pointed observation that she and Nelson had been happy before coming to Europe and that their future salvation involved avoiding the drinking and distractions that had complicated their lives abroad. But this, she acknowledges, is easier said than done: "It's just that we don't understand what's the matter. . . . Why did we lose peace and love and health, one after the other? If we knew, if there was anybody to tell us, I believe we could try. I'd try so hard."[11]

A blue mood of regret hangs heavily over "One Trip Abroad," whose melancholic tone carried Fitzgerald into the last weeks of a difficult 1930, when, in December, he wrote what many people believe to be his best short story, "Babylon Revisited." The American-in-Paris plot is again exploited, though Fitzgerald transforms his protagonist's efforts at rehabilitation into something more than a private struggle. The conflicted Charlie Wales, rather, stands as a kind of Depression-era everyman who must atone for the intemperate twenties with an outlook that is now serious, sober, and contrite.

The story opens with Charlie walking into the Paris Ritz bar looking for old friends, only to find that its formerly conspicuous American clientele either has gone home or is convalescing in Switzerland. He is in town for a few days, hoping to regain custody of his young daughter, Honoria, now living with his former sister-in-law, Marion Peters, and her family. During the boom years, Charlie and his wife, Helen, discovered a Paris that catered to their every indulgence. They drank too much and fought too much, and their fractious marriage ended in Helen's death from a weak heart. Marion blames Charlie. Charlie arrives at the Peterses' to present his case and is shown into the salon, a "comfortably American" room adorned by a warm fire and the welcoming din of Honoria and her cousins playing. He reflexively begins to boast to Marion's husband, Lincoln, about the money he now earns in a Prague-based business—and then suddenly checks himself. He is there to be repentant, not to parade. This scene and the previous one in the Ritz bar give an indication of Charlie's conflicting emotions. He wants to be strong and independent, to be worthy of "comfortably American" homes, but he longs for the alcohol-fueled excitement of his old life. The promising gaiety of the bar and the pleasures of wasting money remain vividly attractive to him. His sole concession to pre-Prague extravagance is the single whiskey he downs each day. The point is to reduce alcohol's power over him, to control his intake, but this nervy ritual hints at Charlie's inability to put drink aside for good or to reconcile his past with his present. Though he mourns Helen's death and regrets Honoria's absence, he is still a prisoner to impulse. "But it was nice while it lasted," he incautiously defends himself to Marion. "We were a sort of royalty, almost infallible, with a sort of magic around us."[12]

Marion and Lincoln, as Fitzgerald scholars have noted, were modeled after Zelda's sister Rosalind and her husband, Newman Smith. Newman worked for the Guaranty Trust Company and helped to open a branch of that bank in Brussels in 1921. He and Rosalind lived there until 1933, overlapping the period of Zelda's breakdown and subsequent treatment at Prangins. Rosalind blamed Fitzgerald for her sister's condition, believed him unfit to raise Scottie (eight at the time), and hoped to adopt the girl. At this point, Scott dropped all pretense: "I know you dislike me," he accurately enough read Rosalind. "I know your ineradicable impression of the life that Zelda and I led, and evident your dismissal of any of the effort, and struggle success or happiness in it and I understand also your real feeling for her—but I have got Zelda + Scotty to take care of now as ever and I simply cannot be upset and harrowed still further."[13] Looking to supplant Rosalind's rendition of family history with his own, Scott returned fire in "Babylon Revisited." His Marion is a resentful, spiteful woman, jealous that Charlie has so much money while she and Lincoln have to make do with less. There is further the strong suggestion that Marion and Helen were not particularly close but that Marion now seeks to use Helen's death to gain the moral high ground on her former brother-in-law.

With Marion's decision on Honoria's custody pending, Charlie resumes his precarious tour of old haunts. At a casino, he watches the bewitching Josephine Baker "go through her chocolate arabesques" and then meanders past a knot of cabarets and bars on his way to Montmartre, "all . . . catering," Fitzgerald writes, "to vice and waste." In effect, Charlie has both renounced his old ways and announced their continued fascination for him. The Montmartre excursion, like his solitary whiskey each day, is part of a reckless courage that gives Charlie the illusion that he can face down temptation and walk away unscathed. And for a time, his Paris plans do appear to come together. Recognizing Honoria's need to be with her father, Marion agrees to her going to Prague. But at the conclusion of this tense negotiation, held in the Peterses' home, an untimely doorbell announces two of Charlie's old acquaintances; both are a little tight. That Charlie should give this all-important address to such questionable company hints again at his inability to separate his old life from his new. Appalled by these gay, grinning ghosts from Charlie's past, Marion will keep Honoria for the time being. Beaten, Charlie retires to the Ritz for his one whisky and soda and to ruminate on the reasons behind his recent misfortunes. From the other side of the bar, a friendly voice asks if Charlie lost money in the crash. "I did," he replies and then adds with sudden insight, "but I lost everything I wanted in the boom."[14]

Like Fitzgerald, Charlie is chasing character. His efforts at redemption are made all the more difficult because the people around him want the old Charlie back. Duncan and Lorraine, the specters who spoil his attempt to recover Honoria, begrudge his efforts at rehabilitation, which call into question their questionable Paris days. And Marion wants to keep Charlie boxed up as a bad man, to validate her scolding sense of justice. Maybe Charlie and Helen did live for a long season as an American prince and princess, but they paid for it in the end. To now see Charlie skip off to Prague with Honoria would be, for Marion, to wreck that beautiful revenge. Charlie will return to Prague—the inference of an Eastern European exile—but he must go alone.

Fitzgerald never lost Scottie, of course, but like Charlie, he was laboring to come to terms with his years abroad. In the new decade, in the new financial climate, with Zelda in and out of hospitals, such paradoxes took on added weight. Leaving Europe for the last time in September 1931, Fitzgerald said good-bye to that part of his life as well as to the early idealism that had marked it. "I not only announced the birth of my young illusions in 'This Side of Paradise,'" he later explained to one editor, "but pretty much the death of them in some of my . . . stories like 'Babylon Revisited.'"[15] The reasons, meanings, and implications behind this "death" make up the underlying argument of this and the preceding sequence of thematically allied chapters. Their titles, "Adrift Abroad," "Emotional Bankruptcy," "Penance," and "Far from Home," reflect the difficult and often directionless path that Scott found himself on following the publication of *Gatsby*. Returning to the United States, he sought to place this period in perspective. Always sensitive to the past, he became increasingly interested in the distinctions between pre- and post-Depression America—and in how his own wavering fortunes seemed almost to mirror those of the country. Determined to endure as an artist, he was moving on; he was coming home.

SEVENTEEN

Jazz Age Jeremiah

It was evident that money and power were falling into the
hands of people in comparison with whom the leader of a village
Soviet would be a gold-mine of judgment and culture.

F. Scott Fitzgerald, "Echoes of the Jazz Age," 1931

In November 1931, two months after Fitzgerald had arrived back in America, *Scribner's Magazine* published his striking retrospective essay "Echoes of the Jazz Age." Its origin can be traced to a letter the previous spring in which Scott, then situated in Lausanne, had insisted to Perkins, "The Jazz Age is over." Fascinated, Perkins replied, "What you say is extremely interesting, and significant," and he arranged for the magazine's managing editor to invite Fitzgerald to write about it.[1] Much as with *Gatsby,* in other words, which had been composed on the Riviera and revised in Rome, Scott produced yet another incisive account of his country from abroad. In "Echoes," however, he did not seek to explain the broad rhythms of historical development, as he had done in *Gatsby;* he hoped instead to capture the more immediate social and cultural circumstances that led to the Great Depression. Having claimed credit for naming the Jazz Age, he now announced its end and his intent to perform its postmortem.

In effect, the essay cast doubt on the alleged "lightness" of the twenties, stressing instead its many ironies and illusions. Fitzgerald questioned, in other words, the idea that a "lost generation" that was disillusioned by the war and the hypocrisies of Victorianism broke from tradition and took up mahjong, sat on poles, demanded bob cuts, became hip to Freudian lingo, indulged in wood-grain alcohol, wore colorful Burberry checkered fabric and sleek drop-waisted dresses, said "boop-boop-a-doop" a lot, and danced the Charleston—if not the Lindy Hop. To be sure, Fitzgerald had helped to popularize this legend, though in "Echoes," he turned it upside down. Now he proclaimed the parents rather than their progeny as the chief beneficiaries of the decade's suddenly emancipated energy.

Maybe the revolution did start with the young, Scott conceded, but as the twenties wore on, "it became," he wrote, "less and less an affair of youth."[2] The envious elders grew tired of watching their children have all the fun and leapt into the general bacchanalianism feet first. In other words, *they* constituted the true lost generation, *they* were the ones who slipped the leash of Victorian propriety, and *they* were the ones who knew better yet preferred the thrill of chatting up a shimmy dancer to playing parental. True, Fitzgerald agreed, juvenilia enjoyed a brief spree, but its influence had peaked in 1922; and all that came after, to the crash of 1929, reflected the grown-ups' appropriation of a children's crusade. The adults called the tunes, and they paid for the party—seniority would now be served. Confused about the new era of dress, dance, and drink, they "employed" cultural compasses like Fitzgerald to translate the brave new world around them, making it less intimidating and more accessible.

The middle-agers' genteel anarchy was no laughing matter, Fitzgerald argued, for it had produced a definite tendency toward decline. He pointed in the essay to a rogue's gallery of casual tragedy—drunkards, suicides, and the institutionalized—noting for effect that "these things happened not during the depression but during the boom."[3] The *having* of one's new American dreams proved to be a dangerous, delusive proposition; it was, rather, as Gatsby learns too late, the eternal wishing, willing, and wanting that keeps hearts pure and minds clear. The country may have indulged in the collective fantasy that a perpetual dollar-driven party beckoned, but Fitzgerald, in writing his Jazz Age jeremiad, lamented capitalism's impact on the national mind. A culture of cupidity had sapped the country's inner resources, broken its pioneer spirit, and caused the economic collapse. Apparently the heady years of hedonism were now to be followed by long days of compulsory contrition.

And this wouldn't be the worst thing, Fitzgerald suggested. To his taste, a strong atmosphere of unreality had hung over the past few years.

Too many ill-mannered Americans were washing up on the Riviera; too many shiny-haired hotel clerks were making a killing in the market. Raised as republicans but eager in their sudden affluence to show off all the toys and travel that money could buy, Americans had lost touch with their hard-won democratic heritage, the most precious thing about them. "It was borrowed time anyhow," Fitzgerald wrote, "the whole upper tenth of a nation living with the insouciance of grand ducs and the casualness of chorus girls."[4] The result, he warned, would be a general deterioration, measured morally, spiritually, and even physically. If the United States continued to enjoy success in the Olympic Games, he contended, it was only because a still striving immigrant class hustled to lay claim to the medals, while the more established stock remained at the bars and cafés to cheer them on. Here Fitzgerald played on the notion—as he had not done in "The Swimmers," "One Trip Abroad," or "Babylon Revisited"— that dissipation had begun at home. Zelda's case to the contrary, one need not leave America to wind up in a "nerve sanitarium."

As the party reached its peak, Scott argued in "Echoes," a solitary hope appeared, literally, on the horizon: "In the spring of '27, something bright and alien flashed across the sky."[5] This was Charles Lindbergh (aka "The Hero"), fresh off capturing the Orteig Prize for flying the *Spirit of St. Louis* from New York City to Paris. The apple-cheeked Lindbergh embodied the Fitzgerald ideal, a boyish midwesterner who won both glory and the girl (Anne Morrow, an ambassador's daughter, no less). In racing from the New World to the Old, Lindbergh had reversed the voyage of the Dutch sailors memorialized in *The Great Gatsby* while matching their brave spirit. And what, Fitzgerald asked, did Americans make of it all? Not enough. Lindbergh's humility, courage, and resourcefulness were at odds with the unserious tone of the day. Rather than people's taking inspiration from his flight and raising their sights a bit higher, they, Scott sighed, offered a polite smile and returned to the party.

The nation's failure to recognize Lindbergh's simple gallantry, Fitzgerald claimed, underscored a larger cultural illness, and he counted himself among the afflicted. "Notoriety," confessed the notorious Scott, "weighed [too heavily] . . . as a social asset," and "writers," he complained, "were geniuses on the strength of one respectable book"—his own fame cemented, of course, by the respectable *This Side of Paradise.*[6] The "better" men, by contrast, opted for quiet spaces and meaningful lives, leaving the corporations and the culture, the power and the politics to be steered by second-tier types. This vacuum in leadership contributed to a gross distortion of proportion and perspective in the public arena. Everything was magnified: the drinking, the dollars, and the corruption, which had always existed yet had never expected to be respectable. But now indulgence took on a new vogue and in its mounting strength saw no reason to apologize.

Fitzgerald's felt and firsthand ruminations in "Echoes" conformed to his "participant" view of the past. No mere observer, he thought his behavior indicative of certain questionable attitudes, appetites, and choices that led America from the Jazz Age to the market crash. "I . . . was pushed into the position not only of spokesman for the time," he once recalled, "but of the typical product of that same moment." And with that moment now passing, Fitzgerald was keen to tally up the returns. The onset of Depressionomics suggested to him the wintering of a nation and a people once nourished on the "fresh green breast of the new world."[7] History's pivot had unquestionably turned; America was growing up, growing old.

Fitzgerald's search for what time had to tell aligned with a broader and longer movement among scholars, intellectuals, and artists on both sides of the Atlantic. Karl Marx's claim that a dialectic of clashing material interests shaped consecutive feudal, capitalist, and socialist ages competed, as we have seen, with the historian Frederick Jackson Turner's insistence that the phases of American development could be charted by the continental progress of its democratic frontier. In 1905, Albert Einstein's theory of relativity altered conventional notions of time and space in ways as inconceivable to the Victorians as the heliocentric model promoted by Galileo had been to the Aristotelian defenders of a geocentric universe. These and a number of other important thinkers shaped Fitzgerald's approach to the past—none, however, was as vital as Henry Adams.

Scott claimed a personal connection to Adams, about whom he once told Perkins, "I knew him when I was a boy." Presumably Father Fay, welcomed in a number of Washington, D.C., salons, introduced Adams to

Scott, who was then at Princeton. There is no conclusive evidence indicating a meeting between the two, though it is suggestive that Adams—as the Honorable Thornton Hancock—appears in *This Side of Paradise* as the "author of an erudite history of the middle ages and the last of a distinguished, patriotic, brilliant family."[8] Adams read human events as responses to the restless pace of energy moving across epochs. Shifting cultural, spiritual, and economic climates—not great men—made history. Those who were in harmony with the reigning zeitgeist thrived, though after a spell, they too fell before a new "spirit of the time." Adams produced a nine-volume history of the nation's formative years, demonstrating in part that his ancestor the quasi-aristocratic John Adams suffered political defeat to a rising Jeffersonianism because he represented a spent force: the Boston-centric parochialism of Puritan New England. The spread of "plain folk" democracy, cotton-belt slavery, and western expansion empowered the followers of Jefferson to victory after victory until 1860, when a host of intensifying historical forces—free labor, abolitionism, and industrialization—crystallized to smash the plantocracy.

Adams emphasized this "dynamic theory" of development in his sparkling *Mont Saint Michele and Chartres* (1904), the "erudite history" that Fitzgerald referred to. Appalled by the apparent "victory" of American machines and science over poetry, art, song, and spirituality, Adams wrote a moving tribute to medieval France. This twelfth-century Gallic resistance to what would later be praised as Yankee "progress" finds its own forms of expression in much of Fitzgerald's work—along with its anticapitalist undercurrent. Like Adams, Scott wanted to understand the source of society's disenchantment, to follow the accelerating pace of its power as it rippled through regions, peoples, and cultures. Both men were interested in observing the dynamo's impact. Adams developed a particular interest in its fifteenth-century European origins; Fitzgerald, by contrast, headed straight to Gotham.

More than a meeting ground for investors and speculators, New York City stood in Fitzgerald's estimation for the dominant expression of contemporary historical change. In tune with the pattern of the new prosperity, the pulse of Manhattan pushed beyond its watery confines, shaping the attitudes and approaches of southerners and midwesterners before reaching the Pacific. This process introduced a new kind of cultural authority. Formerly, Puritans, patriots, and farmers had ruled the textbooks. Now the New York City skyline rose above the earth, suggesting a deeper and more profound change afoot. The buildings, after all, were merely symbols of the cultural imagination that bore them. They were expressions of the modern mind, the secular equivalent of the Great Pyramid of Giza, the Walled City of Shibam, and the Two Towers of Bologna. Bereft of priests and knights, cavaliers and pioneers, they served new gods and new goddesses—among them the flapper, the bootlegger, and the bonds trader.

Fitzgerald's response to New York City moved quickly from a youthful wonderment to a wizened anxiety. New York chaotically mixed the amenities of high culture with the lowbrow fads that swarmed across the country. The underlying superficiality of the metropolis, its concession to the moneymakers and the confidence men, informed Scott's perception, as he put it in a notebook, of "New York's flashing, dynamic good looks, its tall man's quick-step." This suspicion of an essential shallowness lying at the core of the great American city informed Fitzgerald's broader observation that with the conquest of the continent and the closing of the frontier, national life had finally failed to provide avenues for exploration "commensurate," as he eulogized in *The Great Gatsby,* with the seeker's "capacity for wonder." The City represented equally for Scott the potential and the pratfall of American art, literature, fame, and fortune. It all came, he feared, to so much less than it should have. In 1925, while in Paris, he had remarked to the writer Marya Mannes, "You are thrilled by New York—I doubt you will be after five more years when you are more fully nourished from within. I carry the place around the world in my heart but sometimes I try to shake it off in my dreams. America's greatest promise is that something is going to happen, and after awhile you get tired of waiting because nothing happens to people except that they grow old, and nothing happens to American art because America is the story of the moon that never rose."[9]

As with the chimeric Ginevra King, a young Fitzgerald had again overdreamt a situation, attaching to the City great expectations that were impossible to meet. A native New Yorker would have known better, taken the town in proportion, and cannily hidden his heart. But Fitzgerald could claim only a tourist's view. He paraded around Columbus Circle, frequented the Plaza Hotel, and joined Zelda in the Union Square fountain. Of their initial stay in Manhattan (boarding at 38 West Fifty-Ninth Street between October 1920 and April 1921), Fitzgerald wrote, "We felt like small children in a great bright unexplored barn."[10] Like Nick Carraway, Fitzgerald brought a romantic middle-western perspective to New York, one far different from the Hoosier realism of Theodore Dreiser, who dwelled on the City's poverty and vice. Fitzgerald sensed, rather, a different tempo moving on its streets, a boom of buildings and ambition drawing the curious from around the country. *His* New York thus also owed little to Wharton's aristocratic acre of ducal families branched off from distant Dutch descent—like Adams's ancestors, they too were a spent historical force. He focused instead on the new money, the fresh sources of cultural power, and the populistic impulse that gave it all a sharp energy.

Fitzgerald drafted his most cohesive statement of New York—"My Lost City"—in the Depression summer of 1932. A player in the drama, Scott looked on his own "rise" and "fall" as coequal with the kismet of the City. Both man and metropolis registered in their respective ways the decade's wild ride and eventual smashup. Perhaps most astounding to Fitzgerald was how easily it had all happened. From a dingy Claremont Avenue apartment, writing bad advertising copy, he soon emerged as the spokesman for a generation, a mood, and a historical moment. The confusion increased with fame's demands, conditions, and mysteries. "To my bewilderment," Fitzgerald explained, "I was adopted not as a Middle Westerner, not even as a detached observer, but as the very archetype of what New York wanted." And what New York wanted most was to be entertained. This the Fitzgeralds could do, paying for their seats with their studied antics, their reliable appearances in the gossip rags, and their availability for a good quote. "Prohibition," Scott mimed Oscar Wilde for the *New York Evening World*, "is having simply a ruinous effect on young men." "Don't you know," he said, winking at the *New Yorker*'s readers, "I am one of the most notorious drinkers of the younger generation." And a silly 1923 *Metropolitan Magazine* headline teased readers with, "F. Scott

Fitzgerald Says: 'All Women over Thirty-Five Should Be Murdered.'" The mixed mindedness of Fitzgerald's reaction to New York is evident in "My Lost City." Here, he remembered crying in a taxi, he wrote, "because I had everything I wanted and knew I would never be so happy again," but then he admitted, "It was typical of our precarious position in New York that when our child was to be born we played safe and went home to St. Paul—it seemed inappropriate to bring a baby into all that glamour and loneliness."[11]

These early and cautionary reflections foreshadowed for Scott the inevitable end of the great economic surge. Again, Henry Adams is instructive. His 1904 conception of a dystopian New York anticipated key elements of Fitzgerald's later appraisal. Adams wrote, "The city had the air and movement of hysteria, and the citizens were crying, in every accent of anger and alarm, that the new forces must at any cost be brought under control. Prosperity never before imagined, power never yet wielded by man, speed never reached by anything but a meteor, had made the world irritable, nervous, querulous, unreasonable and afraid. All New York was demanding new men, and all the new forces, condensed into corporations, were demanding a new type of man."[12] And Fitzgerald wrote in "My Lost City,"

> The restlessness of New York in 1927 approached hysteria. . . . Young people wore out early—they were hard and languid at twenty-one. . . . Most of my friends drank too much—the more they were in tune with the times the more they drank. . . . I found a moment of utter peace in riding south through Central Park at dark toward where the façade of 59th Street thrusts its lights through the trees. There again was my lost city, wrapped cool in its mystery and promise. But that detachment never lasted long—as the toiler must live in the city's belly, so I was compelled to live in its disordered mind.[13]

Here, New York is portrayed as the urban version of the baby vamp, the icy lover who takes without return. It has collected a census of fragile personalities rather than independent personages, failing to offer the time, reflection, and calm necessary to maturity and growth. More than simply a lightning rod for chaos, the City has internalized the ethics of the prevailing speculative mood and required its subjects to do so as well—this is the price of admittance.

Fitzgerald's September 1931 return to New York, after several years mainly abroad, inspired him to write "My Lost City." Just four months earlier, former governor Alfred Smith had beamed before a mob of photographers at the opening ceremony for the Empire State Building, the massive steel-framed monument to the nation's material advancement. In the cool autumn air, Fitzgerald ascended now to the top of the tower, drawn in the new age of austerity to discover the reason behind the diminishing returns. Adams had once made a similar pilgrimage, chasing the path of industrial power all the way to the Paris Exposition of 1900. In one exhibition hall, he came upon giant electric current generating turbines and suddenly discovered the surprising solution to his search for historical meaning. "As [I] grew accustomed to the great gallery of machines," he wrote, "[I] began to feel the forty-foot dynamos as a moral force, much as the early Christians felt the Cross. . . . Before the end, one began to pray to it; inherited instinct taught the natural expression of man before silent and infinite force." Three decades later, a similar epiphany struck Fitzgerald from atop the Empire State Building. Looking down from 102 stories, he came to see the magical City circumscribed within the borders of its natural environment; an island *"had limits,"* and despite the illusion of its essential perpetuity, Manhattan could project itself only so far. The City, the economy, and the era that could not end were in fact real and subject to age, illness, and even cessation. "And with the awful realization that New York was a city after all and not a universe," Scott wrote, "the whole shining edifice that [the New Yorker] had reared in his imagination came crashing to the ground."[14]

Fitzgerald concludes "My Lost City" with a dramatic inversion of the dying-fall passage found in *The Great Gatsby.* The novel records the transcendent moment when Europeans first arrived in the Western Hemisphere, while "My Lost City" closes with a sober early-morning ferryboat ride along a Hudson River, now bereft of the timeworn magic that formerly drew ancient mariners on: "it no longer whispers of fantastic success and eternal youth."[15] In these subdued pages, Fitzgerald counts the cost of the past decade—New York's, America's, and his own—to answer the questions that he had put to himself: What did it all mean? And why had the country failed to produce a civilization worthy of its initial discoverers' soaring hopes?

What Fitzgerald thought of all of this is not as simple as one might guess. Caveats aside, the Jazz Age still sang out to Scott. Faced with the gray hangover of the 1930s, he could not help but reflect wistfully on the decade that once made him a star. If the ending smelled faintly acrid, the beginning savored of purer, sweeter stuff. Its first fresh stirrings offered a vibrant hope for something different—not necessarily lasting, not essentially serious, yet filled with unalloyed emotion, bright color, and the promise of creative energy. Above all, there was youth. "It all seems rosy and romantic to us who were young then," Fitzgerald wrote, "because we will never feel quite so intensely about our surroundings any more."[16] The brooding memory of first successes brought from him a warm recognition that the short twenties (1919–1922) had paid tribute to the authentic spirit of America's pioneer past, while the longer twenties (1923–1929) trended toward a narrowing of horizons. The shock waves of those days had now subsided, and Fitzgerald's nonfiction writing turned increasingly searching and retrospective. No doubt nostalgia informed his feelings, but something more came to mind. The rare convergence of youth, liberality, innovation, and cultural openness brought, if only for a brief season, a suggestion of what America could be. To write with a full heart of lost cities and lost ages, after all, is to believe in the power of Eden's promise.

EIGHTEEN

Book of Fathers—
Tender Is the Night

The best book he ever wrote, I think, is still "Tender
Is the Night." . . . I read it last year again and it has all the
realization of tragedy that Scott ever found.

Ernest Hemingway to Max Perkins, 1941

In April 1934, Scribner published *Tender Is the Night,* Fitzgerald's fourth
and perhaps finest novel. A study of false starts, the manuscript under-
went years of revision, ranging from a matricide on the Riviera to the
exploits of a disillusioned American film director, before assuming its
final form. The truth is, Fitzgerald had lost track of time. Sensitive to
wrinkles on the social fabric, his earlier books collected their inspiration
from the kaleidoscope of cultural change that had shaped the 1910s. In
them, readers discovered the Gaelic Father Fay, the tempting Ginevra
King, and the professorial John Peale Bishop—each one a glittering ghost
from Scott's impressionable past. By the late 1920s, these ambassadors
of impending love and glory no longer spoke to him with quite the same
clarity. In rapid succession, a series of violent blows—the Wall Street
smash (1929), Zelda's institutionalization (1930), and Edward Fitzgerald's
death (1931)—drew from his pen an altered outlook. His new book took
it all in and took a bit of him in the process.

Fitzgerald finished *Tender* at "La Paix," a roomy, tree-shaded Victorian house just north of Baltimore near the Henry Phipps Psychiatric
Clinic of the Johns Hopkins University Hospital, where, from February

to June 1932, Zelda received care. His uneasy mood during this period may be inferred from a cryptic ledger entry he filed under "Thirty-Six years old": "a strange year of Work + Drink. Increasingly unhappy—Zelda up + down. 1st draft of novel complete[.] Ominous!" A risk-laden enterprise, the book carried the burden of its author's twin intentions: to produce a lasting work of art while responding to more immediate concerns. Zelda's recently published *Save Me the Waltz* had advanced her side of the Fitzgeralds' marital divide while casting considerable doubt on Scott's layman's diagnosis of her condition. He would now have his say. The novel's female protagonist, Nicole Warren, suffers from mental illness, gravitates to a Jozan-like lover "of Latin aspect," and becomes healthier as her husband, the psychiatrist Dick Diver, breaks down. This last plot element reprised Fitzgerald's anxiety that Zelda intended to write her way to health using material that he thought rightfully his. Her reply to this particular charge, expressed in a May 1933 therapy session—"as far as destroying you is concerned I have considered you first in everything I have tried to do in my life"—obviously failed to persuade.[1]

To enrich the novel and give it authenticity, Scott quoted directly from his wife's hospital letters and drafted a crib sheet detailing the "parallel between actual case and case in novel." These included "a woman of 29 [Zelda] has a rivalry complex for success + power competing with her husband" and "a girl of 15 [Nicole] has a father complex deliberately built up by her father, a well-screened degenerate." Other overlaps between the two cases—"collapses," "projects on husband," "invents homosexuality"—are evident. *Tender* approximates the Fitzgeralds to the extent that Scott warned Zelda away from the novel, assuring her of a more hopeful future: "Let me reiterate that I don't want you to have too much traffic with my book, which is a very melancholy work. . . . It represents certain phases of life that are now over. We are certainly on some upsurging wave, even if we don't yet know exactly where it's heading."[2] The result is a book of fears and one that, despite the singular inclusion of Zelda's illness, Fitzgerald had written before—the one in which a man of great potential is destroyed by wealth and beauty.

Diver's gradual decay is the most compelling but certainly not the only transformation of note in *Tender.* These include the deterioration of other characters (for example, the gifted composer-turned-alcoholic Abe North, Scott's salute to Ring Lardner), the passing of historical eras (the end of nineteenth-century unity before twentieth-century multiplicity), and the evolution of traditional gender roles (Nicole's sister, the butch Baby Warren, approximates the new Amazonian). Above them all stands the death of Dick's—Fitzgerald's—father, whose haunting presence in the novel represents the perishing light promise of what America might have been. Shortly after Edward's January 1931 passing, Fitzgerald composed "The Death of My Father," an informal, handwritten tribute that went unpublished until 1951. Just as Scott drew on Zelda's letters when he was writing *Tender,* he would similarly find rich material in his essay. In "The Death of My Father," we encounter, "I loved my father—always deep in my subconscious I have referred judgments back to him, to what he would have thought, or done. He loved me—and felt a deep responsibility for me—I was born several months after the sudden death of my two elder sisters and he felt what the effect of this would be on my mother, that he would be my only moral guide. He became that to the best of his ability. He came from tired old stock with very little left of vitality and mental energy but he managed to raise a little for me." And more concisely in *Tender,* he wrote, "Dick loved his father—again and again he referred judgments to what his father would probably have thought or done. Dick was born several months after the death of two young sisters and his father, guessing what would be the effect on Dick's mother, had saved him from a spoiling by becoming his moral guide. He was of tired stock yet he raised himself to that effort."[3]

Opposite this fading figure of paternal responsibility stands the wholly irresponsible Devereaux Warren, Nicole's father and first lover. A loathsome, morally corrupt man, he conforms to Fitzgerald's tragic vision of an America whose creativity, culture, and sexual codes have recently come under the purview of money and moneymakers. In the "battle" of the fathers, Warren wealth triumphs over Diver integrity. As Nicole's physician, Dick becomes her new lover, directing his patient's emotional transference to himself. This violation of professional ethics, encouraged by Baby Warren's interest in "buying" her sister a doctor, raises the point of a greater generational seduction. For not even the best of fathers could save their sons from the worst of consequences.[4]

Tender's contrasting views of fatherhood serve as a backdrop to equally mixed observations of marriage. And as with so many leads in the novel, this particular line of inquest took root in the circumstances of Fitzgerald's life. His important friendship with Gerald and Sara Murphy is a case in point; models for him of conjugal ease and compatibility, they provided Fitzgerald with a vision of the Divers before Dick and Nicole's descent into Scott and Zelda territory. *Tender's* affectionate dedication to the Murphys—"MANY FÊTES"—paid tribute to the generosity of Villa America's hosts, shown to artists, writers, and expats alike, and it announces their welcome presence in the novel. Gerald's control and self-assurance form the core of the young Dick Diver; Sara's tasteful, simple elegance is evident in Nicole.

Despite the likeness, Sara stubbornly rejected any personal connection to *Tender,* telling Calvin Tomkins in 1961, "I hated the book when I first read it and even more on re-reading. I reject categorically any resemblance to ourselves or to anyone we know." Years later, however, Sara's daughter Honoria, a witness/participant of the "many" Murphy-Fitzgerald "fêtes" on the Riviera, offered a somewhat different view. "In the book," she wrote, "are accurate portrayals of the Murphys on the beach at Antibes." The distinction, "on the beach at Antibes," is important because as the novel proceeds, the Murphys recede. Scott's friend John O'Hara was certainly correct in pointing out to Gerald in 1962, "Sooner or later [Scott's] characters always came back to being Fitzgerald characters in a Fitzgerald world." Disputes over "likeness" aside, Scott knew exactly what he had done, and he wrote to Sara several months after *Tender's* publication explaining his reasons, even his *right* to her image. "I used you again and again in *Tender,*" he stated flatly, excusing the intrusion on the grounds of creative license:

> In a hundred . . . places I tried to evoke not *you* but the effect that you produce on men—the echoes and reverberations—a poor return for what

you have given by your living presence, but nevertheless an artist's (what a word!) sincere attempt to preserve a true fragment rather than a "portrait" by Mr. [John Singer] Sargent. And someday, in spite of all the affectionate skepticism you felt toward the brash young man you met on the Riviera eleven years ago, you'll let me have my little corner of you where I know you better than anybody—yes, even better than Gerald.[5]

Scott exerted his privilege as a writer and leaned heavily in *Tender* on both Sara and Zelda—and even on Lois Moran, the novel's model for Rosemary Hoyt, a young actress attracted to Dick. Put in context, Scott had come to resent Zelda's drag on his artistic and financial resources. Serving as her self-appointed caretaker, editor, and agent took time and vitality away from his work. *Tender* goes over this delicate material in a manner that one might describe as part truth, part self-pity. It would be easy to read into the Diver-Hoyt romance Fitzgerald's years-after-the-fact admission of infidelity, but that seems unlikely. Rather, as Scott identified with Moran as a fellow worker in the arts, Rosemary identifies with Dick in ways that the pampered Nicole never can. The latter, we come to learn, had long been "suckling at [Dick's] lean chest"—this a colloquialism for doctor-patient relations that doubles as Nicole's questionable convalescence from invalid to vamp(ire). Rosemary, by contrast, is a "diver" too. Still young, still respectful of her mother's Victorian precepts, she and Dick speak the same language. "His laws," she reassuringly tells herself, "are like the laws Mother taught me." Whereas Nicole is a reserved Chicago princess, Rosemary is a go-getter, eager to give of herself and determined to please others. While making a movie that calls for her to plunge into a Venice canal, she doesn't think twice: "It was a very expensive set, so I had to dive and dive and dive all morning. Mother had a doctor right there, but it was no use—I got pneumonia."[6] In gravitating toward Rosemary, Dick is attracted less to her youthful flesh than to her enthusiasm and unaffectedness. She is, in a very real sense, a kind of doppelgänger diver whose bloom (like Dick's promise as a physician) will eventually fade. As the reader comes to learn, the corrupting influence of money and celebrity took not her looks but rather the exceptional admixture of innocence and determination that was once her special something.

For all the differences between Rosemary and Nicole, the two eventually take parallel paths. Both are referred to in *Tender* as a "Daddy's girl"—alluding to the title of a film starring Rosemary as well as to Devereaux Warren's taste for sexual taboo. In some sense, Fitzgerald thought of these privileged women as "representative," and he was interested in what their circumstances revealed about America's shifting moral identity. For men like Warren have committed something greater than a private sin; they have, rather, given up their patriarchal responsibilities to establish culture-wide ethical guidelines. Into this breach, Fitzgerald argued, came the new woman, armed, like Rosemary and Nicole, with sudden wealth but lacking the restraint and wisdom to use it wisely. Apparently the failings of men were now to be followed by the false steps of women.

Rosemary's rebellion is particularly instructive on this point, for it is nurtured on newfound economic and erotic freedoms that come with a host of hidden costs. Rather, for example, than discover an authentic occupational independence, she is doomed to repeat the thin list of sex-kitten roles that underlie her relevancy as a Hollywood pinup girl. Nicole's situation, though on the surface much different, is hardly much better. Untethered from Dick but accompanied by the imposing clout of a Warren bank account, she is at liberty to secure any number of transient sexual companions. "New vistas appeared ahead," Fitzgerald says of her abrupt emancipation, "peopled with the faces of many men, none of whom she need obey or even love." The old morality no longer proves compelling, but what more than an easy immunity—and the promise of many interchangeable rooms and partners—does the future hold? "Nicole did not want any vague spiritual romance," Fitzgerald writes, and it seems fitting that this high priestess of the consumer age "crossed herself reverently with Chanel Sixteen" in preparation for her first extramarital affair.[7]

Tender is filled with such dubious improvements. Baby Warren is a cold, insular character, the battle-ax heiress of her father's financial muscle; Abe North's widow, Mary, experiments with shifting class identities by trading her American bona fides for an Italian count who is "not quite light enough to travel in a Pullman south of Mason-Dixon." As Contessa di Minghetti, she is involved in a sexual adventure with a "Lady Caroline" and, hinting at Devereaux Warren's sins, two young girls. One astounded Alsatian observer to the evening comments, "I have never seen women like this sort of women. I have known many of the great courtesans of the world, and for them I have much respect often, but women like these women I have never seen before."[8]

With Fitzgerald, the gender issue cuts two ways, neither of which endorses female autonomy. One might read *Tender* as an unsympathetic review of modern American womanhood, the familiar story of boy meets girl, girl destroys boy that runs throughout Fitzgerald's work. Yet another approach is to see women as reaching a kind of dismal parity with men— victims all of a cynical age. The First World War and subsequent financial takeoff exhausted the country's strength for great crusades while introducing a far more consumer-oriented outlook. The sacrificing spirit, Fitzgerald argues, gave way to self-gratification, and in its course arose the "new woman," the occupant of a sexual middle ground somewhere between paramour and spouse. Rather than applaud the enlarged range of female freedoms, Scott claims that a debilitating personal license now teased two genders. He dramatizes this view in *Tender* with a medical case involving a thirty-year-old female painter with an undiagnosable illness. Trying to make sense of her condition, the afflicted patient says to Diver, "I'm sharing the fate of the women of my time who challenged men to battle. . . . You pick a set-up, or else win a Pyrrhic victory, or you're wrecked and ruined—you're a ghostly echo from a broken wall." Her sickness, Fitzgerald suggests, occurred while "battling" men for a piece of a false paradise. Discussions of *Tender* often and understandably emphasize Dick's downward spiral, but Nicole's descent / ascent is equally compelling. As a young rape victim, she surrendered to Warren chaos but, when "cured," trades consideration and self-control for her father's disordered rules of conduct. In both her Swiss imprisonment and after, she remains at heart a "daddy's girl."[9]

The sudden dominance of Warren privilege in *Tender* suggests a fundamental shift in the American story. Dick's father belonged to a genteel tradition comprising Protestant piety, paternal rule, and liberal politics. For several decades, it set the cultural tempo, suggesting an orderly civilization founded on a sense of shared ethical values. This consensus came undone in the war's wake, leaving the ultrarich to shed the old middle-class morality for a guilt-free code of conduct.[10] Thinking over the origins of this class/cultural transition, Fitzgerald describes the prewar bourgeoisie's eclipse in a striking passage in *Tender* in which Diver contemplates the steep cost of the conflict while surveying Beaumont-Hamel, the site of an intense battle during the Somme offensive:

> This Western-Front business couldn't be done again, not for a long time. The young men think they could do it but they couldn't. They could fight the First Marne again but not this. This took religion and years of plenty and tremendous sureties and the exact relation that existed between the classes. The Russians and Italians weren't any good on this front. You had to have a whole-souled sentimental equipment going back further than you could remember. You had to remember Christmas, and postcards of the Crown Prince and his fiancée, and little cafes in Valence and beer gardens in Unter den Linden and weddings at the mairie, and going to the Derby, and your grandfather's whiskers.... This kind of battle was invented by Lewis Carroll and Jules Verne and whoever wrote Undine, and country deacons bowling and marraines in Marseilles and girls seduced in the back lanes of Würtemburg and Westphalia. Why, this was a love battle—there was a century of middle-class love spent here.[11]

This meditation by Dick works equally on the orders of self-reflection and self-indictment. Indeed, the concept of a "love battle" serves as a kind of grim couplet touching, as it does, on the darkening future of his caste and the narrowing options before him as a now obsolete healer/husband.

In this sense, as the pawn of powerful historical forces, Diver is as much a symbol of the vanishing "West" as Jay Gatsby is. In Dick's fearless student days, he conquered in quick succession Yale, Oxford, and Freud's Vienna. "Most of us have a favorite, a heroic period, in our lives," Fitzgerald writes, "and that was Dick Diver's." Handsome, intelligent, and charmingly naïve, the young doctor harbored intense ambitions in these formative years. When questioned about his plans, he innocently replies, "I've got only one ... and that's to be a good psychologist—maybe to be the greatest one that ever lived." But practicing in a swank clinic for the decadent wealthy on the Zürichsee compromises Dick's professional skills. There, he "cured" homosexuals, helped alcoholics taper off before their next binge, and pasted together the human damage left behind by the world's Devereux Warrens. In this venomous environment, Diver begins an inexorable disintegration. With his golden days now gone, his American idealism expired, all that remains is to identify the reason why. Nicole's new lover performs this service accurately enough, telling her, "You've got too much money. . . . That's the crux of the matter. Dick can't beat that."[12]

And apparently, Fitzgerald tells us, no one else can either. *Tender* ends chronologically in the summer of 1930, several months, that is, after the great market crash had shaken the world. But what does Diver see as he returns one final time to Gausse's placid beach on the bright French Riviera? The rich, of course, richer than ever. Impervious to the fluctuations of a mere stock ticker, they answer to a different economy and thus to different rules entirely. Perhaps no scene in the novel is as powerful as this one. Conceding nothing to sentiment, it tells us definitively that the wealthy are not to be seriously questioned, challenged, or even inconvenienced. The rest of *us* may tremble before the Depression, but not *they*—they are eternal, they are a breed apart, and they are above it all.[13]

Tender Is the Night briefly made the *Publishers Weekly* best-seller list, and it quickly ran through an initial printing of seventy-six hundred copies, thereby launching two further printings that spring. Though it enjoyed a modest commercial success, Fitzgerald, hoping to repair his financial fortunes with a major seller, was greatly disappointed. Four months after *Tender*'s appearance, Scott wrote to Perkins, complaining, "I am terribly unhappy in debt and do not get much comfort out of my personal life if I feel any such shadow over me." *Tender*'s artistic returns fared better. If reviewers caviled here and there about a character's sketchy development or felt themselves unprepared for Diver's rapid bottoming out, they more typically recognized the novel's many felicities in both form and expression. John Chamberlain of the *New York Times* wrote, "Mr. Fitzgerald has not forgotten his craftsmanship, his marvelous sense of what might be called social climate, his sheer writing ability." Gilbert Seldes, always a strong supporter of Scott's, insisted in the *New York Evening Journal* that with *Tender,* Fitzgerald "has stepped again to his natural place at the head of the American writers of our time." And the *Modern Monthly* critic C. Hartley Grattan praised the book's broader cultural observations on the rising money power and its many worshipers: "Only a person utterly insensitive to the grace and beauty of the way of life open to the leisured will fail to see that even in decay these people are infinitely charming, insidiously beguiling to all but sea-green incorruptibles."[14]

One such "utterly insensitive" commentator, the critic Philip Rahv, badly misread Fitzgerald as an apologist for the rich. His May 1934 *Daily Worker* review of *Tender* closed on a hit-the-barricade note: "you can't hide from a hurricane under a beach umbrella."[15] In fact, Fitzgerald was hiding from nothing. In a penetrating few lines, rather, he had offered a shrewd assessment of the exacting global effort it took to maintain the Warrens of the world: "Nicole was the product of much ingenuity and toil. For her sake trains began their run at Chicago and traversed the round belly of the continent to California; chicle factories fumed and link belts grew link by link in factories; men mixed toothpaste in vats and drew mouthwash out of copper hogsheads; girls canned tomatoes quickly in August or worked rudely at the Five-and-Tens on Christmas Eve; half-breed Indians toiled on Brazilian coffee plantations and dreamers were muscled out of patent rights in new tractors—these were some of the people who gave a tithe to Nicole."[16] As an appraisal of capitalism's deep reach, the passage works on two levels. First, it indicates the immensity of private ownership's structure, organization, and exploitation—from the Chicago rail yards to the South American orchards. Second, it identifies Nicole's refined purchasing instincts as wholly trained—she is the selfish offspring of a selfish elect. But absent the more obvious class-conflict signage that one might expect to find in, say, a John Steinbeck novel, *Tender* flew under the critics' radars as a "radical" novel. The workers' struggle dominated the Left in the 1930s, and Fitzgerald was, in some respects, a man of the Right. Approaching capitalism from a more traditionally conservative attitude, he criticized the system for making money the arbiter of power, prestige, and morality. He resented that Edward's courtly southern manners no longer counted or that writers had to entertain the public in order to eat. Both intuitively and more directly, he disliked a system of exchange that took men like Dick Diver and destroyed them.

As a unified statement, *Tender* captures Fitzgerald's historical vision more completely than anything else he ever wrote. He thought highly of the novel, telling his Asheville friend Martha Marie Shank, "*Tender is the Night* [is my] best and *The Great Gatsby* the next best." In a reflective moment, he explained to John Peale Bishop the fundamental difference between the two books. "The dramatic novel [*Gatsby*] has cannons quite different from the philosophical, now called psychological novel [*Tender*]. One is a kind of *tour de force* and the other a confession of faith. It would be like comparing a sonnet sequence with an epic."[17] His marathon finished, his resources spent, Scott found himself in 1934 without a firm idea for a new novel at hand. Ever since he had begun "The Romantic Egotist" as a soldier in the autumn of 1917, he seemed always to have a book in the works. That creative run had come undone. The artist in him endured, but the effort increased.

NINETEEN

Purgatory

For the moment we are both life-tired.

F. Scott Fitzgerald to Beatrice Dance, 1935

Exhausted by the struggle to complete *Tender Is the Night,* Fitzgerald wrestled in the mid-1930s with a mounting sense of failure. He placed fewer stories in the *Saturday Evening Post,* received less money for those he did, and watched as Faulkner, Hemingway, and Steinbeck moved to the front of American letters. In retreat, he now seemed to be sharing Dick Diver's humbling fate—"the spear had been blunted." For several years, Fitzgerald had justified his various humiliations and struggles—the endless appeals to agent and editor for advances, the boozy benders, and the die-hard battle to restrict Zelda's writing—as necessary sacrifices for his art. But that logic held only as long as the old magic still surfaced. Without a novel in the works or a steady income from the well-playing slicks, Scott lost, never to regain, unconditional confidence in his craft. "I wish now," he later wrote to his daughter, Scottie, "I'd *never* relaxed or looked back—but said at the end of *The Great Gatsby:* 'I've found my line—from now on this comes first. This is my immediate duty—without this I am nothing.'"[1]

Troubled in February 1935 by a flair-up of tuberculosis (his first attack occurred, according to his biographer Arthur Mizener, in 1919), Fitzgerald traded the Baltimore area, his home since the spring of 1932, for the clean, cold Appalachian air of Tryon, North Carolina. There, if his *Ledger* is accurate, Scott went on the wagon and brooded over Zelda's uncertain progress at Sheppard-Pratt Hospital, which she had entered the previous year. She led, he confided to Gerald and Sara Murphy, "a poor pitiful life, reading the Bible in the old fashioned manner walking tight lipped and correct through a world she can no longer understand. . . . Part of her mind is washed clean + she is no one I ever knew." The following year, Scott registered Zelda at Highlands Hospital in Asheville, where he had relocated. There, as during their Baltimore days, the two remained near neighbors in a kind of joint convalescence. One might say that they were spouse-patients, pulling a load perhaps now beyond their combined strength. Certainly Scott's bleaker-than-thou reminiscences of this period—"work + worry," "sickness and debt," and "debts terrible"—convey a desperate mood of mixed ailments.[2]

It seems somewhat fitting that a tubercular Fitzgerald could lay claim to a properly poetic affliction. Tuberculosis was thought in the nineteenth century to heighten the senses while purging the body of worldly sins. Some women applied makeup to their skin to achieve a consumptive look, Lord Bryon reportedly announced his desire to die from the disease, and the real deaths of Emily Brontë, Frédéric Chopin, Henry David Thoreau, and Elizabeth Barrett Browning from the "white plague" gave rumor to the illness's romantic properties.

A sojourner in North Carolina, Fitzgerald hoped while there to wean himself off alcohol, rediscover his short-story "trick," and put aside money for the future. None of this happened. He shuttled, rather, between beer and gin, found some small trouble in a messy extramarital affair, and, during particularly low moments, contemplated suicide. Much of what we know about Fitzgerald's struggles during this difficult period comes from Laura Guthrie, a palmist and social hostess of sorts at the Asheville Inn, near Scott's more pricey digs at the Grove Park Inn. Four years Fitzgerald's senior, Guthrie had attended school in Lausanne, visited Russia with her father, and studied journalism at Columbia University. Separated from her husband, who lived in New York with their five-year-old son, she had come to Asheville to take care of her own tubercular lungs. Guthrie became Scott's typist, confidante, and conspirator during the summer of 1935, all the while maintaining a sixty-thousand-word journal of their time together, a considerable portion of which appeared in *Esquire* in 1964.[3]

Though Guthrie brushed aside Fitzgerald's halfhearted sexual over-
tures, she empathized with his lost-little-boy performance. "I feel that
Scott is about the loneliest person in the world," she wrote at the time.
"His mother is old and doesn't understand him at all and he does not care
to see her. His wife is insane and in a sanitarium. He told me he didn't
want to see her again this trip. . . . He is completely alone because no one
is near to him and he has no religion to comfort him. He makes me think
of a lost soul, wandering in purgatory—sometimes hell. He tries so hard
to drown it out with drink and sex." But the sex only caused more troubles. Fitzgerald's contact with a local prostitute stirred up a phobia of
uncleanliness, and a resulting mild skin inflammation made him fear the
worst—syphilis. In secret, he drove to a clinic in Spartanburg, South Carolina, and, under an assumed name, was relieved to be given a clean bill
of health.[4]

Other questionable conquests were soon to follow. Tony Buttitta, the
proprietor of a small bookstore in Asheville's George Vanderbilt Hotel,
befriended Scott and observed firsthand his attractiveness to women:
"He won hearts with . . . a combination of his fame, his ability to make
each one feel she was his only woman, his conversation sprinkled with
praise of their beauty and analysis of their vagrant emotions, and his
tender romantic appeal." Fitzgerald further exuded a youthful charm, part
Princeton, part Peter Pan, complemented by a natural courtliness instilled
by his father. He paid attention to women, asked them questions, and
enjoyed the advantage of striking soft, blue-green eyes fronting a magnetic intelligence. "I was not prepared for the poetic, handsome face,"
one of his secretaries later remembered, adding that after she had been
"exposed to the glimmer of Scott's mind, it was hard . . . to consider a less
luminous man."[5]

Despite such advantages, Fitzgerald earned, among the women he
knew, a reputation as a physically passive partner. He preferred setting a
mood to stripping down. Elizabeth Beckwith Mackie met Scott during
his army days and remembered this celebrated sociologist of the petting
party as a cold fish compared to "the southern boys" she knew, who "at
least understood what it was all about, and were more aggressive and
emotionally satisfying": "In 1917, I'm afraid Scott just wasn't a very lively

animal." Relevantly, an Asheville prostitute remembered Fitzgerald as "nervous": "I thought maybe that was why he was so quick about it. I asked him if that was his usual way and he said, yes, so I didn't take it personally, like he wanted to get it over with. Of course, I've known all kinds, but I expected a man who writes about love to know better." Insecurity might have factored into the reticence that some women detected in Scott. There is some evidence that Fitzgerald mused over, as Hemingway put it, "a matter of measurements." In Hemingway's retelling, an upset Scott confided to him near the end of a Parisian luncheon, "Zelda said that the way I was built I could never make any woman happy." Hemingway claims to have inspected Scott in the eatery's lavatory and reassured him: "You're perfectly fine." The veracity of this story is no certain thing, though it is worth noting that a decade later, Scott's Asheville prostitute, so Buttitta reported, recalled a similar conversation.[6] It seems reasonable to surmise that had Fitzgerald any size "issues," they may have combined with other factors—a native conventionality, middle-class inhibitions, a lingering Catholic consciousness, and lack of a commanding sexual drive—to limit his capacity for erotic pleasure.

Those who were familiar with Fitzgerald's reputation as the high priest of the Jazz Age were sometimes taken aback by his prosy morality. His last lover, Sheilah Graham, remembered "a straitlaced, almost puritanical streak in Scott": "[It] surprised me because it was so contrary to the picture I had gotten of him as daring, nonconforming, and unconventional. He *had* been shocked when I spoke so casually to him of other men I had known. At parties he was acutely uncomfortable if anyone told a suggestive story: his face froze and he invariably walked away." More than a social convention, Fitzgerald's distaste for the off-color informed his literary judgments. After reading John Peale Bishop's coming-of-age novel *Act of Darkness* (1935), which included scenes portraying rape and masturbation, he wrote to Bishop with the following criticism: "I think the book is a little too rough. The insistence on sex-in-the-raw occupies more space than the phenomenun usually does in life. Insofar as this is the story of a boy's awakening to the world of passion, it is justified, but when you launch yourself into an account of the brutal fate that haunts us and the balance is not what it should be." The *New Masses,* on the other hand, described Bishop's novel as "sensitively written," and the *Saturday Review of Literature* called it "honest and straightforward."[7]

Scott, by contrast, wrote almost exclusively above the waistline. One reviewer of *Beautiful and Damned* stated accurately of its author, "He has romance and imagination and a gayety unknown to most of the young moderns, . . . [but] he is not darkly and deeply engaged with the sacred mysteries of Eros." In *Gatsby,* readers encounter layers of sexual insinuation but no details and scant tension. Gatsby's broad hint to Nick, "Daisy comes over quite often—in the afternoons," is as close as the reader comes to espying their illicit congresses. Of Tom and Myrtle's New York apartment tryst, Nick simply announces that "they had disappeared," and after guests suddenly arrive, he states that they "reappeared." True, in *Tender Is the Night,* Dick Diver describes his dying marriage as a case of "making love to dry loins," but Fitzgerald later regretted the line, confiding to the publisher Bennett Cerf, "There is not more than one complete sentence that I want to eliminate [in the book], one that has offended many people and that I admit is out of Dick's character: 'I never did go in for making love to dry loins.' It is a strong line but definitely offensive."[8]

With Scott lacking, as he once wrote of himself in a notebook, a "great animal magnetism," he never outgrew his prep-school code of courtship, namely, playing the gallant with a quick compliment and pleasant manners. Though he engaged in a few affairs during Zelda's years in the hospital, none seemed to have made much of an impression. Graham maintained that he approached women "on a spiritual rather than sexual plane" and reported of their three years together, "I don't remember seeing him naked." More than sex, Scott sought the edge of romance and the always-satisfying challenge of winning over the next golden girl. To him, such sweet pursuits involved the combination of clever letters and cunning conversation designed to set heads swooning. Though Graham may well have seen him as a "spiritual" lover, there is evidence that Fitzgerald regarded himself as a cerebral, analytical companion. One suspects that his assessment of Amory Blaine's cool rules of engagement—"He lacked somehow that intense animal magnetism that so often accompanies beauty in men or women; his personality seemed rather a mental thing"—mirrored his own emotional makeup.[9]

At Asheville, the most golden girl around was Beatrice Dance, the legatee of a wealthy Tennessee family who arrived at the Grove Park Inn in June with her convalescing sister, Eleanor. Married to Du Pres (Hop) Dance, a well-to-do San Antonio businessman, Beatrice was thirty-two and attractive. Her European travels suggested a certain cosmopolitanism. Bored and eager to impress, Fitzgerald charmed Dance only to discover that she had fallen in love. According to Guthrie, Scott described her as "terribly passionate, almost a nymphomaniac," and he acted like a hare (happily) chased by a hound. In the afterglow of their inevitable coupling, he played the regretful fool: "That has happened which I did not want to have happen."[10]

From there followed an anxious few weeks of meetings, letters, and assignations. Guthrie served as confidante to both parties and recorded Fitzgerald's replay of Dance's desperate plea to stay together: "She asked me to go away with her, said she was willing to leave all of her former life and just go with me to any distant point in the world. She said with humility, 'I am rich. I will pay for everything.' So I had to have sense for both of us and told her that never, never would I desert Zelda, especially in her present condition." But Scott's "sense" didn't prevent him from the occasional sexual relapse. At this point Hop arrived in Asheville suspicious of his wife's behavior and mindful of her failure to return his phone messages. Tempting fate or simply maliciously eager for excitement, Scott left a Shirley Temple film with Guthrie and made an early-evening call on the Dances. "Hazy with beer," he paired off and engaged Beatrice in a long conversation, after which—at about 11:30—he imprudently kissed her good night in front of the others and quickly retreated from the room, just beating a furious Hop to the door. Shortly thereafter, Fitzgerald left Asheville for a few days in a halfhearted attempt to break with Beatrice—or perhaps he was looking to ratchet up the intensity. "This is no longer funny," he self-pityingly wrote to Guthrie in a letter postmarked 29 July. "Just what has happened will not surprise you, but it fills me with a profound disgust. I have become involved again + am moving to another hotel, because it means no more work is possible here. Dont women have anything more to do than to sit around and make love + drink beer? This time my emotions arn't even faintly involved and I'm such a wreck physically that I expect the heart, liver and lungs to collapse again at a moment's notice—six weeks of late hours, beer and talk, talk, talk."[11]

In August, Dance finally returned with Hop to Texas. A master of the elegiac adieu, Fitzgerald hoped to end the affair on a "proper" theatrical note. "I guess nobody won + everybody lost," he wrote to her that month. "This is your first tragedy—my second. I think I shall never let my heart go out of myself again." But this only began their sentimental long good-bye; in an undated follow-up letter, Scott sounds as though he were putting the finishing touches on a story for the *Saturday Evening Post:* "Of *course* you were right to go—anything less than a complete separation would have been a perfectly futile temporizing. But you have become the only being with whom I have any desire to communicate any more and when you were gone there was the awful stillness of a desert. Love seems to be like that, unexpected, often tragic, always terribly mortal and fragile." In September, Dance entered a San Antonio hospital, where a drawn-to-the-drama Fitzgerald wrote to her physician, a Dr. Cade, offering, in the name of advancing her recovery, his side of their saga. He obviously remained attracted to the illicitness of their affair and sought to prolong it from a safe distance. "She and I will never meet again in this world," he gravely explained to Cade, "but it was a true deep love between us and to meddle with that would be tinkering with the whole structure of her heart—her feelings, thinkings and perceptions."[12]

This inflated passage is indicative of how little Scott's approach to romance had changed over twenty years. As with Ginevra King, he exaggerated his feelings for Dance, and his defensive plea, "it was a true deep love," comes off as unconvincing. Moreover, in warning her physician not to burrow too deeply into Dance's emotional mechanics ("her feelings, thinkings and perceptions)," Scott reprised his concern, first brought to light during Zelda's treatment, that to "fix" the heart meant neutralizing its capacity for feeling and emotion. Finally, his need to participate in Dance's recuperation calls to mind his earlier efforts to engage Zelda's doctors in amateur analyses. In a second letter to Cade, Fitzgerald angled to intervene directly in her therapy: "I have gathered that a certain person has had a nervous breakdown. You can imagine my feelings. . . . Do you think it would help it if I wrote her a strong moralistic letter. . . . If so will you accept the responsibility for delivering it. I would not put another firecracker under their household for anything."[13]

In the end, Dance's interest in an actual and ongoing love affair—rather than a distant "romance"—far exceeded Fitzgerald's. She played for keeps, fell hard for Scott, and as a result got a bit bruised. He, by contrast, sought an alluring if light diversion to spice up Asheville's dull summer days. Faced with the unwanted prospects of a far more intense situation, he soon tired of Dance's frenetic passion. "I have seen plenty of people disappointed in love," he wrote Guthrie in late September, "but I never saw a girl who *had so much,* take it all so hard. She knew from the beginning there would be nothing more so it could scarcely be classed even as a *dissapointment*—merely one of those semi-tragic facts that must be faced." These lines, substituting "boy" and "he" for "girl" and "she," could have come from *The Great Gatsby*—say, a communiqué from Daisy Fay to Jordan Baker stating the impossibility of a lasting love match with Gatsby. In this instance, Fitzgerald played the role of a careless Daisy. In October, Dance, now out of the hospital, began the difficult process of accepting the situation. "I have my life and responsibilities as Scott has his," she wrote Guthrie, "and when I am a very old lady I shall still be here trying to make Hop happy. . . . I am fundamentally one who takes my responsibilities rather seriously. . . . I had never loved anyone before as I loved Scott and shall love him until I die but as I wrote you when I left Asheville that was all I could do for him or that he could do for me. You know what life is."[14]

Dance and Fitzgerald maintained a scattered correspondence until his death in 1940. She occasionally sent expensive gifts, which he accepted with a certain embarrassment, being unable financially to reciprocate. She later reconnected with Guthrie amid the early-1960s boomlet of Fitzgeraldiana, their few letters circling back to the subject of Scott and their shared summer of '35. Writing to Guthrie in 1964, Dance conceded her now-emptied interest in Fitzgerald's writings: "Scott's books I find no longer readable. I haven't the patience or the interest." She further described herself as "angry" at a recently published Fitzgerald biography by Andrew Turnbull, who depicted her in it as "pretty and wealthy but not otherwise remarkable, and [Scott] resented wasting time on her." Dance also took a swipe at Sheilah Graham, whose memoir of her time with Fitzgerald—*Beloved Infidel*—had been published a few years earlier: "I saw [her] on some silly television recently. She is really returning to her origins unfortunately. She seems insecure and I felt sorry for watching her. It is a pity."[15]

Palmists, prostitutes, and the odd affair aside, Fitzgerald did meet other writers in North Carolina. These included the novelists Margaret Culkin Banning and Marjorie Kinnan Rawlings and the historians Charles and Mary Beard, who were staying in Tryon at the time. Charles was perhaps the most notable, controversial, and popular American historian of the first half of the twentieth century. At the time of his death in 1948, sales of his books had exceeded several million copies. Like Fitzgerald, he was a midwesterner (Indiana), an "Old American" type, and a critic of the nation's anointment of industrial capitalism. He shared Scott's belief that the United States had in some vital sense lost its way since the Civil War.

In the 1936 revised edition of the Beards' widely read textbook *The Rise of American Civilization,* the authors took measure of the market crash, oftentimes sounding a lot like Fitzgerald. In "Echoes of the Jazz Age," for example, Scott had warned of "a whole race going hedonistic, deciding on pleasure," while the Beards spoke of a spreading "virus among all ranks of society, making the spending of money a national mania and casting the stigma of contempt on previous virtues of thrift, toil, and moderation." In a similar fashion, Fitzgerald's commentary, particularly in *The Great Gatsby* and *Tender Is the Night,* on the collapse of older moral codes before the growing cultural influence of moneymakers and movie stars converged with the Beards' claim that "the decline of domestic authority parallel[led] the velocity of mass production and publicity." Finally, the idea of the Jazz Age as some never-to-be-repeated Shangri-La appealed to both the historians and the novelist. Chapter 30 in *Rise,* "The Mirage Dissolves," scrutinizes the 1920s and repeats the metaphor used by Fitzgerald in "My Lost City," also an elegy to the just-passed decade, in which he said, "I can only cry out that I have lost my splendid mirage."[16]

Beard, of course, was a trained historian who visited archives, sampled secondary materials, and appealed to his profession by putting forth hypotheses backed by evidence and footnotes. Fitzgerald in his own way did much the same. His archives were any number of bars, newspapers, beaches, and cities—wherever he picked up stimuli. His secondary source materials included the publications of his fellow writers, whose work he followed closely. As much as Beard—or Veblen or Adams or Turner— he saw in America the end of something that belied the false continuity of textbooks. In 1917, Beard quit his post at Columbia University and, while continuing to write history, retreated to a small dairy farm that he operated in the small western Connecticut town of New Milford. Knocking around the mountain country of North Carolina, Fitzgerald also looked to be in a kind of retreat. New York and Europe were now in his rearview mirror, even as the future remained uncertain.

Underlying Fitzgerald's Asheville limbo were ever-increasing financial difficulties. By 1936, his combined debts to Scribner and Harold Ober had reached some $20,000 (about $350,000 in current dollars). Without a novel in the pipeline and unable to command top price for his stories, Fitzgerald despaired of ever getting his accounts in order. Ober's response to one February request, "I wired your bank $100. today. . . . This will at least give you a little cash to go on while you are working on the new . . . story," hints at Scott's hand-to-mouth existence.[17]

Then, in September, Fitzgerald's mother died of a cerebral hemorrhage. In need of money for Scottie's schooling and Zelda's medical care, he asked his sister, Annabel, for a preprobate transfer of funds to meet his immediate expenses. His letter, the product of a proud man nearing bottom, is worth quoting at length:

I have got to take six weeks rest as the doctors have told me frankly the chances of my lasting out another winter are getting thinner and thinner and I would either be dead or be a jibbering nervous wreck in some sanatorium, in either case leaving very insufficient protection for two helpless dependents. . . . I am already writing again and will continue to write under any circumstances but it would be suicidal to keep on writing at this nervous tensity, often with no help but what can be gotten out of a bottle of gin. . . . I want six to eight weeks of not worrying about a single thing and of not writing under pressure and only for a couple of hours a day.

This story of becoming a nervous wreck at forty is not pretty but I want to make you understand that the only way such a rest can possibly be arranged is the aforesaid conversion of my share of mother's money into protection for my life insurance policy. There is no reproaching me for past extravagances nor for my failure to get control of the liquor situation under the circumstances of strain. . . .

My earning powers have been inevitably dimmed in the last two years by [health concerns and Zelda's care] and by the depression which has cut almost in half my actual income before 1932 up to this year when it was going along at a better clip until mother's collapse and this accident [Fitzgerald had broken his right shoulder two months earlier while diving into a pool]. There is no reason why in decent health I couldn't write myself out of this mess, being still under forty and having the necessary connections and reputation.[18]

Fitzgerald believed the request reasonable, even fitting considering Mollie's adoration for him. He described her to Dance: "a defiant old woman, defiant in her love for me in spite of my neglect of her, and it would have been quite within her character to have died that I might live." Annabel, not on the best of terms with Scott, saw matters differently. As her daughters, Courtney Sprague Vaughan and Patricia Sprague Reneau, later remembered, "The estrangement that existed between Mother and [Scott] was undoubtedly caused, in part, by the different lifestyles each had chosen and had not ended at the time of their mother's death." The matter of Mollie's money now proved to be another point of contention. "We remember," the daughters explained, "Mother telling us that the dispute and hard feelings brought on at the time of our grandmother's death stemmed from . . . Fitzgerald's desire that the money he had earlier borrowed periodically from Grandmother not be deducted from his inheritance. Daddy felt that this was unfair to Mother."[19]

And from the "other side" of the sibling divide, in an interview of 1977, Scottie deepened our understanding of her father and aunt's differences: "Annabelle was an awfully good, strictly brought-up little Catholic girl and remains to this day a very, very fervent Catholic. And Daddy was pretty much flaunting the church, and I think it deeply offended her. I think also he neglected his mother and father pretty badly. . . . And as I have found with other relatives . . . gosh, a lot of people, instead of deriving any pleasure from their relatives being very successful, resent it."[20] What Annabel made of her brother's writing career is a matter of conjecture, but it seems safe to say that by 1936, at least in regard to his finances, Scott thought of himself as anything but successful. In the end, he yielded to Annabel's position and received about $18,000 from an estate valued at around $45,000.

Delay in getting the money, combined with a prolonged artistic miasma, dogged Fitzgerald throughout the fall. In October, back in Asheville, he employed Marie Shank, a local woman with some college, as his secretary. She remembered him as generally soused and unable to write with confidence. "In the very beginning I did not know he was drinking," she later told a biographer. "Had I known, and the extent, I should probably have quit right then. I soon learned that he was an alcoholic, but by that time I was sufficiently interested to stay on. . . . I am sure, though, that he felt his writing ability had left, or was leaving him for good. . . . Apparently he lived on gin and beer—that is what he drank all the time I was there. I have no idea how much gin he averaged a day, but it was plenty." During these difficult months, Shank said, Fitzgerald made two faint attempts to kill himself: first, "he had taken [a phial of morphine] and was found lying on the bathroom floor," and later, he acquired a pistol and threatened to shoot himself.[21] Yet even at this, his lowest point, Fitzgerald showed a devotion to his craft that moved Shank: "One thing that impressed me was his sensitiveness to the beauty of words. Especially toward the latter part of his stay here, I would often go in and find him reading Keats or Shelley, with tears rolling down his cheeks. He would read a little to me and say, 'Did you ever hear anything so beautiful? . . . Occasionally he would ask me to read, and would become very impatient if I put the least expression into what I was reading. He wanted only the words."[22]

The gorgeous Blue Ridge backdrop, by contrast, held for Fitzgerald only a limited and utilitarian attraction. "To my surprise," Shank recalled, "he had little or no appreciation of the beauties of nature, or at least for the beauty of this mountain country, which is lovely beyond description. He said to me he didn't understand why people raved so much about it." Shank's comment aligns with a more general observation made by John Dos Passos regarding Fitzgerald's relentless commitment to his craft: "He didn't look at landscape, he had no taste for food or wine or painting, little ear for music except for the most rudimentary popular songs, but about writing he was a born professional. Everything he said was worth listening to."[23] Scott, of course, had not come to North Carolina for the scenery. He sought to soothe his lungs and ease his expenditures and perhaps, if he could exorcise enough ghosts, put the doubtful atmosphere of *Tender Is the Night* and the lost years of its painful gestation behind him. But for this, he needed still more time.

TWENTY

De Profundis

Me caring about no one and nothing.

F. Scott Fitzgerald, 1936

Early one morning in the spring of 1935, Arnold Gingrich, the thirty-one-year-old editor and cofounder of *Esquire* magazine, arrived at Fitzgerald's 1307 Park Avenue apartment in downtown Baltimore. He was expected. Finding a note pinned to the front door by Scott, Gingrich proceeded up the stairs and into Fitzgerald's flat. There, in a "grubby bathrobe," he later recalled, stood the man whom he considered one of America's greatest writers. But the question now was whether Fitzgerald would ever write—great—again. Nearing forty, Scott was no longer the wunderkind who had knocked off three novels before thirty; nor did he seem a good bet to summon the short-story magic that had delighted a generation of *Saturday Evening Post* readers. "It isn't particularly likely that I'll write a great many more stories about young love," he confessed to the *Collier's* editor Kenneth Littauer. "They have been done with increasing difficulty and increasing insincerity. I would either be a miracle man or a hack if I could go on turning out an identical product for three decades. I know what's expected of me, but in that direction the well is pretty dry and I think I am much wiser in not trying to strain for it but rather to open up a new well, a new vein."[1]

Surprised and flattered by Gingrich's visit, Fitzgerald spoke that morning of his present publishing difficulties, a topic revisited later in the day as the two sat at the airport, near the landing field, awaiting Gingrich's delayed flight. Killing time, they played a kind of verse ping-pong, one starting and the other finishing lines from Rupert Brooke. Falling on "A Channel Passage," Fitzgerald took the opening, reciting the cryptic words "quiet and quick/my cold gorge arose . . ."—and then stopped. "The trouble is," he broke the game, "my cold gorge does, every time I sit down to write a story of young love for *The Saturday Evening Post.* But I'm so overextended that unless I do, the damned ship will do more than lurch and slither; the damned ship will sink." Seeing an opening, Gingrich made his pitch: "Write us just that, and in language as un-buttoned as you like."[2]

In fact, Fitzgerald could already claim some small fame in the field of autobiographical writing—though assuredly of the buttoned-up variety. In "What I Think and Feel at 25" (1922), he imparted life lessons to the graybeards; his epic travels across the wilds of Alabama were duly noted in "The Cruise of the Rolling Junk" (1924); and in "How to Live on $36,000 a Year" (1924), readers smiled at Scott's futile efforts to econo-mize. These were light pieces played for laughs and thus not to be con-fused with their author's "real" writing. But beginning in 1927 with the elegiac "Princeton" and followed by such standouts as "Echoes of the Jazz Age" (1931), "My Lost City" (1932), and "Ring" (1933), Fitzgerald moved his nonfiction writing on to more subtle and searching social commentary. In "One Hundred False Starts" (1933), a dissection of creative inspiration, he anticipated the end of his run as a recorder of first love: "Mostly we au-thors must repeat ourselves—that's the truth. We have two or three great and moving experiences in our lives . . . and we tell our two or three stories—each time in a new disguise—maybe ten times, maybe a hundred, as long as people will listen."[3] With no more "great and moving experi-ences" on the horizon, Fitzgerald faced an uncertain future. He could pla-giarize himself with ever-diminishing returns or move decisively in a dif-ferent direction, in search of a different audience.

Still, if a dozen good reasons begged for Scott to embrace Gingrich's timely overture, one stubborn fact held him back. Compared to the *Sat-urday Evening Post, Esquire* paid a pittance—a going rate of $200 per story (approximately $3,500 in current dollars). Unlike the *Post,* however, *Es-quire* aspired to a higher literary tone and, after bringing Hemingway into its stable, consistently drew the better talent. *Esquire* writers in the 1930s included Thomas Wolfe, John Steinbeck, E. E. Cummings, Sinclair Lewis, Langston Hughes, Thomas Mann, and André Maurois. If association with *Esquire* was something of a financial comedown for Fitzgerald, it would nevertheless put him in the strongest artistic company of his career.[4] In the mood to instruct and always something of an exhibitionist, Scott began drafting in the late fall of 1935 three articles—"The Crack-Up," "Pasting It Together," and "Handle with Care"—eager to take advantage of Gingrich's recommendation that he "write about it." Appearing in *Esquire* the following February, March, and April, this sequence, known collectively as "The Crack-Up," took the temperature equally of its author, his country, and his times.

The sources of Scott's breakdown are easy enough to identify. They include the emotional and financial costs of Zelda's hospitalization, his inability to stop drinking, and the realization that a combination of personal weaknesses and life itself would prevent him from ever being, as he put it in "Handle with Care," an "entire man."[5] In other words, he lacked self-control, felt too much, held onto old dreams too long, and now wished, in his hard-earned wisdom, to pull back. In Asheville, Guthrie had witnessed the crack-up creeping up on Fitzgerald and observed his difficulties from up close. She wrote in her diary, "'Life is not happy,' as he says. It isn't for him. He said it was a good thing he was not a rich man or he would have been dead before now (killing himself with indulgences!) but that the necessity of doing work had kept him going. Now he hopes that life will continue to be just endurable, which will only be if he keeps enough health to work."[6] The connection that Fitzgerald made between health and work seems right. Looking back on the black period 1935–1936, he later noted with some asperity, "all my products were dirges and elegies."[7] Up until then, Scott had, flapper ephemera aside, routinely engaged in material that stimulated him—these included his novels, several sparkling cluster stories that led to *The Great Gatsby* and later *Tender Is the Night,* and in between these, the Basil and Josephine sequence. But now he was stuck, writing fewer memorable stories and unable to sketch out a new novel. He feared, as he had put it to Littauer, that the well was empty.

Even in such an anxious state, however, Scott never really hit bottom, and taken altogether, the "Crack-Up" articles never quite persuaded as candid confessions—they left too much out. Eliding Zelda's more serious "crack-up" and playing down his own dependence on alcohol, Fitzgerald emphasized instead how, like Dick Diver, he was suddenly unable to find sustenance in the world around him: "I had weaned myself from all the things I used to love."[8] He found fault with the culture, with Hollywood, and with all the rich boys who had tormented him in youth and haunted him still. As much as anything, he believed that America had failed to nurture its budding artists, turning them, when possible, into celebrities and giving them no space to mature beyond their initial efforts. "Premature success," he later argued, "gives one an almost mystical conception of destiny as opposed to will power—at its worst the Napoleonic delusion. The man who arrives young believes that he exercises his will because his star is shining. The man who only asserts himself at thirty has a balanced idea of what will power and fact have each contributed."[9] No one enjoyed (or wrote about) early success quite like Fitzgerald did, but he now blamed it for denying him the opportunity to develop a more complete attitude toward life.

One might wonder if *Esquire* really wanted a full confession from Fitzgerald. Presumably without some entertainment value or general appeal in the articles, Gingrich would have passed on them. Their shopworn titles suggest an underlying flippancy meant to draw readers in. Or, put another way, would Scott have dared to refer to Zelda in print as a "crack-up"? But more than a look back, more than purchased words, the articles seemed to help Fitzgerald stake out the emotional terrain for what proved to be the last few years of his life. He began to rein in his old enthusiasm, committed less of himself to others, and gave the distinct impression of marshaling his resources. When he relocated to California, his colleagues and associates there were struck by his quiet countenance. Aware of his reputation, they expected a live wire. But in the "Crack-Up," Fitzgerald promised to take a different path—no longer would he be quite the charmer, quite the chaser, or quite the Scott of old. Long-standing habits were hard to break, however, and he concluded "Pasting It Together" by plainly fishing for reader response: "I have some doubts as to whether this is of general interest but if anyone wants more, there is plenty left, and your editor will tell you."[10]

What saves the "Crack-Up" articles from being mere exercises in self-pity is their connection to a broader world of politics and ideas. In them, we see Fitzgerald linking his current artistic ennui to the coming age of collectivization, which he identified with both the Soviet style of organization and, interestingly, the Hollywood capitalist "factory" that used small teams of writers to produce scripts. Rooting for the individual in an era increasingly committed to what he disdainfully described as the "low gear of collaboration," Scott observed a corporatized attack on imagination: "I saw that the novel, which at my maturity was the strongest and supplest medium for conveying thought and emotion from one human being to another, was becoming subordinated to a mechanical and communal art that, whether in the hands of Hollywood merchants or Russian idealists, was capable of reflecting only the tritest thought, the most obvious emotion. It was an art in which words were subordinate to images. . . . As long past as 1930, I had a hunch that the talkies would make even the best selling novelist as archaic as silent pictures."[11] Relegated to history's ash heap, Fitzgerald steered the "Crack-Up" articles toward a traditional "decline and fall" narrative, suggesting to his readers that they too shared in the tragedy of "the tritest thought." Of course, some people, he conceded, had thrived in the recast moral universe. His own literary examples, however, including Tom Buchanan and Daisy Fay, Nicole Diver and Josephine Perry, amounted to a kind of money-is-the-root-of-all-evil rouges' gallery. Such personalities, Fitzgerald now wrote in the "Crack-Up" essays, had all "made some sort of clean break" with older genteel standards of work and community, sex and spirituality. This transition was irrevocable; it changed the individual forever. Rather than relying on familiar traditions, customs, and institutions, the children of the Victorians severed former ties and ventured into the uncharted future. The clean break, Fitzgerald insisted, anticipating George Orwell's dystopic *1984,* "makes the past cease to exist."[12]

Certainly Scott's crack-up had changed him forever. He seemed to be wrestling with the loss of a romantic idealism that had once served as the rock on which he rested—both emotionally and artistically. Life had intruded, caught him unawares, and broken the kindly illusions of youth, wealth, and success that had for so long sustained him. His faith shattered, he needed now to build up what he could from its fragments. "I don't know whether those articles of mine in *Esquire*—that 'Crack-Up' series—represented a real nervous breakdown," he put the matter to one correspondent. "In retrospect it seems more of a spiritual 'change of life'—and a most unwilling one—it was a protest against a new set of conditions which I would have to face and a protest of my mind at having to make the psychological adjustments which would suit this new set of circumstances."[13]

For Fitzgerald, this "change of life" meant recognizing a cultural condition that would in the decades following his death come under the heading of various descriptive titles including "modernity," "anomie," or "fracture"—that is, the volatile merging of capitalism, secularism, rationalism, and industrialism that had become the dominant impulse propelling Western civilization. And in questioning modernity's efficacy, he joined a number of skeptical artists, historians, and writers. In this sense, "The Crack-Up" is less a lone cry in the dark than one of many examples in a notable cross-cultural antimodernist movement that spanned the last decade of the nineteenth century and the first decades of the twentieth. The Orientalists Lafcadio Hearn and William Sturgis Bigelow found inspiration in Japanese legends and ghost stories, Buddhism and architecture; the painter John La Farge sampled the cultures of the South Seas, visiting Hawaii, Samoa, Tahiti, and Fiji in the early 1890s; and the philosopher George Santayana happily left America's Protestant work ethic behind, resigning from Harvard in 1912 and spending the final decades of his life in Europe. A rather large number of modernity's discontents discovered cultural nourishment in the medieval world. Their numbers included Henry Adams, William Morris, Richard Wagner, James Russell Lowell, Bernhard Berenson, Arthur Kingsley Porter, and, in a minor key, Fitzgerald, whose "Philippe" stories, as has been noted, followed the exploits of a ninth-century Frenchman returning from Moorish Spain to claim his inheritance.

Like some of these men, Fitzgerald had come to see his own indulgences and adventures in escapism as part of a more general cultural ailment. Long past Princeton, he still soothed himself to sleep with the "waking dreams" of football glory. In light of his mounting personal difficulties, he now asked himself if this hitherto-harmless diversion might not have suggested a deeper unwillingness to accept life on its own terms. He raised a similar query on the dangers of escapism in "Babylon Revisited" when he wrote, "if you didn't want it to be snow you just paid some money." This self-indulgent response to reality had inevitably caught up with Fitzgerald—and, he now insisted, had caught up with America, too. As he put it in "Pasting It Together," a country, just like a person, can be wounded by illusions and seek to retreat from the collective hardships of life to the obscure fantasies of "some great material or spiritual bonanza."[14]

To say that America, like the just-shy-of-forty Fitzgerald, had prematurely cracked is to draw attention to its relative youth on the international stage. In 1936, the U.S. Constitution was barely 150 years old, veterans of Gettysburg and Cold Harbor still drew government pensions, and the Nineteenth Amendment, which guaranteed all women the right to vote, had been in effect for only sixteen years. The country, however, now looked ancient and worn. While fresh ideologies—communism and fascism—were on the rise, America's celebrated economic strength seemed unable to overcome the Depression. Had the nation relied too much on capitalism and consumerism? Generations earlier, Abraham Lincoln had in his Second Inaugural Address coupled the country's material prosperity with its long support of slavery and concluded by quoting from the book of Psalms: "Yet, if God wills that it continue, until all the wealth piled by the bond-man's two hundred and fifty years of unrequited toil shall be sunk, and until every drop of blood drawn with the lash, shall be paid by another drawn with the sword, as was said three thousand years ago, so still it must be said 'the judgments of the Lord, are true and righteous altogether.'"[15] Might, in other words, the penalty for slavery be a devastating war that destroyed centuries of ill-gotten gain? In the "Crack-Up" articles, Fitzgerald raises a not-unrelated moral concern; again, a corruptive wealth dreaming and wealth chasing threatens the republic. Tying his personal struggles to those of the country, Scott suggested that his early celebrity, drifting years abroad, and compulsive spending were encouraged by a culture that was too impressed by fame and fortune. In his end, he saw its end. But even as he identified the sources of his discontent, Scott allowed that the golden times, fleeting as they were, still called out to him. What would replace them and serve as the occasional spice and spirit as he aged he could not at the moment say. *"Ye are the salt of the earth,"* he borrowed from the book of Matthew. *"But if the salt hath lost its savour wherewith shall it be salted?"*[16]

⁓

The "Crack-Up" articles stirred an immediate and, among the literati, a generally negative reaction. Many in Fitzgerald's professional orbit—his editor, agent, and fellow writers—were stunned that he had drawn such a raw and painful public portrait. Ober complained, "I think those confounded Esquire articles have done you a great deal of harm," while John Dos Passos thought Scott had sold his talents cheaply. "Christ man how do you find time in the middle of the general conflagration to worry about all that stuff? We're living in one of the damnedest tragic moments in history—if you want to go to pieces I think it absolutely o.k. but I think you ought to write a first rate novel about it (and you probably will) instead of spilling it in little pieces for Arnold Gingrich." Their surprise is curious considering that, as Morris Dickstein has noted, "Fitzgerald's self-knowledge had always been at the heart of his talent."[17]

Beyond Scott's professional circle, however, others appreciated what the *San Francisco Chronicle* described as his effort "to explain the spiritual troubles of many another member of the almost-lost generation." His Baltimore friend and onetime La Paix landlord Margaret Turnbull thought the first "Crack-Up" essay a brilliant "mental snapshot of a rather universal experience," linking a "more or less defeated" Fitzgerald with "a chain of people, stretching around the world, to catch hold of [his] hands."[18] Turnbull spoke with perhaps more authority than she knew. The essays struck a resonant chord among fellow "crack-ups," many of whom contacted Fitzgerald, typically offering a mixture of gratitude, advice, and commiseration. One New Jersey woman counseled Scott to embrace his "spiritual union" with these interested parties: "I cannot resist this strong impulse to write you and I hope that you will forgive me if my letter is unwelcome. I think you will receive letters from all over America, because you have opened the door on a dark chamber of American life. Maybe you will shrink from these writers in something like squeamish unease. But before you turn upon yourself in anger or dismay, perhaps you will see more truly how close, how deep, how intimate, is your spiritual union with other people; how little alone you are actually."[19] And an Arizona man wrote, "You've had some real Grade A anguish now and you think you won't get over it. I've had it—almost exactly the same kind—and the queer thing about it is that we *do* get over it, and that we grow because of it. It's just a waiting game. You'll emerge a mature person. I am not afraid to venture that prophecy. You've been finding out a lot of things that have hurt, like hell, and at the end of it you'll be grown up. You're too young to let it down you."[20] Ever since the publication of *The Great Gatsby,* Fitzgerald had bemoaned his novels' inability to catch the culture and sell in large numbers. Though the "Crack-Up" triptych brought him little money, it did inspire the kind of readers' response that Scott had for several years been missing. These were not artistically critical reactions, of course, but they did impress on Fitzgerald the potential market for confessional writing.

By the 1950s, this genre had moved into the mainstream with such notables as Robert Lowell, Anne Sexton, Norman Mailer, and Sylvia Plath following Fitzgerald. But in the 1930s, publishing houses balked at the public airing of private struggles. At Scribner, a surprised Max Perkins hardly knew what to make of Fitzgerald's performance and chose to deflect its sharpest points. He wrote to Hemingway,

> Nobody would write those articles if they were really true. I doubt if a hopeless man will tell about it, or a man who thinks he is beaten for good. Those people I should think would not say anything at all, just as those who really intend suicide never tell anybody. So I thought that in some deep way, when he wrote those articles, Scott must have been thinking that things would be different with him. He may have lost that passion in writing which he once had, but he is such a wonderful craftsman that he could certainly make out well if he were able to control himself and be reconciled to life.[21]

In fact, it was precisely Fitzgerald's stubborn unwillingness "to reconcile to life" that inspired the sudden spurt of "Crack-Up" essays. And far from symbolizing, as Perkins had put it, Scott's "lost . . . passion in writing," they signaled instead his growth as an author.

On the other side of success, Hemingway replied to Fitzgerald's confession of failure with a superior contempt. His August 1936 short story "The Snows of Kilimanjaro" (also published in Gingrich's *Esquire*) includes a nasty swipe at Scott: "The rich were dull and they drank too much, or they played too much backgammon. They were dull and they were repetitious. He remembered poor Scott Fitzgerald and his romantic awe of them and how he had started a story once that began, 'The very rich are different from you and me.' And how someone had said to Scott, Yes they have more money. But that was not humorous to Scott. He thought they were a special glamorous race and when he found they weren't it wrecked him just as much as any other thing that wrecked him."[22] This speculative, goading, and altogether corrosive caricature of Fitzgerald's supposed reaction to the rich tells us, perhaps, as much about Hemingway as about his subject. Married at the time to the Arkansas heiress Pauline Pfeiffer and holding court in a spacious nineteenth-century Key West home purchased with Pfeiffer money and filled with fine European paintings and antique Spanish furniture, Hemingway nevertheless thought himself dependent artistically on a spartan severity. Accordingly, in disparaging Fitzgerald's "obsession" with wealth, he may well have been chastising himself—seven years had passed since his last novel.

The problem with Hemingway's bon mot is that the incident never happened—or at least it never happened to Scott. Hemingway, rather, had been the one zinged. While dining with Perkins and the Irish-born literary critic Mary Colum, Hemingway somewhat pompously said, "I am getting to know the rich," which prompted Colum to fire back, "The only difference between the rich and other people is that the rich have more money."[23] Cleverly put in his place at the dinner table (by a woman no less), Hemingway could exorcise this minor embarrassment by telling the world that it had happened to someone else, someone the world would recognize, someone who had recently confessed publicly to a host of weaknesses and humiliations.

Fitzgerald took the put-down hard and quickly wrote Hemingway to correct the record. All things considered, he was a gentleman about it:

"Please lay off me in print. If I choose to write de profundis sometimes it doesn't mean I want friends praying aloud over my corpse. No doubt you meant it kindly but it cost me a night's sleep. And when you incorporate it (the story) in a book would you mind cutting my name? It's a fine story—one of your best—even though the 'Poor Scott Fitzgerald ect' rather spoiled it for me." Almost as an afterthought, placed below the body of the letter, below "Ever your friend," Scott tried to set the record straight: "Riches have *never* fascinated me, unless combined with the greatest charm or distinction."[24]

The bit about "poor Scott Fitzgerald" became the story's most notorious line, though earlier in the piece, Hemingway did more than reference Scott; he appeared to address him directly: "But, in yourself, you said that you would write about these people; about the very rich; that you were really not of them but a spy in their country; that you would leave it and write of it and for once it would be written by some one who knew what he was writing of. But he would never do it, because each day of not writing, of comfort, of being that which he despised, dulled his ability and softened his will to work so that, finally, he did no work at all."[25] If, in fact, Hemingway did have Scott in mind when he wrote these lines, he was way off the mark. Fitzgerald's output to this point included four novels, a play, and over one hundred short stories, as well as many hundreds of letters, a substantial number of which were later collected in no fewer than seven edited works.[26] All this and he was still in his thirties.

But with Hemingway's judgment in print, it was now open season on "poor Scott Fitzgerald." That September, the *New York Evening Post* writer Michel Mok interviewed Scott in Asheville on the eve of his fortieth birthday. Recovering from a fractured shoulder suffered in a diving accident, Fitzgerald proceeded to give an off-the-cuff and self-wounding performance that Mok fully exploited. Titled "The Other Side of Paradise: Scott Fitzgerald, 40, Engulfed in Despair," the piece drew a nasty portrait of a pathetically weak man, mothered by a day nurse and habituated to booze. Mok wrote of Fitzgerald's "jittery jumping off and onto his bed, his restless pacing, his trembling hands, his twitching face with its pitiful expression of a cruelly beaten child." Scott's "frequent trips to a highboy, in a drawer of which lay a bottle," were also emphasized for maximum effect. "Each time he poured a drink into the measuring glass on his bedside table," wrote Mok, "he would look appealingly at the nurse and ask, 'Just one ounce?' "[27]

One on one with Mok, Fitzgerald seemed eager to unburden himself and naïvely presumed that the journalist would ignore his austere surroundings and unsteady physical condition. These were precisely the things that Mok homed in on. As a result, the reader is left with the distinct impression that, whatever was ailing Fitzgerald, he had it coming. And this may not be an altogether false read. During the dark days of 1935–1936, Fitzgerald did exhibit symptoms of self-loathing; it was as if, as he wrote in the "Crack-Up" essays, he wanted to make "some sort of clean break" and needed to immolate the old self in order to do so. Intended or not, he did give Mok the match. After the article appeared, Scott wrote Ober an epistle of half truths justifying his willingness to cooperate with the story:

> I was in bed with temp about 102 when the . . . phone rang and a voice said that this party had come all the way from N. Y. to interview me. I fell for this like a damn fool, got him up, gave him a drink + accepted his exterior good manners. He had some relative with mental trouble (wife or mother) so I talked to him freely about treatments symptoms ect, about being depressed at advancing age and a little desperate about the wasted summer with this shoulder and arm—perhaps more freely than if [I] had been well. I hadn't the faintest suspicion what would happen + I've never been a publicity seeker + never gotten a raw deal before. When that thing [the article] came it seemed about the end and I got hold of a morphine file and swallowed four grains enough to kill a horse. It happened to be an overdose and almost before I could get to the bed I vomited the whole thing and the nurse came in + saw the empty phial + there was hell to pay. [F]or awhile + afterwards I felt like a fool.[28]

But had Fitzgerald told Ober the full story? Did he himself understand the full story? It seems at least an even bet that he used the interview, like he used the "Crack-Up" articles, for his own ends. By killing off the old man—one thinks of Scott's questionable suicide attempt following Mok's visit—perhaps he hoped a new one might rise.

Over time, some of the darkness that had descended on Fitzgerald gradually lifted. "The writing of the articles helped me," he informed one correspondent, but he acknowledged their limitations as well: "In my case the disease wore itself out." What remained is Scott's testimony to the power of his "illness" and to the set of cultural circumstances in which it flourished. In time and in the fullness of his life, Fitzgerald's "crack-up" took on an added poignancy. A year after his death, Perkins began to appreciate the articles' important therapeutic role and intrinsic artistic value in a way that had once eluded him. "I hated it when it came out, just as you did," he wrote Edmund Wilson, "but I have found several intelligent people that think highly of it. There was more truth and sincerity in it, I suppose, than we realized at the time."[29]

TWENTY-ONE

Life in a Company Town

Isn't Hollywood a dump—in the human sense of the word.
A hideous town, pointed up by the insulting gardens of its rich,
full of the human spirit at a new low of debasement.

F. Scott Fitzgerald, 1940

As early as December 1919, prior even to the publication of *This Side of Paradise,* Fitzgerald had Hollywood on his mind. "Is there money in writing movies?" he asked his agent of a few weeks, Harold Ober. Could a man with a smart pen and a modern sensibility make it in films? Just a babe on the literary scene, Fitzgerald was already looking for new worlds to conquer—but this one would have to wait. Not until January 1927 did Scott take his first Hollywood plunge, penning "Lipstick" for United Artists, a silly college-humor script about an aphrodisiac face paint; the film never made it into production. "Everyone thinks the beginning or premise contains exceptionally fine material," one UA official wrote Fitzgerald, "but that rest of story is weak."[1] A return trip in the autumn of 1931 also ended in a white flag. Scott's screenplay for the Jean Harlow vehicle *Red-Headed Woman* lost out to the cleverer and censure-defying draft submitted by Anita Loos, author of the popular comic novel *Gentlemen Prefer Blondes* (1925). Only on his third and final Hollywood venture (1937–1940) did Fitzgerald receive his single screen credit, this for a fine adaptation of Erich Maria Remarque's *Three Comrades.*

In the spring of 1937, with Fitzgerald's publishing options narrowed, he once again entertained the idea of writing for the movies. He contacted his agent, Harold Ober, who contacted Ober Associates' Hollywood representative, H. N. Swanson, who contacted Edwin Knopf, then heading the script department at MGM and a Fitzgerald acquaintance since the late 1920s. Knopf and the director King Vidor had once contemplated making a film based loosely on the lives of Scott and Zelda. And the 1935 movie *The Wedding Night,* a romantic drama starring Gary Cooper and Anna Sten for which Knopf provided the story of a financially strapped novelist, took Scott as its inspiration. Swanson's overture led to a late-June interview-luncheon in New York, after which Knopf, convinced of Scott's sobriety, offered him a six-month contract starting at $1,000 a week—an incredible sum for an unproven screenwriter. Less than two weeks later, Fitzgerald was aboard a Southern Pacific passenger train heading to Los Angeles.

There, all did not go smoothly. Fitzgerald was unable to decipher what directors wanted from him and lacked any organic connection to the region, its people, or its perspectives, so he treated Hollywood like a foreign land. Even its mild weather seemed to confuse him. Consider the following anecdote from Frances Kroll, Scott's secretary during these final years:

> I have a dark impression that lingers—of a walk we took up the street at one day's end. I was going to my car; he was going to Schwab's Drug Store on Sunset Boulevard, just a couple of blocks away. He was wearing a dark topcoat and a grey homburg hat. As we kept pace, I looked over at him and was chilled by his image, like a shadowy figure in an old photograph. His outfit and pallor were alien to the style and warmth of Southern California—as if he were not at home here, had just stopped off and was dressed to leave on the next train.[2]

We might recall that Fitzgerald had also resisted the appeal of the Carolina Appalachians, whose natural beauty had failed to move him. Then again, neither Asheville nor Hollywood was exactly a vacation spot for Scott; the former promised to heal his lesioned lungs, and the latter held out the hope of resurrecting his ever-shaky finances.

To say, however, that Hollywood offered Scott little more than money would be unjust. Since *Tender Is the Night*'s publication, Fitzgerald had lived in various homes, inns, and hotels in Baltimore and North Carolina, but this movement had inspired neither peace nor productivity. The regimen of mountain retreats and resting cures had brought him no relief; he grew bored, sought stimulation, and wrestled with a septic mix of guilt and debt that at times gave way to depression. Only a radical change could alter his circumstances, and California proved to be the most convenient lifeboat available. His North Carolina friend Margaret Culkin Banning captured the essence of his apathy during this period: "In Tryon, he often talked deeply and revealingly about work and, to some extent, about himself. I don't believe I feel qualified to try to explain why he went back to Hollywood. But I knew there were two contributing factors. One, of course, was money and the constant fear of losing what markets he had. The other was a terrible loneliness that came over him at being away from people of his own craft and with so few people who understood what his major preoccupation was."[3] Put another way, it might be said that Fitzgerald, mired in a negating and self-defeating self-seclusion, needed Hollywood far more than Hollywood needed him.

Even at this low point, however, Fitzgerald remained confident of his skills and, Scott being Scott, stormed the movie industry with typically grandiose expectations for success, believing that he could dominate his situation by sheer application of will. A pedagogue at heart, he studied movies like an earnest schoolboy, much as he had once reviewed Zelda's medical treatments; now, instead of advising doctors, he assumed to instruct directors. No doubt a good bit of this audacity had to do with Fitzgerald's innate "bossiness," his desire to lead rather than to follow; it is equally true, however, that as aesthetic statements, movies absorbed him on their own intrinsic merits. He thought the industry fell far short of its potential, even as its possibilities for dramatic expression genuinely excited him. In a sense, Scott's relationship to the cinema mirrored his reaction to the rich: it promised much but delivered little. With seemingly endless dollars, talent, and time, Hollywood's film industry, he supposed, too rarely rose above the easy and the formulaic. Others noticed his disenchantment. "There were many things that delighted him," remembered the actress Helen Hayes, "but all in all, I think Scott was unhappy there from the start. . . . He hated the awful discipline of the studios. Pictures took writers right back to the working climate of high school. And he was not in the best shape spiritually; he was afraid that his writing gift was going through a tunnel."[4]

The collaborative process in particular frustrated Fitzgerald. He had to clock in to the studio each morning, suffered through a series of story conferences, and quickly discovered that his skills and reputation as a writer—the very things that Hollywood apparently coveted—counted for little when arguing with a director over the insertion of a few key words in a script. Lacking creative license only typified for Fitzgerald the broader comedown of the Hollywood experience. The magic of the West Coast rarely touched him; he mistrusted its paradisiacal overtones, which he read as a grand and empty seduction. "I find, after a long time out here, that one develops new attitudes," he complained to Gerald Murphy in 1940. "It is, for example, such a slack *soft* place—even its pleasure lacking the fierceness of Provence. . . . This is an unhealthy condition of affairs. Except for the stage-struck young girls people come here for negative reasons—all gold rushes are essentially negative—and the young girls soon join the vicious circle. There is no group, however small, interesting as such. Everywhere there is, after a moment, either corruption or indifference." Along the same lines, he wrote to Beatrice Dance of his determination to "accept the fact that movies are a game—entertainment for children and nothing more. If one didn't constantly remind oneself of this one would be continually heartbroken thinking what they might be and very occasionally have been."[5]

As usual, where Fitzgerald found romance lacking, he made it up on the spot. In Hollywood, he identified the 1936 death of the MGM producer Irving Thalberg as *the* crucial turning point in the movie industry's brief history. Known for his youth and talent, Thalberg, only thirty-seven at the time of his passing, was a consummate professional with a seemingly unerring eye for choosing the right actors, scripts, and directors. His true job title might more accurately have read "Impresario." Drawn to "literary" subjects, Thalberg clashed with the MGM titan Louis B. Mayer, who preferred to crank out profitable crowd pleasers—one sees his fingerprints on the Andy Hardy and Dr. Kildare series. Thalberg's death (by pneumonia and lung failure, a "romantic" illness close to Scott's own tuberculosis scare) signified to Fitzgerald something larger than the climax of a private Hollywood power struggle. Instead he saw it, as he had seen Gatsby's death, as part of a passing phase in American life—the end of the old dream that men might come to the New World and create work of profound and personal meaning. Or, as the film historian Mark A. Vieira has put it, "the thoughtful, quirky, innovative cinema of Irving Thalberg died with him."[6]

It took little time for Hollywood's corporate regimen to eat away at Scott's spirit. In his correspondence, he sometimes referred to the studios as "factories," and in a letter to Zelda's sister Rosalind, he dismissed his one screen credit when he declared the movie "awful," its script "*entirely* rewritten by the producer." His friend the novelist John O'Hara recalled that during these difficult years, Fitzgerald "had lost confidence, was wounded, insecure and uncertain."[7] Aiming to give the industry what he presumed it wanted in a writer—sobriety, conviviality, and collegiality—Scott took on a quieter and more withdrawn countenance in southern California. He knew that in the small film colony, contracts were indirectly if inescapably tied to off-the-clock reputations, and he struck an altogether less conspicuous pose. There were to be no more confessionals, no more emotional bankruptcies, and certainly no more crack-ups.

His reward for deferring to Hollywood's Left Coast puritanism was a measure of financial independence that he had not known for years. "The only great satisfaction I've had [in Hollywood]," he observed to an old Princeton classmate, "has been paying off my debts."[8] During his eighteen-month tenure at MGM, Fitzgerald earned nearly $90,000—about $1.4 million in contemporary dollars. When including his freelance work at Twentieth Century-Fox, Columbia Studios, Goldwyn, and Paramount Universal, the figure jumps to some $125,000, or about $2 million in current earnings. Taken altogether, one might say that Fitzgerald's California withdrawal proved a great help financially (he died solvent in 1940, leaving Zelda a small life-insurance policy), while the artistic returns are more difficult to gauge. He embarked on a new short-story line, the Pat Hobby tales, and was working on a novel, *The Last Tycoon,* at the time of his death. Given a different context, this might have been a prime writing period for Scott (ages forty to forty-four), though it is impossible to separate his work from his drinking and his drinking from his declining health. Thus, to imagine a more "productive" Fitzgerald, either in Hollywood or elsewhere, during these final years is something of a stretch. What we know is that he published only one novel after the age of twenty-eight.

Fitzgerald was searching for a spark in his new surroundings and began a semisecretive love affair with the syndicated gossip columnist Sheilah Graham. Both parties were naturally reticent to go public with their relationship; Fitzgerald was married, and it wouldn't do for Graham, a scandal-sheet writer, to be caught in her own scandal. Outside of Hollywood, however, Fitzgerald introduced "Sheilo," as he sometimes called her, to a number of his East Coast friends including Perkins, Wilson, Ober, and the Murphys. For Scott, the relationship complemented his curious double-life existence in California. As he made a show of sobriety for his bosses and dialed down the wild antics that were once his calling card, so he quietly took up with Graham, herself a West Coast transplant dealing with a host of hidden demons.

Born Lily Shiel in 1904 to a Jewish Ukrainian family newly arrived in England, Graham survived a series of early hardships. She was left fatherless before the age of one, and her first memories, according to her son Robert Westbrook, were of hunger, sexual abuse, and running away from an enormous dog: "they were the images that formed her and they stayed with her for the rest of her life."[9] Lily's already difficult childhood took a decidedly Dickensian turn at the age of six, when her mother placed her in an orphanage for Jewish children near London. There, she showed both a tenacious resolve and an instinct to please, captaining the girls' cricket team and distinguishing herself in the classroom. At fourteen, she returned home, and at seventeen, after her mother had died of cancer, she embarked for London's West End and what she presumed would be a dancing career. Unable to make a go of it, she married, at eighteen, Major John Graham Gillam, DSO.

Observers of the Graham-Fitzgerald relationship invariably comment on Scott's efforts to educate the gossip columnist with a program of reading and discussion that the two came to call "A College of One." In fact, Fitzgerald was Graham's *second* mentor. As Graham's daughter,

Wendy Fairey, has noted, Gillam was "a kindly older man who proved impotent, went bankrupt, and looked the other way when [Graham] went out with other men, but under whose Pygmalionesque tutelage she improved her speech and manners, enrolled in the Royal Academy of Dramatic Arts, and changed her name." In effect, Graham found a sponsor who recognized the value of her beauty and was willing to invest in it. The author of *Gallipoli Diary* and a sometime attendee of court functions, Gillam introduced Graham to high social circles, and that included a June 1931 presentation at Buckingham Palace. Decked out in a Norman Hartnell gown, tiara, and white ostrich plumes, Graham entered the throne room and curtsied to a bored Queen Mary and a more attentive King George V before backing out for champagne and cakes. This and other less regal engagements encouraged Graham to protect her past from coming to light, and where the truth proved awkward, fiction served quite well.[10] She later wrote,

> The story I allowed to get about was that I was the daughter of John Lawrence and Veronica Roslyn Graham—both solid-sounding names. We had lived in Chelsea, a fashionable yet Bohemian section of London. This slightly unconventional background could account for any oddness, any slips, in my social behavior. My father, who owned considerable property in the City, died on a business trip to Germany when I was little. I had had tutors, then gone to finishing school in Paris. My mother died when I was seventeen; I had married Major Gillam . . . almost immediately thereafter.[11]

The overtones here are really quite Gatsbyesque. "I'll tell you God's truth," Gatsby says, trotting out a string of untruths. "I am the son of some wealthy people in the middle-west—all dead now. I was brought up in America but educated at Oxford because all my ancestors have been educated there for many years. It is a family tradition. . . . My family all died and I came into a good deal of money." And like Gatsby, Graham too lived in some anxiety that her self-inventions would be exposed. "Time and again when I attached myself to a group at someone's home and hopefully ventured a few words," she later remembered, "the group seemed to dissolve and I would be left standing alone. Again the horror of rejection, of feeling *outside,* of being *scorned*—as if these people knew instinctively that I was of commoner clay—came over me."[12]

Graham was moving toward a divorce and eager to abandon an England that demanded for the upkeep of her hard-won status an elaborate inventory of lies, so she migrated to America in 1933. Having, as Fairey notes, "earned a modest reputation as a freelance journalist, [Graham] bluff[ed] her way into jobs as a New York staff reporter, getting scoops and writing eye-catching features such as 'Who Cheats Most in Marriage?'" Three years later, she was in Hollywood making good money as a nationally syndicated columnist. It was there that Graham and Fitzgerald met at a house party in the summer of 1937. Scott left early that night, and Graham later professed not to have known his identity; the encounter, however, may well have hit Fitzgerald with the force of a nearly forgotten recognition. It is possible that he saw, for a second, the Zelda of old—young, assured, and beautiful. What we know is that he later wrote into *The Last Tycoon* a similar scene: "Smiling faintly at him from not four feet away was the face of his dead wife, identical even to the expression. . . . The eyes he knew looked back at him, a curl blew a little on a familiar forehead; the smile lingered, changed a little according to pattern, the lips parted—the same. An awful fear went over him, and he wanted to cry aloud."[13]

Days later, at a Writers' Guild dinner dance at the Coconut Grove in Los Angeles, Scott and Sheilah made a lasting connection. "I don't know how it happened," she later recalled, "but a moment came when I found myself sitting all alone at [a] long table, and at [another table] sat a man I recognized as Scott Fitzgerald, all alone. . . . He appeared to be in his forties but it was difficult to know; he looked half-young, half-old: the thought flashed through my mind, he should get out into the sun, he needs light and air and warmth. Then he leaned forward and said, smiling across the two tables, 'I like you.'"[14]

Blond, attractive, and at the time engaged to hereditary nobility— Edward Arthur Donald St. George Hamilton Chichester, sixth Marquess of Donegall—Graham represented for Fitzgerald a fresh challenge, a new golden girl. A few days later, they met again and went with friends to the Clover Club. That night, Graham fell in love with Fitzgerald. "It is hard to put into words how Scott . . . worked this magic," she later recalled.

"He gave me the delightful feeling that hundreds of attractive men were just waiting for the chance to cut in on him and to snatch me away because I was so irresistible—and the feeling, too, that he would not let me out of his arms if he had to fight every one of them." More than a physical reaction, Fitzgerald won Graham over by making this beautiful woman, long accustomed to unwanted sexual advances, feel as though her opinions were worthy of serious consideration. Scott, she realized that night, *"appreciate[d] my mind as well as my face."* She soon broke with the Marquess.[15] Aside from Scott's skillful wooing, another consideration factored into Graham's decision to end her engagement: marrying Donegall would mean returning to England. Graham, in effect, chose career over marriage or, to put it somewhat differently, chose career and a lover who enhanced her self-esteem over marriage.

Within a few weeks, Fitzgerald, a chronic interrogator, had squeezed from Graham the real story about her background—or most of the real story. Reticent of his response, she characterized herself as only "part Jewish" and never told him her true age or, knowing his puritanical streak, the full catalogue of her sexual history. In fact, the charade, or as much as Fitzgerald knew of it, sealed their bond. Delighted in Graham's efforts to jump class, he outlined a course of study—the aforementioned "College of One"—designed to arm the "Hollywood Today" columnist with a fundamental education in the classics of Western literature and music. As Fairey has written, "My mother spent hours each day reading books and discussing them with [Scott]. The curriculum had history in it—the aim was to work up to reading Spengler—and art and music, but above all it was the study and appreciation of literature. Keats, Shelley, Swinburne, T. S. Eliot—Fitzgerald and my mother recited the poems together and pretended to be famous characters from novels by Dickens and Thackeray and Tolstoy."[16] The adventure appealed to Fitzgerald's pedagogical side (at the same time, he was advising Scottie on what courses to take at Vassar) while drawing him back to the books and authors that had shaped his own literary tastes. As he began to conceptualize a new novel arising from the circumstances of his life in Hollywood, it must have been intellectually reassuring for Fitzgerald to reflect on those writers whom he had known best and longest.

The exercise might further have brought to memory other youthful endearments. Years before, Scott had won the hand of a bona fide southern belle, and now he claimed the "property" of a nobleman, a reversal of the droit du seigneur complex that had long bothered him. If Graham lacked the innocence, spontaneity, and reckless promise that were once Zelda's calling cards, she possessed other qualities that impressed Fitzgerald. Foremost, she was a worker, a writer in fact, who enjoyed financial independence, earned the respect of her peers, and claimed a clear if somewhat-further-down-the-line seat at the Hollywood table. In this sense, one might say that she was *his* superior. If not as interesting as Zelda, she was more emotionally stable, and Fitzgerald, the post-crack-up penitent, needed stability in his life now. As Edmund Wilson observed some years after Scott's death,

> Where Zelda had the charm of a sophisticated child—imaginative, amusing, capricious—and the lack of inhibitions of an Alabama belle, Sheilah Graham was quite mature: sober and self-controlled. . . . Graham had had to learn slowly and to make herself a place in the world. Where Zelda would have flown away with any topic of conversation, no matter how little she knew about it, and enchanted—though she occasionally exasperated—the company with her opalescent fancies, Sheilah Graham would sit in silence, or, if she would hazard an inept remark, at once become aware of her error and be deeply embarrassed by it. When Fitzgerald set out to instruct her, she mastered what he had to teach with an accuracy that gave her in Hollywood a reputation of being exceptionally well informed. So not only did she rouse in him the sense of romance without which he could not flourish; she was able, with her affection and her common sense, to do everything a woman could to console him, to keep up his morale and to provide him with the necessary conditions for work—all of which meant making it possible for Fitzgerald to insulate himself from the distracting and, for him, the humiliating life of the moving-picture world.[17]

If setting up a smaller, secluded world with Graham proved for Scott a palliative of sorts, it offered Graham something as well. As Frances Kroll remembered, Graham "needed to feel that she was responsible for his sobriety. And in a sense, she was. They had worked out a relationship that was peaceful enough to give him the mind to work and to make escape to full time alcoholism unnecessary."[18] Together, they fell into a stable after-work rhythm: dinner at home or at a favorite restaurant, discussion of the assigned book, and then to bed in their respective apartments. To help himself sleep, Scott used the sedatives chloral and Nembutal; he took Benzedrine tablets each morning.

Despite Graham's stable presence, Fitzgerald never found traction in California. He lived in four separate residences, returned east several times, and spent a good many of his working hours freelancing on short-term projects. Needing to present a sober face to the film industry and used to having a drink in hand, he consumed Coca-Cola as he once consumed beer. He sometimes attended parties and occasionally rediscovered his old magic. At one affair, he spoke quite knowledgably about the work of Thomas Mann, with Mann in the room. Now and then, Graham would be at the same party, and Scott felt strength and perhaps some relief in her company. After visiting California, Scottie came to know and respect Graham's role in her father's life:

> More than anything, I think my father needed somebody who was eminently practical, someone with her feet on the ground, someone with an inward calm and stability—someone perhaps like Sheilah Graham. . . . A genius needs peace and quiet to be inventive, a balance to his own inner turmoil. . . . I didn't resent her being with him. Why should I? I thought it was marvelous that he had somebody to look after him, somebody whose company he enjoyed. She was immensely loyal and devoted, obviously adored him, and I was naturally happy for him. Without her, I can't imagine how he would have survived Hollywood—Hollywood let him down so.[19]

Wilson also saw, if only briefly, Fitzgerald and Graham together. His remarks to John Peale Bishop on the two are by turns insightful and snide—a reversion to the "stupid old woman" swipe he took nearly twenty years earlier:

> Have I told you that Scott came to see us on a visit from Hollywood? He is transformed in the most amazing way. Hollywood and strict non-drinking have changed him—believe it or not—into something in the

nature of a well-meaning Middle Western businessman who takes a diffident interest in the better kind of books. He had his girl with him—a pretty little blond English girl who writes a syndicated movie column. She is a very steadying influence but not awfully interesting—I think that his present morality and tameness are partly due to her. It occurred to me for the first time that his madness [that is, his "crack-up"] had probably partly been due to Zelda. I realized also that he had never before a technique for meeting the world sober. He is now evolving one in a groping way. It is as if he were learning to walk for the first time among grown-ups. Maybe he will emerge into a later period and accomplish something remarkable.[20]

In fact, the "new" Fitzgerald had for some time been in the making. The "Crack-Up" essays were a deliberate and important part of that process, with the decision to move to California constituting another piece in a slowly forming puzzle. Now, in reaching out to Graham, Scott sought, as both Scottie and Wilson noted, someone who could bring stability to his life.

A part of him, however, resented the relationship, and that came through to others. Helen Hayes believed that "Sheilah . . . was good to Scott, but he wasn't nice enough to her—ever."[21] There is, in the remarks of both Hayes and Wilson, the suggestion that Fitzgerald regarded his relationship with Graham as something of an anticlimax. He associated the warm innocence of the twenties with what he memorably called "early success," and he contrasted that decade favorably to the colorless-by-comparison thirties. The Jazz Age—Zelda's age—sparkled; the Depression era—its later years spent by Scott moving about small North Carolina towns and trying to find his footing in the Hollywood hierarchy—carried with it the faint trace of contrition. For all Graham's good qualities, she may well have constituted a relationship of atonement for Fitzgerald. Accordingly, he both loved and begrudged her as the devoted caregiver whose mere presence affirmed his fallen star. When Zelda initially refused marriage, a part of him respected her for holding out for "the best." Graham, by contrast, had taken him at his worst, and as loving and as admirable as that fact is, Fitzgerald despised feeling like someone's second prize.

Other disconnects were perhaps inevitable. While Graham's Jewish origins and early life in the London slums fascinated Scott, they also rubbed uneasily against his sense of class and racial privilege. Certainly he kept his commitment to her measured. Never in their more than three years together did he suggest they share an apartment. "My feeling is that Scott was somewhat put off by Jews as a group," Graham later wrote, "however much he liked Eddie Mayer and almost canonized Thalberg and had many Jewish friends in Hollywood. But the Jews, for him, were not the Beautiful People." The astuteness of Graham's observation might be gleaned from a self-conscious entry that Fitzgerald wrote in a notebook during this period: "Hell, the best friend I have in Hollywood is a Jew— another of my best dozen friends is a Jew. Two of the half dozen men I admire most in America are Jews and two of my half dozen best men in History are Jews. But why do they have to be so damned conceited. That minority conceit—like fairies."[22]

Though Scott and Graham stayed together until his death, their relationship remains, despite her writing several books on the topic, something of a mystery. Her feelings for him were obviously genuine; his were more complex. He would never divorce Zelda while she remained ill, and he saw little hope for her recovery. And he almost certainly associated "Sheilo" with a "dissipated" Hollywood where, as he had said to Murphy, "the young girls soon join the vicious cycle." He also couldn't shake the specter of what he guessed about her sexual past. He kept a framed photo of Graham, and after his death, she discovered the ugly words "Portrait of a Prostitute" scrawled on its reverse side. What particular demons—guilt or drink, snobbishness or self-loathing—inspired such a sharp anger can only be conjectured. He had known better days, and he knew they were not coming back.

{ TWENTY-TWO }

Sentimental Education

I want you to be among the best of your race and not waste
yourself on trivial aims. To be useful and proud—
is that too much to ask?

F. Scott Fitzgerald to Scottie Fitzgerald, 1936

In my next incarnation, I may not choose again to be
the daughter of a Famous Author.

Scottie Fitzgerald Lanahan, 1965

When one thinks of Fitzgerald "places," certain romantic images invariably come to mind: a Prohibition-defying party in Gatsby's Great Neck,
a sun-dripped beach in Dick Diver's Provence, or perhaps a quiet St. Paul
Sunday with Scott busily putting the finishing touches on his first novel.
Very few people would picture the author of the Jazz Age in an academic
setting, unless one considers a Princeton football game an academic setting. But Fitzgerald thought of himself as a teacher; he loved to instruct.
While in Hollywood, he took it upon himself to oversee the educations
of both Sheilah Graham and—back in the East—Scottie. The former, a
gossip columnist hoping to graduate from *Vogue* to Proust, welcomed the
attention; Fitzgerald's daughter did not. Scottie gamely suffered through
Fitzgerald's many lettered queries and suggestions with the practiced eye
of a prep-school veteran. With "father," she had her hands full.

In different ways, Graham did too, though, like Eliza Doolittle, she
was eternally grateful for Scott's efforts, memorializing his Henry
Higgins–like turn in her reverential book *College of One* (1967), whose title

comes from the playful term they used for their joint venture in reading. Heavy on the humanities and fine arts, the curriculum of the College of One emphasized poetry, history, novels, and classical music. Areas in which Fitzgerald had little interest or aptitude—and these included the hard sciences, mathematics, and foreign languages—were left off his carefully constructed syllabi. On the surface, Scott and Sheilah embarked on a simple and one-sided academic program: he was the professor, and she was his pupil. For both parties, however, something more than a run-through of great books beckoned. "In the beginning," Graham remembered of her early days with Scott, "I had hoped we could marry." But Fitzgerald, in his own way, remained a devoted husband to Zelda. In a 1938 letter to one of her physicians, he declared, "So long as she is helpless, I'd never leave her or ever let her have a sense that she was deserted."[1] As the "other" woman in Scott's life, Graham settled for something less, a companionship that included a distinctly Pygmalion element. For Fitzgerald, on the other hand, their studies must have afforded a certain diversionary satisfaction during his generally unsatisfactory Hollywood days. He never really made it as a screenwriter, and word soon got out that he drank. Undoubtedly more than a few acquaintances viewed him as a defeated man, a role he sometimes gave the appearance of living down to. In tutoring Graham, however, he was in complete control, mapping out a curriculum that showcased his literary taste, historical perspective, and moral sensibility. In a very real sense, the subject of Scott's seminar was . . . Scott.

Fitzgerald anticipated the College of One running for "about two years" and promised Graham a ceremonial graduation in the spring of 1941. He drew up for her an ambitious reading list alternating chapters of H. G. Wells's encyclopedic *The Outline of History* (published in 1920 and followed by subsequent revised editions) with what Fitzgerald considered to be the giants of modern literature. These included Theodore Dreiser ("He's the best of our generation"), Henry James ("too complex and intricate"), and Gustave Flaubert ("who is eternal"). In all, Scott thought sixty books would suffice, and these included *Tender Is the Night* as well as novels by personal favorites Hemingway, Ring Lardner, and Compton Mackenzie. The inclusion of Mackenzie, perhaps Fitzgerald's first serious model as a writer but not one to make many "serious" lists, suggests that beyond introducing Graham to the classics, he hoped to review old and formative acquaintances. Certainly as their course neared its end, she had learned at least as much about what Scott thought of the books and authors they discussed as about the books and authors themselves. And this was fine with Graham. She enjoyed the advantage of a motivated and knowledgeable instructor whose remarks, asides, and more lengthy commentary must have been enormously helpful to a woman earning rent and grocery money by day and reading *Madame Bovary* by night. As she later recalled, the idea was to do a traditional undergraduate degree in about half the time: "This education was for a woman who had to learn in a hurry."[2]

Scott was in a hurry too—eager to secure his place in American letters with another novel and to put the misery of his "crack-up" years behind him. Reading Mackenzie and company anew perhaps alleviated some of these pressures, as they encouraged Fitzgerald to reconnect with the books and ideas of his youth. As one might expect, however, the nostalgic element of this enterprise did not translate particularly well across generational lines, and when Fitzgerald pushed his expectations on Scottie, the results were decidedly mixed. Concerned that she might one day inherit her mother's mental illness or her father's drinking, he wished for her to be educated morally as well as intellectually. At times, his demanding attention to Scottie upset Zelda, who complained that Scott had turned their daughter against her. There is more than a little merit in the accusation. Fitzgerald always thought of Scottie as sharing his mental and emotional makeup, and his decisions about how to dress, educate, and more generally raise her predominated, even before Zelda's illness. In a May 1933 conversation that quickly turned combative, Scott said to Zelda, "you know that Scottie relies on me utterly and completely now." Zelda replied, "She has got nobody else to rely on. You alienated her affections from me years ago."[3]

In the fall of 1936, Fitzgerald enrolled Scottie in the Ethel Walker School, an all-girls' prep school in Simsbury, Connecticut. Here, she might presumably get a liberal dose of the Yankee work ethic that Scott associated with New England. The class dimensions of the enterprise, however, reminiscent as they were of his own experiences as a poor boy at a rich boys' school, bothered Fitzgerald. Scottie later wrote observantly of her father's conflicting emotions in sending her to the East to be educated,

> The choosing of what was then one of the five or six best-known rich girl's schools in the country illustrates once again that curious conflict of attitudes he had about money and Society with a capital "S." In one sense, I think he would have hated it if I hadn't been at a "chic" school, but no sooner was I there than he started worrying about its bad influence on me. Of course no young person nowadays could understand the closed upper strata of Eastern Seaboard Society in those days. Either you went to the right school and made your debut, or in the case of a boy went to an Ivy League college, or you couldn't be in what was in effect a club to which you belonged all your life. . . . So I think Daddy was torn between trying to make up for my lack of stability at home with the sense of belonging that comes from being a member of a club, and his own instinctive lack of respect for the values of that club.[4]

Overly sensitive to Scottie's weaknesses, Fitzgerald determined to instill in his daughter the discipline that had eluded him as Mollie's spoiled baby boy. Many of his communications to Scottie have a sermonizing tone, written with love to be sure but unmistakably intent on initiating her early into the struggles of life. At the tender age of eleven, she received his solemn assurance that happiness was essentially an illusion:

> I feel very strongly about you doing [your] duty. . . . I am glad you are happy—but I never believe much in happiness. I never believe in misery either. Those things you see on the stage or the screen or the printed page, they never really happen to you in life.
>
> All I believe in in life is the rewards for virtue (according to your talents) and the *punishments* for not fulfilling your duties, which are doubly costly. If there is such a volume in the camp library, will you ask Mrs. Tyson to let you look up a sonnet of Shakespeare's in which the line occurs "*Lilies that fester smell far worse than weeds.*"[5]

Fitzgerald proceeded in this particular letter to identify for Scottie a small list of "things" she should "worry about," and these included "courage," "cleanliness," and "efficiency." He then offered a significantly longer catalogue of "things not to worry about." These included "pleasures" and "satisfactions," "triumph" and "failure," unless, he continued, the failure "comes through your own fault." He closed the letter on a pitch that strained to be playful yet carried a slightly menacing subtext. He thought, in reference to her teasingly calling him "Pappy," he might saddle her with the questionable nickname "Egg," which, he wrote, "implies that you belong to a very rudimentary state of life and that I could break you up and crack you open at my will and I think it would be a word that would hang on if I ever told it to your contemporaries. 'Egg Fitzgerald.' How would you like to go through life with—'Eggie Fitzgerald' or 'Bad Egg Fitzgerald' or any form that might occur to fertile minds?" Scott wanted to encourage Scottie, though he was prepared to cut her down to size when he thought she behaved selfishly or exhibited, as he once put it, "a tremendous self-esteem."[6]

As Scottie entered her teen years, Fitzgerald's interest in her development grew, and naturally he wrote about it. In December 1935, while mired in a health-imposed purgatory near Hendersonville, North Carolina, he began drafting the Gwen stories, a series with a Scottie-like character that he hoped would have an extended run in the *Saturday Evening Post*. It did not. Deep in the personal crisis that produced the "Crack-Up" essays and physically ill, Fitzgerald struggled to rediscover his short-fiction magic. As James West has noted, "Characterization" in the Gwen sequence "is murky, and plotting is confused." The *Post* did in fact take, after substantial revision, the first and third Gwen stories ("Too Cute for Words" and "Inside the House"), though others were rejected. Gwen and Scottie both were fourteen, were "motherless," and loved to hear Fred Astaire crooning "Cheek to Cheek" to Ginger Rogers in *Top Hat*. Like Scott, Gwen's father, Bryan Bowers, was strict on his daughter. "I want to tell you about your father," one of Bryan's friends tells Gwen. "He never got over your mother's death, never will. If he is hard on you, it is because he loves you."[7]

Fitzgerald wove his paternal concerns into the Gwen narrative, and the series carries the considerable weight of its author's uncertainties. Bryan Bowers is "old American" in the courtly sense that one might describe Edward Fitzgerald—he has taught Gwen the genteel manners of his youth and wants her to aspire to a career in the sciences, observing her interest in movies and movie stars with suspicion. He is further concerned that he has made life too materially comfortable for Gwen and constantly urges her to fight against the conspiracy of ease that would make her "a romantic little snob." When Gwen dreams of a perfect existence, it is one without work, without school. "I don't want a career," she thinks. "I want to be a belle, a belle, a belle."[8] Bryan is determined to disabuse Gwen of this empty fantasy—as Scott wished that he had managed to restrain Zelda, his own "belle," from dallying in the arts.

Fitzgerald's concern for Scottie only deepened during his Hollywood days. His letters to her were steady, controlling, and intense. He wanted to know about her academic progress, of course, but more personal issues were not beyond his purview. In one communication, during her sophomore year at Vassar, he asked why she had gone "completely overboard" when coloring her hair:

> A letter from Baltimore disturbed me this morning—what have you done to your hair? Three different people have seen fit to correspond with me about it. Can't you tone down the effect a little? You heightened it so gradually that I don't think you realize yourself now just what it looks like. Nobody minds if a woman over thirty wants to touch hers up but why imitate a type that is passé even in pictures? It was a cute trick when you had one blond strand that looked as if the sun might have hit it, but going completely overboard defeats any aesthetic purpose.[9]

One finds in such remarks the echo of unasked-for advice he had once offered his sister Annabel on the aesthetics of eyebrows ("you should brush them or wet them and train them every morning and night").[10] The difference is that Fitzgerald felt responsible for Scottie in a way that he never felt responsible for anyone else. Annabel's brushed eyebrows might attract a beau or not, but Scott was not deeply invested in the outcome. His advice to Scottie came with all the subtlety of a papal bull.

Another notable and not particularly healthy feature of the relationship between father and daughter was a competitive tension all on Scott's side. Early on, Scottie showed interest in writing, and Fitzgerald tended to play down such prospects, hoping she would gravitate toward something more "serious." He worried about her picking up the bad "habits" of a writer, thinking no doubt of his own punishing relationship with the bottle, though he also showed irritation at what he perceived to be her cavalier approach to publication. He wanted to impress upon her that writing was difficult, demanding work. "Nobody," he once told her, "ever became a writer just by wanting to be one." Here, one cannot help but be reminded of Scott's efforts to steer another amateur—Zelda—away from writing. In Scottie's case, he had altogether different occupational plans. "I want her," he informed an official at the Walker School, "to follow some such line as a premedical course or one that will equip her for scientific research. If she is going to write (which God forbid!) I'd rather the necessity came from anything except a fundamentally literary training. The world seems full of people seeking for self-expression with nothing to express."[11]

The magic of the Fitzgerald name ensured, however, that Scottie would receive invitations to publish, and one came from *Mademoiselle* in the spring of 1939. The magazine asked her to write an article on modern youth, an obvious variation on her father's "flaming youth" pieces in the twenties. Fitzgerald was not amused and wired her from Hollywood in an attempt to derail the venture: "Dearest Scottie that Mademoiselle business is a way of getting something from you for fifty dollars that they would have to pay ten times that sum for me. I have to make a living for us all and you must not write them anything without submitting it first to me. It might be an unconscious duplication of a thought of mine. If they had asked for something about Vassar that would have been your business."[12] Sure of her "business," Scottie sent the completed essay, "A Short Retort," to *Mademoiselle* without delay. In it, she vigorously defended her generation while taking a few scattered shots at her father's. "In the speak-easy era," she wrote, "we were left pretty much to ourselves and allowed to do as we pleased. And so, we 'know the score.'" Perhaps reflecting on her constant shuttling between prep schools while

Zelda and Scott struggled to piece together their health, marriage, and work, Scottie argued a bit loftily about her peers, "We've had to make our own decisions, invent our own standards, establish our own code of morals. The fact that we've turned out as well as we have is more to our credit than that of our parents." And in what might be taken as something of a personal reply to her father's questioning of her judgment and resilience, she insisted, "We have the toughness that comes from knowing the world wasn't made to order for us. . . . People exaggerate our defects, anyway. They think we're a wild set and have lost all sense of proportion."[13]

Fitzgerald read the article as an attack both on his generation and on himself. Returning fire, he wrote Scottie a short retort of his own. "I grant you the grace of having been merely a dupe as I warned you you would be—for I cannot believe that you would announce that you pursued your education yourself while I went around to the speakeasies. . . . You must have wanted fifty dollars awfully bad to let them print such a trite and perverted version of your youth." Compounding matters was the fact that the byline read, "by Frances Scott Fitzgerald, daughter of F. Scott Fitzgerald, whose novels of the Jazz Age are definitive records of an era." Scott saw nothing but opportunism in the use of *his* name and told her so—"You chose to ride on my shoulder and beat me on the head with a wooden spoon. . . . [In the] future please call yourself by any name that doesn't sound like mine in your writings." Rather than let matters lie, Scott soon responded with "My Generation," a short piece that went unpublished for nearly thirty years, in which he compared the now remote world of his father ("one of hope") with the modern world inherited by Scottie ("one of disillusion"). Crossing swords, he declared, "I do not 'accept' that world, as for instance my daughter does."[14]

Years later, in a 1977 interview, Scottie looked back on her father's reaction to the *Mademoiselle* essay as an illustrative episode. It negatively conjoined his private and professional insecurities, she argued, yet also offered insight into how these tangled emotions contributed to his creative process. "He interpreted that [essay] as being an enormous effort to demolish him," she explained, "whereas I wasn't thinking about him at all. It was an extremely immature silly little piece, and I probably shouldn't have printed it. But he certainly overreacted to it, as he did to everything. He was so sensitive to slights and injuries, which, I suppose, is part of the point, isn't it? Without that terrible, agonizing sensitivity, we wouldn't have the stories of Basil being so acutely aware of class differences and so forth."[15]

Bylines and angry words aside, Fitzgerald's rejection of the "disillusionment" he believed enfeebled his daughter's generation merged with a more particular paternal concern—that Scottie be "hard as nails." He wanted her in college, in a demanding major, and he wanted her to graduate. He was reconciled to the distinct possibility that, like many young women, she might drop out in order to marry, but he hoped she would not. Believing that he had wasted his talent, he wanted something better for Scottie. Zelda thought that perhaps two years at Vassar would be enough, but Scott would not hear of it. "Her promise is unusual," he assured Zelda in a March 1940 letter that contained much of the parental praise he carefully kept from Scottie. He argued that she had "raised herself from a poor scholar to a very passable one" and further "introduced with some struggle a new note" to the class-ridden campus. He further played both sides of the recent "Short Retort" dustup by saluting her sale of "a professional story at eighteen."[16]

Fitzgerald obviously enjoyed reliving his college years through Scottie. In correspondence, he sometimes compared her experiences at Vassar (or what he believed them to be) to his at Princeton. "You are doing exactly what I did," he lectured her in one communication. "I wore myself out on a musical comedy . . . [and] slipped way back in my work . . . [and] lost a year in college." Just a few weeks before his death in December 1940, Fitzgerald wrote sentimentally to Scottie of listening to the recent Princeton-Harvard football game on the radio: "the old songs remind[ed] me of the past that I lived a quarter of a century ago and that you are now living."[17] He imagined Scottie attending the game, open to its raw excitement and feeling the same warm wave of emotions that had washed over him during that unforgettable freshman fall of 1913.

Fitzgerald further hoped that the rigor and discipline of college might toughen Scottie for the coming hardships he foresaw for her generation in a world then preparing for war. "A whole lot of people have found life a whole lot of fun," he wrote to her. "I have not found it so." Doubting that she would find it so either, he advised her to "accept the sadness, the tragedy of the world we live in, with a certain *esprit*."[18] He offered himself as an example of one whose potential had been sacrificed to an early and permanent error. That error's name was Zelda Sayre.

One is struck when reading the Scott-Scottie correspondence how freely Fitzgerald discusses his marriage, often in unsparing ways that could only have brought certain pain or doubt to his daughter. More than passing on relationship advice, these exchanges indulged Scott's need to work through his own well-rehearsed lines of marital anger, regret, and self-pity. In one letter, he drew for Scottie the torn portrait of a defeated man, taken down, like Dick Diver, by his weakness for a woman who did not understand the virtue of work:

> When I was your age I lived with a great dream. The dream grew and I learned how to speak of it and make people listen. Then the dream divided one day when I decided to marry your mother after all, even though I knew she was spoiled and meant no good to me. I was sorry immediately I had married her but, being patient in those days, made the best of it and got to love her in another way. You came along and for a long time we made quite a lot of happiness out of our lives. But I was a man divided—she wanted me to work too much for *her* and not enough for my dream. She realized too late that work was dignity, and the only dignity, and tried to atone for it by working herself, but it was too late and she broke and is broken forever.[19]

Determined that Scottie not break, Fitzgerald pressed her to be self-sufficient, an equal partner, and to carry her share—all the things that he had wished for in Zelda. "The mistake I made was in marrying her," he explained to Scottie with a sharp, unnecessary honesty. "We belonged to different worlds—she might have been happy with a kind simple man in a southern garden. She didn't have the strength for the big stage— sometimes she pretended, and pretended beautifully, but she didn't have it. She was soft when she should have been hard, and hard when she should have been yielding. She never knew how to use her energy—she's passed that failing on to you."[20]

Looking to wean Scottie from her mother's influence, Fitzgerald sent her to a string of academically challenging private schools. At the same time, his inexhaustible resentment of the rich continued to burn, and he never let Scottie forget where "they" stood on that subject. When Fitzgerald thought he saw indications in her letters that she had misread the class codes around her, he pounced. In one note, she had innocently referred to some of the girls at the Walker School as "nice." This irritated Scott, who considered the old Maryland Fitzgeralds, with their faded gentility and haute bourgeois good manners, as "nice" people in the true sense; he dismissed Scottie's classmates, by comparison, as gate-crashers. "I will bet two-thirds of the girls," he wrote her, "have at least one grandparent that peddled old leather in the slums of New York, Chicago or London, and if I thought you were accepting the standards of the cosmopolitan rich, I would much rather have you in a southern school, where scholastic standards are not so high and the word 'nice' is not debased to such a ludicrous extent." He warned her not to go "Park Avenue."[21]

How was Scottie supposed to feel about this? Her father had marched her off to mix with the "cosmopolitan rich" but then cautioned her from getting too close. She survived by deflection. She ignored her father's drinking, his efforts to enroll her in yet another "College of One," and his many resentments. "These . . . letters . . . would arrive at Vassar," she later remembered, "and I'd simply examine them for checks and news, then stick them in my lower right-hand drawer."[22] Importantly, she kept them, and in 1963, many of the letters were published, offering insight into their author's heightened sense of honor, obligation, and responsibility. Here was Fitzgerald the uncompromising moralist who wished to make his daughter impervious to the weaknesses and temptations that had compromised his career. He did this out of love, he did this out of anger, and he did this out of fear.

If Fitzgerald's bossy parenting seemed to have brought rather inconclusive returns in his lifetime, a longer view suggests a stronger influence. In 1943, Scottie married Samuel Jackson ("Jack") Lanahan, a Golden Gloves tournament boxer with a Princeton degree. Jack was from a well-to-do Baltimore family and had lived in a Greek Revival mansion in Towson, not far from La Paix. For several years, he and Scottie resided in Washington, DC, near, that is, to the former homesteads of the Mary-land Keys and Fitzgeralds. Presumably, Scott would have been pleased. In the winter of 1964, Scottie and Jack's oldest son, Tim, was applying to colleges, and his mother pressed him to visit Cornell. Arthur Mizener, Fitzgerald's first biographer, taught in Cornell's English Department, and Scottie confided in him with some small chagrin that she too had turned into a "bossy" parent. "Sometimes I feel creepy, I remind myself so of Daddy, and you cannot nag about EVERYTHING, which I must say is a lesson Daddy never learned."[23]

TWENTY-THREE

Stahr Fall

I'm not going to perish before one more book.

F. Scott Fitzgerald, 1937

In Hollywood, Fitzgerald felt the pivot of history making one of its occasional turns. The long run of laissez-faire individualism—defined variously as rule by a robber baron, a titan, or, as Fitzgerald would have it, a
tycoon—had come to an end. Now, in the Depression-era twilight of the
old capitalist order, he began to develop the idea that two mighty com-
petitors battled for control of production and power: the corporations
and the unions. Though regarded by most people in the 1930s as impla-
cable ideological enemies, both in fact shared a common goal: establishing
large-scale bureaucracies to manage the great fortunes that were once the
family fiat of Morgans, Rockefellers, and Fords. In Hollywood, a variation of this theme played out before Scott's eyes. The day of the great
film impresario, a creative pioneer on the scale of a D. W. Griffith or a
Charlie Chaplin, was passing; in the push for profits, other players began
to edge them aside. And no matter who gained the upper hand in this
struggle for points and percentages—white collar or blue—the "collective" had now come into its own as a reckoning force in America.

Though Scott self-identified with the political Left, his artistic instincts trended "individual" rather than "masses." "I could never be a
Communist," he said to Sheilah Graham. "I could never be regimented.
I could never be told what to write."[1] Such independence did not make
him look favorably on the business wing of the GOP, however. Fitzgerald,
rather, regarded the profit motive and the endless chasing of dollars

(something the bone-tired short-story writer knew all too well) as symptomatic of a larger cultural illness corrupting the West. It is instead more accurate to locate Scott ideologically as a man of an older, precapitalist Right, as a champion of the military heroes and merchant princes who appealed to his fundamentally romantic sensibilities. This sharp break between past ("heroic") and present ("communal") had long been a fixture of Fitzgerald's writing. Now situated in Hollywood, as he began to slowly regain his creative footing, Fitzgerald felt again the old itch to comment on laissez-faire's progress in the New World.

Before embarking on a fresh novel, Fitzgerald had first to shore up his perpetually imperiled finances. Perhaps as much as $40,000 in the red when he left the East Coast for Hollywood, Scott was earning a handsome $1,250 a week when MGM refused, in December 1938, to renew his contract. After that, he had gone about, hand in hat, taking freelance scriptwriting jobs at various studios. During these difficult months, his scattered impressions of Hollywood—the improbable meeting place of Gentiles and Jews, artists and businessmen—began to gel. Here, on the continent's edge, he was coming to believe, where the last American frontier once offered opportunity, dwelled a vast film factory now in the process of running to a kind of spiritual ruin. This is the story he wanted to get down, uncompromised by the need to divide his failing energies on other projects. But this was not to be. A *Saturday Evening Post* writer no more, Scott approached *Collier's* in the fall of 1939 with a synopsis of his unwritten novel, asking the magazine's fiction editor, Kenneth Littauer, to purchase its serial rights. "I would rather do this for a minimum price," Fitzgerald confessed, "than continue this in-and-out business with the moving pictures where the rewards are great, but the satisfaction unsatisfactory and the income tax always mopping one up after the battle." Several weeks later, Littauer agreed to read a six-thousand-word sample of the book, but he thought it "pretty cryptic" and declined to serialize without seeing more. "IF IT HAS TO BE NOW," he wired an impatient Fitzgerald, "IT HAS TO BE NO."[2]

This is where the Pat Hobby stories come in. The series, appearing in *Esquire* between January 1940 and May 1941 (five months after Fitzgerald's death), helped Scott meet his most persistent financial obligations.

He received from Arnold Gingrich's magazine $250 for each of the seventeen stories, representing a total outlay of $4,250 (roughly $4,000 and $68,000, respectively, in current dollars). Though he frequently asked Gingrich to increase his pay ("I can't believe," he wrote of one Hobby offering, "it isn't worth $400.00"), the undemanding format was part of the point. Fitzgerald's *Post* stories were far more elaborate productions, typically running some six thousand words and necessitating their author's attention to complex themes and plot development. The Hobby cycle, by contrast, required no such grand effort. They ran to only about two thousand words and tended to focus on a single, simple incident.[3]

The running one-liner is that Pat is a rat—and a rummy, womanizer, liar, and cheat—but he is also a pitiable Hollywood hack, once a successful screenwriter now just trying to cadge enough money out of producers to play the ponies and salvage a bit of pride. "The series is characterized by a really bitter humor," Fitzgerald wrote to one correspondent, "and only the explosive situations and the fact that Pat is a figure almost incapable of real tragedy or damage saves it from downright unpleasantness." Some critics later insisted that the stories lack merit and bear the damning and sloppy fingerprints of a rush job. Matthew J. Bruccoli, Fitzgerald's major biographer, writes that on balance, the Hobby stories are "disappointing" and "mainly travesties."[4] This, however, seems a bit excessive. Yes, Fitzgerald wrote the Hobby stories in some haste, but he did revise them before publication. And if their quality is uneven, they stand nevertheless in tone and mood as expressive statements of his acerbic response to the film industry. Moreover, several of the themes that scaffold Scott's unfinished Hollywood novel—the insecurity of the movie producers, the cynicism of the screenwriters, and, more generally, the language, attitudes, and material culture of the region—are anticipated in the Hobby episodes. To be fair, these stories, weak as several of them are, went beyond simply financing the writing of *The Last Tycoon;* they served, further, as a kind of minor-key apprentice piece for the greater work.

Because Fitzgerald was during his final Hollywood stint a sometimes-employed screenwriter writing about a sometimes-employed screenwriter, the question persists to this day as to how much of himself he put into Pat. The answer is not much. Though it's true he once, with considerable gallows humor, signed off on a telegram to Gingrich as "Pat Hobby Fitzgerald," Scott never identified in any meaningful sense with Hobby, who is basically a comedic creation without a shred of romantic sensibility.[5] Whereas Pat loves the Hollywood lifestyle—the swimming pools and servants, the easy women and (not so) easy money—Fitzgerald detested Tinseltown and had only come to work and to manage his debts. Together the Hobby stories and *Tycoon* form fresh chapters in their author's ongoing saga—the one about the man, the generation, and the country that had fallen short.

Pat is a negligible if telling casualty in this narrative. To succeed in profit-driven Hollywood requires a self-control and sobriety beyond the capacity of his thirsty constitution. This rises to the level of a minor human tragedy because Pat has in every other way dutifully accepted the pecking-order prerequisites of his hive. He knows, if not always from firsthand experience, the right colleges, country clubs, and neighborhoods to inhabit. As a younger man, he had played the game well enough to grab his own small piece of the Hollywood pie: a succession of wives, Filipino servants, and a coveted swimming pool. But the years—and a lotusland-induced dissipation—catch up to the "old-timer," and at forty-nine and soft around the middle, he struggles simply to hang on. Unable to wheedle a coveted studio pass, he finds himself one day standing paralyzed outside the towering gates of the grand fantasyland that was once both his happiness and his home. "For the first time in his life," Fitzgerald writes, "he began to feel a loss of identity."[6]

A prisoner of Hollywood, Pat cannot conceive of any other reality. To "exist" means to be near the spotlight, the dollars, and the drama. He is a paradoxical figure in that, as a Hollywood insider, he understands how the "real" film industry operates and yet is drawn to its special magic as passionately as any Iowa tourist. In effect, Pat's Hollywood is as unattainable as Gatsby's Daisy. As a young man, Pat had made his mark, grabbing dozens of silent-film screen credits before he was rendered obsolete by the talkies, the competition, and the changing times. Just shy of fifty, he understands the bleakness of his future. Though his thinning Hollywood connections are embarrassed by his antics and keep him at arm's length, he cannot give the industry up, cannot move on, and will beg, borrow, cheat, or steal to remain in its golden kingdom. He is a desperate man, unable to conceive of a world beyond the studio's doors. The day that he is locked out for good is the day that he begins to die.

The Pat Hobby series is reminiscent of Fitzgerald's cluster of expat stories that began appearing in the late 1920s and culminated artistically with "Babylon Revisited" (1931). What unites them is a thematic emphasis on dissipation. As Europe has broken down, say, Charlie Wales of "Babylon Revisited," so has Hollywood had its way with Pat. His daily routine includes boozing, betting on the ponies, and trying to bed the secretaries. But the issue of his "corruption" really cuts two ways. The film industry, after all, aspired to something more than mere entertainment, yet in constantly keeping a writer of dubious talent like Pat around—to touch up a scene here, add a bit of dialogue there—it highlighted its essential reliance on unoriginal and clichéd material. This trafficking in mediocrity raises the larger question of Hobby's "role" and "meaning": who, ultimately, is the real shaper of American popular culture, Hollywood or the army of Hobbys it employs?

Even if the Pat Hobby stories occupy a lower rung on the Fitzgerald canon, their merits should not be discounted on the grounds that they were written to pay bills. One could, after all, say the same of all Scott's stories. And in any case, they did more than make rent, for while Fitzgerald never enjoyed a stretch of uninterrupted writing time in Hollywood, he felt financially stable enough in the summer of 1939 to begin work on *Tycoon*. From his letters and outlines, we know that he anticipated writing a book that resembled in structure, economy, and scope *The Great Gatsby*, that is, a relatively thin novel that could nevertheless convey a story of broad historical dimensions. In *Tycoon*'s tragic hero, the producer Monroe Stahr, Fitzgerald created a character that promised to be every bit as compelling as Gatsby. Of East Coast, Jewish origin, Stahr repeats the historical trek of the old Atlantic Dutch sailors who were once in search of a New World. And like Gatsby, when confronted with the brute force of the modern world, this dreamer, too, would have to die.

As with all of Fitzgerald's novels, he drew on personal experiences and relationships for color and context. It should come as no surprise that Sheilah Graham (as Kathleen Moore) is featured prominently in *Tycoon*.

Stahr's beloved wife, Minna Davis, had died three years earlier, and he remains a prisoner to her memory. Enter Moore, a secretive young woman who physically resembles Minna. Other episodes, including Stahr's reluctance to remarry and Moore's mysterious past as the paramour of a king (or, in Graham's case, the lover of a lord), were taken from life. Structurally, Fitzgerald's employment of a *Gatsby*-like participant-narrator—Cecelia Brady—to retrospectively tell Stahr's story is yet another borrowing. Brady, the daughter of a powerful Hollywood producer, is in college when she meets and falls in love with Stahr. She recounts his heroic if losing battle to elevate art over commerce in Hollywood, his powerful interest in Minna, and his inevitable decline before illness and overwork. Attractive to women and respected by men, Stahr is young and has dark curly hair and intelligent eyes. He is physically slender, with a large, but not loud, presence. He seems inured to lack of sleep or rest, and others naturally defer to his judgments. One character, seeing him on an airplane, assumes he might be one of the pilots.

Though unfinished, the forty-four-thousand-word manuscript is the closest Fitzgerald ever came to depicting his concept of the "whole man." Amory Blaine and Basil Duke Lee are too young for us to glimpse anything more than the outline of their adult lives, and Gatsby is compromised by fatal flaws; Anthony Patch and Dick Diver are victims of their own respective weaknesses. But Stahr retains the strengths and virtues of a great commander who leads by the force of his genius and the appeal of his vision. These romantic properties, however, are no longer enough to save him. Uninterested in mere moneymaking, Stahr chooses art over commerce in what will be a losing battle with the studios and the unions for control of Hollywood.

As noted earlier, Fitzgerald's politics were the product of a sentimental outlook. Though he read some Marx, his criticisms of the machine age were typically of an artistic rather than economic nature. He feared the triumph of conformity over spontaneity, the pride of profits over imagination. Best known for his stories in the *Saturday Evening Post,* Fitzgerald could display an aversion to capitalism that was surprising to those who bothered to look deeply into his work. This was apparently the case with Budd Schulberg, a screenwriter whose list of credits came to include *On the Waterfront* (1954), for which he won an Oscar. Schulberg worked briefly with Fitzgerald on the script for *Winter Carnival* (1939) and later wrote a best-selling Hollywood satire of these experiences, *The Disenchanted* (1950). A onetime member of the Communist Party, Schulberg expected Fitzgerald to be something of a political naïf and recorded in *The Disenchanted* his surprise at discovering otherwise. In one scene, Shep, a young and ambitious screenwriter, stumbles on an untitled draft written by Manley Halliday, a once-great novelist now reduced to providing copy for the movies:

> Shep knew why . . . Halliday hadn't published in nearly a decade: because he was defeatist, an escapist, cut off from "vital issues," from "The People," a disillusioned amanuensis of a dying order—oh, Shep hadn't read his *New Masses* for nothing! Yet here were these eighty-three pages. My God, this was *alive,* while the writers who were not defeatist, not escapist, not bourgeois apologists and not "cut off from the main stream of humanity" were wooden and lifeless. Was it possible—and here heresy really struck deep—for an irresponsible individualist, hopelessly *confused,* to write a moving, maybe even a profound, revelation of social breakdown?[7]

Social breakdown had, of course, always been at the center of Fitzgerald's writing. The collapse of once-dominant classes, values, and taboos had given his work an immediacy that worked on two levels, most obviously as ruminations on topical issues and, more importantly, as deeper meditations on historical change. *Tycoon,* along with Fitzgerald's best fiction and nonfiction alike, can be and should be read with this duality in mind.

In the end, Stahr, like Gatsby, is sacrificed to stronger forces, and, considering his craft, the irony is striking. The cinema creates images of an iconic American individualism, after all, that are mass-produced by clock-punching bureaucrats. Fitzgerald wants us to know, however, that there was a time when giants really did walk the earth, and one particularly signal episode in *Tycoon* underscores Stahr's credentials as a titan. An earthquake bursts the studio's water mains, and Stahr, with his sets in danger of being washed away, fires off a series of orders that results in the valve being shut off, the rescue of numerous props, and the cleanup of the studio. Here, Stahr is briefly master of his studio, of the penny-counting bosses who threaten his reign, and even of the elements. It is his last hurrah.

Stahr's fatherly concern for his studio, his actors, and the moviegoing public make him that rare literary figure, a sympathetic businessman. In fact, one might read *Tycoon* as a meditation on the industrialist as hero—providing that said hero runs his operations less like George Babbitt than like Julius Caesar. Prior to Fitzgerald, writers routinely drew unflattering portraits of executives yet typically without explaining their actual work. Stahr, by contrast, is all studio. He dismisses an ineffective director, discusses marketing strategies at a lunch meeting, and lights a creative fire under his writers. No mere capitalist, Stahr, Fitzgerald insists, is "the last of the princes." His obligation extends beyond a small group of investors to encompass the entire industry, and that includes audiences. Facing down a group of skeptical colleagues, Stahr lobbies hard for the completion of a movie that he knows will tank at the box office. The room erupts—"It'll lose money," one suit correctly points out. But Stahr brushes their dollars-and-cents objections aside: "it's a quality picture," he counters. He argues that the studios cheated moviegoers by playing it safe with formulaic scripts: "we have a certain duty to the public." This paternalistic stress on corporate responsibility extends everywhere Stahr goes and touches everything he does. Unlike other producers, he keeps no secretary-concubine, a Communist Party organizer recognizes him as a hardworking and fundamentally fair "boss," and his power to heal recalls Dick Diver in his better days. When an actor is humiliated by impotency, or failing vision plagues a cameraman, or a screenwriter falls into a depression, Stahr restores each through his wisdom, counsel, and confidence. Fitzgerald writes that to all of these men, "a great purposefulness" had been brought back into their lives.[8]

Scott is eager to portray his hero as a true American type, and so if Monroe Stahr is a prince, he is, within the country's democratic traditions, a prince of the people. His presidential given name suggests qualities shared by Andrew Jackson and Abraham Lincoln, fellow strong leaders who figure in the book. One impressed visitor to the studio, Prince Agge from Denmark, takes an immediate liking to Stahr—a case, the implication is clear, of royalty recognizing royalty. "This then was Lincoln," Agge realizes. "This then, he thought, was what they all meant to be." Lincoln, without the benefit of a West Point education, proved to be a better intuitive general than were many of the officers serving under him; the cause brought out his best. And Stahr, though always the youngest man in the room, inspires his writers and designers, actors and directors to produce films of superior quality. Like Lincoln, he builds an impressive "army." The upshot is that he is the last paternalist in a profit-driven industry. "You're no merchant," one of his screenwriters comments. "I knew a lot of them when I was a publicity man and I agree with Charles Francis Adams [the son and grandson of presidents]. . . . He knew them all—Gould, Vanderbilt, Carnegie, Astor—and he said there wasn't one he'd care to meet again in the hereafter. Well—they haven't improved since then, and that's why I say you're no merchant."[9]

Fitzgerald modeled Stahr on Irving Thalberg (1899–1936), the producer of such classics as *Grand Hotel, Mutiny on the Bounty, Romeo and Juliet,* and the Marx Brothers' *A Night at the Opera.* As Scott reported to Littauer shortly after beginning the novel, "Thalberg has always fascinated me. His peculiar charm, his extraordinary good looks, his bountiful success, the tragic end of his great adventure. . . . He is one of the half-dozen men I have known who were built on the grand scale." The tensions between Thalberg and his Metro-Goldwyn-Mayer boss, the iconic producer and "star system" creator Louis Mayer, provided Fitzgerald with the obvious creativity-versus-commerce dichotomy situated at the heart of *Tycoon.* Of their differences, Bruccoli writes, "Bad feelings developed between Thalberg and Mayer over the division of the M-G-M profits, as Thalberg insisted that his share be commensurate with his responsibilities. Mayer, who had a powerful ego, felt that he was being disparaged and overshadowed by his protégé. In 1933, while Thalberg was in Europe recuperating from a collapse caused by overwork, Mayer removed him as M-G-M production head, although Thalberg retained his own production unit."[10] Known in Hollywood as the "Boy Wonder," Thalberg had the youth, looks, talent, and mental alertness that Fitzgerald respected. As a prince, Thalberg/Stahr employs the energy and resources of a profit-driven industry much, one might say, as the Florentine Medici family had once used its banking fortune to inspire Renaissance art and architecture. In creating Stahr, Fitzgerald envisioned one last lofty attempt by an individual to put his aesthetic imprint on an entire civilization.

Not everyone was as enamored with Thalberg as Scott was. As Graham recalled, most of the writers she knew "detested" the Boy Wonder for opposing their efforts to unionize. According to Thalberg's biographer Bob Thomas, he broke a potential strike by the Screen Writers Guild by promising to "*close down the entire plant,* without a single exception." Where Fitzgerald saw in Thalberg a true captain of industry, others thought the producer's "paternalism" cloaked the heart of a cold-blooded capitalist who fundamentally distrusted his employees.[11]

Stahr's closest purely fictional kin is Jay Gatsby. Both characters were grail chasers who inevitably smashed against the modern world's indifference to their grand dreams. *Gatsby* closes with the elegiac cadence of Dutch sailors coming to the New World, more to fill their imaginations than their pockets. In *Tycoon,* a boyish, untried Stahr arrives in Hollywood with the same searching impulse. Years later, as a successful executive, he now flies first class into Los Angeles, but as the book's narrator makes clear, that golden glow of discovery still surrounds him:

> The motors were off and all our five senses began to readjust themselves for landing. I could see a line of lights for the Long Beach Naval Station ahead and to the left, and on the right a twinkling blur for Santa Monica. The California moon was out, huge and orange over the Pacific. However I happened to feel about these things—and they were home after all—I know that Stahr must have felt much more. These were the things I had first opened my eyes on, like the sheep on the back lot of the old Laemmle studio; but this was where Stahr had come to earth after that extraordinary illuminating flight where he saw which way we were going, and how we looked doing it, and how much of it mattered. You could say that this was where an accidental wind blew him but I don't think so. I would rather think that in a "long shot" he saw a new way of measuring our jerky hopes and graceful rogueries and awkward sorrows, and that he came here from choice to be with us to the end. Like the plane coming down into the Glendale airport, into the warm darkness.[12]

Certain words and images that Fitzgerald had used in *Gatsby* came again to life as he was writing *Tycoon*. Gatsby "had come a long way to this blue lawn," while one producer in *Tycoon* "had come a long way from some ghetto." In *Gatsby*, Dutch sailors once found their spiritual sustenance in the "fresh, green breast of the new world"; while in *Tycoon*, "at both ends of life," a man may discover he needs "nourishment—a breast—a shrine."[13]

Both Gatsby and Stahr are migrants of a kind, and the pioneer theme takes on a particularly strong resonance for Fitzgerald in Hollywood. Encamping along the Pacific and meeting the Jewish, Brit-born Sheilah Graham had given him a fresh perspective on his country and its prospects. Like Stahr, he had come west—financial obligations aside—seeking inspiration. And despite the sundry disappointments he experienced in the film colony, its underlying vitality and attraction to artists, writers, and directors from around the world made Scott feel a part of the great historical pilgrimage that he associated with those sailors of centuries before. "I look out at it—and I think it is the most beautiful history in the world," he wrote in a random note found after his death. "It is the history of me and my people. And if I came here yesterday like Sheilah I should still think so. It is the history of all aspiration—not just the American Dream but the human dream and if I came at the end of it that too is a place in the line of pioneers."[14]

~~~~~~

Like Stahr, whose shattered health meant the end of his artistic vision, Fitzgerald too worked on borrowed time. Always sensitive to changing perspectives, he hoped in *The Last Tycoon* to capture his strongest impressions of Hollywood while they were still fresh. "It may be the last novel I'll ever write," he informed Zelda two months before his death, "but it must be done now because after fifty one is different. One can't remember emotionally, I think except about childhood but I have a few more things left to say." At the same time, he was reading, with some disappointment, Hemingway's just-released Spanish Civil War novel, *For Whom the Bell Tolls*. He recognized its virtues but thought it lacked the inventiveness and poetry of *A Farewell to Arms*. "I suppose life takes a good deal out of you," he wrote, sounding a bit like Nick Carraway, "and you never can quite repeat."[15]

Fitzgerald suffered a heart attack in late November 1940 at Schwab's Drugstore on Sunset Boulevard and afterward put the novel before everything else. This was, his secretary later remembered, "the only time he really stopped drinking": "He took precautions, remained in bed a good deal of time and buckled down to real work on *The Last Tycoon*. I feel he wanted desperately to finish it before anything might happen to his life." Under doctor's orders to avoid undo exertion, Scott moved into Graham's first-floor apartment a block east of his own two-story flat on North Laurel Avenue. There, a writing board nestled on his lap, he spent his final weeks contemplating the fate of his tragic hero. In notes for the manuscript, Fitzgerald, the symbol of a long-lost Jazz Age, had written of Stahr, "Suddenly outdated he dies."[16]

Scott's death came on December 21, 1940, a Saturday. Enjoying a quiet afternoon at Graham's, he sat in a green armchair eating a Hershey chocolate bar and making notes of football players in the latest copy of the *Princeton Alumni Weekly;* Beethoven's "Eroica" played on the phonograph. Without warning, he suddenly sprang up and grabbed the mantelpiece before collapsing to the floor. A terrified Graham tried to revive him by pouring brandy through his clenched teeth, but Scott was gone, pronounced dead at 5:15 P.M. Whether he knew just how little time he had is an unanswerable question. A few days earlier, he had expressed to Zelda some slight optimism after seeing the results of a cardiogram taken after his first attack. He spoke of months of recuperation and of the chance for better health. "It is odd," he wrote to her, "that the heart is one of the organs that does repair itself."[17]

In Scott's final "sad" years, even with his ongoing money troubles, he found a way to pay Zelda's medical bills and (with the assistance of the Murphys and the Obers) keep Scottie in Vassar. In all, he had earned in California about $125,000, a sum that allowed him to relinquish most of his debts while maintaining a life-insurance policy for Zelda's security. Though obviously a sick man during this period, he published over thirty stories and articles, worked on more than a dozen movie scripts, and wrote a publishable and promising *Tycoon*. Like Stahr, he kept his enterprise afloat, refusing to give way until he could do nothing else.[18]

Fitzgerald's body was taken to Pierce Brothers Mortuary on West Washington Boulevard. The poor embalming job made him look like a mannequin. Considering his low-key lifestyle in Los Angeles, it was not surprising that a sparse crowd turned out for the viewing. Still, the journalist Frank Scully was struck by the discrepancy between Fitzgerald's achievements in life and his neglect in death: "There lay American genius . . . [and] not a soul was in the room. Except for one bouquet of flowers and a few empty chairs, there was nothing to keep him company except his casket. I've seen some pretty magnificent funerals in Hollywood, both on the screen and in churches and temples, but I never saw a sadder one than the end of the father of all the sad young men."[19]

Graham had phoned Harold Ober shortly after Fitzgerald's death and, telling him that Scott "really hated California," thought his body should be brought back east, "where his father is buried because he admired him." But where was the money to come from to transport the remains? Kroll knew that Scott had kept $700 in cash hidden in a book. Expenses came to $613.28. Taken to Rockville, Maryland, Fitzgerald's remains were laid to rest at Rockville Union Cemetery after the Baltimore Diocese refused permission for a burial at the city's St. Mary's Church, on account of Scott's long-lapsed Catholicism. About thirty mourners showed up; neither Graham (counseled by Scottie to remain in California) nor Zelda was present. Max Perkins, one of the attendees, wrote to John Peale Bishop, "The day was rather distressing. It was one of those terrible funeral home funerals. Awful." Zelda's sister Rosalind, the only Sayre at the burial, recalled some years later that the ceremony was attended by "about everybody who could have been reasonably expected for a funeral in a Maryland Village, on a winter day, for one who had been years away."[20]

Zelda, now living with her mother in Montgomery, mourned for Scott, missing him terribly. He had returned east to visit her three times since moving to California, but these were stressful, unsuccessful holidays in which he ended up getting drunk. They had no connection to his new life in Hollywood and with Sheilah Graham. In "Sheilo," he had found a woman who loved him unconditionally and would serve as his caretaker, as he saw himself caring for Zelda and Scottie. Frances Kroll, just four years older than Fitzgerald's own Frances, played an important role as well, doubling as both secretary and confidante during Scott's California days. If not exactly a second family, the presence of these two women brought a certain peace and comfort to Fitzgerald. He was lucky to have them. Zelda was probably aware that Scott had "a girl" in California, though *The Last Tycoon*'s publication in 1941 would have erased any doubt. She took it in stride: "I confess that I didn't like the heroine," she wrote to Margaret Turnbull, her onetime La Paix landlord and neighbor; "she seems the sort of person who knows too well how to capitalize. . . . However, I see how Stahr might have found her redolent of the intimacies of forgotten homely glamour, and his imagination have endowed her with the magical properties of his early authorities."[21] Stunned at the sudden loss of Scott, Graham married the following year, and the year after that, she gave birth to a daughter: Wendy Frances.

── PART IV ──

Ghosts and Legends, 1940 and After

I am the last of the novelists for a long time now.

F. Scott Fitzgerald, circa 1940

TWENTY-FOUR

Zelda after Scott

The voices fainter and fainter—How is Zelda,
how is Zelda—tell us—how is Zelda

F. Scott Fitzgerald, late 1930s

In the early spring of 1940, Dr. Robert Carroll, a pioneering psychiatrist and the founder of Highland Mental Hospital in Asheville, discharged Zelda from his care. Returning to Montgomery to live with her mother, Minnie, she spent her days painting and writing, in effect retreating into the kind of slow "southern" routine that Scott thought was her limited due. Not that anyone in Montgomery confused her for conventional. Zelda's strong interest in religion, curio conversation, and distracted manner (the unhappy inheritance, perhaps, of electro- and insulin shock treatments—memory-robbing "cures") gave her away as an eccentric. She appeared to the Sayres as something of a modern-day Icarus, the foolish youth who tried to escape his Cretan captivity on wings of wax but flew too close to the sun and fell into the sea. Now, after the riotous years, there would be pieces to pick up.

Zelda's release from Highland had capped a protracted skirmish between Scott and the Sayres. Fitzgerald was by this time working in Hollywood and seeing Sheilah Graham. Though he felt a sharp sense of responsibility for Zelda and was unwilling to cut either financial or emotional ties (in the context of a largely epistolary relationship), he knew that they would never live together again. He also understood that Zelda wanted to be with him. In an April 1938 appeal to Dr. Carroll, Scott wrote with some panicky exaggeration, "I am in the best working time of my life, my mind never quicker nor more desperately anxious to store a little security for old age and to write a couple more decent books before that light goes out, and I cannot live in the ghost town which Zelda has become."[1] One wonders the extent to which Scott may have "worked" on Carroll to persuade him to his point of view. Did Carroll accept the argument that Scott could do best for Zelda by doing best for himself and perhaps grant his patient's famous husband time to complete his life's work?

What we do know is that Carroll remained skeptical of Zelda's prospects outside a hospital setting, and Scott emphasized the physician's concerns when writing to the Sayres, sometimes making himself out to be no more than an interested third party. In a May 1938 letter apprising Rosalind of where matters stood, he insisted that Carroll and Minnie composed the two warring sides: "I am," he wrote with an uncharacteristic passivity, "almost as much the football as Zelda." Cautiously agreeing with what he called "the Montgomery point of view," he too wanted more freedom for Zelda, he told Rosalind, but refused to overrule a trained physician's opinion. In any case, there seemed to be only two options in the matter: either he or Minnie would have to assume responsibility for Zelda. Both possibilities, he insisted, were nonstarters. "I have proven my incapacity for the job," he frankly observed, and he dismissed the idea of the elderly, indulgent Minnie taking command as "fantastic."[2]

In October, in light of the Sayres' continued call for Zelda's release, Fitzgerald again consulted Carroll. Her prognosis, he reported, following up with Rosalind, was not positive. According to Scott, Carroll had deemed Zelda "incurable," certainly unable to live on her own, and in need of the regimented order and structure—in regard to diet, daily exercise, and supervised activities—that she could receive only in a hospital. Scott assured Rosalind that his own health ("I have been to a doctor twice a week for a year trying to keep together my lungs and heart") was none too sure, and with Minnie, as he coldly put it, "on the edge of her dotage," there was no one, in any event, who could provide Zelda with the care she apparently still required. "Cure her I cannot and simply *saying* she's cured must make the Gods laugh."[3]

Over the next year and a half, however, Zelda's liberties increased. She was allowed to travel alone to Montgomery for the 1939 Christmas holiday, and the following March, Carroll recommended that she be permitted to live with Minnie. "It is wonderful to be able to write you this," Scott gave her the good news. "Dr. Carroll has for the first time and at long last agreed that perhaps you shall try to make a place for yourself in the world. In other words, that you can go to Montgomery the first of April and remain there indefinitely or as long as you seem able to carry on under your own esteem." After four years at Highland, Zelda felt like a prisoner on the threshold of freedom: "I will be very, very happy to escape the spiritual confines of medical jurisdiction." On 6 April, Carroll wrote a "To Whom It May Concern" letter in which he praised Scott— always a great cultivator of his wife's physicians—for having "made provision for every helpful treatment. . . . Mrs. Fitzgerald has gradually improved to the point that we are now cooperating with the husband in paroling her."[4] A few days later, Zelda was back in Montgomery; eight months after that, Scott was dead.

Living with Minnie, Zelda remained an active and original painter; on several occasions, she exhibited her various portraits and flower sketches as well as her paper dolls at Montgomery's Museum of Fine Arts. As usual, money was tight, and she yearned to support herself by filling a canvas or a page. The Fitzgerald estate provided her with about $50 per month. Chafing under Minnie's watchful eye and wanting her own home, she petitioned Judge John Biggs Jr., Scott's executor, in 1942 for additional funds, but this proved unfeasible. Pressing on, Zelda began a new novel, *Caesar's Things,* destined, like Scott's *The Last Tycoon,* never to be finished. Her preoccupation with Christianity framed the work ("render unto Caesar the things that are Caesar's, and unto God . . ."), a point she emphasized to Biggs in a subsequent communication: "I am writing a book about the social structure being only manifestations of the Christian precepts to show how *every* deed we do is included within some principle of Christ." Zelda's first biographer, Nancy Milford, described *Caesar's Things* as, above all, a glimpse into its author's troubled mind: "Its subject was once again the story of Zelda's life. Only this time the reader confronts the rigidity of Zelda's psychosis head on, and the novel moves at a strained pace, swinging in and out of fantasies whose meanings are known only to the author. It is a sort of collage of autobiographical writing, fantasy, and religiosity. There is no sum of the parts of this novel, but only the parts themselves, truncated and wildly incoherent." Minnie simply concluded that her daughter had "gone off the deep end about religion."[5]

Over the next few years, Zelda periodically returned to Highland Hospital, checking herself in for two months in 1944, some three months in 1946, and again in November 1947 for several months. "She remained a highly nervous person and occasionally had to return to the hospital to get herself under control," Rosalind remembered, "but she also had many long good periods when she was able to follow her interests, keep up with her friends, and live a fairly normal life." And as in any "normal life," a certain degree of reflection and regret crept in. "I wish," she wrote to Scottie in 1945, "that I had been better able to do one thing and not so given to running into cul-de-sac with so many." Here, she seemed to acknowledge Scott's old claim that she had merely been a dabbler, a generalist in various arts but artistically proficient in none. On the whole, she defended her marriage, thought Scott had been a good provider, and saw no need to justify their large living in the now-remote 1920s. Zelda assured Scottie that her parents, despite their difficulties, remained dedicated to each other: "We had a good time. His devotion to me is a noble and a moving manifestation of faithful faith in an idea. I was his wife and he wanted not to lose the precious associations of what the same could have meant. He made and spent a million dollars, largely on hospital bills & schools toward the end and always on 'largess' rather than comfort. We always lived in cheap hotels and made up the difference in night-clubs; in not having to apologize; and in a *great* deal of expensive and unpremeditated moving about." There were times, she confessed, when her memory lingered back to the old and pure pleasures of "vintage Antibes."[6]

Helping Zelda to stir up the past was a visit by a young Fitzgerald scholar, Henry Dan Piper (Princeton, '39). In early March 1947, having been recently discharged from the Fort McClellan army base at Anniston, some two hours north of Montgomery, Piper phoned Zelda, spoke enthusiastically of Scott's work, and requested an interview. She consented, and he drove down for a weekend. Zelda presented her card—"Mrs. F. Scott Fitzgerald"—to the young man on their initial meeting, telling him somewhat unpromisingly, "I don't have much to tell you." Then, noticing his camel's-hair polo coat, she remembered that Scott wore one just like it.[7]

Zelda's two-day conversation with Piper went in fits and starts. Sometimes Zelda was expansive, other times reticent; she was most attentive when her young guest praised her late husband. "In our brief talk of Scott," Piper wrote in a notebook, "I had emphasized the disparity between his good and bad stories—some were full of poetry, others of forced writing and a concocted plot. But she didn't get my point. . . . Only when I mentioned the marvelous passages at the opening of Gatsby, with the wind rippling coolly and setting everything in motion was she really alert—listening to me with more than half an ear." In a subsequent letter to Biggs, Piper related that surprisingly much of Scott's biography was unknown to Zelda. "I realize from talking with her," he wrote, "that there is a great deal of Scott Fitzgerald's life with which she is unacquainted, particularly the pre-1918 and post-1932 years." He also recognized Zelda's still-felt closeness to Scott. "Certainly during our several days' conversations she seemed to be getting a definite pleasure from talking about the various early novels and stories, and of their early life together," he observed. "So long as our discussions were guided into these channels I noticed she was most animated and rational, and the old charm and gift for words returned." But when Zelda strayed from her scripted anecdotes, Piper continued, she engaged in "weird religious conjectures and philosophical ruminations." Taking his leave, he felt sorry for her, respected her brave front, and thought she suffered from having too little to "consume her tremendous physical energy."[8] As a parting gift, Zelda presented Piper with a self-portrait.

Once the baby belle of the Great War, Zelda, nearly two years post-Hiroshima, had entered the era of Cold War nuclear anxiety. In a follow-up note to Piper, she wished him well in the spirit of the day: "Hoping your atomic pulsations and your pulsating atoms progress according to the dynamic tempos of this dramatic age." In less theatrical terms and with a measure of the old grace and southern hospitality, she closed, "Ma enjoyed meeting you also and there is always a chicken whenever a friend stops in."[9]

Nearly a year to the day after Piper's visit, Zelda died in a fire at High-land Hospital, where she had checked herself in the previous November. Probably asphyxiated, perhaps in her sleep, she was one of nine patients who perished that night. The *New York Herald Tribune* reported the horri-fying scene: "Chains and padlocks which prevented the windows from being opened far enough for patients to escape hampered rescuers. Firemen, hospital attendants and volunteers hacked through some of the chains with fire axes and carried women to safety. Other patients were saved by attendants who unlocked their doors and led them through the smoke filled halls. . . . Several women patients, clad in night dress, were rounded up by the townspeople as they wandered into near-by woods. . . . The fire leaped upward through the roof, and six patients were trapped on the fourth floor."[10]

Days after the fire, Zelda was buried with Scott at Rockville Union Cemetery. Scottie thought it fitting, even reassuring, that after years of struggle and separation, her parents should now and forever be united. Writing to "Dearest Grandma," she thanked Minnie for consenting to this arrangement and thus giving her parents a kind of postmortem ease and amity that had eluded them in life. "I was so glad you decided she should stay with Daddy, as seeing them buried together gave the tragedy of their lives a sort of classic unity and it was very touching and reassuring to think of their two high-flying and generous spirits at peace together at last."[11]

TWENTY-FIVE

Life after Death

But to die, so completely and unjustly after having given
so much. Even now there is little published in American
fiction that doesn't slightly bare my stamp—in a
small way I was an original.

F. Scott Fitzgerald, 1940

Some years after Scott Fitzgerald's death, Edmund Wilson struggled to understand the postwar deification of his old friend. Because of his well-known association with Scott, Wilson reported having found himself "for years the recipient of a flow of letters of a very curious kind. It was evident that it was not merely, or perhaps primarily, as the author of *The Great Gatsby* and *Tender Is the Night* that Fitzgerald interested these correspondents but that he had become the object of a cult which had gone beyond mere admiration for the author of some excellent books. He had taken on the aspect of a martyr, a sacrificial victim, a semi-divine personage."[1] And, perhaps after all, he became an oracle of sorts—though the scope of Fitzgerald's vision extended beyond the "Roaring Twenties" to encompass the whole of American history. This he read as a story of building up and breaking down, the April-to-autumn exhaustion captured in the old Spenglerian cycle of decay and decline. The wonder is that, in a nation premised on progress, such a fundamentally tragic interpretation should have resonated so deeply among "the very curious kind" who wrote to Wilson—or that it should continue to echo among the curious to this day.

Fitzgerald's apotheosis is all the more remarkable considering the depths to which his reputation had fallen. His last received royalty statement (August 1940) docked in at an inauspicious $13.13; only seventy-two copies of his books sold in 1940, and he owed Scribner nearly $7,000. Over the next decade, however, Fitzgeraldiana both old and new began to find a market and build momentum. *The Last Tycoon* appeared posthumously in 1941, followed four years later by *The Crack-Up*, containing essays, selections of his notes, and a sampling of letters; both were edited by Wilson. The Viking Press brought out *The Portable F. Scott Fitzgerald* in 1945, and it included an appreciative introduction by John O'Hara. Making a definitive judgment that carried weight, the irrepressible O'Hara called Fitzgerald "our best novelist, one of our best novella-ists, and one of our finest writers of short fiction."[2]

The Great Gatsby and *The Diamond as Big as the Ritz and Other Stories* were reissued in 1945 and '46 by Editions for the Armed Services and given to U.S. service members at home and abroad, which helped to create a new generation of readers for Fitzgerald's novels and stories. With interest continuing to build, 1950 proved to be a particularly eventful year for the Fitzgerald revival. It was the same year in which Malcolm Cowley's landmark volume *The Stories of F. Scott Fitzgerald* and Budd Schulberg's compulsively readable roman à clef *The Disenchanted* (the author's tragicomic account of working with Fitzgerald on a screenplay) appeared. Also in 1950, Scottie Lanahan donated her father's papers to the Princeton University Library—another step on Fitzgerald's path to, as he might have put it, a posthumous "personage hood." Princeton offered $2,500 for Fitzgerald's papers in 1949, but after agreeing to the sale, Scottie decided to make the papers an "outright gift." Finally, in 1951, Alfred Kazin's *F. Scott Fitzgerald: The Man and His Work,* an edited volume of criticism, and Arthur Mizener's *The Far Side of Paradise: A Biography of F. Scott Fitzgerald* were published. Both books made the case for Scott's inclusion in a small circle of great American writers. Kazin's study still sparkles with thoughtful reflections by Lionel Trilling, T. S. Eliot, and Gertrude Stein—gatekeepers of the Western literary tradition. A reviewer for the *New York Times* called the collection "an instructive and intensely interesting book, one to be placed on your permanent shelf."[3]

Though nurtured mainly by intellectuals, the Fitzgerald boom ranged far beyond the custodians of high culture. Both Scott's books and books about him began selling in surprising numbers. Mizener's biography sold 20,000 copies in its first few days of sales, *The Stories of F. Scott Fitzgerald* sold 13,000 units in six months, and Random House moved some 5,000 copies of Schulberg's *The Disenchanted* in January 1951 alone. That same year, Scribner's records show orders for works by Fitzgerald closing in on 30,000 units; by 1960, that figure had leapt to 177,000. A 2013 news story in *USA Today* estimated that approximately twenty-five million copies of *The Great Gatsby* have been sold worldwide.[4]

Interest in Fitzgerald's writing spurred interest in his life. In 1934, while teaching English at Yale, Arthur Mizener, Fitzgerald's first biographer, discovered *Tender Is the Night* sitting on the "new-books" shelf at the library. "I started to read myself to sleep with it at about eleven o'clock," he later recalled, "and I finished it around six the next morning."[5] After a stint at Wells College in New York's Finger Lakes district, he found a more secure post at Carleton College in Northfield, Minnesota—some forty miles south of Scott's St. Paul—where he began to write *Far Side of Paradise*. Its publication made Mizener a minor celebrity, as reviews and serializations of the book appeared in major media outlets and the author found himself the subject of a profile piece in the *New York Times*. Mizener's astonished wife, Rosemary, wrote her sister that the biography had unleashed a pent-up demand among Fitzgerald fans: "Arthur's mail is staggering. The book's success has stirred up everyone we have ever known, plus every Fitzgerald admirer in the country and every psychotic. There are letters from astrologists, from unhappy seventeen-year-olds whose fathers don't understand them and who feel that Arthur might, from widows still missing their husbands who want to know which Fitzgerald book to buy, and from the Butch's and the Joe's that Arthur knew twenty-five years ago."[6] A few months after *Far Side of Paradise*'s publication, Mizener accepted a position at Cornell. His biography of Scott remains to this day an approachable, engaging account, even if its author accepts at face value Fitzgerald's estimation of himself as a "feeler" rather than a "thinker." In this regard, Mizener echoes the envy-born claim made by Wilson in the twenties that Fitzgerald somehow became a major writer in spite of his limited intellect. It is ironic, then, that Wilson thought the biography, for all its shrewd insights, had failed.

That assessment must have been a blow to Mizener, who had sought Wilson's support and blessing. Mizener writes in the foreword to *Far Side of Paradise* that he would never have attempted to write Scott's story "without the approval and the help of Mr. Edmund Wilson." These generous words disguise the fact that Wilson had written a substantially negative report on the book when it was in manuscript. In it, he candidly expressed his disappointment to Mizener: "I do feel certain objections . . . to the way you have treated the subject which are more serious than I had expected and which I hope you won't resent my expressing frankly." From there, Wilson proceeded to critique the introduction (too long and too academic) as well as Mizener's lengthy discussion of the romantic personality type ("as if you were unloading an old lecture"). "I was hoping that you would aim at something more distinguished and less routine," Wilson admonished.[7]

After this opening skirmish, Wilson advanced a more significant criticism: "But the thing that worries me most is the general tone of the book." While recognizing Mizener's appreciation of Fitzgerald's writing, Wilson thought the biographer gave a skewed impression of Scott the man by focusing on the most egregious examples of his bad behavior. "With his life," Wilson wrote, "you seem to dwell on everything that is discreditable or humiliating, almost to the point of ghoulishness." Wilson believed that Mizener's relative youth worked against him. Having matured in the difficult 1930s, Mizener lacked a vital connection to the ebullient Jazz Age—Scott's heyday: "You have the disadvantage of not having known the Fitzgeralds or seen anything of the gaiety of the twenties, whereas you must have had a firsthand impression of the desperate hangover of the thirties. But you can't really tell the story without somehow doing justice to the exhilaration of the days when Scott was successful and Zelda at her most enchanting. You do slight the positive elements."[8] Why, Wilson asked, did Mizener have to emphasize Scott's cowardice on the football field and, more generally, "maladjustments and defeats"? And why did he not approach Zelda with sensitivity rather than censor? Wilson informed Mizener that despite her illness, Zelda was a unique artist of distinct ability: "Even when her mind was going, the writing and painting she did had her curious personal quality of imaginative iridescence and showed something of real talent. In the earlier days of her married life this talent came out mainly in her conversation, which was so full of felicitous phrases and unexpected fancies that, in spite of the fact that it was difficult to talk to her consecutively about anything, you were not led, especially if you yourself had absorbed a few Fitzgerald highballs, to suspect any mental unsoundness from her free 'flight of ideas.'"[9] Wilson assured Mizener that his criticisms were meant to strengthen the biography and hoped they might result in a more generous portrait of Scott. He recognized the manuscript's real strengths in literary criticism ("you have convinced me—what I didn't admit before—that *Tender is the Night* is Scott's most important book") but thought it got the human context out of proportion, "defer[ring]," as he caustically put it, "too much to the prejudices of the *Kenyon Review.*"[10]

A few weeks later, Scottie, having also read the manuscript, gave her approval for Mizener to quote from the Fitzgerald Papers, even as she voiced strong reservations reminiscent of Wilson's:

> You *will* think me, I know, anxious for filial reasons not to have Daddy appear in a "bad light" . . . but you have missed the charm, and the goodness, and the . . . heroic side of the man—which even I, as a far from loving daughter, felt as strongly as everybody who knew him—or at least you have sacrificed it overwhelmingly in favor of the Mr. Hyde, the vain, self-indulgent, eternally immature side of him. And you have done so even more in the case of mother, bringing out not at all her remarkable and absolutely marvelous qualities which were obvious even to people who knew her when she was very sick.[11]

If *Far Side of Paradise* failed to win over those who were close to Fitzgerald, however, it earned strong praise from reviewers and proved to be of great interest to general readers. Aside from putting Fitzgerald's story "on record," Mizener's biography treated Scott seriously as a writer and initiated a long and still-ongoing line of scholarly biographies, edited volumes, and monographs dedicated to the man, his times, and his talent.

Published almost simultaneously with *Far Side of Paradise,* Schulberg's *The Disenchanted* added another layer to the Fitzgerald legend. Fitzgerald and Schulberg met in 1939 after Schulberg, just twenty-five at the time, turned in a tired screenplay for *Winter Carnival,* a college romance set in New England. Looking to kick-start the film, the producer Walter Wanger assigned Schulberg to write a fresh script with Fitzgerald. At first, Schulberg thought the order from on high a joke. "Somehow I got the impression," he noted years later, "that Scott had died." Apparently Wanger liked the idea of bringing together a couple of writers who "knew" the Ivy League. At the two writers' first lunch, a slightly starstruck or perhaps simply polite Schulberg told Fitzgerald that he had read all of his books in college (Dartmouth '36). "I'm surprised that you know who I am," Scott evenly replied.[12]

Wanger wanted his writers to get a feel for the New England winter prep scene and so ordered the two men east, much against Fitzgerald's wishes. Scott's efforts at sobriety relied then on a daily routine that he had carved out with Sheilah Graham's help, which would now be disrupted. The cross-country flight was long and included two stops for refueling; to help pass the time, Schulberg's father had given them two bottles of Mumm champagne, which they accordingly polished off in the air. Only warming to the cause, Fitzgerald kept drinking in what turned out to be a bender that lasted the next three days. A furious Wanger fired Scott, and there the miserable episode ended, hidden for eleven years, until Schulberg mined their misadventures in *The Disenchanted.* Allowing for some poetic license, the novel's antihero, the writer T. Manley Halliday, is modeled after Fitzgerald (circa 1939). Fabulously successful in the 1920s, Halliday is now a homburg-hatted ghost, all but forgotten by the literary establishment. He resides at the Garden of Allah apartments (Scott's old Sunset Boulevard address), where he is attempting to pick up the emotional crumbs after a disastrous marriage (Jere stands in for Zelda) with the assistance of a new love who tries to keep him sober (Anne Loeb, playing a passable Sheilah Graham). The Dartmouth disaster is revisited in excruciating detail (the film *Love on Ice* substitutes for *Winter Carnival*), with Scott's garden-variety anti-Semitism, drunken speechifying, and occasionally loutish behavior made transparent for all the book-reading world to see.

Far from a hatchet job, however, *The Disenchanted* struggled between its author's veneration for Fitzgerald and the man Fitzgerald had now become. Schulberg's insights into Scott's character, politics (or lack thereof), and wounded if resilient outlook demonstrate a careful reading of the writer that adds a certain tenderness and pathos to what might otherwise have been an all-too-bitter send-up. In observations such as "Despite Manley's reputation as one of the least restrained flambeaux of his age, he had a deep streak of bourgeois conventionality" and "He couldn't even be sure if Halliday were conservative, liberal or radical. He simply seemed to be standing off and observing his world with an indefinable blend of romanticism and cynicism," Schulberg got Scott just right.[13]

Scottie recognized her father's intoxicated speech in Schulberg's novel—and it frightened her. After reading *The Disenchanted,* she wrote to Mizener, telling him, "The reporting job is absolutely terrific—I wish you would tell me whether he took notes after Dartmouth. I really felt I was in the room with Daddy the entire time during the drunken scenes— that was *exactly* the way he talked and acted during those bouts and it really gave me an eerie sensation." One example of Schulberg's "terrific" reportage is a scene in which Manley tries to get his writing partner Shep to forget their mounting troubles and find the next party: "S really a beau'ful night. Wonnerful night. . . . Come on, Baby, le's not worry about that sonuvabish. Le's have a li'l fun. We oughta get a li'l fun outa this expedition. We worked. Day 'n night. I don' feel guilty. Be damned if I'm gonna feel guilty."[14]

In response to these warts-and-all studies of Fitzgerald, Sheilah Graham's protective, heartfelt *Beloved Infidel* (1958) emphasized Scott's humor, humanity, and brave effort to finish his last novel. The book opens with a protest of sorts, a deck clearing of what others—"outsiders," she calls them—had written of Fitzgerald. "As the years passed and I read increasingly about [Scott] in books and magazines," Graham observes, "I found myself thinking, 'This is not the Scott I knew.' From those pages there emerged a man who was often a stranger to me. The man they put together from [his] correspondence, [and his] books, the quick, fugitive glimpses they caught of [him] toward the end—this was not Scott Fitzgerald as I knew him." Graham offers her readers a friendly "insider" account of Scott's Hollywood years that approached the subject of his alcoholism and demons with more compassion than either Mizener or Schulberg had managed. Wilson thought the narrative so spot-on that he praised it in a lengthy *New Yorker* essay as "the very best portrait of Fitzgerald that has yet been put into print."[15] Here was a flawed if fully human Fitzgerald and one that future readers would now come to know not merely through his books and letters but through the warm remembrances of Graham. In her, Scott had an effective advocate, just as the debate over the "meaning" of his life was beginning to take shape.

For many years, literary detectives have kicked around Wilson's old question: why the enduring interest in Fitzgerald? Some have argued for simple nostalgia, a yearning among readers to escape the banality of everyday life for a glamorous bygone era of jazz and gin. Others contend that the concerns facing Fitzgerald's generation, the first to wrestle with a host of anxieties linked to the perils of prosperity, have remained vital to succeeding generations ensnared in their own struggles to establish "higher" goals. Both observations are correct as far they go, though neither, to my mind, goes quite far enough.

In Fitzgerald's writings, rather, we encounter an America unusually thick with fallen heroes, martyrs to a powerful social-mobility mythology. Embedded in these offerings is the disquieting notion that we have drifted far from our inheritance as the children of pioneers to fashion a culture that teaches its young to love too much the privileges and protections of wealth. It is thus painful to see Gatsby, "a son of God," ape the East Egg pretensions of the arrogant, irresponsible Tom Buchanan, the "one percent" at its worst. Certainly other post–Great War commentators captured this critical tone, but perhaps none did so with quite the panoramic eye and situational "feel" that lent to Fitzgerald's novels, stories, and essays a remarkable precision, insight, and accessibility. He worked hard to achieve such sparkling constructions, hoping to be read, remembered, and taken seriously. "My whole theory of writing I can sum up in one sentence," he explained at an already knowing twenty-three: "An author ought to write for the youth of his own generation, the critics of the next, and the schoolmasters of ever afterward."[16]

With this daunting enterprise in mind, Fitzgerald sought to record in some definite sense the history of America. Time and again, his writings raised serious questions about the uneven progress of the New World's peoples. The growing power of industrialists and financers offended his romantic sensibility, and he wondered if this rising republic of consumers could ever recover its old idealism. Such sharp doubts are famously depicted in the shimmering green light that watches silently over Gatsby's grand illusion. That striking image contains the suggestion of what four centuries of western voyagers have gained and what they have surrendered. It is in this candid appraisal, remembered in the golden late afternoons of lost cities, decades, and generations, that Fitzgerald appealed to readers who shared his skepticism of that grandest of illusions, the "American Dream." They—we—remain both captivated by its promise and restlessly aware of its burdensome historical weight. This dilemma Fitzgerald captured so gracefully, so indelibly in the final true lines of *Gatsby:* "So we beat on, boats against the current, borne back ceaselessly into the past."[17]

NOTES

Manuscript Collection Abbreviations

AMPD   Arthur Mizener Papers Delaware, Special Collections, University of Delaware Morris Library

AMPP   Arthur Mizener Papers Princeton, Department of Rare Books and Special Collections, Princeton University Firestone Library

CHMR   Craig House Medical Records, Department of Rare Books and Special Collections, Princeton University Firestone Library

FSFP   F. Scott Fitzgerald Papers, Department of Rare Books and Special Collections, Princeton University Firestone Library

FSFAP   F. Scott Fitzgerald Additional Papers, Department of Rare Books and Special Collections, Princeton University Firestone Library

HDPP   Henry Dan Piper Papers, Special Collections Research Center, Southern Illinois University Carbondale

JPBP   John Peale Bishop Papers, Department of Rare Books and Special Collections, Princeton University Firestone Library

MJBP   Matthew J. Bruccoli Papers, Irvin Department of Rare Books and Special Collections, University of South Carolina Thomas Cooper Library

ZFP   Zelda Fitzgerald Papers, Department of Rare Books and Special Collections, Princeton University Firestone Library

Introduction: Clio and Scott

1. F. Scott Fitzgerald, *The Notebooks of F. Scott Fitzgerald,* ed. Matthew J. Bruccoli (New York: Harcourt Brace Jovanovich/Bruccoli Clark, 1978), 159.

2. F. Scott Fitzgerald to Edmund Wilson, 10 January 1918, in *The Letters of F. Scott Fitzgerald,* ed. Andrew Turnbull (New York: Charles Scribner's Sons, 1963), 323.

3. F. Scott Fitzgerald to Scottie Fitzgerald, July 1938, in *F. Scott Fitzgerald: Letters to His Daughter,* ed. Andrew Turnbull (New York: Charles Scribner's Sons, 1965), 57; F. Scott Fitzgerald to Harold Ober, 21 February 1938, in *As Ever, Scott-Fitz—: Letters between F. Scott Fitzgerald and His Literary Agent, Harold Ober, 1919–1940,* ed. Matthew J. Bruccoli (Philadelphia: J. B. Lippincott, 1972), 357.

4. Edmund Wilson, *The Shores of Light: A Literary Chronicle of the Twenties and Thirties* (New York: Farrar, Straus and Young, 1952), 31.

5. John Biggs Jr., "Fitzgerald in Wilmington—The Great Gatsby at Bay," *(Wilmington) Sunday Bulletin,* 6 January 1974, 9. While living in Delaware, Fitzgerald, playing on the "landed gentleman" idea identified by Biggs, sent a postcard to daughter, Scottie, addressed to "Mlle Scotty Joan of Arc Fitzgerald Ellerslie

Castle." He signed off, "yours Louis XIV (le roi soliel)." Fitzgerald to Dear Pie, 24 February 1929, in Bruccoli Collection, MJBP. The palace idea came up again when the Fitzgeralds were staying in France. "One thing I remember very vividly," Scottie recalled, "is the castle in the backyard in Cannes, at the Villa Fleur de Bois, I believe it was, and this very elaborate castle constructed in the backyard." The Fitzgeralds stayed at the Villa Fleur de Bois from June 1929 until October. "Scottie Fitzgerald Interview," Montgomery, AL, 1977, MJBP.

6. Anonymous reviewer in the *Times Literary Supplement*, "This Side of Paradise," in *F. Scott Fitzgerald in His Own Time: A Miscellany*, ed. Matthew J. Bruccoli and Jackson R. Bryer (Kent, OH: Kent State University Press, 1971), 313.

7. F. Scott Fitzgerald to Max Perkins, 27 October 1924, in *Dear Scott/Dear Max: The Fitzgerald-Perkins Correspondence*, ed. John Kuehl and Jackson Bryer (New York: Charles Scribner's Sons, 1971), 80.

8. F. Scott Fitzgerald, "The Swimmers," in *Taps at Reveille*, ed. James L. W. West III (New York: Cambridge University Press, 2014), 243.

9. Malcolm Cowley, *A Second Flowering: Works and Days of the Lost Generation* (New York: Viking, 1973), 30; F. Scott Fitzgerald, "My Lost City," in *My Lost City: Personal Essays, 1920–1940*, ed. James L. W. West III (New York: Cambridge University Press, 2005), 110.

10. Richard Lehan, *The Great Gatsby: The Limits of Wonder* (New York: Twayne, 1995), 1–10.

11. Milton R. Stern, *Tender Is the Night: The Broken Universe* (New York: Twayne, 1994), 4, 12.

12. Ruth Prigozy, ed., *The Cambridge Companion to F. Scott Fitzgerald* (New York: Cambridge University Press, 2001); Kirk Curnutt, ed., *A Historical Guide to F. Scott Fitzgerald* (New York: Oxford University Press, 2004).

13. Bryant Mangum, ed., *F. Scott Fitzgerald in Context* (New York: Cambridge University Press, 2013).

14. Robert Sklar, *F. Scott Fitzgerald: The Last Laocoön* (New York: Oxford University Press, 1967), 3. Sklar adapted the Fitzgerald-as-Laocoön idea from Malcolm Lowry, who introduced it in his novella "Through the Panama," published posthumously in *Hear Us O Lord from Heaven Thy Dwelling Place* (Philadelphia: J. B. Lippincott, 1961).

15. F. Scott Fitzgerald to Anne Ober, 4 March 1938, in *F. Scott Fitzgerald: A Life in Letters*, ed. Matthew J. Bruccoli (New York: Simon and Schuster, 1994), 352.

16. F. Scott Fitzgerald, *Tender Is the Night*, ed. James L. W. West III (New York: Cambridge University Press, 2012), 68.

17. Edmund Wilson, *The Bit between My Teeth: A Literary Chronicle of 1950–1965* (New York: Farrar, Straus and Giroux, 1965), 17.

18. F. Scott Fitzgerald to Scottie Fitzgerald, 5 October 1940, in Turnbull, *Letters to His Daughter*, 155–56.

19. Fitzgerald, "My Lost City," in *My Lost City*, 107.

1. Prince and Pauper

1. F. Scott Fitzgerald to John Jamieson, 15 April 1934, b50, FSFP. On Gatsby's origins, see Richard Lehan, *The Great Gatsby: The Limits of Wonder* (New York: Twayne, 1995), 60–61, 64–66, 82–90.

2. F. Scott Fitzgerald, *The Great Gatsby,* ed. Matthew J. Bruccoli (New York: Cambridge University Press, 1991), 140; F. Scott Fitzgerald, *Tender Is the Night,* ed. James L. W. West III (New York: Cambridge University Press, 2012), 136.

3. Andrew Turnbull, *Scott Fitzgerald* (New York: Charles Scribner's Sons, 1962), 4.

4. André Le Vot, *F. Scott Fitzgerald: A Biography,* trans. William Bryon (New York: Doubleday, 1983), 8.

5. Ibid., emphasis added.

6. Archbishop Dowling to "My Dear Monsignor," 3 June 1921, b39b, FSFP. Manhattanville College sold its campus to City College of New York and moved to suburban Purchase, New York, in 1952. A "Kennedy college," its alumnae include Rose Kennedy and her daughters Eunice and Jean and daughters-in-law Ethel Skakel Kennedy and Joan Bennett Kennedy.

7. Henry Dan Piper, *F. Scott Fitzgerald: A Critical Portrait* (New York: Holt, Rinehart and Winston, 1965), 8; F. Scott Fitzgerald, "An Author's Mother," in *My Lost City: Personal Essays, 1920–1940,* ed. James L. W. West III (New York: Cambridge University Press, 2005), 181; Jeffrey Meyers, *Scott Fitzgerald: A Biography* (New York: HarperCollins, 1994), 5, 4; Scottie Smith to Matthew J. Bruccoli, internal evidence suggests early 1970s, b25, MJBP.

8. F. Scott Fitzgerald, *This Side of Paradise,* ed. James L. W. West III (New York: Cambridge University Press, 1996), 78.

9. F. Scott Fitzgerald, foreword to *Colonial and Historic Homes of Maryland,* by Don S. Swann Jr. (Baltimore: Johns Hopkins University Press, 1975).

10. Turnbull, *Scott Fitzgerald,* 7; Fitzgerald, "Author's House," in *My Lost City,* 169.

11. F. Scott Fitzgerald to Mollie Fitzgerald, 18 July 1907, in *F. Scott Fitzgerald: A Life in Letters,* ed. Matthew J. Bruccoli (New York: Simon and Schuster, 1994), 5; Turnbull, *Scott Fitzgerald,* 35.

12. Fitzgerald, *Paradise,* 11; F. Scott Fitzgerald to Annabel Fitzgerald, June 1936, in *The Letters of F. Scott Fitzgerald,* ed. Andrew Turnbull (New York: Charles Scribner's Sons, 1963), 535; Fitzgerald, "An Author's Mother, in *My Lost City,* 181–82.

13. Scott Donaldson, *Fool for Love: A Biography of F. Scott Fitzgerald* (New York: Delta, 1983), 13–14.

14. Michel Mok, "The Other Side of Paradise: Scott Fitzgerald, 40, Engulfed in Despair," in *Conversations with F. Scott Fitzgerald,* ed. Matthew J. Bruccoli and Judith S. Baughman (Jackson: University Press of Mississippi, 2004), 122–23; John Biggs Jr., "Fitzgerald in Wilmington—The Great Gatsby at Bay," *(Wilmington) Sunday Bulletin,* 6 January 1974, 9. James J. Hill (1938–1916) was nicknamed "The

Empire Builder" for his control of the Great Northern Railway, a series of lines running from the upper Midwest to the Pacific Northwest.

15. F. Scott Fitzgerald, "The Death of My Father," in *A Short Autobiography,* ed. James L. W. West III (New York: Scribner, 2011), 120. Edward's attention to his son's manners is captured in an entry in Fitzgerald's *Ledger:* "When you enter a room speak first to the oldest lady, says father." F. Scott Fitzgerald, *F. Scott Fitzgerald's Ledger: A Facsimile,* ed. Matthew J. Bruccoli (Washington, DC: Bruccoli Clark / NCR Microcard Editions, 1972), 165.

16. Fitzgerald, *Gatsby,* 5; Fitzgerald, *Tender,* 232.

17. F. Scott Fitzgerald, "Minnesota's Capital in the Rôle of Main Street," *Literary Digest International Book Review,* March 1923, *in F. Scott Fitzgerald in His Own Time: A Miscellany,* ed. Matthew J. Bruccoli and Jackson R. Bryer (Kent, OH: Kent State University Press, 1971), 141.

18. Fitzgerald, *Gatsby,* 137. The foundling-child theme is evident in *Paradise.* With Amory's glamorous mother too ill for parental duties, he is farmed out to relatives in the "crude, vulgar" climes of Minneapolis. Fitzgerald, *Paradise,* 15.

19. Fitzgerald, "Author's House," in *My Lost City,* 168, 169. While on a trip to Quebec, Fitzgerald sent his daughter, Scottie, a postcard, playfully informing her, "I have been elected President of Canada but am too busy as King of the World to take the job." Fitzgerald to "Dear Pie," 25 January 1928, Bruccoli Collection, MJBP.

20. F. Scott Fitzgerald to Alida Bigelow, September 1919, in Bruccoli, *Life in Letters,* 33. The line "In a room below the roof" refers to the upstairs space in Fitzgerald's parents' brownstone row house (599 Summit Avenue), where, in the summer of 1919, he completed *This Side of Paradise.*

2. Celtic Blood

1. Sam Kennedy, "Personals," *St. Paul Academy Now and Then,* Easter 1909, 4; F. Scott Fitzgerald, "The Freshest Boy," in *The Basil, Josephine, and Gwen Stories,* ed. James L. W. West III (New York: Cambridge University Press, 2009), 57.

2. Andrew Turnbull, *Scott Fitzgerald* (New York: Charles Scribner's Sons, 1962), 29.

3. F. Scott Fitzgerald, "Who's Who—and Why," in *A Short Autobiography,* ed. James L. W. West III (New York: Scribner, 2011), 1.

4. *A Handbook of the Best Private Schools of the United States and Canada 1915* (Boston: P. E. Sargent, 1915), 53.

5. Turnbull, *Scott Fitzgerald,* 34–35. Fitzgerald's prep-school alter ego, Amory Blaine, repeated Scott's catalogue of strengths and weaknesses nearly verbatim. See F. Scott Fitzgerald, *This Side of Paradise,* ed. James L. W. West III (New York: Cambridge University Press, 1996), 24–25.

6. Fitzgerald, "Freshest Boy," in *Basil, Josephine, and Gwen,* 56; Charles Donahoe to Arthur Mizener, 10 January 1948, b1, AMPP; G. Ingersoll Lewis to Henry Dan Piper, internal evidence suggests 1945–1947, b2, HDPP.

7. F. Scott Fitzgerald, "FOOTBALL," in *F. Scott Fitzgerald in His Own Time: A Miscellany,* ed. Matthew J. Bruccoli and Jackson R. Bryer (Kent, OH: Kent State University Press, 1971), 3–4.

8. F. Scott Fitzgerald, "Author's House," in *My Lost City: Personal Essays, 1920–1940,* ed. James L. W. West III (New York: Cambridge University Press, 2005), 170.

9. Turnbull, *Scott Fitzgerald,* 38.

10. Margaret Chanler, *Autumn in the Valley* (Boston: Little, Brown, 1936), 80; Charles Donahoe to Arthur Mizener, 10 January 1948, b1, AMPP.

11. C. Edmund Delbos to Arthur Mizener, 18 March 1948, b1, AMPP; Father Sigourney Fay to F. Scott Fitzgerald, 22 August 1917, in *Correspondence of F. Scott Fitzgerald,* ed. Matthew J. Bruccoli and Margaret M. Duggan (New York: Random House, 1980), 19–21; Jeffrey Meyers, *Scott Fitzgerald: A Biography* (New York: HarperCollins, 1994), 40.

12. Matthew J. Bruccoli, *Some Sort of Epic Grandeur: The Life of F. Scott Fitzgerald* (New York: Harcourt Brace Jovanovich, 1981), 19.

13. Fitzgerald, *Paradise,* 31. Jacobites hoped to restore the Stuart dynasty to the throne of England after James II was deposed in the Glorious Revolution of 1688. "Bonnie Prince Charlie," James II's grandson, led a Jacobite uprising that was put down at the Battle of Culloden in 1746.

14. Fitzgerald, *Short Autobiography,* 5, 8; F. Scott Fitzgerald, *The Great Gatsby,* ed. Matthew J. Bruccoli (New York: Cambridge University Press, 1991), 116.

15. F. Scott Fitzgerald to John O'Hara, 18 July 1933, in *The Letters of F. Scott Fitzgerald,* ed. Andrew Turnbull (New York: Charles Scribner's Sons, 1963), 503.

16. Joan Allen, *Candles and Carnival Lights: The Catholic Sensibilities of F. Scott Fitzgerald* (New York: NYU Press, 1978), 20–21.

17. Bruccoli, *Some Sort of Epic Grandeur,* 38.

18. Shane Leslie, "Scott Fitzgerald's First Novel," *Times Literary Supplement,* 6 November 1959, 643; Shane Leslie, "Some Memories of Scott Fitzgerald," *Times Literary Supplement,* 31 October 1958, 632.

19. F. Scott Fitzgerald to Shane Leslie, February 1918, in *F. Scott Fitzgerald: A Life in Letters,* ed. Matthew J. Bruccoli (New York: Simon and Shuster, 1994), 20. Fitzgerald had originally trotted out the "arithmetical progression" line for Wilson, though in this version, he included a dig at Leslie: "Too bad I haven't a better man for 31." F. Scott Fitzgerald to Edmund Wilson, Fall 1917, in Turnbull, *Letters,* 320; Edmund Wilson, "Thoughts on Being Bibliographed," in *Classics and Commercials: A Literary Chronicle of the Forties* (New York: Farrar, Straus, 1950), 110.

3. Forever Princeton

1. Fitzgerald wrote in *This Side of Paradise* that Amory, mulling over his boyhood conceit, "wondered how people could fail to notice that he was a boy marked

for glory." F. Scott Fitzgerald, *This Side of Paradise*, ed. James L. W. West III (New York: Cambridge University Press, 1996), 24.

2. Ibid., 41; Andrew Turnbull, *Scott Fitzgerald* (New York: Charles Scribner's Sons, 1962), 42. F. Scott Fitzgerald, *The Great Gatsby*, ed. Matthew J. Bruccoli (New York: Cambridge University Press, 1991), 9.

3. Martin Duberman, *Paul Robeson: A Biography* (New York: Knopf, 1988), 6.

4. F. Scott Fitzgerald, *F. Scott Fitzgerald's Ledger: A Facsimile*, ed. Matthew J. Bruccoli (Washington, DC: Bruccoli Clark / NCR Microcard Editions, 1972), 167. On "cribbing," Fitzgerald wrote a decade after leaving college, "Personally I have never seen or heard of a Princeton man cheating in an examination. . . . I can think of a dozen times when a page of notes glanced at in a wash room would have made the difference between failure and success for me, but I can't recall any moral struggles in the matter." F. Scott Fitzgerald, *A Short Autobiography*, ed. James L. W. West III (New York: Scribner, 2011), 99.

5. John D. McMaster, "As I Remember Scott," *Confrontation*, Fall 1973, 4.

6. John Peale Bishop, "The Missing All," *Virginia Quarterly Review*, Winter 1937, 115; F. Scott Fitzgerald to Edmund Wilson, 25 November 1940, in *F. Scott Fitzgerald: A Life in Letters*, ed. Matthew J. Bruccoli (New York: Simon and Schuster, 1994), 471.

7. F. Scott Fitzgerald, "Winter Dreams," in *All the Sad Young Men*, ed. James L. W. West III (New York: Cambridge University Press, 2007), 47. As Bishop noted, Scott's relationship with the rich was always that of an outsider: "He made money, and like Gatsby remained an intruder in the moneyed world." Bishop, "Missing All," 116.

8. Fitzgerald, *Paradise*, 130.

9. F. Scott Fitzgerald, "Princeton," in *My Lost City: Personal Essays, 1920–1940*, ed. James L. W. West III (New York: Cambridge University Press, 2005), 10, 6.

10. Ibid., 7.

11. Edmund Wilson, *A Prelude: Landscapes, Characters and Conversations from the Earlier Years of My Life* (New York: Farrar, Straus and Giroux, 1967), 180.

12. Matthew J. Bruccoli, *Some Sort of Epic Grandeur: The Life of F. Scott Fitzgerald* (New York: Harcourt Brace Jovanovich, 1981), 43; Arthur Mizener, *The Far Side of Paradise: A Biography of F. Scott Fitzgerald* (New York: Houghton Mifflin, 1951), 31.

13. Bruccoli, *Some Sort of Epic Grandeur*, 43.

14. F. Scott Fitzgerald to Scottie Fitzgerald, February 1938, in *F. Scott Fitzgerald: Letters to His Daughter*, ed. Andrew Turnbull (New York: Charles Scribner's Sons, 1965), 34–35. The verse, Horace, Ode 1.22, should read,

"Integer vitae, scelerisque purus,
Non eget Mauris jaculis
Fusce, neque arcu, Nec . . ."

"He who is upright in life and pure of sin does not need Moorish spears nor bow." Though Fitzgerald pressed Scottie to bear down academically he had, during his own college career, understood and seemed to accept the fact that his attention to extracurriculars left him time only for a truncated education. In "The Spire and Gargoyle," a contribution to the *Nassau Literary Magazine* published in February 1917, Fitzgerald wrote knowingly of himself, "he had neither the leisure to browse thoughtfully on much nor the education to cram thoughtfully on little." F. Scott Fitzgerald, "The Spire and the Gargoyle," in *Spires and Gargoyles: Early Writings, 1909–1919*, ed. James L. W. West III (New York: Cambridge University Press, 2010), 164.

15. Matthew J. Bruccoli, Scottie Fitzgerald Smith, and Joan P. Kerr, eds., *The Romantic Egoists: A Pictorial Autobiography from the Scrapbooks and Albums of F. Scott and Zelda Fitzgerald* (New York: Charles Scribner's Sons, 1974), 44; Fitzgerald, "Who's Who—and Why," in *Short Autobiography*, 1; Fitzgerald, *Ledger*, 168; F. Scott Fitzgerald, *Fie! Fie! Fi-Fi!*, in *F. Scott Fitzgerald in His Own Time: A Miscellany*, ed. Matthew J. Bruccoli and Jackson R. Bryer (Kent, OH: Kent State University Press, 1971), 4.

16. Turnbull, *Scott Fitzgerald*, 54; Wilson, *Prelude*, 68.

17. Sara Mayfield, *Exiles from Paradise: Zelda and Scott Fitzgerald* (New York: Delacorte, 1971), 37.

18. Fitzgerald, "The Spire and the Gargoyle," in *Spires and Gargoyles*, 162. Fitzgerald's introduction to metropolitan amenities included outfitting himself at Brooks Brothers in New York and at Jacob Reed's Sons in Philadelphia.

19. Christian Gauss to Arthur Mizener, 17 October 1944, b1, AMPP; Turnbull, *Scott Fitzgerald*, 65.

20. Fitzgerald, "Pasting It Together," in *My Lost City*, 146.

21. Mizener, *Far Side of Paradise*, 35.

22. Bishop, "Missing All," 108; Turnbull, *Scott Fitzgerald*, 52.

23. F. Scott Fitzgerald to Edmund Wilson, 25 November 1940, in Bruccoli, *Life in Letters*, 471.

24. F. Scott Fitzgerald to Scottie Fitzgerald, 3 August 1940, in Turnbull, *Letters to His Daughter*, 142.

25. F. Scott Fitzgerald, *The Crack-Up*, ed. Edmund Wilson (New York: New Directions, 1945), 345.

26. Turnbull, *Scott Fitzgerald*, 61.

27. Fitzgerald, "Pasting It Together," in *My Lost City*, 148; Edmund Wilson, *The Shores of Light: A Literary Chronicle of the Twenties and Thirties* (New York: Farrar, Straus and Young, 1952), 27.

28. F. Scott Fitzgerald to Christian Gauss, 7 September 1934, in *The Letters of F. Scott Fitzgerald*, ed. Andrew Turnbull (New York: Charles Scribner's Sons, 1963), 386. Princeton became a notorious place for Scott gossip. Some years after Fitzgerald's death, John Davies, then editor of the *Princeton Alumni Weekly*, informed a biographer, "I've talked to some old Cottage types about those house parties when he and Zelda were chaperones, and personally, I think both of them were crazy;

there is something pathological, depraved, [and] unnice about this cartwheels with no bloomers routine that all the literary tolerance in the world can't excuse." John Davies to Henry Dan Piper, internal evidence suggests late 1950s, b1, HDPP.

29. John Biggs Jr., "Fitzgerald in Wilmington—The Great Gatsby at Bay," *(Wilmington) Sunday Bulletin,* 6 January 1974, 9; McMaster, "As I Remember Scott," 6.

30. Edmund Wilson to Christian Gauss, 15 May 1944, in *Edmund Wilson: Letters on Literature and Politics, 1912–1972,* ed. Elena Wilson (New York: Farrar, Straus and Giroux, 1977), 335.

31. Morris Dickstein, *Dancing in the Dark: A Cultural History of the Great Depression* (New York: Norton, 2009), 261.

32. Marjorie Kinnan Rawlings to Arthur Mizener, 18 March 1948, b2, AMPP.

33. Fitzgerald, "Princeton," in *My Lost City,* 15.

4. Golden Girl

1. F. Scott Fitzgerald, *F. Scott Fitzgerald's Ledger: A Facsimile,* ed. Matthew J. Bruccoli (Washington, DC: Bruccoli Clark / NCR Microcard Editions, 1972), 165.

2. F. Scott Fitzgerald, "The Scandal Detectives," in *The Basil, Josephine, and Gwen Stories,* ed. James L. W. West III (New York: Cambridge University Press, 2009), 20.

3. Ibid., 35; F. Scott Fitzgerald to Marie Hersey, 28 October 1936, in *The Letters of F. Scott Fitzgerald,* ed. Andrew Turnbull (New York: Charles Scribner's Sons, 1963), 545.

4. Dinitia Smith, "Love Notes Drenched in Moonlight: Hints of Future Novels in Letters to Fitzgerald," *New York Times,* 8 September 2003.

5. Ginevra King Pirie to Arthur Mizener, 7 November 1947, b1, AMPP.

6. F. Scott Fitzgerald to Scottie Fitzgerald, 11 April 1940, in *F. Scott Fitzgerald: A Life in Letters,* ed. Matthew J. Bruccoli (New York: Simon and Schuster, 1994), 440.

7. F. Scott Fitzgerald, *The Great Gatsby*, ed. Matthew J. Bruccoli (New York: Cambridge University Press, 1991), 6; James L. W. West, *The Perfect Hour: The Romance of F. Scott Fitzgerald and Ginevra King, His First Love* (New York: Random House, 2005), 43.

8. West, *Perfect Hour,* 43, 133; Fitzgerald, *Ledger,* 170.

9. Fitzgerald, *Gatsby,* 9.

10. West, *Perfect Hour,* 64–65. Ginevra appears to have told Scott the truth—none of his letter to her survive.

11. In 1950, ten years after Fitzgerald's death, his daughter, Scottie, gave these typed copies to Ginevra. In 2003, Ginevra King Chandler, one of Ginevra's granddaughters, donated the transcriptions along with her grandmother's diary to Princeton University's Firestone Library.

12. F. Scott Fitzgerald, *Tender Is the Night,* ed. James L. W. West III (New York: Cambridge University Press, 2012), 312; F. Scott Fitzgerald, *The Beautiful and Damned,* ed. James L. W. West III (New York: Cambridge University Press, 2008), 72;

Fitzgerald, "Emotional Bankruptcy," in *Basil, Josephine, and Gwen*, 269–70. After Scott's death, Ginevra replied to a biographer's query about their romance by stating that Fitzgerald "emphasized—and overemphasized" her "thoughtless" and flirtatious behavior in the Josephine stories. She acknowledged, however, "it is only fair to say I asked for some of them." Arthur Mizener, *The Far Side of Paradise: A Biography of F. Scott Fitzgerald* (New York: Houghton Mifflin, 1951), 327n15.

13. West, *Perfect Hour,* 50.

14. Ibid., 51–56.

15. Ibid., 65–66.

16. For Mitchell's obituary, see the 25 March 1987 *Chicago Tribune.*

17. Fitzgerald, *Ledger,* 173; Matthew J. Bruccoli, Scottie Fitzgerald Smith, and Joan P. Kerr, eds., *The Romantic Egoists: A Pictorial Autobiography from the Scrapbooks and Albums of F. Scott and Zelda Fitzgerald* (New York: Charles Scribner's Sons, 1974), 27.

18. West, *Perfect Hour,* 84–85; Elizabeth Friskey, "Visiting the Golden Girl," *Princeton Alumni Weekly*, 8 October 1974, 11.

19. F. Scott Fitzgerald to Scottie Fitzgerald, 5 July 1937, in *F. Scott Fitzgerald: Letters to His Daughter,* ed. Andrew Turnbull (New York: Charles Scribner's Sons, 1965), 23.

20. Mizener, *Far Side of Paradise,* 275; F. Scott Fitzgerald to Scottie Fitzgerald, 4 November 1937, in Turnbull, *Letters to His Daughter,* 32; Smith, "Love Notes." Ginevra and William Mitchell, parents of three children, were divorced in 1939. She remarried, taking the last name of her husband, John T. Pirie Jr.; Ginevra died in 1980 at the age of eighty-two.

5. Opposites Alike

1. Chester B. Sikking to Alexander P. Clark, 4 September 1971, b5, FSFP.

2. Devereaux Josephs to Henry Dan Piper, 1 May 1947, b2, HDPP.

3. F. Scott Fitzgerald to Cousin Ceci, 19 June 1917, b5, FSFP.

4. F. Scott Fitzgerald, "Who's Who—and Why," in *A Short Autobiography,* ed. James L. W. West III (New York: Scribner, 2011), 2.

5. F. Scott Fitzgerald to Edmund Wilson, 10 January 1918, in *The Letters of F. Scott Fitzgerald,* ed. Andrew Turnbull (New York: Charles Scribner's Sons, 1963), 321; F. Scott Fitzgerald to Shane Leslie, 22 December 1917, in *F. Scott Fitzgerald: A Life in Letters,* ed. Matthew J. Bruccoli (New York: Simon and Schuster, 1994), 14.

6. Matthew J. Bruccoli, *Some Sort of Epic Grandeur: The Life of F. Scott Fitzgerald* (New York: Harcourt Brace Jovanovich, 1981), 84.

7. F. Scott Fitzgerald to Edmund Wilson, January 1922, in Bruccoli, *Life in Letters,* 51.

8. Major Dana Palmer to Arthur Mizener, 1 February 1951, b2, AMPP; Sally Cline, *Zelda Fitzgerald: Her Voice in Paradise* (London: John Murray, 2002), 47; Nancy Milford, *Zelda* (New York: Harper and Row, 1970), 33.

9. F. Scott Fitzgerald, *The Great Gatsby*, ed. Matthew J. Bruccoli (New York: Cambridge University Press, 1991), 117; Zelda Fitzgerald to F. Scott Fitzgerald, 13 February 1940, b27, MJBP.

10. Sam Broomfield to Arthur Mizener, internal evidence suggests 1951, b1, AMPP.

11. Edmund Wilson to Arthur Mizener, 11 November 1949, b1, f10, AMPD.

12. F. Scott Fitzgerald to Ruth Sturtevant, 4 December 1918, in Turnbull, *Letters,* 454.

13. F. Scott Fitzgerald, *The Notebooks of F. Scott Fitzgerald,* ed. Matthew J. Bruccoli (New York: Harcourt Brace Jovanovich/Bruccoli Clark, 1978), 79.

14. Charles Lawton Campbell, "Scott and Zelda Were His Friends," *Villager* (Bronxville, NY), April 1971, 8, 20.

15. F. Scott Fitzgerald, "Pasting It Together," in *My Lost City: Personal Essays, 1920–1940,* ed. James L. W. West III (New York: Cambridge University Press, 2005), 146–47. On the "money-maker" theme, sometime during that busy autumn of 1919, Zelda had owned up to her doubts, writing Scott, "I am very proud of you—I hate to say this, but I don't *think* I had much confidence in you at first." Zelda Fitzgerald to F. Scott Fitzgerald, Fall 1919, in *Dear Scott, Dearest Zelda: The Love Letters of F. Scott and Zelda Fitzgerald,* ed. Jackson R. Bryer and Cathy W. Barks (New York: St. Martin's, 2002), 38.

16. F. Scott Fitzgerald to Isabelle Amorous, 26 February 1920, in *Correspondence of F. Scott Fitzgerald,* ed. Matthew J. Bruccoli and Margaret M. Duggan (New York: Random House, 1980), 53.

17. F. Scott Fitzgerald to Ruth Sturtevant, 26 March 1920, in Turnbull, *Letters,* 459.

18. R. L. Samsell, "The Falsest of the Arts," *Fitzgerald/Hemingway Annual* 3 (1971): 178.

19. James Thurber, *Credos and Curios* (New York: Harper and Row, 1962), 154.

20. André Le Vot, *F. Scott Fitzgerald: A Biography,* trans. William Bryon (New York: Doubleday, 1983), 87; Fitzgerald, "My Lost City," in *My Lost City,* 110.

21. Campbell, "Scott and Zelda," 8, 20. Scottie Fitzgerald once remarked to a biographer, "very few people realize how much of Daddy's writing was literally influenced by mama, not just inspired." Scottie Fitzgerald Lanahan to Arthur Mizener, 1 June 1948, b27, MJBP.

22. Kendall Taylor, *Sometimes Madness Is Wisdom: Zelda and Scott Fitzgerald, a Marriage* (New York: Ballantine Books, 2001), 57; George Jean Nathan, "Memories of Fitzgerald, Lewis and Dreiser," *Esquire,* October 1958, 148–49. Scott's *Ledger* for December 1918 includes the (misspelled) entry "Zelda's dairy." F. Scott Fitzgerald, *F. Scott Fitzgerald's Ledger: A Facsimile,* ed. Matthew J. Bruccoli (Washington, DC: Bruccoli Clark/NCR Microcard Editions, 1972), 173.

6. Trouble in Paradise

1. F. Scott Fitzgerald, "Early Success," in *My Lost City: Personal Essays, 1920–1940,* ed. James L. W. West III (New York: Cambridge University Press, 2005), 185.

Fitzgerald did not make big money off *This Side of Paradise* per se, earning a more than respectable but certainly not life-changing $6,000 in royalties in 1920—roughly $70,000 in current dollars. Its success, however, increased his asking price in the short story market, which is where he would draw the bulk of his earnings.

2. F. Scott Fitzgerald, *This Side of Paradise,* ed. James L. W. West III (New York: Cambridge University Press, 1996), 37, 23, 25.

3. Ibid., 92, 178, 260.

4. F. Scott Fitzgerald, *The Great Gatsby,* ed. Matthew J. Bruccoli (New York: Cambridge University Press, 1991), 20; Fitzgerald, *Paradise,* 260.

5. Fitzgerald, *Paradise,* 256.

6. Ibid., 11.

7. Stanley Coben, *Rebellion against Victorianism: The Impetus for Cultural Change in 1920s America* (New York: Oxford University Press, 1991), 4.

8. George Santayana, *"The Genteel Tradition in American Philosophy" and Character and Opinion in the United States,* ed. James Seaton (New Haven, CT: Yale University Press, 2009).

9. Fitzgerald, *Paradise,* 137, 117.

10. Ibid., 90.

11. Ibid., 165, 170, 183, 184.

12. Ibid., 221.

13. Ibid., 206, 220, 217.

14. Ibid., 62.

15. Ibid., 63. "P.D." is shorthand for "Popular Daughter"—a girl who, in the "looser" moral environment of the period, might drink, smoke, and casually kiss men. She is the daughter of the "Victorian Mother," who grew up in the more tightly controlled time of the belle and the gentleman caller.

16. Ibid., 78, 86.

17. Ibid., 111, 226.

18. Shane Leslie to Charles Scribner, internal evidence suggests April 1918, b50, FSFP.

19. Shane Leslie, *Long Shadows: Memoirs of Shane Leslie* (London: John Murray, 1966), 251; Roger Burlingame, *Of Making Many Books: A Hundred Years of Reading, Writing and Publishing* (New York: Charles Scribner's Sons, 1946), 67–68.

20. Perkins's effort to place a rejected manuscript with another press is, of course, an unusual practice. According to Burlingame, "Perkins peddled the revised manuscript to other publishers, terrified that they would accept it, for all the time he saw how vitally it might still be improved." Burlingame, *Of Making Many Books,* 67.

21. A. Scott Berg, *Max Perkins: Editor of Genius* (New York: E. P. Dutton, 1978), 15–16.

22. Max Perkins to F. Scott Fitzgerald, 16 September 1919, in *Dear Scott/Dear Max: The Fitzgerald-Perkins Correspondence,* ed. John Kuehl and Jackson Bryer (New York: Charles Scribner's Sons, 1971), 21.

23. Fitzgerald, "Early Success," in *My Lost City,* 186.

7. Corruptions: The Early Stories

1. F. Scott Fitzgerald, *The Notebooks of F. Scott Fitzgerald,* ed. Matthew J. Bruccoli (New York: Harcourt Brace Jovanovich/Bruccoli Clark, 1978), 131.

2. Horace Bushnell, *Christian Nurture* (New York: Charles Scribner, 1861), 32.

3. Randolph Bourne, *The Radical Will: Selected Writings* (New York: Urizen Books, 1977), 97.

4. Booth Tarkington, *Seventeen* (New York: Harper and Brothers, 1916), 228; "A Novelist's Humorous View of Youth: Delicious Lampoon by Booth Tarkington," *New York Times,* 5 March 1916; William Lyon Phelps, *The Advance of the English Novel* (New York: Dodd, Mead, 1916), 281.

5. Owen Johnson, *Stover at Yale* (New York: Frederick A. Stokes, 1912), 350.

6. Bruce Bliven, "Flapper Jane," *New Republic,* 9 September 1925.

7. F. Scott Fitzgerald to Christian Gauss, 2 February 1933, in *The Letters of F. Scott Fitzgerald,* ed. Andrew Turnbull (New York: Charles Scribner's Sons, 1963), 384.

8. F. Scott Fitzgerald, "Bernice Bobs Her Hair," in *Flappers and Philosophers,* ed. James L. W. West III (New York: Cambridge University Press, 2000), 114.

9. Ibid., 111, 119–20; F. Scott Fitzgerald to Annabel Fitzgerald, c. 1915, in *Correspondence of F. Scott Fitzgerald,* ed. Matthew J. Bruccoli and Margaret M. Duggan (New York: Random House, 1980), 15, 18, 16.

10. Fitzgerald, "Bernice Bobs Her Hair," in *Flappers and Philosophers,* 121, 122, 129, 131–32.

11. Ibid., 122, 132.

12. F. Scott Fitzgerald, "The Diamond as Big as the Ritz," in *Tales of the Jazz Age* (New York: Cambridge University Press, 2002), 129.

13. Patricia Nelson Limerick, *The Legacy of Conquest: The Unbroken Past of the American West* (New York: Norton, 1987), 18.

14. For Fitzgerald's time in Montana, see Landon Y. Jones, "Babe in the Woods: F. Scott Fitzgerald's Unlikely Summer in Montana," *Montana: The Magazine of Western History*, Autumn 2007, 34–45.

15. Fitzgerald, "A Table of Contents," in *Tales of the Jazz Age,* 6.

16. Fitzgerald, "May Day," ibid., 66–67, 63.

17. F. Scott Fitzgerald, "My Lost City," in *My Lost City: Personal Essays, 1920–1940,* ed. James L. W. West III (New York: Cambridge University Press, 2005), 108.

18. Fitzgerald, "Early Success," in *My Lost City* 185.

19. Matthew J. Bruccoli, Scottie Fitzgerald Smith, and Joan P. Kerr, eds., *The Romantic Egoists: A Pictorial Autobiography from the Scrapbooks and Albums of F. Scott and Zelda Fitzgerald* (New York: Charles Scribner's Sons, 1974), 71.

20. Andrew Turnbull, *Scott Fitzgerald* (New York: Charles Scribner's Sons, 1962), 227.
21. Fitzgerald, "May Day," in *Tales of the Jazz Age,* 106.

8. The Knock-Off Artist

1. Ernest Hemingway to Arthur Mizener, 22 April 1950, in *Ernest Hemingway: Selected Letters, 1917–1961,* ed. Carlos Baker (New York: Charles Scribner's Sons, 1981), 689; Frances Kroll Ring, *Against the Current: As I Remember F. Scott Fitzgerald* (San Francisco: Ellis / Creative Arts, 1985), 23–24; Michel Mok, "The Other Side of Paradise: Scott Fitzgerald, 40, Engulfed in Despair," in *Conversations with F. Scott Fitzgerald,* ed. Matthew J. Bruccoli and Judith S. Baughman (Jackson: University Press of Mississippi, 2004), 126. A recent small collection of Fitzgerald's writings takes drinking as its theme: *On Booze* (New York: New Directions, 2011). An earlier work, Ray Canterbery and Thomas C. Birch's *F. Scott Fitzgerald: Under the Influence* (St. Paul, MN: Paragon House, 2006), also plays off the drinking theme, though its focus is on Fitzgerald's social and economic thought.
2. F. Scott Fitzgerald to Max Perkins, internal evidence suggests 10 October 1924, in *Dear Scott / Dear Max: The Fitzgerald-Perkins Correspondence,* ed. John Kuehl and Jackson Bryer (New York: Charles Scribner's Sons, 1971), 78.
3. F. Scott Fitzgerald to Edmund Wilson, January 1922, in *The Letters of F. Scott Fitzgerald,* ed. Andrew Turnbull (New York: Charles Scribner's Sons, 1963), 330.
4. The notable exceptions are the "Crack-Up" essays, published in early 1936.
5. Alexander Boyd to F. Scott Fitzgerald, internal evidence suggests 1922 or 1923, b39, FSFP; Thomas Alexander Boyd, "Literary Libels: Francis Scott Key Fitzgerald," in Bruccoli and Baughman, *Conversations,* 13, 21.
6. F. Scott Fitzgerald, "A Short Autobiography," in *A Short Autobiography,* ed. James L. W. West III (New York: Scribner, 2011), 107.
7. F. Scott Fitzgerald, *F. Scott Fitzgerald's Ledger: A Facsimile,* ed. Matthew J. Bruccoli (Washington, DC: Bruccoli Clark / NCR Microcard Editions, 1972), 160.
8. Louis Bromfield to Arthur Mizener, internal evidence suggests 1951, b1, AMPP.
9. Laura Guthrie Hearne, "A Summer with F. Scott Fitzgerald," *Esquire,* December 1964, 260.
10. Sheilah Graham, *The Real F. Scott Fitzgerald: Thirty-Five Years Later* (New York: Grosset and Dunlap, 1976), 100.
11. F. Scott Fitzgerald, *The Beautiful and Damned,* ed. James L. W. West III (New York: Cambridge University Press, 2008), 78.
12. F. Scott Fitzgerald, draft of letter to Dr. Oscar Forel, internal evidence suggests 1930, b49, FSFP; F. Scott Fitzgerald to Rosalind Sayre Smith, 19 July 1934, in *Correspondence of F. Scott Fitzgerald,* ed. Matthew J. Bruccoli and Margaret M. Duggan (New York: Random House, 1980), 374; F. Scott Fitzgerald, "A New Leaf," in *Taps at Reveille,* ed. James L. W. West III (New York: Cambridge University Press, 2014), 332.

13. F. Scott Fitzgerald, "Echoes of the Jazz Age," in *My Lost City: Personal Essays, 1920–1940,* ed. James L. W. West III (New York: Cambridge University Press, 2005), 136.

14. F. Scott Fitzgerald, "An Alcoholic Case," in *The Lost Decade: Short Stories from Esquire, 1936–1941,* ed. James L. W. West III (New York: Cambridge University Press, 2008), 31.

15. F. Scott Fitzgerald to Max Perkins, 11 March 1935, in Kuehl and Bryer, *Dear Scott/Dear Max,* 218–19.

16. Frances Kroll to Arthur Mizener, 14 June 1948, b1, AMPP.

17. Heywood Broun, "Books," in Bruccoli and Baughman, *Conversations,* 3; Marguerite Mooers Marshall, "F. Scott Fitzgerald, Novelist, Shocked by 'Younger Marrieds' and Prohibition," ibid., 26; Zelda Fitzgerald to Dearest Scottie, 1945, b4, ZFP.

18. A. Scott Berg, *Max Perkins: Editor of Genius* (New York: E. P. Dutton, 1978), 147.

19. Edmund Wilson to F. Scott Fitzgerald, 5 July 1921, in *Edmund Wilson: Letters on Literature and Politics, 1912–1972,* ed. Elena Wilson (New York: Farrar, Straus and Giroux, 1977), 63.

20. Edmund Wilson, *The Shores of Light: A Literary Chronicle of the Twenties and Thirties* (New York: Farrar, Straus and Young, 1952), 27.

21. Edmund Wilson to F. Scott Fitzgerald, 4 December 1933, b54, FSFP.

22. F. Scott Fitzgerald to Edmund Wilson, 16 May 1939, in *F. Scott Fitzgerald: A Life in Letters,* ed. Matthew J. Bruccoli (New York: Simon and Schuster, 1994), 391.

9. Rich Boy, Poor Boy

1. F. Scott Fitzgerald, *The Love of the Last Tycoon,* ed. Matthew J. Bruccoli (New York: Cambridge University Press, 1994), 10.

2. Matthew J. Bruccoli, Scottie Fitzgerald Smith, and Joan P. Kerr, eds., *The Romantic Egoists: A Pictorial Autobiography from the Scrapbooks and Albums of F. Scott and Zelda Fitzgerald* (New York: Charles Scribner's Sons, 1974), 223.

3. F. Scott Fitzgerald to Mollie Fitzgerald, June 1930, in *The Letters of F. Scott Fitzgerald,* ed. Andrew Turnbull (New York: Charles Scribner's Sons, 1963), 496.

4. In 1939, Budd Schulberg briefly collaborated with Fitzgerald on the screenplay for *Winter Carnival.* Schulberg later mined his remembrances of Scott for his novel *The Disenchanted,* noting Fitzgerald's penchant for giving outsized tips: "Manley wouldn't let Shep pay for the cab. He pulled out a crushed handful of bills, selected one at random and flung it to the driver. It happened to be a five-dollar bill. 'Manley, you ought to hang on to some of that money.' 'Fi drove a cab [Manley replied], that's how I'd like to be paid.'" Budd Schulberg, *The Disenchanted* (New York: Random House, 1950), 187.

5. F. Scott Fitzgerald, "The Offshore Pirate," in *Flappers and Philosophers,* ed. James L. W. West III (New York: Cambridge University Press, 2000), 16.

6. Ibid., 17.

7. Ibid., 29.

8. F. Scott Fitzgerald to Ludlow Fowler, March 1925, in *Correspondence of F. Scott Fitzgerald,* ed. Matthew J. Bruccoli and Margaret M. Duggan (New York: Random House, 1980), 152.

9. F. Scott Fitzgerald, Appendix 1, in *All the Sad Young Men,* ed. James L. W. West III (New York: Cambridge University Press, 2007), 502; F. Scott Fitzgerald to Harold Ober, October 1925, in *As Ever, Scott-Fitz——: Letters between F. Scott Fitzgerald and His Literary Agent, Harold Ober, 1919–1940,* ed. Matthew J. Bruccoli (Philadelphia: J. B. Lippincott, 1972), 81.

10. Fitzgerald, "The Rich Boy," in *Sad Young Men,* 5.

11. Ibid., 16.

12. Ibid., 19.

13. Ibid., 34.

14. Ibid., 19.

15. F. Scott Fitzgerald, "How to Live on $36,000 a Year," in *My Lost City: Personal Essays, 1920–1940,* ed. James L. W. West III (New York: Cambridge University Press, 2005), 28, 31.

16. Ibid., 35.

17. F. Scott Fitzgerald to Edmund Wilson, 7 October 1924, in Turnbull, *Letters,* 341.

18. Honoria Murphy Donnelly with Richard N. Billings, *Sara & Gerald: Villa America and After* (New York: Times Books, 1982), 10, 11.

19. Calvin Tomkins, *Living Well Is the Best Revenge* (New York: Modern Library, 1998), 38.

20. Fitzgerald, "Early Success," in *My Lost City,* 190.

21. Donnelly and Billings, *Sara & Gerald,* 100.

22. F. Scott Fitzgerald, *Tender Is the Night,* ed. James L. W. West III (New York: Cambridge University Press, 2012), 9.

23. Edward Fitzgerald to Master Scott Fitzgerald, 30 July 1909, in Bruccoli and Duggan, *Correspondence,* 5.

10. The Wages of Sin: The Beautiful and Damned

1. H. L. Mencken, "Books More or Less Amusing," *Smart Set,* August 1920, 140; H. L. Mencken, *The Vintage Mencken,* ed. Alistair Cooke (New York: Vintage Books, 1955), 162; F. Scott Fitzgerald, *The Beautiful and Damned,* ed. James L. W. West III (New York: Cambridge University Press, 2008), 239, 194. While composing *The Beautiful and Damned,* Fitzgerald practiced his Mencken voice in a *St. Paul Daily News* review of John Dos Passos's *Three Soldiers.* The review, he stated to a friend, is "written in Mencken's manner which I don't mind parodying for St. Paul consumption." F. Scott Fitzgerald to Thomas Boyd, 19 September 1921, in

Correspondence of F. Scott Fitzgerald, ed. Matthew J. Bruccoli and Margaret M. Duggan (New York: Random House, 1980), 85.

2. F. Scott Fitzgerald to Carl Van Vechten, 1 March 1924, in *The Letters of F. Scott Fitzgerald,* ed. Andrew Turnbull (New York: Charles Scribner's Sons, 1963), 476–77; Brian Way, *F. Scott Fitzgerald and the Art of Social Fiction* (New York: St. Martin's, 1980), 64; F. Scott Fitzgerald to Moran Tudury, 11 April 1924, in Bruccoli and Duggan, *Correspondence,* 139.

3. Fitzgerald, *Beautiful and Damned,* 12, 179.

4. Ibid., 12.

5. Ibid., 248.

6. André Le Vot, *F. Scott Fitzgerald: A Biography,* trans. William Bryon (New York: Doubleday, 1983), 83, 90.

7. Fitzgerald, *Beautiful and Damned,* 117, 102; F. Scott Fitzgerald to Zelda Fitzgerald, internal evidence suggests summer 1930, in Bruccoli and Duggan, *Correspondence,* 241.

8. F. Scott Fitzgerald to Scottie Fitzgerald, 14 June 1940, in *F. Scott Fitzgerald: A Life in Letters,* ed. Matthew J. Bruccoli (New York: Simon and Schuster, 1994), 453.

9. Fitzgerald, *Beautiful and Damned,* 52; Marguerite Mooers Marshall, "F. Scott Fitzgerald, Novelist, Shocked by 'Younger Marrieds' and Prohibition," in *Conversations with F. Scott Fitzgerald,* ed. Matthew J. Bruccoli and Judith S. Baughman (Jackson: University Press of Mississippi, 2004), 28; F. Scott Fitzgerald, "Echoes of the Jazz Age," in *My Lost City: Personal Essays, 1920–1940,* ed. James L. W. West III (New York: Cambridge University Press, 2005), 136.

10. Marshall, "F. Scott Fitzgerald, Novelist," in Bruccoli and Duggan, *Conversations,* 28.

11. Ibid., 27.

12. Fitzgerald, *Beautiful and Damned,* 333, 351.

13. Ibid.

14. Fitzgerald's critique of privilege in elite institutions of higher learning remains a great concern in our own day. See, for example, Steven Pinker's "The Trouble with Harvard: The Ivy League Is Broken and Only Standardized Tests Can Fix It," in the 4 September 2014 *New Republic,* http://www.newrepublic.com/article/119321/harvard-ivy-league-should-judge-students-standardized-tests; and William Deresiewicz's *Excellent Sheep: The Miseducation of the American Elite and the Way to a Meaningful Life* (New York: Free Press, 2014). In a passage that could have had any number of Anthony Patches in mind, Deresiewicz writes that that the nation's better schools have encouraged a system that "manufactures students who are . . . anxious, timid, and lost, with little intellectual curiosity and a stunted sense of purpose: trapped in a bubble of privilege" (3).

15. Fitzgerald, *Beautiful and Damned,* 160.

16. Ibid., 64.

17. F. Scott Fitzgerald to Carl Hovey, 22 April 1921, in Bruccoli and Duggan, *Correspondence,* 82; F. Scott Fitzgerald to Max Perkins, c. 10 December 1921, in *Dear*

Scott/Dear Max: The Fitzgerald-Perkins Correspondence, ed. John Kuehl and Jackson Bryer (New York: Charles Scribner's Sons, 1971), 47.

18. Max Perkins to F. Scott Fitzgerald, 31 December 1921, in Kuehl and Bryer, *Dear Scott/Dear Max,* 50.

19. Fitzgerald, *Beautiful and Damned,* 368.

20. Ibid., 335, 341; see West's introduction to Fitzgerald, *Beautiful and Damned,* xvii; F. Scott Fitzgerald to Max Perkins, 9 January 1922, in Kuehl and Bryer, *Dear Scott/Dear Max,* 51.

21. Max Perkins to F. Scott Fitzgerald, 17 April 1922, in Kuehl and Bryer, *Dear Scott/Dear Max,* 58.

22. W. Collins Sons & Co. London to F. Scott Fitzgerald, 23 March 1922, b39, FSFP.

23. Fanny Butcher, *Chicago Sunday Tribune,* 5 March 1922, part 8, p. 15; N. P. Dawson, "The Beautiful and Damned," *New York Globe and Commercial Advertiser,* 4 March 1922, 10; John Peale Bishop, "Mr. Fitzgerald Sees the Flapper Through," *New York Herald,* 5 March 1922, sec. 8, p. 1; Henry Seidel Canby, "The Flapper's Tragedy," *Literary Review of the New York Evening Post,* 4 March 1922, 463.

24. Fitzgerald, *Beautiful and Damned,* 251.

11. Exile in Great Neck

1. The "in one town or another" claim comes from the final sentence of *Tender Is the Night* and links Fitzgerald's childhood uprootings with Dick Diver's adult fall from grace. F. Scott Fitzgerald, *Tender Is the Night,* ed. James L. W. West III (New York: Cambridge University Press, 2012), 352. The "nifty-little Babbitt house" nickname is Zelda's; see her letter to Sandy and Charles Kalman, 13 October 1922, b5, ZFP; F. Scott Fitzgerald to Cecie Taylor, internal evidence suggests late 1922, in *Correspondence of F. Scott Fitzgerald,* ed. Matthew J. Bruccoli and Margaret M. Duggan (New York: Random House, 1980), 117; Zelda Fitzgerald to Charles Kalman, summer 1923, b5, ZFP.

2. Edith Wharton, *The House of Mirth* (New York: Random House, 1999), 27; F. Scott Fitzgerald, *The Beautiful and Damned,* ed. James L. W. West III (New York: Cambridge University Press, 2008), 333.

3. Edith Wharton, *The Custom of the Country* (New York: Bantam, 2008), 64, 65.

4. Ibid., 129.

5. André Le Vot, *F. Scott Fitzgerald: A Biography,* trans. William Bryon (New York: Doubleday, 1983), 198–99.

6. John Dos Passos, *The Best of Times: An Informal Memoir* (New York: New American Library, 1966), 129; Fitzgerald, *Tender,* 15.

7. Jonathan Yardley, *Ring: A Biography of Ring Lardner* (New York: Random House, 1977), 184.

8. Andrew Turnbull, *Scott Fitzgerald* (New York: Charles Scribner's Sons, 1962), 137; F. Scott Fitzgerald, "How to Live on $36,000 a Year," in *My Lost City: Personal*

Essays, 1920–1940, ed. James L. W. West III (New York: Cambridge University Press, 2005), 29.

9. Fitzgerald, "Ring," in *My Lost City,* 92; Ring Lardner Jr., *The Lardners: My Family Remembered* (New York: Harper & Row, 1976), 164.

10. Fitzgerald, *Tender,* 96.

11. F. Scott Fitzgerald to Max Perkins, 27 December 1921, in Bruccoli and Duggan, *Correspondence,* 90; F. Scott Fitzgerald to Harold Ober, 2 March 1922, in *As Ever, Scott-Fitz—: Letters between F. Scott Fitzgerald and His Literary Agent, Harold Ober, 1919–1940,* ed. Matthew J. Bruccoli (Philadelphia: J. B. Lippincott, 1972), 39.

12. H. L. Mencken, "On Being an American," in *The American Scene: A Reader,* ed. Huntington Cairns (New York: Knopf, 1965), 12.

13. Sara Mayfield, *Exiles from Paradise: Zelda and Scott Fitzgerald* (New York: Delacorte, 1971), 87; Fitzgerald, "How to Live on $36,000 a Year," in *My Lost City,* 33; F. Scott Fitzgerald to Beatrice Dance, early 1937, in Bruccoli and Duggan, *Correspondence,* 472.

14. F. Scott Fitzgerald to Max Perkins, c. January 1923, in *Dear Scott/Dear Max: The Fitzgerald-Perkins Correspondence,* ed. John Kuehl and Jackson Bryer (New York: Charles Scribner's Sons, 1971), 66.

12. After the Gold Rush: The Great Gatsby

1. F. Scott Fitzgerald to Max Perkins, c. 20 June 1922, in *Dear Scott/Dear Max: The Fitzgerald-Perkins Correspondence,* ed. John Kuehl and Jackson Bryer (New York: Charles Scribner's Sons, 1971), 61; F. Scott Fitzgerald, *The Great Gatsby,* ed. Matthew J. Bruccoli (New York: Cambridge University Press, 1991), 137.

2. Fitzgerald, *Gatsby,* 14.

3. Ibid., 69.

4. Ibid., 72, 71.

5. Ibid., 51; Thorstein Veblen, *The Theory of the Leisure Class* (New York, Penguin, 1986).

6. Fitzgerald, *Gatsby,* 33.

7. On Fitzgerald and Veblen, see E. Ray Canterbery, "Thorstein Veblen and *The Great Gatsby,*" *Journal of Economic Issues* 33 (June 1999): 297–304. "Our Irresponsible Rich" was published under a number of titles, the most accessible copy of the essay can be found in F. Scott Fitzgerald, "What Kind of Husbands Do 'Jimmies' Make?," in *F. Scott Fitzgerald in His Own Time: A Miscellany,* ed. Matthew J. Bruccoli and Jackson R. Bryer (Kent, OH: Kent State University Press, 1971), 188, 191.

8. Fitzgerald, *Gatsby,* 104–5.

9. Maureen Corrigan, *So We Read On: How The Great Gatsby Came to Be and Why It Endures* (New York: Little, Brown, 2014), 45; Fitzgerald, *Gatsby,* 126, 140.

10. J. Hector St. John de Crevecoeur, *Letters from an American Farmer: And Sketches of Eighteenth-Century America* (New York: Penguin Books, 1986), 59; Thomas Jefferson to Roger C. Weightman, 24 June 1826, in *The Portable Thomas Jefferson*, ed. Merrill D. Peterson (New York: Penguin Books, 1975), 585; Abraham Lincoln, *Abraham Lincoln: Speeches and Writings, 1859–1865*, ed. Roy P. Basler (New York: Library of America, 1989), 85.

11. Sinclair Lewis, *Babbitt* (New York: Modern Library, 2002), 8, 27; Theodore Dreiser, *An American Tragedy* (New York: Signet, 2000), 325, 365.

12. James Truslow Adams, *The Epic of America* (Boston: Little, Brown, 1933), 416; Herbert Hoover, "Rugged Individualism Speech, October 22, 1928," in *Great Issues in American History: From Reconstruction to the Present Day, 1864–1981*, ed. Richard and Beatrice K. Hofstadter (New York: Vintage Books, 1982), 330, 335.

13. F. Scott Fitzgerald to Thomas Boyd, March 1923, in *Correspondence of F. Scott Fitzgerald*, ed. Matthew J. Bruccoli and Margaret M. Duggan (New York: Random House, 1980), 126; Henry Dan Piper, *F. Scott Fitzgerald: A Critical Portrait* (New York: Holt, Rinehart and Winston, 1965), 130; Joseph Conrad, *Nostromo: A Tale of the Seaboard* (New York: Penguin Books, 1986), 199.

14. Joseph Conrad, "Youth," in *Youth/Heart of Darkness/The End of the Tether* (New York: Penguin Books, 1995), 38; F. Scott Fitzgerald to H. L. Mencken, May or June 1925, in *The Letters of F. Scott Fitzgerald*, ed. Andrew Turnbull (New York: Charles Scribner's Sons, 1963), 482.

15. Fitzgerald, *Gatsby*, 140.

16. Conrad, "Youth," in *Youth/Heart of Darkness/The End of the Tether*, 43; H. L. Mencken, "New Fiction," in *American Mercury*, July 1925, 383; F. Scott Fitzgerald to John Peale Bishop, 7 April 1934, in Turnbull, *Letters*, 363; Fitzgerald, *Gatsby*, 141.

17. Fitzgerald, *Gatsby*, 140, 115.

18. Ibid., 138.

19. Ibid., 75. On Franklin's "Scheme of Employment," see Benjamin Franklin, *The Autobiography of Benjamin Franklin*, ed. Leonard W. Labaree (New Haven: Yale University Press), 154.

20. T. S. Eliot, *Christianity & Culture* (San Diego, CA: Harcourt Brace, 1976), 51.

21. Richard Lehan, *The Great Gatsby: The Limits of Wonder* (New York: Twayne, 1995), 82; F. Scott Fitzgerald to Max Perkins, 6 June 1940, in Kuehl and Bryer, *Dear Scott/Dear Max*, 263.

22. Oswald Spengler, *The Decline of the West* (New York: Oxford University Press, 1991), 345; Fitzgerald, *Gatsby*, 123.

23. Frederick Jackson Turner, *The Frontier in American History* (New York: Henry Holt, 1920), 38.

24. Ibid., 3.

25. F. Scott Fitzgerald to Ernest Boyd, 1 February 1925, in Turnbull, *Letters*, 478; Max Perkins to F. Scott Fitzgerald, 20 April 1925, in Kuehl and Bryer, *Dear Scott/Dear*

Max, 101. Stage and screen versions of *Gatsby* netted Fitzgerald some $25,000 in 1926—roughly $305,000 in current dollars.

26. Max Perkins to F. Scott Fitzgerald, 20 November 1924, in Kuehl and Bryer, *Dear Scott/Dear Max,* 84.

13. Adrift Abroad

1. F. Scott Fitzgerald, *F. Scott Fitzgerald's Ledger: A Facsimile,* ed. Matthew J. Bruccoli (Washington, DC: Bruccoli Clark/NCR Microcard Editions, 1972), 178; F. Scott Fitzgerald, *The Notebooks of F. Scott Fitzgerald,* ed. Matthew J. Bruccoli (New York: Harcourt Brace Jovanovich/Bruccoli Clark, 1978), 113. On Jozan's "denial," see Sara Mayfield, *Exiles from Paradise: Zelda and Scott Fitzgerald* (New York: Delacorte, 1971), 96.

2. F. Scott Fitzgerald to Max Perkins, c. October 1924, in *F. Scott Fitzgerald: A Life in Letters,* ed. Matthew J. Bruccoli (New York: Simon and Schuster, 1994), 82; F. Scott Fitzgerald to Ernest Hemingway, 23 December 1926, in *The Letters of F. Scott Fitzgerald,* ed. Andrew Turnbull (New York: Charles Scribner's Sons, 1963), 298. As Fitzgerald's note to Perkins attests, he had a difficult time spelling "Hemingway"; he also sometimes substituted "Earnest" for "Ernest." As readers of this book are by now aware, Fitzgerald was a notoriously poor speller.

3. Matthew J. Bruccoli, *Scott and Ernest: The Fitzgerald/Hemingway Friendship* (New York: Random House, 1978), 45; Mayfield, *Exiles from Paradise,* 112; Ernest Hemingway, *A Moveable Feast* (New York: Scribner, 2003) 186. In a 1932 letter to Max Perkins, Hemingway wrote, "Poor old Scott—He should have swapped Zelda when she was at her craziest but still saleable back 5 or 6 years ago before she was diagnosed as nutty." Ernest Hemingway to Max Perkins, 27 July 1932, in *The Only Thing That Counts: The Ernest Hemingway–Maxwell Perkins Correspondence,* ed. Matthew J. Bruccoli (Columbia: University of South Carolina Press, 1996), 175.

4. Hemingway, *Moveable Feast,* 147, 149.

5. Malcolm Cowley, *Exile's Return: A Literary Odyssey of the 1920s* (New York: Viking, 1956), 102.

6. F. Scott Fitzgerald, "The Swimmers," in *Taps at Reveille,* ed. James L. W. West III (New York: Cambridge University Press, 2014), 243.

7. Fitzgerald, "Babylon Revisited," ibid., 157; Edmund Wilson to F Scott Fitzgerald, 5 July 1921, in *Edmund Wilson: Letters on Literature and Politics, 1912–1972,* ed. Elena Wilson (New York: Farrar, Straus and Giroux, 1977), 63.

8. Louis Bromfield to Arthur Mizener, internal evidence suggests 1951, b1, AMPP.

9. Fitzgerald, "The Swimmers," in *Taps,* 235.

10. F. Scott Fitzgerald, "How to Live on Practically Nothing a Year," in *My Lost City: Personal Essays, 1920–1940,* ed. James L. W. West III (New York: Cambridge University Press, 2005), 41, 45, 46, 47.

11. Ibid., 48; F. Scott Fitzgerald to Thomas Boyd, March 1923, in *Correspondence of F. Scott Fitzgerald,* ed. Matthew J. Bruccoli and Margaret M. Duggan (New York: Random House, 1980), 127.

12. John David Smith, "The Place of Ulrich Bonnell Phillips in American Historiography," in *Ulrich Bonnell Phillips: A Southern Historian and His Critics,* ed. John David Smith and John C. Inscoe (Athens: University of Georgia Press, 1990), 2.

13. Earl Wilkins to F. Scott Fitzgerald, 23 July 1934, b40a, FSFP.

14. H. R. Stoneback, "A Dark Ill-Lighted Place: Fitzgerald and Hemingway, Philippe Count of Darkness and Philip Counter-Espionage Agent," in *F. Scott Fitzgerald: New Perspectives,* ed. Jackson R. Bryer, Alan Margolies, and Ruth Prigozy (Athens: University of Georgia Press, 2000), 232.

15. Harold Ober to F. Scott Fitzgerald, 5 December 1934, in *As Ever, Scott-Fitz—: Letters between F. Scott Fitzgerald and His Literary Agent, Harold Ober, 1919–1940,* ed. Matthew J. Bruccoli (Philadelphia: J. B. Lippincott, 1972), 205–6.

16. Gilmore Millen, "Scott Fitzgerald Lays Success to Reading," in *Conversations with F. Scott Fitzgerald,* ed. Matthew J. Bruccoli and Judith S. Baughman (Jackson: University Press of Mississippi, 2004), 84.

17. Max Perkins to F. Scott Fitzgerald, 18 June 1926, in *Dear Scott/Dear Max: The Fitzgerald-Perkins Correspondence,* ed. John Kuehl and Jackson Bryer (New York: Charles Scribner's Sons, 1971), 142–43.

18. Zelda Fitzgerald, "Show Mr. and Mrs. F. to Number—," in *Zelda Fitzgerald: The Collected Writing,* ed. Matthew J. Bruccoli (New York: Scribner, 1991), 425.

19. John Biggs Jr., "Fitzgerald in Wilmington—The Great Gatsby at Bay," *(Wilmington) Sunday Bulletin,* 6 January 1974, 9. A 1934 newspaper article on Wilmington history states, "There are a number of curiously named streets in Wilmington, and the progress of time has likewise changed the atmosphere and personnel of what were once fine neighborhoods. There is, for example, Lafayette Street, better known as Bloodfield, a short lane which is a rendezvous for drug addicts and the abiding place of all sorts of Negro desperadoes." *(Wilmington) Delmarva Star,* 11 February 1934, 1.

20. Fitzgerald, "My Lost City," in *My Lost City,* 113.

14. Emotional Bankruptcy

1. Henry Dan Piper, *F. Scott Fitzgerald: A Critical Portrait* (New York: Holt, Rinehart and Winston, 1965), 184.

2. F. Scott Fitzgerald, *Tender Is the Night,* ed. James L. W. West III (New York: Cambridge University Press, 2012), 141.

3. F. Scott Fitzgerald, "Emotional Bankruptcy," in *The Basil, Josephine, and Gwen Stories,* ed. James L. W. West III (New York: Cambridge University Press, 2009), 286.

4. F. Scott Fitzgerald, "Penrod and Sam," in *F. Scott Fitzgerald in His Own Time: A Miscellany,* ed. Matthew J. Bruccoli and Jackson R. Bryer (Kent, OH: Kent State

University Press, 1971), 113; Donald William Dotterer, "The Privileged and Precocious: A Study of F. Scott Fitzgerald's Basil and Josephine Stories" (master's thesis, Drew University, 1977), 14.

5. Fitzgerald, "Basil and Cleopatra," in *Basil, Josephine, and Gwen,* 184.

6. "Emotional Bankruptcy," ibid., 271.

7. Fitzgerald, "The Freshest Boy," 59, "A Snobbish Story," 262, "First Blood,"189 in *Basil, Josephine, and Gwen*; F. Scott Fitzgerald, *The Great Gatsby,* ed. Matthew J. Bruccoli (New York: Cambridge University Press, 1991), 86.

8. Fitzgerald, "He Thinks He's Wonderful," in *Basil, Josephine, and Gwen,* 96, 98.

9. Fitzgerald, "The Freshest Boy," ibid., 68, 75.

10. Fitzgerald had first tried out the concept of emotional bankruptcy in *This Side of Paradise.* Demonstrating more caution than Josephine, Rosalind said to Amory, "I'm yours. . . . For the first time I regret all the other kisses; now I know how much a kiss can mean." F. Scott Fitzgerald, *This Side of Paradise* (New York: Vintage, 2009), 175.

11. Fitzgerald, "First Blood," in *Basil, Josephine, and Gwen,* 191; Rochelle S. Elstein, "Fitzgerald's Josephine Stories: The End of the Romantic Illusion," *American Literature* 51 (March 1979): 75, 77, 81.

12. Fitzgerald, "A Woman with a Past," in *Basil, Josephine, and Gwen,* 243.

13. F. Scott Fitzgerald to Max Perkins, 21 July 1928, in *The Letters of F. Scott Fitzgerald,* ed. Andrew Turnbull (New York: Charles Scribner's Sons, 1963), 212; Fitzgerald to Betty Markell, 16 September 1929, ibid., 495; Fitzgerald to Max Perkins, 21 May 1930, ibid., 221.

14. F. Scott Fitzgerald to Harold Ober, 8 April 1930, in *As Ever, Scott-Fitz—: Letters between F. Scott Fitzgerald and His Literary Agent, Harold Ober, 1919–1940,* ed. Matthew J. Bruccoli (Philadelphia: J. B. Lippincott, 1972), 168.

15. F. Scott Fitzgerald to Max Perkins, 15 May 1934, in *F. Scott Fitzgerald: A Life in Letters,* ed. Matthew J. Bruccoli (New York: Simon and Schuster, 1994), 260.

16. F. Scott Fitzgerald to Max Perkins, 21 May 1934, in *Dear Scott / Dear Max: The Fitzgerald-Perkins Correspondence,* ed. John Kuehl and Jackson Bryer (New York: Charles Scribner's Sons, 1971), 199.

17. Ginevra King Pirie to Henry Dan Piper, 8 July 1947, b2, HDPP; Jackson R. Bryer and John Kuehl, introduction to *The Basil and Josephine Stories,* by F. Scott Fitzgerald (New York: Scribner, 1973), 22.

18. Paul Goodman, *Growing Up Absurd: Problems of Youth in the Organized System* (New York: Random House, 1960), dust jacket.

19. Fitzgerald, "The Captured Shadow," in *Basil, Josephine, and Gwen,* 119–20.

15. Penance

1. F. Scott Fitzgerald, *F. Scott Fitzgerald's Ledger: A Facsimile,* ed. Matthew J. Bruccoli (Washington, DC: Bruccoli Clark / NCR Microcard Editions, 1972), 184.

2. Zelda Fitzgerald to F. Scott Fitzgerald, internal evidence suggests September 1930, in *Dear Scott, Dearest Zelda: The Love Letters of F. Scott and Zelda Fitzgerald,* ed. Jackson R. Bryer and Cathy W. Barks (New York: St. Martin's, 2002), 69–70. Fitzgerald wrote in marginalia on the side of a circa 1937–1940 letter, "AFFAIR (unconsummated) with ACTRESS (1927)." F. Scott Fitzgerald to Clayton Hutton, b10, FSFAP.

3. Harold Ober to F. Scott Fitzgerald, 14 March 1930, in *As Ever, Scott-Fitz—: Letters between F. Scott Fitzgerald and His Literary Agent, Harold Ober, 1919–1940,* ed. Matthew J. Bruccoli (Philadelphia: J. B. Lippincott, 1972), 166.

4. Eleanor Lanahan, *Scottie: The Daughter of . . . : The Life of Frances Scott Fitzgerald Lanahan Smith* (New York: Harper Perennial, 1995), 59; F. Scott Fitzgerald to Dr. Robert Carroll 4 March 1938, in *Correspondence of F. Scott Fitzgerald,* ed. Matthew J. Bruccoli and Margaret M. Duggan (New York: Random House, 1980), 487.

5. Sara Mayfield, *Exiles from Paradise: Zelda and Scott Fitzgerald* (New York: Delacorte, 1971), 60; John Dos Passos, *The Best of Times: An Informal Memoir* (New York: New American Library, 1966), 130; Andrew Turnbull, *Scott Fitzgerald* (New York: Charles Scribner's Sons, 1962), 343–44.

6. Edmund Wilson, *The Shores of Light: A Literary Chronicle of the Twenties and Thirties* (New York: Farrar, Straus and Young, 1952), 379–80.

7. Rosalind Sayre Smith to F. Scott Fitzgerald, 8 and 16 June 1930, b53, FSFP; Scottie Fitzgerald Lanahan to Arthur Mizener, 5 July 1950, b1, AMPP.

8. F. Scott Fitzgerald, "Two Wrongs," in *Taps at Reveille,* ed. James L. W. West III (New York: Cambridge University Press, 2014), 38.

9. Ibid., 39.

10. Ibid., 44.

11. Ibid., 39, 41.

12. Zelda Fitzgerald to F. Scott Fitzgerald, March 1920, in Bryer and Barks, *Dear Scott, Dearest Zelda,* 44–45.

13. Matthew J. Bruccoli, *Some Sort of Epic Grandeur: The Life of F. Scott Fitzgerald* (New York: Harcourt Brace Jovanovich, 1981), 163.

14. F. Scott Fitzgerald to Lubov Egorova, 22 June 1930, in *F. Scott Fitzgerald: A Life in Letters,* ed. Matthew J. Bruccoli (New York: Simon and Schuster, 1994), 186; Bruccoli, *Some Sort of Epic Grandeur,* 306, 305; Zelda Fitzgerald to F. Scott Fitzgerald, August 1930, in Bryer and Barks, *Dear Scott, Dearest Zelda,* 90.

15. Zelda Fitzgerald to F. Scott Fitzgerald, March 1932, in Bryer and Barks, *Dear Scott, Dearest Zelda,* 156.

16. Zelda Fitzgerald, *Save Me the Waltz,* in *Zelda Fitzgerald: The Collected Writing,* ed. Matthew J. Bruccoli (New York: Scribner, 1991), 46, 13, 98.

17. Ibid., 47.

18. Bruccoli, *Some Sort of Epic Grandeur,* 274.

19. Zelda Fitzgerald, *Save Me the Waltz,* 32, 39, 82, 37, 86. Along with Jacque, another Zelda dig at Scott may have been her likely naming David Knight after Richard

(Dick) Knight, a New York lawyer whom she met while living at Ellerslie. In a letter addressed to Scott in the late summer or early fall of 1930, she wrote, "you went to New York to see Lois and I met Dick Knight the night of that party for [the French diplomat and writer] Paul Morand. Again, though you were by then thoroughly entangled sentimentally, you forbade me seeing Dick and were furious about a letter he wrote me." Zelda Fitzgerald to F. Scott Fitzgerald, internal evidence suggests September 1930, in Bruccoli, *Life in Letters,* 193. Two years later, while Zelda was at Phipps and directly after she had written *Save Me the Waltz,* she was asked to write about herself. Among other items in this document, she addressed her attraction to Dick Knight: "One lost afternoon in a black lace dress we drank cocktails in a New York apartment and sat afterwards a long time on the stairway, oblivious with a kind of happy desperation. . . . We would have made scenes but there was trouble. . . . I forgot him during rehearsals for the Opera Ballet. I was too tired to care and too full of brooding except when something external drove me to him: the night Scott came home drunk from Princeton and smashed my nose about some conflict of his own and my sister left the house and never forgave him, poor man. I telephoned Dick. He has the most magnetic voice I've ever known." Nancy Milford, *Zelda* (New York: Harper and Row, 1970), 249.

20. Zelda Fitzgerald, *Save Me the Waltz,* 115, 138.
21. F. Scott Fitzgerald to Dr. Mildred Squires, 14 March 1932, in Bruccoli, *Life in Letters,* 209.
22. Ibid.
23. F. Scott Fitzgerald to Max Perkins, 30 April 1932, ibid., 217; for Zelda's contract, see b6, ZFP.
24. Geoffrey Hellman, "Beautiful and Damned," *Saturday Review of Literature,* 22 October 1932, 190; McFee's review is in Sally Cline, *Zelda Fitzgerald: Her Voice in Paradise* (London: John Murray, 2002), 320.
25. Donald Hutter to Henry Dan Piper, 2 February 1960, b1, HDPP; Ruth Prigozy, "Introduction: Scott, Zelda, and the Culture of Celebrity," in *The Cambridge Companion to F. Scott Fitzgerald,* ed. Ruth Prigozy (New York: Cambridge University Press, 2001), 21.
26. F. Scott Fitzgerald to Sara Murphy, 30 March 1936, in *The Letters of F. Scott Fitzgerald,* ed. Andrew Turnbull (New York: Charles Scribner's Sons, 1963), 425–26.
27. F. Scott Fitzgerald to Dr. Oscar Forel, internal evidence suggests 1930, b49, FSFP.
28. F. Scott Fitzgerald to Dr. Oscar Forel, 29 January 1931, in Bruccoli, *Life in Letters,* 204, 207.
29. Dr. Oscar Forel to F. Scott Fitzgerald, 10 March 1932, b39, FSFP.
30. F. Scott Fitzgerald to Dr. Clarence Slocum, 2 April 1934, b1, CHMR; F. Scott Fitzgerald to Dr. Thomas Rennie, October 1932, in Bruccoli, *Life in Letters,* 220, 219.

31. Matthew J. Bruccoli, Scottie Fitzgerald Smith, and Joan P. Kerr, eds., *The Romantic Egoists: A Pictorial Autobiography from the Scrapbooks and Albums of F. Scott and Zelda Fitzgerald* (New York: Charles Scribner's Sons, 1974), 190.

32. Zelda Fitzgerald to Scottie Fitzgerald, February–March 1927, b4, ZFP; Zelda Fitzgerald to Dearest Nanny, March 1927, b4, ZFP.

33. F. Scott Fitzgerald to Dr. Thomas Rennie, October 1932, in Bruccoli, *Life in Letters,* 220–21.

34. F. Scott Fitzgerald to Dr. Adolf Meyer, 10 April 1933, ibid., 231.

35. Stenographic Report of conversation between Mr. and Mrs. F. Scott Fitzgerald and Dr. Thomas A. C. Rennie, 28 May 1933, b1, CHMR.

36. Ibid.

37. Ibid.

38. Ibid.

39. H. L. Mencken, *The Diary of H. L. Mencken,* ed. Charles A. Fecher (New York: Vintage, 1989), 56. Ginevra King Pirie's 1947 observation, "I am surprised that Scott didn't get into the hands of a psychiatrist before his death, for they would have had a field day with his emotional tie-up," might not be far off the mark. Ginevra King Pirie to Henry Dan Piper, 8 July 1947, b2, HDPP.

40. Mary Jo Tate, *F. Scott Fitzgerald, A to Z* (New York: Facts on File, 1998), 166; Thelma Nason, "Afternoon (and Evening) of an Author," *Johns Hopkins Magazine,* February 1970, 7, 12; F. Scott Fitzgerald to Dr. Oscar Forel, internal evidence suggests summer 1930, in Bruccoli, *Life in Letters,* 197.

41. Zelda Fitzgerald to F. Scott Fitzgerald, internal evidence suggests September 1930, ibid., 194; F. Scott Fitzgerald to Zelda Fitzgerald, [summer?] 1930, ibid., 189.

42. F. Scott Fitzgerald to Dr. Harry M. Murdock, 28 August 1934, in Bruccoli and Duggan, *Correspondence,* 381.

43. F. Scott Fitzgerald to Dr. Clarence Slocum, 22 March 1934, b1, CHMR.

44. Sheilah Graham, *The Real F. Scott Fitzgerald: Thirty-Five Years Later* (New York: Grosset and Dunlap, 1976), 50; F. Scott Fitzgerald to Zelda Fitzgerald, April 1938, in Bruccoli, *Life in Letters,* 355.

16. Far from Home

1. The Count de Buffon, *The Natural History of Quadrupeds,* vol. 2 (Edinburgh: Thomas Nelson and Peter Brown, 1830), 31, 39.

2. Thomas Jefferson, "Anecdotes of Dr. Franklin," in *The Writings of Thomas Jefferson: Being His Autobiography, Correspondence, Reports, Messages, Addresses, and Other Writings, Official and Private,* vol. 8, ed. H. A. Washington (New York: Taylor and Maury, 1861), 501.

3. Thomas Jefferson, *Notes on the State of Virginia,* in *The Portable Thomas Jefferson,* ed. Merrill D. Peterson (New York: Penguin Books, 1975), 134, 102.

4. Thomas Paine, "Common Sense," in *The Thomas Paine Reader,* ed. Michael Foot and Isaac Kramnick (New York: Penguin Books, 1987), 65; Ralph Waldo Emerson, "The American Scholar," in *Selected Writings of Ralph Waldo Emerson,* ed. William H. Gilman (New York: Signet, 1965), 228; Abraham Lincoln, "'A People's Contest': Message to Congress, July 4, 1861," in *This Fiery Trial: The Speeches and Writings of Abraham Lincoln,* ed. William E. Gienapp (New York: Oxford University Press, 2002), 105.

5. Henry Adams to Charles Francis Adams Jr., 21 November 1861, in *The Letters of Henry Adams,* vol. 1, *1858–1868,* ed. J. C. Levenson, Earnest Samuels, Charles Vandersee, and Viola Hopkins Winner (Cambridge, MA: Harvard University Press, 1982), 315.

6. E. E. Cummings, in *American Writers in Paris, 1920–1939,* ed. Karen Lane Rood (Detroit: Gale Research, 1980), 106.

7. F. Scott Fitzgerald, "The Swimmers," in *Taps at Reveille,* ed. James L. W. West III (New York: Cambridge University Press, 2014), 230.

8. Ibid., 224, 238–39, 241.

9. Fitzgerald, "One Trip Abroad," in *Taps,* 267–68, 278.

10. Ibid., 279.

11. Ibid., 283, 286.

12. Fitzgerald, "Babylon Revisited," in *Taps,* 159, 160.

13. F. Scott Fitzgerald to Rosalind Sayre Smith, 8 June 1930, in *Correspondence of F. Scott Fitzgerald,* ed. Matthew J. Bruccoli and Margaret M. Duggan (New York: Random House, 1980), 236. Regarding Rosalind and Newman Smith in Brussels, see Thaddeus Holt, *The Deceivers: Allied Military Deception in the Second World War* (New York: Skyhorse, 2004).

14. Fitzgerald, "Babylon Revisited," in *Taps,* 161, 177.

15. F. Scott Fitzgerald to Kenneth Littauer, [July?] 1939, in *F. Scott Fitzgerald: A Life in Letters,* ed. Matthew J. Bruccoli (New York: Simon and Schuster, 1994), 402.

17. Jazz Age Jeremiah

1. F. Scott Fitzgerald to Max Perkins, c. 15 May 1931, and Perkins to Fitzgerald, 21 May 1931, in *Dear Scott / Dear Max: The Fitzgerald-Perkins Correspondence,* ed. John Kuehl and Jackson Bryer (New York: Charles Scribner's Sons, 1971), 171.

2. F. Scott Fitzgerald, "Echoes of the Jazz Age," in *My Lost City: Personal Essays, 1920–1940,* ed. James L. W. West III (New York: Cambridge University Press, 2005), 132.

3. Ibid., 136.

4. Ibid., 138.

5. Ibid., 136

6. Ibid., 138.

7. Fitzgerald, "My Lost City," in *My Lost City*, 109–10; F. Scott Fitzgerald, *The Great Gatsby*, ed. Matthew J. Broccoli (New York: Cambridge University Press, 1991), 140.

8. F. Scott Fitzgerald to Max Perkins, 4 September 1919, in *F. Scott Fitzgerald: A Life in Letters,* ed. Matthew J. Bruccoli (New York: Simon and Schuster, 1994), 32; F. Scott Fitzgerald, *This Side of Paradise,* ed. James L. W. West III (New York: Cambridge University Press, 1996), 31.

9. F. Scott Fitzgerald, *The Notebooks of F. Scott Fitzgerald,* ed. Matthew J. Bruccoli (New York: Harcourt Brace Jovanovich/Bruccoli Clark, 1978), 31; F. Scott Fitzgerald to Marya Mannes, October 1925, in *The Letters of F. Scott Fitzgerald,* ed. Andrew Turnbull (New York: Charles Scribner's Sons, 1963), 488.

10. Fitzgerald, "My Lost City," in *My Lost City,* 110.

11. Ibid., 109, 111; Marguerite Mooers Marshall, "F. Scott Fitzgerald, Novelist, Shocked by 'Younger Marrieds' and Prohibition," in *Conversations with F. Scott Fitzgerald,* ed. Matthew J. Bruccoli and Judith S. Baughman (Jackson: University Press of Mississippi, 2004), 26; John Chapin Mosher, "That Sad Young Man," in Bruccoli and Baughman, *Conversations,* 78; B. F. Wilson, "F. Scott Fitzgerald Says: 'All Women over Thirty-Five Should Be Murdered,'" in Bruccoli and Baughman, *Conversations,* 55.

12. Henry Adams, *The Education of Henry Adams* (New York: Modern Library, 1999), 499.

13. Fitzgerald, "My Lost City," in *My Lost City,* 112–13.

14. Adams, *Education,* 380; Fitzgerald, "My Lost City," in *My Lost City,* 115.

15. Fitzgerald, "My Lost City," in *My Lost City,* 115.

16. Fitzgerald, "Echoes of the Jazz Age," ibid., 138.

18. Book of Fathers: Tender Is the Night

1. F. Scott Fitzgerald, *F. Scott Fitzgerald's Ledger: A Facsimile,* ed. Matthew J. Bruccoli (Washington, DC: Bruccoli Clark/NCR Microcard Editions, 1972), 187; Stenographic Report of Conversation between Mr. and Mrs. F. Scott Fitzgerald and Dr. Thomas A. C. Rennie, 28 May 1933, b1, CHMR.

2. Matthew J. Bruccoli and George Parker Anderson, eds., *F. Scott Fitzgerald's Tender Is the Night: A Documentary Volume* (Detroit: Bruccoli Clark Layman/Thompson Gale, 2003), 155; F. Scott Fitzgerald to Zelda Fitzgerald, 26 April 1934, in *Dear Scott, Dearest Zelda: The Love Letters of F. Scott and Zelda Fitzgerald,* ed. Jackson R. Bryer and Cathy W. Barks (New York: St. Martin's, 2002), 193.

3. F. Scott Fitzgerald, "The Death of My Father," in *A Short Autobiography,* ed. James L. W. West III (New York: Scribner, 2011), 118; F. Scott Fitzgerald, *Tender Is the Night,* ed. James L. W. West III (New York: Cambridge University Press, 2012), 232.

4. Rena Sanderson, "Women in Fitzgerald's Fiction," in *The Cambridge Companion to F. Scott Fitzgerald,* ed. Ruth Prigozy (New York: Cambridge University Press, 2001), 159. Baby later decides that Nicole would be better off without Dick and lets him know that a separation could easily be arranged. Interestingly, Rosalind Sayre Smith's May 1938 letter to Fitzgerald regarding Zelda's future has certain Baby overtones, including aggressiveness, an eagerness to separate the spouses, and an appeal to practical business sense. Sayre Smith writes, "Then there is the final and, in my own opinion, the best suggestion I can make. . . . Why not give her back to us, with allowance enough for normal support, and let us do the best we can for her? Then all these complexities would be simplified, whatever bitterness there is, if any, would be washed out, and you would be free to go ahead with the business of living and preparing of the future of yourself. . . . That is the really sensible thing to do, the only thing that will ever enable all involved to find whatever measure of peace may still be alive somewhere under all this tragedy." Rosalind Sayre Smith to F. Scott Fitzgerald, 29 May 1938, b53, FSFP.

5. Honoria Murphy Donnelly with Richard N. Billings, *Sara & Gerald: Villa America and After* (New York: Times Books, 1982), 38, 37, 39; F. Scott Fitzgerald to Sara Murphy, 15 August 1935, in *The Letters of F. Scott Fitzgerald,* ed. Andrew Turnbull (New York: Charles Scribner's Sons, 1963), 423.

6. Fitzgerald, *Tender,* 312, 45, 24.

7. Ibid., 328, 326, 325.

8. Ibid., 291, 342.

9. Ibid., 210; Milton R. Stern, *Tender Is the Night: The Broken Universe* (New York: Twayne, 1994), 49.

10. Robert Sklar, *F. Scott Fitzgerald: The Last Laocoön* (New York: Oxford University Press, 1967), 282.

11. Fitzgerald, *Tender,* 67–68.

12. Ibid., 134, 151, 327.

13. On the chronology question, see James West's introduction to the Cambridge edition of *Tender,* particularly pages xxxvi–vii.

14. F. Scott Fitzgerald to Max Perkins, 23 August 1934, in *Dear Scott/Dear Max: The Fitzgerald-Perkins Correspondence,* ed. John Kuehl and Jackson Bryer (New York: Charles Scribner's Sons, 1971), 206; John Chamberlain, "Books of The Times," *New York Times,* 13 April 1934, 17; Gilbert Seldes, "True to Type—Scott Fitzgerald Writes Superb Tragic Novel," *New York Evening Journal,* 12 April 1934, 23; C. Hartley Grattan, *Modern Monthly,* July 1934, 375–77.

15. Philip Rahv, "You Can't Duck Hurricane Under a Beach Umbrella," *Daily Worker,* 5 May 1934, 7.

16. Fitzgerald, *Tender,* 65.

17. Martha Marie Shank to Arthur Mizener, 26 October 1949, b2, AMPP; F. Scott Fitzgerald to John Peale Bishop, 7 April 1934, in *F. Scott Fitzgerald: A Life in Letters,* ed. Matthew J. Bruccoli (New York: Simon and Schuster, 1994), 255.

19. Purgatory

1. F. Scott Fitzgerald, *Tender Is the Night*, ed. James L. W. West III (New York: Cambridge University Press, 2012), 229; F. Scott Fitzgerald to Scottie Fitzgerald, 12 June 1940, in *F. Scott Fitzgerald: Letters to His Daughter*, ed. Andrew Turnbull (New York: Charles Scribner's Sons, 1965), 128.

2. Arthur Mizener, *The Far Side of Paradise: A Biography of F. Scott* Fitzgerald (Boston: Houghton Mifflin, 1951), 53; F. Scott Fitzgerald to Gerald and Sara Murphy, summer 1940, in *F. Scott Fitzgerald: A Life in Letters*, ed. Matthew J. Bruccoli (New York: Simon and Schuster, 1994), 458; F. Scott Fitzgerald, *F. Scott Fitzgerald's Ledger: A Facsimile*, ed. Matthew J. Bruccoli (Washington, DC: Bruccoli Clark / NCR Microcard Editions, 1972), 189.

3. On Guthrie's background, see Arnold Gingrich, "Will the Real Scott Fitzgerald Please Stand Up and Be Counted?," *Esquire*, December 1964, 10.

4. Laura Guthrie Hearne, "A Summer with F. Scott Fitzgerald," *Esquire*, December 1964, 165, 252.

5. Tony Buttitta, *After the Good Gay Times: Asheville—Summer of '35, a Season with F. Scott Fitzgerald* (New York: Viking, 1974), 53; Frances Kroll Ring, *Against the Current: As I Remember F. Scott Fitzgerald* (San Francisco: Ellis / Creative Arts, 1985), 23, 41. Fitzgerald conceded in a notebook that he lacked "the two top things," money and raw sex appeal, but boasted of having "the two second things, . . . good looks and intelligence": "So I always got the top girl." F. Scott Fitzgerald, *The Notebooks of F. Scott Fitzgerald*, ed. Matthew J. Bruccoli (New York: Harcourt Brace Jovanovich / Bruccoli Clark, 1978), 205.

6. Elizabeth Beckwith Mackie, "My Friend Scott Fitzgerald," *Fitzgerald / Hemingway Annual* 2 (1970): 20. On Fitzgerald in Asheville, see Buttitta, *After the Good Gay Times*, 56, 113. According to Buttitta, "Lottie," Scott's Asheville "girl," said to him, "Years ago [Zelda] told [Scott] he could never satisfy her or any other woman because he was built so small. Can you beat that? It really hit him hard. And he believed her because he thought she was smart, and because he knew little about it himself." Ernest Hemingway, *A Moveable Feast* (New York: Scribner, 2003), 190.

7. Sheilah Graham and Gerold Frank, *Beloved Infidel: The Education of a Woman* (New York: Henry Holt, 1989), 248; F. Scott Fitzgerald to John Peale Bishop, 30 January 1935, in Bruccoli, *Life in Letters*, 276; "Brief Review," *New Masses*, 18 June 1935; and Berry Fleming, "John Peale Bishop's Novel of the South," *Saturday Review of Literature*, 9 March 1935.

8. N. P. Dawson, "The Beautiful and Damned," *New York Globe and Commercial Advertiser*, 4 March 1922, 10; F. Scott Fitzgerald, *The Great Gatsby*, ed. Matthew J. Bruccoli (New York: Cambridge University Press, 1991), 88, 26; F. Scott Fitzgerald to Bennett Cerf, 13 August 1936, Bruccoli, *Life in Letters*, 306.

9. Fitzgerald, *Notebooks*, 205; Sheilah Graham, *The Real F. Scott Fitzgerald: Thirty-Five Years Later* (New York: Grosset and Dunlap, 1976), 117, 30; F. Scott Fitzgerald,

This Side of Paradise, ed. James L. W. West III (New York: Cambridge University Press, 1996), 63.

10. Hearne, "Summer with F. Scott Fitzgerald," 161–62.

11. Ibid., 164; F. Scott Fitzgerald to Laura Guthrie, 29 July 1935, in *Correspondence of F. Scott Fitzgerald,* ed. Matthew J. Bruccoli and Margaret M. Duggan (New York: Random House, 1980), 417.

12. F. Scott Fitzgerald to Beatrice Dance, August 1935, in Bruccoli and Duggan, *Correspondence,* 419, 420; F. Scott Fitzgerald to Dr. Cade, September 1935, b5, FSFAP.

13. F. Scott Fitzgerald to Dr. Cade, September 1935, b5, FSFAP.

14. F. Scott Fitzgerald to Laura Guthrie, 23 September 1935, in Bruccoli, *Life in Letters,* 290; Beatrice Dance to Laura Guthrie, 25 October 1935, b11, FSFAP.

15. Beatrice Dance to Laura Guthrie Hearne, 5 July 1964, b11, FSFAP; Andrew Turnbull, *Scott Fitzgerald* (New York: Charles Scribner's Sons, 1962), 262–63.

16. Charles Beard and Mary Beard, *The Rise of American Civilization,* vol. 2 (New York: Macmillan, 1936), 757, 758; F. Scott Fitzgerald, "Echoes of the Jazz Age," in *My Lost City: Personal Essays, 1920–1940,* ed. James L. W. West III (New York: Cambridge University Press, 2005), 132; "My Lost City," ibid, 115. On the Beard and Fitzgerald overlap, see Ronald Berman, *Fitzgerald-Wilson-Hemingway: Language and Experience* (Tuscaloosa: University of Alabama Press, 2003), 25–26, 35.

17. Harold Ober to F. Scott Fitzgerald, 14 February 1936, in *As Ever, Scott-Fitz—: Letters between F. Scott Fitzgerald and His Literary Agent, Harold Ober, 1919–1940,* ed. Matthew J. Bruccoli (Philadelphia: J. B. Lippincott, 1972), 253.

18. F. Scott Fitzgerald to Annabel 10 September 1936, in Bruccoli and Duggan, *Correspondence,* 448–49.

19. F. Scott Fitzgerald to Beatrice Dance, 15 September 1936, in *The Letters of F. Scott Fitzgerald,* ed. Andrew Turnbull (New York: Charles Scribner's Sons, 1963), 541; Patricia Sprague Reneau and Courtney Sprague Vaughan, *Remembered and Honored: Clifton A. F. "Ziggy" Sprague, U.S.N., 1896–1955* (Santa Cruz, CA: privately printed, 1992), 69, as quoted in Jeffrey Meyers, *Scott Fitzgerald: A Biography* (New York: HarperCollins, 1994), 277.

20. Scottie Fitzgerald interview, Montgomery, AL, 1977, MJBP.

21. Marie Shank to Arthur Mizener, 26 October 1949, b12, FSFAP.

22. Marie Shank to Arthur Mizener, 20 November 1949, b12, FSFAP.

23. Ibid.; John Dos Passos, *The Best of Times: An Informal Memoir* (New York: New American Library, 1966), 129.

20. De Profundis

1. Arnold Gingrich, "Will the Real Scott Fitzgerald Please Stand Up and Be Counted?," *Esquire,* December 1964, 12; F. Scott Fitzgerald to Kenneth Littauer, [late July?] 1939, in *The Letters of F. Scott Fitzgerald,* ed. Andrew Turnbull (New York: Charles Scribner's Sons, 1963), 588.

2. Gingrich, "Real Scott Fitzgerald," 16.

3. F. Scott Fitzgerald, "One Hundred False Starts," in *A Short Autobiography,* ed. James L. W. West III (New York: Scribner, 2011), 127.

4. On Fitzgerald's relationship with *Esquire,* see James L. W. West III, "Fitzgerald and *Esquire*," in *The Short Stories of F. Scott Fitzgerald: New Approaches in Criticism,* ed. Jackson R. Bryer (Madison: University of Wisconsin Press, 1982), 149–66.

5. F. Scott Fitzgerald, "Handle with Care," in *My Lost City: Personal Essays, 1920–1940,* ed. James L. W. West III (New York: Cambridge University Press, 2005), 153.

6. Scott Donaldson, "The Crisis of Fitzgerald's 'Crack-Up,'" *Twentieth Century Literature* 26 (Summer 1980): 177.

7. F. Scott Fitzgerald to Zelda Fitzgerald, August 1939, in *F. Scott Fitzgerald: A Life in Letters,* ed. Matthew J. Bruccoli (New York: Simon and Schuster, 1994), 405.

8. Fitzgerald, "The Crack-Up," in *My Lost City,* 142.

9. Fitzgerald, "Early Success," ibid., 190.

10. Fitzgerald, "The Crack-Up," ibid., 149

11. Ibid., 148.

12. Fitzgerald, "Handle with Care," in *My Lost City,* 151.

13. F. Scott Fitzgerald to Mrs. Laura Feley, 20 July 1939, in Turnbull, *Letters,* 589.

14. Fitzgerald, "The Crack-Up," in *My Lost City,* 139; F. Scott Fitzgerald, "Babylon Revisited," in *Taps at Reveille,* ed. James L. W. West III (New York: Cambridge University Press, 2014), 177; Fitzgerald, "Pasting It Together," in *My Lost City,* 146.

15. Abraham Lincoln, "'With Charity for All': Second Inaugural Address, 4 March 1865," in *This Fiery Trial: The Speeches and Writings of Abraham Lincoln,* ed. William E. Gienapp (New York: Oxford University Press, 2002), 221.

16. Fitzgerald, "The Crack-Up," in *My Lost City,* 144.

17. Harold Ober to F. Scott Fitzgerald, 21 August 1936, in *As Ever, Scott-Fitz—: Letters between F. Scott Fitzgerald and His Literary Agent, Harold Ober, 1919–1940,* ed. Matthew J. Bruccoli (Philadelphia: J. B. Lippincott, 1972), 279–80; John Dos Passos to F. Scott Fitzgerald, September 1936, in *The Fourteenth Chronicle: Letters and Diaries of John Dos Passos* (Boston: Gambit, 1973), 488; Morris Dickstein, *Dancing in the Dark: A Cultural History of the Great Depression* (New York: Norton, 2009), 259.

18. Scott Donaldson, *Fool for Love: A Biography of F. Scott Fitzgerald* (New York: Delta, 1983), 147.

19. Jule B to F. Scott Fitzgerald, 25 September 1936, b40a, FSFP.

20. Julian Street to F. Scott Fitzgerald, 12 February 1936, b53, FSFP.

21. A. Scott Berg, *Max Perkins: Editor of Genius* (New York: E. P. Dutton, 1978), 282.

22. Ernest Hemingway, "The Snows of Kilimanjaro," *Esquire,* August 1936, 200.

23. Berg, *Max Perkins,* 305.

24. F. Scott Fitzgerald to Ernest Hemingway, 16 July 1936, in Bruccoli, *Life in Letters,* 302. Hemingway substituted "Julian" for "Scott Fitzgerald" when the story

appeared in *The Fifth Column and the First Forty-Nine Stories,* an anthology of Hemingway's writings published by Scribner in 1938.

25. Hemingway, "Snows of Kilimanjaro," 195.

26. Selections of Fitzgerald's letters appear in three general collections, edited by Andrew Turnbull (1963), Matthew J. Bruccoli and Margaret M. Duggan (1980), and Bruccoli (1994). These are supplemented by more specialized volumes pertaining to Fitzgerald's letters to his daughter (edited by Turnbull, 1965); to his editor, Max Perkins (edited by John Kuehl and Jackson Bryer, 1971); to his literary agent, Harold Ober (edited by Bruccoli, 1972); and to his wife, Zelda (edited by Bryer and Cathy W. Barks, 2002). Full citations of these volumes appear elsewhere in these notes.

27. Michel Mok, "The Other Side of Paradise: Scott Fitzgerald, 40, Engulfed in Despair," in *Conversations with F. Scott Fitzgerald,* ed. Matthew J. Bruccoli and Judith S. Baughman (Jackson: University Press of Mississippi, 2004), 120.

28. F. Scott Fitzgerald to Harold Ober, 5 October 1936, in Bruccoli, *Life in Letters,* 308.

29. F. Scott Fitzgerald to Mr. Roger Garis, 22 February 1938, b40a, FSFP; Max Perkins to Edmund Wilson, 16 February 1941, in *Edmund Wilson: Letters on Literature and Politics, 1912–1972,* ed. Elena Wilson (New York: Farrar, Straus and Giroux, 1977), 337.

21. Life in a Company Town

1. F. Scott Fitzgerald to Harold Ober, 19 December 1919, in *As Ever, Scott Fitz—: Letters between F. Scott Fitzgerald and His Literary Agent, Harold Ober, 1919–1940,* ed. Matthew J. Bruccoli (Philadelphia: J. B. Lippincott, 1972), 6; Ruth Prigozy, "Fitzgerald's Flappers and Flapper Films of the Jazz Age: Behind the Morality," in *A Historical Guide to F. Scott Fitzgerald,* ed. Kirk Curnutt (New York: Oxford University Press, 2004), 144.

2. Frances Kroll Ring, *Against the Current: As I Remember F. Scott Fitzgerald* (San Francisco: Ellis/Creative Arts, 1985), 99. Fitzgerald told Graham that he covered himself because he feared a flair-up of tuberculosis. Sheilah Graham and Gerold Frank, *Beloved Infidel: The Education of a Woman* (New York: Henry Holt, 1989), 235.

3. Margaret Culkin Banning to Henry Dan Piper, 17 July 1944, HDPP.

4. Aaron Latham, *Crazy Sundays: F. Scott Fitzgerald in Hollywood* (New York: Viking, 1971), 127.

5. F. Scott Fitzgerald to Gerald Murphy 14 September 1940, in *The Letters of F. Scott Fitzgerald,* ed. Andrew Turnbull (New York: Charles Scribner's Sons, 1963), 429–30; F. Scott Fitzgerald to Beatrice Dance, 6 November 1940, FSFAP.

6. Mark A. Vieira, *Irving Thalberg: Boy Wonder to Producer Prince* (Berkeley: University of California Press, 2010), 395.

7. F. Scott Fitzgerald to Rosalind Sayre Smith, 27 May 1938, in *Correspondence of F. Scott Fitzgerald,* ed. Matthew J. Bruccoli and Margaret M. Duggan (New York:

Random House, 1980), 503; Jeffrey Meyers, *Scott Fitzgerald: A Biography* (New York: HarperCollins, 1994), 289.

8. F. Scott Fitzgerald to John Biggs Jr., spring 1939, in Turnbull, *Letters,* 581.

9. Robert Westbrook, *Intimate Lies: F. Scott Fitzgerald and Sheilah Graham, Her Son's Story* (New York: HarperCollins, 1995), 139.

10. For biographical material, see Wendy Fairey's brief piece on her mother, "Sheilah Graham, 1904–1988," Jewish Women's Archive, http://jwa.org/weremember /graham-sheilah, accessed 4 November 2016.

11. Graham and Frank, *Beloved Infidel,* 133.

12. F. Scott Fitzgerald, *The Great Gatsby,* ed. Matthew J. Bruccoli (New York: Cambridge University Press, 1991), 52; Graham and Frank, *Beloved Infidel,* 166.

13. Fairey, "Sheilah Graham"; F. Scott Fitzgerald, *The Love of the Last Tycoon,* ed. Matthew J. Bruccoli (New York: Cambridge University Press, 1994), 26.

14. Graham and Frank, *Beloved Infidel,* 175.

15. Ibid., 177–78.

16. Fairey, "Sheilah Graham."

17. Edmund Wilson, *The Bit between My Teeth: A Literary Chronicle of 1950–1965* (New York: Farrar, Straus and Giroux, 1965), 21–22.

18. Ring, *Against the Current,* 97.

19. Eleanor Lanahan, *Scottie: The Daughter of . . . : The Life of Frances Scott Fitzgerald Lanahan Smith* (New York: Harper Perennial, 1995), 95.

20. Edmund Wilson to John Peale Bishop, 1 February 1939, b23, JPBP.

21. Latham, *Crazy Sundays,* 187.

22. Sheilah Graham, *The Real F. Scott Fitzgerald: Thirty-Five Years Later* (New York: Grosset and Dunlap, 1976), 41; F. Scott Fitzgerald, *The Notebooks of F. Scott Fitzgerald,* ed. Matthew J. Bruccoli (New York: Harcourt Brace Jovanovich / Bruccoli Clark, 1978), 333.

22. Sentimental Education

1. Sheilah Graham, *College of One: The Story of How F. Scott Fitzgerald Educated the Woman He Loved* (Brooklyn, NY: Melville House, 2013), 62; Nancy Milford, *Zelda* (New York: Harper and Row, 1970), 317.

2. Graham, *College of One,* 93, 95, 94, 77.

3. Stenographic Report of Conversation between Mr. and Mrs. F. Scott Fitzgerald and Dr. Thomas A. C. Rennie, 28 May 1933, b1, CHMR, 59. On the subject of Scottie's "overcoming" her parentage, Scott wrote, "People will be quick to deck you out with my sins. . . . [They] would like to be able to say, and would say, on the slightest provocation: 'There she goes—just like her papa and mama.'" F. Scott Fitzgerald to Scottie Fitzgerald, 19 September 1938, in *F. Scott Fitzgerald: Letters to His Daughter,* ed. Andrew Turnbull (New York: Charles Scribner's Sons, 1965), 58.

4. Eleanor Lanahan, *Scottie: The Daughter of . . . : The Life of Frances Scott Fitzgerald Lanahan Smith* (New York: Harper Perennial, 1995), 76–77.

5. F. Scott Fitzgerald to Scottie Fitzgerald, 8 August 1933, in Turnbull, *Letters to His Daughter,* 3. Fitzgerald referred to Shakespeare's Sonnet 94.

6. Ibid., 3, 4, 5; F. Scott Fitzgerald to Margaret Turnbull, 11 October 1938, b5, FSFAP.

7. James L. W. West III, introduction to *The Basil, Josephine, and Gwen Stories,* by F. Scott Fitzgerald (New York: Cambridge University Press, 2009), xv; Fitzgerald, "Inside the House," in *Basil, Josephine, and Gwen,* 316.

8. Fitzgerald, "Inside the House," in *Basil, Josephine, and Gwen,* 313.

9. F. Scott Fitzgerald to Scottie Fitzgerald, 27 March 1940, in Turnbull, *Letters to His Daughter,* 109.

10. F. Scott Fitzgerald to Annabel Fitzgerald, c. 1915, in *Correspondence of F. Scott Fitzgerald,* ed. Matthew J. Bruccoli and Margaret M. Duggan (New York: Random House, 1980), 18.

11. F. Scott Fitzgerald to Scottie Fitzgerald, 20 October 1936, in Turnbull, *Letters to His Daughter,* 16; F. Scott Fitzgerald to Ethel Walker Smith, 17 August 1936, in Bruccoli and Duggan, *Correspondence,* 444.

12. Lanahan, *Scottie,* 103.

13. Frances Scott Fitzgerald, "A Short Retort," *Mademoiselle,* July 1939, 41.

14. F. Scott Fitzgerald to Scottie Fitzgerald, July 1939, in Turnbull, *Letters to His Daughter,* 96, 98. F. Scott Fitzgerald, "My Generation," *Esquire,* October 1968, 121.

15. "Scottie Fitzgerald Interview," Montgomery, AL, 1977, MJBP.

16. F. Scott Fitzgerald to Zelda Fitzgerald, 19 March 1940, in *Dear Scott, Dearest Zelda: The Love Letters of F. Scott and Zelda Fitzgerald,* ed. Jackson R. Bryer and Cathy W. Barks (New York: St. Martin's, 2002), 331.

17. F. Scott Fitzgerald to Scottie Fitzgerald, 12 April 1940, in Turnbull, *Letters to His Daughter,* 113; F. Scott Fitzgerald to Scottie Fitzgerald, 2 November 1940, ibid.,157.

18. F. Scott Fitzgerald to Scottie Fitzgerald, 17 November 1936, ibid., 18.

19. F. Scott Fitzgerald to Scottie Fitzgerald, 7 July 1938, ibid., 51. In another letter to Scottie on the "broken" theme, Fitzgerald wrote of Zelda, "the insane are always mere guests on earth, eternal strangers carrying around broken decalogues that they cannot read." F. Scott Fitzgerald to Scottie Fitzgerald, December 1940, ibid. 164.

20. F. Scott Fitzgerald to Scottie Fitzgerald, 7 July 1938, ibid., 52.

21. F. Scott Fitzgerald to Scottie Fitzgerald, undated fragment, ibid., 166.

22. Frances Fitzgerald Lanahan, introduction, ibid., xiii. The checks—Scottie's allowance—amounted to $13.85 per week.

23. Frances Fitzgerald Lanahan to Arthur Mizener, 21 January 1964, b1 AMPP.

23. Stahr Fall

1. Sheilah Graham, *College of One: The Story of How F. Scott Fitzgerald Educated the Woman He Loved* (Brooklyn, NY: Melville House, 2013), 137–38.

2. F. Scott Fitzgerald to Kenneth Littauer, 29 September 1939, in *Correspondence of F. Scott Fitzgerald,* ed. Matthew J. Bruccoli and Margaret M. Duggan (New York: Random House, 1980), 549; Kenneth Littauer to F. Scott Fitzgerald, 28 November 1939, ibid., 561.

3. Bryant Mangum, "The Short Stories of F. Scott Fitzgerald," in *The Cambridge Companion to F. Scott Fitzgerald,* ed. Ruth Prigozy (New York: Cambridge University Press, 2001), 76.

4. F. Scott Fitzgerald to Nathan Kroll, 6 May 1940, in Bruccoli and Duggan, *Correspondence,* 595; Matthew J. Bruccoli, introduction to *The Love of the Last Tycoon,* by F. Scott Fitzgerald (New York: Cambridge University Press, 1994), xxxvi.

5. F. Scott Fitzgerald, *The Pat Hobby Stories* (New York: Scribner, 1995), xv.

6. F. Scott Fitzgerald, "Pat Hobby and Orson Wells," in *The Lost Decade: Short Stories from Esquire, 1936–1941,* ed. James L. W. West III (New York: Cambridge University Press, 2008), 122. *Tycoon*'s Wylie White, like Hobby a screenwriter, attended a Hollywood party at which no one spoke to him. "I didn't feel I had any rightful identity," he recalled the humiliation. Fitzgerald, *Tycoon,* 11. In a March 1940 letter to Zelda, Scott referenced his own loss of "identity": "Nothing has developed here. I write these 'Pat Hobby' stories—and wait. . . . But my God I am a forgotten man." F. Scott Fitzgerald to Zelda Fitzgerald, 19 March 1940, in *Dear Scott, Dearest Zelda: The Love Letters of F. Scott and Zelda Fitzgerald,* ed. Jackson R. Bryer and Cathy W. Barks (New York: St. Martin's, 2002), 331.

7. Budd Schulberg, *The Disenchanted* (New York: Random House, 1950), 368.

8. Fitzgerald, *Tycoon,* 27, 48, 43. Ever the hero worshiper, Scott, Graham remembered, read James Anthony Froude's biography *Julius Caesar* before starting *Tycoon.* Graham, *College of One,* 85.

9. Fitzgerald, *Tycoon,* 49, 17. On Scott's interest in the presidential theme, Sheilah Graham noted, "He explained to me why Stahr's first name was Monroe; 'Jewish parents often gave their sons the names of American Presidents.'" Graham, *College of One,* 80.

10. F. Scott Fitzgerald to Kenneth Littauer, 29 September 1939, in Bruccoli and Duggan, *Correspondence,* 546, 549; Bruccoli, introduction to *Tycoon,* xix.

11. Graham, *College of One,* 59; Bruccoli, introduction to *Tycoon,* xix.

12. Fitzgerald, *Tycoon,* 20–21.

13. F. Scott Fitzgerald, *The Great Gatsby,* ed. Matthew J. Bruccoli (New York: Cambridge University Press, 1991), 141, 140; Fitzgerald, *Tycoon,* 13.

14. F. Scott Fitzgerald, *The Notebooks of F. Scott Fitzgerald,* ed. Matthew J. Bruccoli (New York: Harcourt Brace Jovanovich / Bruccoli Clark, 1978), 332.

15. F. Scott Fitzgerald to Zelda Fitzgerald, 11 October 1940, in Bryer and Barks, *Dear Scott, Dearest Zelda,* 370; F. Scott Fitzgerald to Zelda Fitzgerald, 26 October 1940, ibid., 374.

16. Frances Kroll Ring to Arthur Mizener, 14 June 1948, b1, AMPP; Matthew J. Bruccoli, *"The Last of the Novelists": F. Scott Fitzgerald and the Last Tycoon* (Carbondale: Southern Illinois University Press, 1977), 142.

17. F. Scott Fitzgerald to Zelda Fitzgerald, 13 December 1940, in Bryer and Barks, *Dear Scott, Dearest Zelda,* 382.

18. Frances Kroll Ring and R. L. Samsell, "Sisyphus in Hollywood," *Fitzgerald/Hemingway Annual* 5 (1973): 102. After the repayment of various debts, Fitzgerald's estate was worth less than $35,000.

19. Frank Scully, *Rogues' Gallery: Profiles of My Eminent Contemporaries* (Hollywood, CA: Murray and Gee, 1943), 268–69.

20. Sheilah Graham to Harold Ober, 21 December 1940, in *As Ever, Scott Fitz—: Letters between F. Scott Fitzgerald and His Literary Agent, Harold Ober, 1919–1940,* ed. Matthew J. Bruccoli (Philadelphia: J. B. Lippincott, 1972), 423; Max Perkins to John Peale Bishop, 28 December 1940, b22, JPBP; Rosalind Sayre Smith to Arthur Mizener, 26 June 1950, b2, AMPP.

21. Zelda Fitzgerald to Margaret Turnbull, 13 November 1941, b5, ZFP.

24. Zelda after Scott

1. F. Scott Fitzgerald to Dr. Robert Carroll, 19 April 1938, *Correspondence of F. Scott Fitzgerald,* ed. Matthew J. Bruccoli and Margaret M. Duggan (New York: Random House, 1980), 495–96.

2. F. Scott Fitzgerald to Rosalind Sayre Smith, 27 May 1938, ibid., 502.

3. F. Scott Fitzgerald to Rosalind Sayre Smith, 21 December 1938, b53, FSFP.

4. F. Scott Fitzgerald to Zelda Fitzgerald, 8 March, in *Dear Scott, Dearest Zelda: The Love Letters of F. Scott and Zelda Fitzgerald,* ed. Jackson R. Bryer and Cathy W. Barks (New York: St. Martin's, 2002), 328; Zelda Fitzgerald to F. Scott Fitzgerald, March 1940, ibid., 329; Dr. Robert S. Carroll to Whom It May Concern, 6 April 1940, b49, FSFP.

5. Sally Cline, *Zelda Fitzgerald: Her Voice in Paradise* (London: John Murray, 2002), 389; Nancy Milford, *Zelda* (New York: Harper and Row, 1970), 355; Cline, *Zelda Fitzgerald,* 390.

6. Eleanor Lanahan, *Scottie: The Daughter of . . . : The Life of Frances Scott Fitzgerald Lanahan Smith* (New York: Harper Perennial, 1995), 185; Zelda Fitzgerald to "Dearest Scottie," internal evidence suggests 1945, b4, ZFP; Lanahan, *Scottie,* 155. Around the same time, Gerald Murphy wrote to Scottie, "no one can say that according to their own unusual laws they [Scott and Zelda] did not have a great deal of what they valued in life." 1 June 1945, MJBP; Zelda Fitzgerald to Scottie Fitzgerald, internal evidence suggests early 1940s, b4, ZFP.

7. Piper majored in chemistry at Princeton, though he found time to write for the *Daily Princetonian* and the *Nassau Lit.* He began graduate work in English in 1946 and published his revised University of Pennsylvania dissertation as *F. Scott Fitzgerald: A Critical Portrait* in 1965. Milford, *Zelda,* 379.

8. Milford, *Zelda,* 380; Henry Dan Piper to Judge John Biggs Jr., 17 March 1947, b2, HDPP. Biggs had written to Piper before the latter's meeting with Zelda, "It is a fact that she gets very much worked up when she thinks of Scott and his death." Biggs to Piper, 17 February 1944, b2, HDPP.

9. Zelda Fitzgerald to Henry Dan Piper, internal evidence suggests 1947, b2, HDPP.

10. *New York Herald Tribune,* 12 March 1948.

11. Scottie Fitzgerald Lanahan to Mrs. A. D. Sayre, "Dearest Grandma," 19 March 1948, b6, ZFP.

25. Life after Death

1. Edmund Wilson, *The Bit between My Teeth: A Literary Chronicle of 1950–1965* (New York: Farrar, Straus and Giroux, 1965), 16.

2. Royalties on Books, b55, FSFP. The nearly $7,000 would amount to some $115,000 in present-day dollars. Elaine P. Maimon, "F. Scott Fitzgerald's Book Sales: A Look at the Record," *Fitzgerald/Hemingway Annual* 5 (1973): 166; John O'Hara, introduction to *The Portable F. Scott Fitzgerald,* ed. Dorothy Parker (New York: Viking, 1945), xiv.

3. Eleanor Lanahan, *Scottie: The Daughter of . . . : The Life of Frances Scott Fitzgerald Lanahan Smith* (New York: Harper Perennial, 1995), 141, 198; Charles Jackson, "The Critics and Fitzgerald," *New York Times,* 29 April 1951, http://www.nytimes.com/books/00/12/24/specials/fitzgerald-kazin.html.

4. Maimon, "F. Scott Fitzgerald's Book Sales," 169, 172; Deirdre Donahue, "'The Great Gatsby' by the Numbers," *USA Today,* 7 May 2013, http://www.usatoday.com/story/life/books/2013/05/07/the-great-gatsby-is-a-bestseller-this-week/2133269/.

5. Rosemary Mizener Colt, "My Father, My Mother, *The Far Side of Paradise,* and Me," *F. Scott Fitzgerald Review* 2 (2003): 12.

6. Ibid., 9.

7. Arthur Mizener, *The Far Side of Paradise: A Biography of F. Scott Fitzgerald* (New York: Houghton Mifflin, 1951), v; Edmund Wilson to Arthur Mizener, 22 February 1950, b1, f10, AMPD. Wilson's read-through of the manuscript produced one criticism that embodied his general problem with the biography: its sly infantilizing of Fitzgerald. Contradicting Mizener's physical description of Scott, Wilson inked in the margin, "He was very broad-shouldered and did not like the impression of being small." Edmund Wilson, Comments to Arthur Mizener, draft of *The Far Side of Paradise,* page 38, b1, f1, AMPD.

8. Wilson gave a specific example of Mizener's "misreading" of Zelda: "Your account of her dancing 'appallingly' with her skirt over her head. I understand that Sara Murphy says that this spectacle was not appalling but strangely beautiful." Edmund Wilson to Arthur Mizener, 22 February 1950, b1, f10, AMPD.

9. Ibid. In fact, Mizener believed that he had offered a restrained portrait of Zelda's illness. Days after the tragic fire at Highland Hospital, he wrote to one correspondent, "Mrs. Fitzgerald's death is . . . a great simplifier for the book; it means that I can tell the whole story of her illness and its effect on Fitzgerald; or, perhaps not the whole story, but as much of it as will ever be publishable; some of the details are too terrible ever to be gone into print." Arthur Mizener to Dorothy Hillyer, 18 March 1948, b1, AMPP.

10. Edmund Wilson to Arthur Mizener, 22 February 1950, b1, f10, AMPD.

11. Scottie Fitzgerald Lanahan to Arthur Mizener, 10 March 1950, b1, AMPP.

12. "Budd Schulberg on F. Scott Fitzgerald," YouTube, 9 November 2016, http://www .youtube.com/watch?v=XMbtr_25XZI.

13. Budd Schulberg, *The Disenchanted* (New York: Random House, 1950), 33–34, 49.

14. Scottie Fitzgerald Lanahan to Arthur Mizener, 22 October 1950, b1, AMPP; Schulberg, *Disenchanted,* 352. Mizener replied to Scottie's letter, "You certainly are right about Budd's reporting, if that's the right word. Anyhow, about things he's experienced he does write magnificently. I know that he did not keep any notes on the Dartmouth trip at all. That's what I mean about 'reporting.' What he seems to remember is the quality, the feel, of experience, and then when he begins to write or to talk about it, the particulars are called back by the feelings." Arthur Mizener to Scottie Fitzgerald Lanahan, 27 October 1950, b2, MJBP.

15. Sheilah Graham and Gerold Frank, *Beloved Infidel* (New York: Henry Holt, 1989), viii; Wilson, *Bit between My Teeth,* 24.

16. The quote appeared, as part of "The Author's Apology," in the third printing (May 1920) of *This Side of Paradise.*

17. F. Scott Fitzgerald, *The Great Gatsby,* ed. Matthew J. Bruccoli (New York: Cambridge University Press, 1991), 141.

ACKNOWLEDGMENTS

A few years ago, in a used bookstore in Madison, Wisconsin, I came across an edition of F. Scott Fitzgerald's letters. The openness of his emotions combined with the almost haunting quality of his writing to produce a lingering effect that I have, in some respects, yet to shake. It is a sensation, I suppose, that I share with countless readers. On a more personal note, I find myself indebted not merely to Fitzgerald but to those scholars and biographers who have researched his life and works and thus made this present study possible. One can find in these pages a listing of the many books, essays, and edited volumes that inform Fitzgerald historiography, though I should like to say here that I found particularly helpful the scholarship of Cathy Barks, Ronald Berman, the late Matthew J. Bruccoli, Jackson R. Bryer, Kirk Curnutt, Scott Donaldson, the late John Kuehl, Richard D. Lehan, Bryant Mangum, Nancy Milford, Ruth Prigozy, the late Robert Sklar, the late Milton R. Stern, and James L. W. West III.

I am further grateful to Professor West for commenting on an early iteration of the introduction and one of the chapters. His questions and observations ("Fitzgerald's optimism and hope, were always there. At various times in his life, he hit bottom and vowed to rid himself of that troublesome idealism . . . but he was never really successful at turning himself into a nihilist, or even a cynic") helped me to produce a more focused, thoughtful, and, I hope, interesting manuscript.

I also want to recognize the really effective criticism I received from two anonymous reviewers for the Harvard University Press. Their well-considered comments improved both the argument and the presentation of the project, which grew in response to their remarks.

A fair amount of archival research helped to shape this book, and the staffs of the following institutions holding Fitzgerald related materials made easy the acquisition of documents, images, and artifacts: the Department of Rare Books and Special Collections at Princeton University's Firestone Library; the Irvin Department of Rare Books and Special Collections at the University of South Carolina's Thomas Cooper Library;

the Special Collections department at the University of Delaware's Morris Library; and the Special Collections Research Center at Southern Illinois University, Carbondale.

My home institution, Elizabethtown College, supported the project by providing its author with release time, faculty development funds, and, through a generous Dean's budget, supplementary funds; colleagues in the school's High Library responded to my many requests with courtesy and skill.

At Harvard University Press Joy Deng, Julia Kirby, and Stephanie Vyce attended to a number of late queries and loose ends that kept the manuscript moving against calendar and clock. Andrew Katz of Westchester Publishing Services combed over the edited files with a remarkable eye for detail.

What I owe to my editor, John Kulka, can only be imperfectly expressed. He made every aspect of this book, from the language, to the organization, to the illustrations, both fuller and finer. In a world filled with words, his is a rare talent. "I feel I've certainly been lucky," to quote a young Fitzgerald, "to find a publisher who seems so interested generally in his authors."

INDEX